D1519822

Madame le Professeur

Madame le Professeur

WOMEN EDUCATORS IN
THE THIRD REPUBLIC

Jo Burr Margadant

PRINCETON UNIVERSITY PRESS • PRINCETON, NEW JERSEY

Copyright © 1990 by Princeton University Press
Published by Princeton University Press, 41 William Street,
Princeton, New Jersey 08540
In the United Kingdom: Princeton University Press, Oxford

All Rights Reserved

Library of Congress Cataloging-in-Publication Data

Margadant, Jo Burr, 1939–
Madame le professeur : women educators in the Third Republic /
Jo Burr Margadant.
p.   cm.
Includes bibliographical references.
ISBN 0-691-05593-9 — ISBN 0-691-00864-7 (pbk.)
1. Women teachers—France—Biography 2. Women educators—
France—Biography. 3. Women in education—France—History—
19th century. 4. Women in education—France—History—20th
century. 5. France—History—Third Republic, 1870–1940. I. Title.
LA2375.F7M37   1990
378.1'2'0944092—dc20
[B]   89-70243 CIP

Publication of this book has been aided by the Whitney Darrow
Fund of Princeton University Press

This book has been composed in Linotron Melior

Princeton University Press books are printed
on acid-free paper, and meet the guidelines for
permanence and durability of the Committee on
Production Guidelines for Book Longevity
of the Council on Library Resources
Printed in the United States of America by
Princeton University Press, Princeton, New Jersey

1   2   3   4   5   6   7   8   9   10
(Pbk.) 1   2   3   4   5   6   7   8   9   10

For Ashley, Thad, and Ted

Contents

Tables

Acknowledgments

WHEN STARTING this project fourteen years ago, I had just discovered in a seminar with Barbara Kanner the excitement generated by the enterprise of women's history. A study of the first graduates of the Ecole Normale of Sèvres, which Karen Offen suggested, turned out to be exceptionally suited to a long gestation. Through years of research, writing, and revising, I never lost interest in the Sévriennes whose lives provide the content of this book. Part of that appeal grew out of natural similarities between their experiences as teachers with family obligations and my own, though the differences were equally intriguing. In part, the significance of their achievements kept my mind engaged. Equally important, though, was the inventiveness of other historians working in the fields of women, gender, and the family whose explorations led me to think in new ways about the material I had gathered. The debt I owe them fills the footnotes of this study.

Of the many people who knowingly helped me bring this project to fruition, I want to thank my mentor and friend Roy Willis first, who, despite his own unfamiliarity with the field of women's history, provided exceptionally good advice as an editorial critic. Closer to my field, Susanna Barrows offered continuously perceptive comments on the arguments developed here as well as her wonderful gift for words whenever my prose stumbled. To her imaginative flair, I also owe the title of this book. André Burguière spent long hours wading through an early version of this work. Karen Offen, Bonnie Smith, and Steven Hause all read the next-to-final version; to them especially I owe thanks for excellent advice as specialists in the field. Each of them made substantive contributions to the final product and also alerted me to oversights and errors. I take full responsibility, of course, for any mistakes that still remain. Several other friends and scholars have read all or portions of this work in various stages and offered helpful comments. They include Daniel Brower, Rachel Fuchs, Louise Tilly, Marjorie Murphy, Michelle Perrot, Herrick Chapman, Rosemary Wakeman, Tyler Stovell, and my colleagues at Santa Clara University Mary Gordon and Barbara Molony. The intellectual encouragement that all these individuals offered me has meant as much to the completion of this manuscript as did their advice.

The Social Science Research Council provided the funds that made the original research for this project possible. The unfailing goodwill of staff members at the National Archives and at the Ecole Normale Supérieure de Sèvres, several of whom made special efforts to locate material or make helpful contacts for me, proved invaluable. The Directrice of Sèvres, Mme Serre, and the school's librarian, Mme Putois, were particularly generous with their counsel, as was the archivist for the Alumnae Association, Mme Chenot. Françoise Mayeur lent me a copy of her thesis for the *doctorat d'état* on the foundation of girls' secondary schools, which made my research immeasurably easier. Finally, seven retired Sévriennes graciously agreed to recount their experiences in personal interviews. I am deeply grateful to Mlle Courtain, Mlle Félix, Mlle Fontaine, Mlle Galle, Mlle Guiscafré, Mlle Lods, and Mme Scheid. Their recollections gave a much appreciated voice to the silent testimony of the archives.

In members of my family, I found the support most needed for such a demanding undertaking, beginning with my mother, who, having asked me to write something interesting to nonprofessionals, proofread the entire manuscript. To the three people whose lives have been most touched by the writing of this book I owe the most: Ashley Dunning, who made her mother's book a matter of filial pride; Thad Dunning, who accepted it all with perfect grace because he never knew his mother otherwise; and Ted Margadant, whose many insights in conversation were equaled only by his wise decision not to read the text until I had completed the entire manuscript. That this project ever became a book owes much to his unstinting faith in me.

Abbreviations

A.N.	Archives nationales
BAES	Bulletin de l'Association des élèves de Sèvres
BMAES	Bulletin mensuel de l'Association des élèves de Sèvres
BTAES	Bulletin trimestriel de l'Association des élèves de Sèvres
E.N.S.	Ecole Normale Supérieure des jeunes filles
ESDJF	L'Enseignement secondaire des jeunes filles
RESDJF	Revue de l'enseignement secondaire des jeunes filles
RU	Revue universitaire

Madame le Professeur

Introduction

THIS BOOK takes as its subject the first generation of women who, over a century ago, broke the gender barrier that traditionally divided male *professeurs* from women schoolteachers. Those educators faced an extraordinary challenge. Even today, the tradition of the male professeur remains so dominant in French culture that the masculine title "le professeur" applies to the thousands of women who practice this profession. Such a paradox represents more than the inertia of linguistic habits. Early in the Third Republic, educational reformers, determined to upgrade and secularize the education of daughters of the *bourgeoisie*,[1] legislated into existence a female counterpart of the men who taught in secondary schools for boys. A special Ecole Normale Supérieure, housed in the former porcelain factory at Sèvres, became responsible for training a novel category of teacher delineated by the title "Madame le Professeur." She was not to be a carbon copy of male colleagues. Instead, this new professional would replicate inside girls' schools domestic images of femininity. The School of Sèvres, under the tutelage of its formidable first *directrice*, would, indeed, fashion a professional persona with a distinctive ethos. Its first graduates,[2] eager to bring a feminine face to their profession, moved quickly into positions of influence in the new girls' *collèges* and *lycées* that as a generation they would dominate for half a century. Their work as professeurs and directrices established a fundamental context for change in bourgeois feminine culture from the 1880s through the First World War. These Sévriennes also managed in this period, by dint of talent and determination, to turn their own profession into a respectable career for middle-class women. Ultimately, however, both efforts—to create a feminine version of secondary education and a female professeur—failed. Just as girls' secondary schools renounced a feminized curriculum to prepare their students for the *baccalauréat* designed for boys, in the final decade of the

[1] The term *bourgeois* could be used loosely to refer to any man who had passed the baccalauréat exam or more restrictively to designate the well-to-do business, official, professional, and proprietary elites. It was in the latter sense that the sponsors of girls' secondary education used the term to describe the clientele they hoped to attract to the new schools.

[2] This study covers the classes from the entering year 1881 through 1890. Classes are designated by year of entry to Sèvres, as is customary in the French system.

3

Third Republic, "Madame le Professeur" lost her distinctive mission and became an educator patterned after masculine traditions.

Embedded in the history of this generation and the profession they founded, though, there lies another, more personal story, one that resonates with private pathos. It recounts not what these Sévriennes accomplished but what as individuals, confined to a marginal social world, they felt and endured. Raised in a society that placed great value on stability, especially in its social mores, these teachers placed themselves in a position that for young and single women held real social perils. Ostracism figured first among them. Disapproved of for their excessive learning, ignored as strangers in communities where they worked, yet suspected of loose morals whenever they went out, perforce, alone, many of them anguished through their early professional years. By the time they reached mid-life, girls' secondary education had become more generally accepted, in large part through their own selfless dedication. Most of them could claim positions of respect in both their communities and their schools. The irony of this achievement was that just when these pioneering women might have expected to reap the honor due them for their arduous endeavors, demands inside their own profession changed. Quite suddenly they found themselves as aging professionals cast in the role of uncomprehending and incomprehensible "old fogies."

In their personal struggle to come to terms with change, these women felt and suffered like other ordinary people. That alone inspires interest in their thoughts and feelings. When, in addition, we begin to see this private side of their experience as a reflection of the society in which they lived, their personal motives and responses take on new layers of meaning.

What can a history of 213 pioneering professional women contribute to the historiography of modern France?[3] More, perhaps, than is immediately apparent. There can be little doubt of the potential interest of this study for historians of women. In the history of working women, this marks the first attempt to write a comprehensive history of French women in a middle-class profession. Not just any profession, either: in the nineteenth and twentieth centuries, teaching represented the most exalted profession for daughters of the middle class. Furthermore, this generation of Sèvres's alumnae came from the politically dominant class of France's Third Republic. As public teachers, they worked within its institutional heart; and as an educational elite, they fundamentally

---

[3] This number represents 80 percent of the first ten classes. The staff of the Archives nationales (A.N.) could not locate the *dossiers personnels* of the other graduates. Their dossiers, stored in series F17, are organized into cartons by date of death rather than under the name of the person.

marked the course of development of girls' secondary schools. Inevitably, a reconstruction of their personal and professional lives casts light on other themes within the Third Republic's history.

With respect to women's history, this work may be compared to current theoretical perspectives in the field. Broadly speaking, two approaches to women's historical experience have dominated recent literature. The older of them, growing out of feminist polemics, assumes that women were hapless victims of conditions imposed on them by men within a patriarchal social order.[4] Certainly this study in some ways reinforces that view of the modern feminine condition. As state employees in public secondary schools for girls, these Sévriennes belonged to a bureaucratized profession under the control of men. Moreover, they pursued a career track not only separate from the men's teaching profession but also inferior to it in status and opportunities. Both discrimination and subordination form an integral part of this professional generation's history. Yet as an explanatory device, this way of understanding women's experience proves inadequate and misleading. It denies the part that women had in determining the course of their own history, and it overlooks the changes resulting from conflict between men and women in their different social roles.

A more fruitful approach, recently explored by American and European historians, rejects this dichotomous view of women's history, with women as victims and men as their oppressors.[5] These historians assume instead that women in the past had considerable influence over their own destinies, albeit in ways that society circumscribed. To understand women's experience in the past, they argue, we must adopt the perspective of the women studied and investigate their world and their values from within. Increasingly, that realization has led historians into the particular domains of women, those of family, the home, and reproduction. Conceptually, what such scholars have in common is their identification of a clear polarity in the social experience of women. On the one hand lies the private sphere of family and family obligations, on the other hand, the public sphere of community and work.

All major contributors to this methodological approach have predicated their work on the primacy of family life for women and on the

---

[4] This view received an early and brilliant treatment by Simone de Beauvoir, *The Second Sex*, trans. and ed. H. M. Parshley (New York: Bantam, 1961). For a more recent and rancorous statement of this position, see Sheila Rowbotham, *Women, Resistance and Revolution* (New York: Vintage, 1972).

[5] For a particularly well-stated view of this position, see the introduction to Bonnie G. Smith, *Ladies of the Leisure Class: The Bourgeoises of Northern France in the Nineteenth Century* (Princeton: Princeton Univ. Press, 1981), 3–17.

subordination of their public lives to family duties. They reason that activities in the public sphere, which for men appear to have a public character, for women either derive from familial obligations or project domestic roles onto the community. Olwen Hufton's study of the eighteenth-century poor in France and Louise Tilly and Joan Scott's book on women from the industrial working class maintain that familial values determined the decisions of women about when and where to work.[6] Looking at a different social class, the industrial bourgeoisie of the nineteenth-century Nord, Bonnie Smith discovered that the leisured women of this milieu also had a strictly familial frame of reference. Thus, she argues that the charity work in which these women engaged merely extended into public life their maternal and domestic obligations.[7]

Impressed by these results, I chose a similar line of inquiry for the study of a radically different social type: the career woman. Of course, domestic duties and domestic values did profoundly shape these women's experience both because of expectations they placed upon themselves and because of what their families, their superiors, and the school community wanted from them. Many aspects of their lives bear witness to that orientation. Yet unlike the women whom Hufton, Scott, and Tilly have described, Sévriennes who stayed in their profession did not consistently subordinate their work to family. In balancing work and family obligations, they foreshadowed calculations of women in the later twentieth century who, having pursued careers that require a high level of training, adopt a masculine model of performance and success. Not surprisingly, Sévriennes were, in this development, transitional figures. Even by the end of their careers, these educators had not entirely renounced a notion of feminine achievement modeled after the bourgeois ideal of the domestic woman.

[6] Olwen Hufton, *The Poor of Eighteenth Century France, 1750–1789* (Oxford: Clarendon, 1974). See also Olwen Hufton, "Women and the Family Economy in Eighteenth Century France," *French Historical Studies* 9, no. 3 (1975): 1–22; and Louise A. Tilly and Joan W. Scott, *Women, Work and Family* (New York: Holt, Rinehart, 1978), 104–46. Two recent companion collections of articles on women's work and women's role in the family in England suggest the ongoing influence of this approach: Jane Lewis, ed., *Women's Experience of Home and Family, 1840–1914* (Oxford: Basil Blackwell, 1986), and Angela V. John, ed., *Unequal Opportunities: Women's Employment in England, 1800–1918* (Oxford: Basil Blackwell, 1986).

[7] B. Smith, *Ladies*, 123–64. For a similar argument, see Leonore Davidoff and Catherine Hall, *Family Fortunes: Men and Women of the English Middle Class, 1780–1850* (Chicago: Univ. of Chicago Press, 1987), and Barbara Corrado Pope, "Angels in the Devil's Workshop: Leisured and Charitable Women in Nineteenth-Century England and France," in *Becoming Visible: Women in European History*, ed. Renate Bridenthal and Claudia Koonz (Boston: Houghton Mifflin, 1977), 296–324.

In much the same way, the public image of these women offered an ambiguous social message. Sévriennes as teachers and directrices were agents of a state eager to shape the public life of the republic through its schools. Inevitably, this drew them into tasks and issues that their counterparts in boys' schools also shared. On such occasions, they were acting in their capacity as civil servants, not as women whose roles in the family defined their public acts. Yet the social acceptability of this profession grew directly out of its resemblance to demands on bourgeois mothers in the home. For decades, expectations placed on teachers and directrices reflected that maternal reference. Over the course of Sévriennes' careers, however, a professional model not linked to gender began to change these expectations in the classroom, upsetting what had always been in practice an uneasy balance between the teacher or directrice as civil servant and as surrogate "mother." Once again the results of the present study situate this generation on a bridge between a nineteenth-century ideal and a late twentieth-century model of the public woman.

I have also taken from my predecessors in the field the goal of writing women's history from within. In fact, a reconstruction of these Sévriennes' hopes and fears, their triumphs and their anguish, sheds a novel light on established issues in French history. The professional experience of this generation coincided with the crucial years in the formation of a new educational tradition, years when secondary schools for girls first introduced a separate secondary track for girls, then gradually changed the educational expectations of the middle classes so completely that even Catholic schools for girls had to shift their goals. Finally, in the 1920s, public secondary schools for girls gave way themselves to mounting public pressure for a secondary system modeled after boys' schools. Necessarily, to tell these women's story means recounting the history of that transformation. Yet the results do not simply repeat the findings of earlier institutionally focused studies. Following institutional developments through the lives of teachers and directrices provides a fresh perspective on themes in educational history.

Of special interest for institutional studies is the relationship brought to light here between attitudes of functionaries in the civil service and values promoted in the bosom of the middle-class home. Two modi operandi fundamental to modern French society confront each other across the troubled lives of this female generation, one drawn from the middle-class family, the other from the operations of a bureaucratic state. To the extent that family values and the bureaucratic ethos reinforced each other, Sévriennes become the model of the dedicated civil servant; to the extent that they conflicted, these women lacked the mental outlook required to defend their own professional interests. The dilemma did not last the course of their careers, but its very existence suggests a latent clash of values between the public and private experience of individuals from the middle classes that could well have affected the lives of men as well as women in this period.

From a comparative point of view, the most noteworthy findings of this study relate to issues in the history of the professions. Professional elites have recently assumed a central place in social histories of the modern period.[8] Into this burgeoning literature historians of women have inserted their own questions about the fate of middle-class females who tried to follow fathers and brothers into new arenas of secular expertise and public service.[9] Rarely theoretical, these investigations focus rather on the success or failure of strategies for professional acceptance that women in different generations and professional fields adopted. In England and the United States, the most intensively studied countries, these strategies boiled down to three in the decades before the First World War. Some pioneering women parlayed traditionally "feminine" talents into a professional field that segregated women's work from men's in a subordinated status.[10] Others claimed the same expertise as men in a common professional culture but carried out their tasks in sep-

[8] Burton Bledstein, *The Culture of Professionalism: The Middle Class and the Development of Higher Education in America* (New York: W. W. Norton, 1976; Christophe Charle, *Les Elites de la République 1880–1900* (Paris: Fayard, 1987); Gerald L. Geison, ed., *Professions and the French State, 1700–1900* (Philadelphia: Univ. of Pennsylvania Press, 1983); Thomas L. Haskell, *The Authority of Experts: Studies in History and Theory* (Bloomington: Indiana Univ. Press, 1984).

[9] Martha Vicinus, *Independent Women: Work and Community for Single Women 1850–1920* (Chicago: Univ. of Chicago Press, 1985); Barbara J. Harris, *Beyond Her Sphere: Women and the Professions in American History* (Westport, Conn.: Greenwood Press, 1978); Penina Migdal Glazer and Miriam Slater, *Unequal Colleagues: The Entrance of Women into the Professions, 1890–1940* (New Brunswick, N.J.: Rutgers Univ. Press, 1987); Margaret W. Rossiter, *Women Scientists in America: Struggles and Strategies to 1940* (Baltimore: Johns Hopkins Univ. Press, 1982); Mary Roth Walsh, *"Doctors Wanted: No Women Need Apply": Sexual Barriers in the Medical Profession, 1835–1975* (New Haven: Yale Univ. Press, 1977); Joan Jacobs Brumberg and Nancy Tomes, "Women in the Professions: A Research Agenda for American Historians," *Reviews in American History* 10, no. 2 (1982): 275–96; Regina G. Kunzel, "The Professionalization of Benevolence: Evangelicals and Social Workers in the Florence Crittenton Homes, 1915 to 1945," *Journal of Social History* 22, no. 1 (1988): 21–43. For studies of French professional women, see Arlette Farge and Christiane Klapisch-Zuber, eds., *Madame ou Mademoiselle? itinéraires de la solitude féminine 18e–20e siècle* (Paris: Editions Montalba, 1984), 163–202; Yvonne Knibiehler, *Nous les assistantes sociales* (Paris: Aubier-Montaigne, 1980).

[10] Nursing followed this pattern of development. See Vicinus, *Independent Women*, 85–120.

arate institutions serving female clienteles.[11] A third group tried to enter a male profession and advance by merit.[12] The results of all these efforts to secure for women a permanent position in the emergent professional elite proved disappointing. By World War II in Anglo-Saxon countries, women had lost their earlier toehold in the men's professions, while male professionals increasingly challenged the cultural imperative that a female clientele be served by women.[13] What remained for educated women in search of a career were the poor pay and low status of femininized sectors of professions controlled and dominated by a male elite.

The trajectory of the new women's profession of secondary teaching in France pursued a similar course but with a different outcome. Women professeurs began, like nurses, social workers, and teachers in American women's colleges, with a professional image modeled after domestic roles assigned to women. As elsewhere, that strategy succeeded marvelously with the general public; but professionally, it marginalized female professeurs within the nation's teaching corps. Impatient with this subordination, women teaching in lycées fought successfully after World War I to introduce to girls' education the same professional tasks and standards as characterized boys' schools. This achievement gradually equalized rewards for male and female teachers between the wars. Yet in contrast to what happened in the liberal professions, the merging of the two professional worlds at the level of rewards neither crowded women out of the profession nor lessened its appeal for men. By World War II, women professeurs had taken their place permanently alongside men as experts in a prestigious public service.

Two circumstances permitted this exceptional result. In the first place, the bureaucratic practices of the state made it difficult in the short run and impossible over the longer term to distinguish between male and female teachers. A tendency to fashion the women's corps into a likeness of the male profession appeared right from the start in the procedures for licensing and supervising women teachers. This tendency increased as a scientific outlook gained ascendance over the morally grounded pedagogy of the early Third Republic. Finally, once boys' and girls' lycées had the same curriculum, the rationale for treating men and women teachers differently would collapse under the pressure of the state's own merito-

[11] Mary E. Wooley and her entirely female faculty at Mount Holyoke College for Women pursued this course for a time. Glazer and Slater, *Unequal Colleagues*, 25–68.

[12] This approach produced the occasional eminent woman doctor like Sara Josephine Baker or scientist like Florence R. Sabin. Ibid., 119–65.

[13] Nancy F. Cott, *The Grounding of Modern Feminism* (New Haven: Yale Univ. Press, 1987), 213–40; Patricia M. Hummer, *The Decade of Elusive Promise* (Ann Arbor, Mich.: UMI Research Press, 1979).

cratic ethos. What then prevented male teachers from invading girls' schools? The answer this time lies in the politics of education in the Third Republic. The rivalry between Church and state over girls' education forced republicans to defend their schools by copying the model offered by the clergy, and that meant leaving women in charge of educating girls. In sum, a struggle between factions within the political elite permitted women professeurs to insert themselves into the professional power structure.

On a conceptual level, this outcome fits neatly into the model of professionalization recently proposed by Andrew Abbott.[14] The professions belong, in Abbott's view, to an interdependent system in which jurisdictional boundaries are in perpetual dispute. The evolution of any particular group of experts depends on their successful competition with other professions over the arenas in which their expertise applies. Ordinarily, conflicts over jurisdiction result either in an amalgamation of two professions into a single larger field or in a new, hierarchical subdivision of jurisdictions. Rarely do two professions claiming equal expertise share a common jurisdiction, but this can happen if they serve different clienteles. Because the cultural resistance to mixing sexes in the classroom proved so strong in France, men and women secondary teachers would follow just that course.

How, then, can one characterize this study? Neither an institutional nor a cultural history, it belongs to that genre of social history included under the unwieldy label *prosopography*. As the biography of a group, it shares with much larger quantitative studies certain common features. The most obvious is its aggregative treatment of individual experiences. Throughout my research I have sought quantifiable evidence in order to construct a collective profile of this group of women. In that respect, this study resembles the quantitatively more ambitious works of Françoise Mayeur, Paul Gerbod, and Gérard Vincent, each of whom has also studied secondary teachers.[15] Unlike most other prosopographies, however, this study is not limited to the workplace, and it broadens its perspective to embrace the life cycle of a single generation of teachers and direc-

[14] Andrew Abbot, *The System of Professions: An Essay on the Division of Expert Labor* (Chicago: Univ. of Chicago Press, 1988), 6–7, 20, 71–74, 102–22, 219–21.

[15] Françoise Mayeur, *L'Enseignement secondaire des jeunes filles sous la Troisième République* (Paris: Presses de la fondation nationale des sciences politiques, 1977); Paul Gerbod, *La Condition universitaire en France au XIXe siècle* (Paris: Presses universitaires de France, 1965); Gérard Vincent, "Les Professeurs de l'enseignement secondaire dans la société de la Belle Epoque," *Revue d'histoire moderne et contemporaine* 13 (January–March 1966): 49–86; and Gérard Vincent, "Les Professeurs du second degré au début du XXe siècle, essai sur la mobilité sociale et la mobilité géographique," *Mouvement social* 69 (1969): 124–27.

trices. While Mayeur, Gerbod, and Vincent provide a relatively static profile of their teachers within a professional milieu, the collective portrait developed in this study moves back and forth between private and professional experience and changes over time.

Like the cultural anthropologist, I have also tried to reconstruct the mental and emotional world of this professional generation, something statistics on behavior do not show. In recognition of that fact, social historians have recently begun to use the tools of disciplines other than sociology in order to interpret their results. A good example is Bonnie Smith's attempt to understand the cultural implications of the leisured bourgeoise's rising fertility in the Nord throughout the nineteenth century. Lacking evidence that private correspondence or diaries might have held, she looks instead for cultural explanations in the symbolic meaning of the artifacts surrounding women's lives—their clothes, their furniture, the architectural layout of their homes.[16] But this approach still involves an inference that the testimony of her subjects might belie. Another new approach, inspired by semiotics and literary theory, returns to language as the traditional source of evidence in history. Historians influenced by this linguistic turn in cultural studies explore the mental outlook of a group by reconstructing the way that language expresses and organizes power within any social field through which a person moves.[17] In my own more modest effort to reenter another cultural world, to recover the meaning in the life of women that they themselves attached to it, I have drawn intermittently on both of these approaches.

The organization of this study reflects my interest in these women's history as they lived it. Chapters follow a developmental logic linked explicitly to the life cycle, hence to experience as it progressively unfolds. As biography, it is at one and the same time a personal history that traces this generation of women from their adolescence through maturity to old age and a career study that follows their professional lives through successive stages, beginning with their training and moving through their experiences first as new teachers, later as knowledgeable professionals, and finally as a generation heading for retirement. Yet along with these biological and professional permutations, other changes occurred in the institutions where these women worked, changes that impinged directly on their attitudes and lives. Thus, woven into a chapter organization based on personal and professional development are themes re-

---

[16] B. Smith, *Ladies*, 53–92.

[17] For an important application of this approach to the history of women, see Joan Wallich Scott, *Gender and the Politics of History* (New York: Columbia Univ. Press, 1988).

flecting broader transformations both in girls' schools and in the local and professional communities of which these women were a part.

To set the stage for these much larger shifts, I begin the study with the foundation of girls' secondary schools and the Ecole Normale at Sèvres. This introduction explores the contradictions inherent in a schooling system that was ideologically committed to upholding a separate educational and professional sphere for women within a centralizing, bureaucratic state. Three following parts chronicle the lives and careers of the first generation of Sèvres's graduates.

The first, which covers their young adulthood and early careers, opens with a social analysis of students recruited into Sèvres. A discussion of the school itself examines the professional training and institutional style that students found there as well as the self-sacrificing, even heroic ethos encouraged by the first directrice. The analysis then develops a multisided portrait of young Sévriennes as teachers in the classroom, as colleagues and subordinates in their schools, and as outsiders in communities to which the Ministry of Education sent them. The results reveal a generation trapped in a professional milieu where loneliness and conflict were endemic. A combination of their status as pariahs and a social training that encouraged personal aloofness isolated them from society and from each other, while professional rivalries and an inherently unstable model of success strained their relations with superiors. One response to this experience involved an all-out effort by Sévriennes to find posts closer to their families, if necessary at the expense of their careers. Marriage offered some teachers a similar kind of haven. Yet the emotional comfort home life promised came at the expense of added duties that these young professionals undertook as women in their families. Much evidence suggests conscious and unconscious resistance among young teachers to the demands that work and family placed upon them.

A second part concerns this generation's professional mid-life, when several rose to posts of real importance. Both personally and professionally, Sévriennes after 1900 entered a new era. No longer fledgling teachers, they emerged as leaders in their schools, in the broader community of educators, and, ultimately, in a nation at war. Many Sévriennes now pursued professional advancement boldly while preserving a corporate ethos based on self-denying dedication. Especially as directrices of girls' schools, they would defend the ethos that they themselves had learned at Sèvres and that in key respects extended familial values into public institutions. The experience of war dramatically revived their old heroic values, redefining in the process their vision for women in the nation. As the war swept thousands of male public servants into the army, municipalities and the central government turned to directrices of girls' schools for vital service on the civilian front. For the first time, directrices moved outward from the school itself to become leaders in the public eye. In tribute to the dedication of these women, France would offer several of them honors that only men had previously received. Yet directrices perceived their mission as maternal figures in the nation's hour of deepest need, and as before, familial values continued to dominate their discourse.

A third and final part situates this aging generation of educators within a world transformed in its cultural values and its educational expectations for middle-class women by the social consequences of the war. The focus shifts here from directrices to outspoken teachers who after 1910 expressed a mounting restlessness within the women's corps over its inferior status in a paternalistic, bureaucratic profession. Their dissatisfaction combined with that of parents over the economic implications of a peripheral female track would in due course drive girls' secondary schools to adopt the baccalauréat program. Aging Sévriennes, still in prominent positions, now stood at an institutional crossroads that for some of them perplexed their final years. Under the eye of state inspectors and the influence of younger teachers, girls' schools teetered between the aggressively individualistic ethos of preprofessional studies and the familial style of education still fostered by the older generation. Once retired, this pioneering generation returned to private life, where, for the first time in the records left behind, they appear apart from institutional pressures. The results confirm what this study repeatedly discovers. A single moral vision shaped this generation's attitudes as professionals, as individuals, and as members of their families, and it derived from definitions of femininity and service engendered in their homes.

The Invention of the Woman Professeur

ASSEMBLED on July 19, 1881 to debate a bill creating a national *école normale* for women secondary teachers, the Senate of the National Assembly had just heard a favorable report from the spokesman for the parliamentary commission. "Is there anyone who wants to speak?" queried the president. Baron d'Emond Dufaur de Gavardie rose from the far right side of the room: "I request the dismissal of this proposal. . . . It envisages a completely novel institution. A lay seminary for girls who would be lady professeurs, I am not familiar with that monster!"[1] In an unexpected foretaste of what awaited women secondary teachers, a burst of laughter exploded from all sides of the hall. Immediately, however, the shared amusement at Gavardie's wit subsided into the partisan jeers and acclamations typical of debates on education over the three preceding years as republicans had sought to found a national schooling system free of Church control.[2] In fact, Gavardie's protest amounted to a futile gesture in a major struggle already lost by Catholic royalists seven months earlier, when republican majorities in both legislative houses had approved a law creating public secondary schools for girls.[3] Having enacted the legal framework for these schools the previous December, those majorities now had merely to provide a way to train the women teachers who would staff them.

Gavardie's objection did raise, nonetheless, a fundamental issue about the nature of this new profession. The problem he implicitly discerned

[1] July 19, 1881 session of the Senate in *Lycées et collèges de jeunes filles. Documents, rapports et discours à la Chambre des députés et au Sénat. Décrets, arrêtés, circulaires, etc. Tableau du personnel des lycées et collèges par ordre d'ancienneté . . .* , préface par Camille Sée (Paris: Cerf, 1884), 447.

[2] Republicans in 1881 fell into three parliamentary groupings: the moderates led by men like Jules Ferry and Jules Simon, the Opportunists led by Léon Gambetta, and the Radicals. After the election of 1876, these groups constituted a majority in the Chamber of Deputies, a majority that was confirmed in the all-out struggle with the royalist Right led by President MacMahon in the elections of May 16, 1877. Two years later the republicans captured a majority of the seats in the Senate as well. The moderates, merged with the Opportunists, would remain in control of the government until the crisis over the Dreyfus Affair brought the Radicals to power in the 1890s. Gordon Wright, *France in Modern Times*, 3d. ed. (New York: W. W. Norton, 1981), 240–62.

[3] The Senate approved a final version on December 10, 1880. The Chamber of Deputies approved the Senate's version of the bill on December 16, 1880.

in the law creating Sèvres was the likeness that this new school bore to convents. What professional style did the state intend these women teachers to adopt? The secular standards of the male lycée professeur or the cloistered ideal associated with religious education? The oldest and most influential version of the model teacher came, of course, from Catholic teaching orders. Teachers of the cloth had dominated the public image of the teacher since the Middle Ages. For much of the nineteenth century, the state had chosen to impose a similar style on public education by insisting that all staff in boys' lycées, excepting only professeurs, remain unmarried and reside at school,[4] and even professeurs had to take their meals within the institution.[5] Republican ascendance in the 1870s marked the end in public schools of that religiously inspired model for male teachers. As fervent anticlericals, republicans intended to replace the cloister with the family in the popular imagination as the proper source of moral inspiration.[6] Teachers under the republic would be the living proof of that new secular ideal. Beginning in the 1880s, therefore, public teachers were expected to adopt a professional ethos that engaged them with the world and a social image which identified them as members of a family. For men in this profession, the transition to a new, more worldly ideal proceeded smoothly in the last two decades of the nineteenth century.[7] But women teachers, whose gender made them the object of severe social constraints, could not throw off the cloistered style so quickly. In that dilemma, we see beginning to emerge the profile of the women's normal school that found a home at Sèvres and the distinctive features of the initial corps of teachers who would train there.

Graduates of Sèvres faced yet another problem as a result of their identity as women. Gavardie's sneer at "lady professeurs" raised an issue of great importance for women bold enough to enter this profession. Outside Paris, and to a degree even within the capital, polite bourgeois society had not developed an accepted role for educated women. The decline of the aristocratic salon and the emergence of the all-male bourgeois club (*cercle*) had undercut the one respectable arena for such

---

[4] Antoine Prost, *L'Histoire de l'enseignement en France, 1800–1967* (Paris: A. Colin, 1968), 25, 77.

[5] Ibid.

[6] Katherine Auspitz, *The Radical Bourgeoisie: The Ligue de l'Enseignement and the Origins of the Third Republic, 1866–1885* (Cambridge: Cambridge Univ. Press, 1982), 20–22.

[7] For an excellent account of this process as it affected the intellectual and social life within the Ecole Normale Supérieure of the rue d'Ulm, see Robert J. Smith, *The Ecole Normale Supérieure and the Third Republic* (Albany: State Univ. of New York Press, 1982), 59–72, 79–84.

women in the nineteenth century.[8] Within the Catholic bourgeoisie, at least, a cultivated woman, unless connected with Parisian salon life, might now have few occasions to display her knowledge freely.[9] Artistic circles, like those in which the writer George Sand moved, could offer well-read women intellectual friendships, but the social independence required in this milieu closed them to "respectable" women fearful for their reputations. For men, by contrast, intellectual credentials linked to higher education would become over the course of the nineteenth century an ever firmer base for social status, a trend the Third Republic would decidedly advance. Indeed, by 1914, among the most respected leaders in political and even journalistic life, many could hark back to training as a lycée professeur.[10] Such was the social background to Gavardie's joke about the "lady professeur." His epithet itself mocked this new profession with the clash between two such different social images.

But why did republicans vote to train a corps of women secondary teachers if the royalist and Catholic opposition could so easily ridicule them as misfits? After all, the precedent of other European countries to which the author of the bill, the deputy Camille Sée, had looked for guidance,[11] spoke for having male instructors.[12] Indeed, in France itself, tradition pressed for that arrangement. In the only previous public offering of advanced studies for girls, the municipal secondary courses for girls launched in 1867 by the minister of education Victor Duruy, the state relied on men to teach the girls' classes.[13] Moreover, private schools for

---

[8] Maurice Agulhon, *Le Cercle dans la France bourgeoise: 1810–1848* (Paris: A. Colin, 1977).

[9] B. Smith, *Ladies*, 53–92. In describing the families of the business elite of the Nord in the second half of the nineteenth century, Smith depicts a female world that operated alongside of but intellectually and even socially separate from that of husbands. After dinner parties, according to Smith, men withdrew from women's company for a smoke and to talk of matters about which women were ignorant, indifferent, or had diametrically opposing views.

[10] For the classic statement of this view, see Alfred Thibaudet, *La République des professeurs* (Paris: B. Grasset, 1927). Christophe Charle includes among the ruling class those teachers promoted from secondary teaching into university posts in Paris in *Les Elites de la République*.

[11] "Proposition de loi de M. Camille Sée . . . ," in *Lycées et collèges de jeunes filles*, 67–133.

[12] The German educator Dr. Jacob Wychgram, a professor of secondary studies for girls at Leipzig who wrote an account of the founding years of girls' secondary education in France, considered that the decision not to use male teachers was a serious pedagogical error. *L'Instruction publique des filles en France*, trans. E. Esparcel (Paris: Delagrave, 1885).

[13] Sandra Horvath-Peterson, *Victor Duruy and French Education: Liberal Reform in the Second Empire* (Baton Rouge: Louisiana State Univ. Press, 1984). For general studies of nineteenth-century educational history before the Third Republic, see Robert An-

girls and even convent schools, in the not-so-distant past, had also hired men to give advanced instruction. Pursuing answers to that question will lead us back into the history of girls' private schools in France and to the impact of the Falloux Law of 1850 on staffing practices in public schools for girls. It will also take us onto the major battleground of politics throughout the early Third Republic, where we shall find republicans locked in combat with the Church. Ultimately, it will bring us to the fountainhead of republican attitudes toward women in the discourse— dating from the French Revolution and, originally, Rousseau—that linked domestic roles of women to the civic virtue of their sons and husbands. In the 1880s, progressives set out to harness that old republican ideal to the new goal of upgrading bourgeois girls' education.

As the story of Sèvres and its first progeny unfolds, however, it will become apparent that at the core of this profession lay an ambiguity. Republicans expected women in this new profession to create distinctly feminine traditions based on expectations for their sex within the home. They easily imagined the perpetuation through secondary schools, aided by their laws and their decrees, of gender-specific social roles and values. In that belief, they failed to reckon with the long-term influence of the elitist, meritocratic ethos of the *Université*, the professional corporation of secondary and university male teachers. Republicans did not foresee the problems inherent in expecting a professional corporation steeped in the liberal ideology of individual merit and standardized degrees to apply the principle of separate spheres to secondary teaching. For years the men and women who ran this educational system kept the contradiction hidden by continuous compromise, in a labyrinth of administrative readjustments. In the end, however, such piecemeal adaptations failed because the logic of the unitary outlook of the men's profession kept girl students and women teachers from getting equal treatment, while at the same time encouraging them to seek it. Under the weight of the resulting disaffection, the notion of a separate educational sphere for girls inevitably would collapse.

The Weight of History

A brief examination of the history of girls' education in the nineteenth century makes clear that precedent played as great a part in shaping the reforms of 1880–1881 as did invention. The very idea of schooling girls in secondary studies had antecedents dating back as far as the

---

derson, *Education in France, 1848–1870* (Oxford: Oxford Univ. Press, 1975), and Maurice Gontard, *L'Enseignement secondaire en France de la fin de l'Ancien Régime à la loi Falloux, 1750–1850* (Aix-en-Provence: Edisud, 1984).

1830s when, at least in Paris, some private schools for girls offered secondary instruction to daughters of the well-to-do. Françoise Mayeur, on whose study most of our knowledge of these developments depends, discovered that the Conseil royal d'instruction, which exercised the right to inspect all private schools, recognized a two-tiered institutional structure for schooling girls in the department of the Seine.[14] One level, called *pensions*, offered girls an elementary education and fell under the jurisdiction of the royal government's primary school inspectors. A second group of schools known as *institutions* gave their students more advanced instruction. In recognition of that fact, in 1837 the Conseil royal d'instruction turned their supervision over to inspectors from the Université.[15]

Admittedly, the subjects taught in institutions were not the same as those in boys' collèges and lycées. French literature and language constituted the core curriculum of girls' secondary studies. Girls might study a miscellany of other subjects, variable among schools, including the biological sciences, history, and modern languages.[16] But Latin and Greek, the foundation of masculine instruction, found no place in girls' secondary studies. Instead, a considerable part of every day went to developing their skills in the feminine domestic and social arts of music, drawing, dancing, and needlework. From a long-term perspective, the distinctive mark of girls' education in this period was not the feminization of the secondary curriculum; that would remain a constant trait of advanced instruction for girls up to 1924. The peculiarity of girls' secondary studies in this period lay in the fact that most private girls' schools hired men, not women, to teach their courses.

In contrast to the practice after 1850, male teachers monopolized private instruction for girls in the vicinity of Paris in all but the most elementary classes. According to a survey in the department of the Seine in 1846, male teachers filled two-thirds of the teaching posts in girls' boarding schools known as *pensionnats*.[17] Only positions in teaching the social graces (*arts d'agréments*) or math and reading to the youngest children customarily went to women instructors.[18] Rather than being

[14] Françoise Mayeur, *L'Education des jeunes filles en France au XIXe siècle* (Paris: Hachette, 1979), 59–63, 104–12. See also Octavius Gréard, *L'Enseignement secondaire des filles; mémoire présenté au Conseil académique de Paris dans la séance du 27 juin 1882* (Paris: Delagrave, 1883), 18–41.

[15] Mayeur, *L'Education des jeunes filles*, 90.

[16] Ibid., 61, 90.

[17] Ibid., 73.

[18] Women apparently taught music, needlework, and drawing. Of the feminine social arts, only dancing was taught in girls' schools by male instructors. Ibid., 81.

full-fledged teachers, women worked more often as assistant teachers (ré-pétitrices), responsible for supervising students' work and play outside the classroom. Indeed, so broad was the consensus on this staffing practice in girls' schools that even convent schools apparently observed it, hiring men to teach their older classes.[19]

Mayeur concludes that this monopoly by men of girls' instruction in the upper elementary and secondary classes of private schools for girls in Paris stemmed partly from the lack of schools for training women teachers. Beginning in 1819, the state required all lay women teachers to possess an elementary teaching certificate called the brevet de capacité.[20] Although the law did not apply to nuns in teaching orders, who merely needed a "letter of obedience" from their mother superior to certify their competence as teachers,[21] this law might have opened a significant professional avenue for women teachers. Unfortunately, authorities did not make the acquisition of this credential easy. Because organizing teacher-training schools for women educators was left entirely up to local efforts, few écoles normales primaires d'institutrices appeared. By 1838, in fact, when every department had an école normale primaire for men as required under law, only one such school for women existed anywhere in France. Ten years later, the total had increased to a mere eight. In order to prepare for the state's credentialing exam, aspiring women teachers most often had either to study on their own or to enroll at their personal expense in private courses, called cours normaux.[22] Both alternatives constituted substantial obstacles for the impecunious women who commonly sought their livelihood in teaching.

Even those who overcame these hurdles and managed to acquire the brevet still found their prospects for good teaching posts restricted, since their credential qualified them for only elementary teaching. By contrast, male competitors for jobs in private girls' schools would generally have passed the baccalauréat, signaling a successful conclusion to a masculine secondary education.[23] However meager a professional credential, the baccalauréat gave men an edge in competing with women for teaching posts in girls' institutions. There did exist in Paris by the 1840s an alternative to the brevet de capacité for women going into teaching. At the

[19] The Assumptionists were the only congregation that staffed their schools entirely with women. Ibid., 73.

[20] Anne Therese Quartararo, "The Ecoles Normales Primaires d'Institutrices: A Social History of Women Primary School Teachers in France, 1879–1905" (Ph.D. diss., Univ. of California, Los Angeles, 1982), 37.

[21] Ibid., 36.

[22] Prost, L'Histoire de l'enseignement, 180.

[23] Mayeur, L'Education des jeunes filles, 74.

Hôtel de Ville, twice a year, the Université administered exams and gave diplomas to women who aspired to operate or teach in girls' institutions.[24] But neither the prestige of these degrees nor the numbers who acquired them were enough to challenge men in girls' classrooms. For in the last analysis, the force that kept women teachers out of secondary instruction was cultural, not professional. Women teachers before midcentury found themselves confined to tasks perceived as suited to their image as maternal figures: teaching little girls to read and write; instructing older ones in social graces; and supervising girls of all ages in their activities outside the classroom.

The Second Empire would witness a radical transformation of this profile of girls' schools in Paris. In the first place, starting in the 1850s, the incipient movement toward secondary schools for girls there collapsed. Coincidentally, male teachers began to disappear from feminine instruction.[25] The central catalyst in this metamorphosis was the Falloux Law of 1850. This law, the brainchild of Vicomte Frédéric de Falloux, then minister of education, laid down new governing rules within which girls' schools would operate for the next three decades. Three features of this law would shape developments in girls' education up to 1880. In the first place, in the aftermath of the workers' insurrection of June 1848, Falloux, like other moderate republicans, looked to the Church to help restore respect for state authority.[26] He reversed, therefore, an effort undertaken in the early Second Republic to force nuns to take the brevet and reinstated the "letter of obedience" as a proof of competence to teach.[27] Even before midcentury this privilege had placed the Church in a position to dominate girls' primary education. Afterward, it would carry even greater weight since the right to train and certify religious teachers positioned the Church well in just those decades when interest in girls' formal schooling soared dramatically. The Church responded by flooding France with teaching nuns and religious schools. Between 1852 and 1859 alone, the imperial government under Louis Napoleon III authorized the founding of 923 new female religious orders. As a result, by 1863, religious orders instructed 56 percent of all female students in primary schools.[28]

[24] Ibid., 76.

[25] In the 1860s, Victor Duruy counted three thousand convents and girls' boarding schools or pensionnats that still allowed male professeurs from boys' secondary schools to teach occasional courses in their schools. John Moody, *French Education since Napoleon* (Syracuse: Syracuse Univ. Press, 1978), 83 n. 99.

[26] Ibid., 5–7.

[27] Prost, *L'Histoire de l'enseignement*, 173.

[28] Quartararo, "The *Ecoles Normales Primaires d'Institutrices*," 45–46. On the expan-

Vicomte Falloux had actually hoped to spur the growth of public elementary schools for girls as well as convent schools. Indeed, the law of 1850 required an *école de filles* in every commune of eight hundred inhabitants or more. But because the law did not insist that local townships pay for these new schools, municipal officials often left their creation to religious congregations.[29] Even where municipalities did set up primary schools for girls, they might well hire women in religious orders to staff them. Nuns apparently proved far more willing than lay women to accept the physical hardships enforced upon them by the pitiable salaries that frugal municipal councils offered.[30] Because the law did not provide for public normal schools for women either, professional training fell into Catholic sisters' hands almost everywhere, except in those few areas where Protestants were strong enough to operate a normal school for women of their faith.[31] Already by 1863, two-thirds of the teachers with lay professional degrees had gone to cours normaux directed by religious congregations or as adolescents had attended boarding schools run by nuns.[32] The result by 1878 was that the Catholic church could boast a virtual monopoly over primary schooling for girls and the training of women elementary teachers.

Falloux's Law not only gave the Church the opportunity to take control of girls' education, it also restricted girls' education to an elementary level. The law of 1850 did not abolish institutions. It simply ignored their existence and thereby nipped in the bud the incipient secondary education for girls growing up in Paris in the 1840s. With no legal recognition of secondary studies, there ceased to be any need for supervision of girls' schools by the Université or for higher professional degrees for women teachers.[33] This feature of the Falloux Law proved to be the second catalyst reshaping the course of girls' schooling in the succeeding decades. Without the state's involvement, girls' private schools gradually renounced any serious effort to offer a full curriculum of secondary studies, all the more inevitably as nuns armed merely with a letter of obedience took over the major role in feminine instruction.

Economic trends in the 1850s reinforced the move away from secondary schooling. Property values in major urban centers rose sharply after

---

sion of convents throughout the century, see Claude Langlois, *Le Catholicisme au féminin* (Paris: Cerf, 1984), 307–42.

[29] Prost, *L'Histoire de l'enseignement*, 103.

[30] Quartararo, "The *Ecoles Normales Primaires d'Institutrices*," 48–50.

[31] According to Antoine Prost, there were eleven public normal schools for women in 1868. *L'Histoire de l'enseignement*, 180.

[32] Ibid., 46.

[33] Mayeur, *L'Education des jeunes filles*, 75–76, 104–5.

1848, driving up the costs of pensionnats, which, unlike convent schools, rarely owned their buildings. Faced with higher rents, many of these schools had to close their doors.[34] Those that did survive succeeded only by taking drastic measures to cut expenses, so drastic, in fact, that they were transformed as educational institutions in the process. Unable to raise tuition fees above what convents charged, lay boarding schools chose instead to lower teachers' salaries.[35] Men, as a result, deserted girls' instruction for better paid positions elsewhere. Thus, just when Catholic teaching orders for women entered a period of rapid growth, men were leaving jobs in girls' schools for greener pastures. The combined effect of the proliferation of teaching sisters, the desertion of private girls' schools by male instructors, and the disappearance of advanced professional degrees for women teachers signaled the end in girls' schools of secondary studies.

The only exceptions to this institutional transformation were a few private courses, called cours, designed for day students from the wealthy classes and taught by men in Paris. The inspiration for these cours dated back to the 1780s when an enterprising monk named Abbé Gaultier conceived the idea of offering courses to well-to-do young ladies in Paris without requiring that they live away from home. Following the pedagogical tradition of the seventeenth-century Bishop Fénélon,[36] Abbé Gaultier insisted that an adolescent girl needed the guiding presence of her mother and should not, therefore, be sent away to school. Unlike the bishop, though, Gaultier did not believe that mothers by themselves could teach their daughters all they would have to know as matrons. Convinced of the importance of some intellectual training, he devised an educational setting to which girls could come accompanied by their mothers. Well into the nineteenth century, classes modeled after Gaultier's cours still enjoyed a considerable following among Parisians of the upper bourgeoisie.[37]

Falloux's Law changed little in the organization of these cours except that they, like all girls' schools after 1850, had to name a woman as administrative head.[38] In other ways, however, cours did not reflect the trends underway in schools for girls in the aftermath of Falloux's Law.

[34] Ibid., 106.

[35] Ibid.

[36] François de Salignac de la Mothe Fénélon, *Fénélon on Education: A Translation of the "Traité de l'éducation des filles" and Other Documents Illustrating Fénélon's Educational Theories and Practice*, ed. H. C. Barnard, (Cambridge: Cambridge Univ. Press, 1960).

[37] Gréard, *L'Enseignement secondaire des filles*, 22.

[38] Mayeur, *L'Education des jeunes filles*, 106–7.

Women did not take over course instruction, and although a cleric had conceived the cours for girls, they did not remain a Catholic institution. Instead, over the course of the Second Empire, the politics surrounding girls' education would transform the cours from an institutional form approved and sometimes even run by churchmen to one noxious to the Church and defended fiercely by the anticlerical Left.[39]

The turnabout occurred in 1867 when Victor Duruy as minister of education announced as an official goal the spread of public secondary studies for girls in France. A liberal Bonapartist and former educator himself, Duruy determined that the deplorable state of girls' education provided mainly by the Church needed to be remedied at once.[40] To that end, he set about promoting the idea of public secondary cours for girls that municipalities would organize and fund. Given the financial constraints on local governments, cours had indisputable advantages over schools since they required little administrative supervision and nothing more than a rented hall for lectures. Furthermore, professeurs from boys' lycées, eager to make a little money on the side, could be recruited easily and inexpensively as teachers.

As guardian for the nuns, the Church responded to Duruy's innovation with hostility, attacking both the idea of the cours and Duruy's view that girls needed secondary education. In the battle that ensued, Bishop Dupanloup of Orléans mounted the Church's main attack. Ignoring his own earlier complaints over the superficiality of feminine education, Dupanloup insisted on the moral dangers to girls of advanced instruction and, above all, of introducing males into their classrooms.[41] Only nuns, the Church implied, could safely educate an adolescent girl. In his campaign to preserve the nuns' control of girls' education, Dupanloup succeeded manifestly. At least a dozen municipal cours had emerged in major cities during the closing years of the Second Empire. Over the succeeding decade, only a handful of these courses survived.[42] Decidedly, the Church had won the first round in the struggle for control of girls' education. But in this initial skirmish, the battle lines between the Left and Right emerged redrawn. As the allies of the Church rallied behind the cause of convent education and the educational status quo, the anticlerical Left took up the case for secondary studies and with it a strong preference for day schools.

[39] This is a major thesis of Mayeur's. Ibid., 67, 106, 118, 140–41.

[40] Horvath-Peterson, *Victor Duruy and French Education*, 25–51, 151–73.

[41] Ibid., 161–67.

[42] The only cours secondaires dating from Duruy's time still extant in 1880 were located in Paris, Oran, Bordeaux, Saint-Etienne, Dijon, and Montpellier. Mayeur, *L'Enseignement secondaire*, 144.

Thus, in 1879, when republicans were at last in a position to impose their political program on the Right, the baggage of the past weighed heavily on the plans advanced by men like Camille Sée and Jules Ferry for girls' schooling. Any effort, on the one hand, to expand public education for girls constituted ipso facto an assault on the position of the Church. This was particularly true for secondary studies since in the wake of Duruy's efforts on behalf of secondary cours for girls, the Church had sided with its most reactionary prelates in favor of keeping girls' education elementary. Whatever their private views on this instruction, republican politicans generally approved girls' secondary schools because they challenged a stronghold of the Church. On the other hand, the very success achieved by women's teaching congregations during the Second Empire placed constraints on their potential rivals. To return men to girls' classrooms once nuns had feminized instruction, as Duruy tried to do, risked offending sensibilities in the middle classes. But if the state resolved to staff its secondary schools for girls with women, that placed its teachers in the difficult position of competing in the public's eyes with nuns. The more public schools tried to mimic convents, the more the public would compare them. All of these considerations figured in the debates that led in 1880 to the law creating secondary schools for girls and in 1881 to the law that founded the Ecole Normale de Sèvres.

Political and Ideological Considerations

To understand the motives that propelled republican majorities in both the Chamber of Deputies and the Senate into taking such remarkably progressive steps requires distinguishing between two groups among these laws' defenders. Most politicians who supported secondary schools for girls did so in defense of the republic. They had accepted the view propounded by the men around Jules Ferry: the only way to guarantee that future generations would not again betray the French republic was to give them a solid civic education in state schools. Having watched two earlier regimes destroyed by popular consent, republicans were most concerned to woo the lower classes. That resolve would lead them to create a system of free (June 16, 1881) and compulsory (March 18, 1882) primary education for children up to age thirteen, and in connection with that program to undertake at last to train women primary school teachers in écoles normales in each department (August 9, 1879). In 1880, with Ferry's blessing, Camille Sée succeeded in extending the argument of guarantees for the republic to daughters of the upper middle class.[43] Since bourgeois parents refused to educate their children with the lower classes, that required the creation of separate schools with, not incidentally, high tuition.

In a celebrated speech delivered at the Salle Molière in 1870, Ferry himself insisted on the menace to progressive causes of leaving to the Church the task of educating bourgeois girls. "There is going on today a silent but persistent struggle," Ferry warned his listeners,

> *between the society of the past . . . with its edifice of regrets, beliefs, and institutions that do not accept modern democracy, and the society which emerged from the French Revolution. There remains within our midst an "old regime" that still persists, and when this struggle, which is the very foundation of modern anarchy, when this intimate struggle ends, the political struggle will be over in one stroke. Moreover, women cannot be neutral in this combat any longer; optimists, who do not want to see the reality of things, imagine that the role of the woman counts for nothing, that she does not figure in the fray; but they do not perceive the secret and continuous help that women bring to this waning society which we [republicans] are seeking to expel.*[44]

Returning to a theme first raised by Jules Michelet in 1845 when he attacked the influence of the priest on bourgeois wives,[45] Ferry conjured up the specter of a matron grown more influential in the family since the days when Michelet initially described her. Over the intervening decades, the bourgeois mother had become the central figure in the education of young children,[46] and her opinions even influenced where her older offspring went to school.[47] Ferry also feared the weight of her convictions on her husband. "Whoever holds the woman holds all," he de-

[43] In the preface to *La Loi Camille Sée, documents, rapports et discours relatifs à la loi sur l'enseignement secondaire des jeunes filles* (Paris: J. Hetzel, 1881), Louis Bauzon argues that Sée's proposal for secondary schools for girls took the elite of the republican cause by surprise. They were forced to support it because, given the defense that Sée made for the idea, it was impossible for republicans to find any grounds other than prejudice for opposing it.

[44] Jules Ferry delivered this speech in the Salle Molière on April 10, 1870. Quoted in Mayeur, *L'Enseignement secondaire,* 17–18.

[45] Jules Michelet, *Du prêtre, de la femme et de la famille* (Paris: M. Lévy, 1845).

[46] Laura S. Strumingher, "L'Ange de la Maison: Mothers and Daughters in Nineteenth-Century France," *International Journal of Women's Studies,* 2, no. 1 (1979): 51–71; Marie-Françoise Lévy, *De mères en filles: l'education des françaises 1850–1880* (Paris: Calmann-Lévy, 1984).

[47] Camille Sée referred specifically to this danger in his report to the Chamber of Deputies that accompanied his bill. *Lycées et collèges de jeunes filles,* 198–99.

clared, "first because he holds the child, and then because he holds the husband, not perhaps the youthful husband still fired by a storm of passions, but the husband exhausted and disillusioned by life."[48] The loud applause that greeted this remark suggests that others recognized in Ferry's words a familiar portrait of domestic life. Ten years later hope of turning domestic bourgeois women into admirers of the Republic would constitute the central factor in persuading republican majorities in the National Assembly to support reforms proposed by Camille Sée.

Two other themes embedded in this speech explain why Jules Ferry and several close associates personally favored secondary schools for bourgeois girls. One of these concerned their views on marriage. To certain of these reformers, "a real marriage" meant, as Ferry put it to his audience in the Salle Molière, "a marriage of the minds." "There exists today," Ferry insisted, "a barrier between the woman and the man, between the wife and husband, which means that many marriages which are harmonious in appearance hide the most profound discord in feelings, tastes, and views." Five years before his own marriage introduced him personally to the joys of living with an educated wife, Ferry sketched this scene of domestic strife born of mismatched intellects.[49] In 1880, Jean-Baptiste Ferrouillat, responding to the presentation of Sée's bill before the Senate, vividly repeated the same point: "Graduates of two opposing schools, one oriented toward the past, the other toward the future, [husbands and wives] often are like strangers who speak different tongues. I am mistaken; they are in a worse predicament, for they understand each other well enough to quarrel constantly with neither truce nor rest."[50] "This profound, intellectual divorce," he went on to argue, was the result of "the inequality of their educations."[51] For men like Ferrouillat, the purpose of a secular education designed for bourgeois girls was to reinforce the influence of husbands over wives inside the home. For those who shared the views of Jules Ferry, it was to bring companionship to marriage.

Undoubtedly, in 1880, with the debate over the legalization of divorce already underway, pleas for a new harmony in marriage resonated forcefully for all deputies on the Left. But for Protestants, in particular, Ferry's vision of a companionate marriage based on education must have struck deep cultural chords. To be sure, not all Protestant deputies supported

---

[48] Quoted in Mayeur, *L'Enseignement secondaire*, 18.

[49] Françoise Mayeur, "La Femme dans la société selon Jules Ferry," in *Jules Ferry, fondateur de la République: actes du colloque*, ed. François Furet (Paris: Editions des hautes études en sciences sociales, 1985), 79–87.

[50] *Lycées et collèges de jeunes filles*, 293.

[51] Ibid.

the new law.[52] But several from the liberal wing of Protestantism figured conspicuously in the movement for reform.[53] Ferry himself had married the daughter of a freethinking Protestant family in 1875.[54] Thus, in addition to the more typically republican concern to secularize the education of future wives and mothers, the traditional Protestant ideal of spouses with a common education won converts for reform.

One further consideration shaped Ferry's thinking on the subject. For him as for others in his entourage under the sway of Auguste Comte, the issue of a secular education had more than a domestic or even political dimension.[55] Its importance lay, above all, in the role that secular education played in pushing civilization forward toward the scientific age. Auguste Comte had argued for a view of history in which humanity gradually transcended earlier cognitive stages, informed by superstition and religion, to arrive finally in the nineteenth century at the highest stage of civilization, when science ordered human reflections on the world. In light of this development, Ferry considered the control of education by the Church to be an obstacle to civilization's progress that the state would have to overcome. To compromise was to slow the march of history. "Citizens, it is imperative to choose," he warned in closing his impassioned plea for girls' schooling in the Salle Molière, "either woman belongs to science or she belongs to the Church."[56]

Indisputably, in their desire to raise the intellectual level of feminine instruction and to encourage intellectual companionship in marriage,

---

[52] Douglas Johnson, "Jules Ferry et les protestants," in Furet, *Jules Ferry*, 73–78.

[53] Especially prominent among Ferry's Protestant supporters were Paul Broca, P. Chalamet, and Ferdinand Buisson. Arguing before the Senate, Broca called for a new ideal of marriage in which a wife would be "capable of understanding [her husband], of putting her mind in unison with his, to be, in the words of Jules Simon, his 'intellectual companion.'" *Lycées et collèges de jeunes filles*, 257. Notice that the reference to the spiritualist Jules Simon proves that the ideal appealed to non-Protestant republican reformers as well as Protestants. For an analysis of attacks on Protestant influence by spokesmen for the Right, see Steven C. Hause, "Anti-Protestant Rhetoric in the Early Third Republic," *French Historical Studies* 16, no. 1 (1989): 183–201.

[54] Mayeur, "La Femme dans la société," in Furet, *Jules Ferry*, 85.

[55] For a discussion of the influence of positivism on French intellectuals in the nineteenth century, see Theodore Zeldin, *France 1848–1945*, vol. 2, *Intellect, Taste and Anxiety* (Oxford: Clarendon Press, 1977), 595–608; Evelyn Acomb, *The French Laic Laws, 1879–1889: The First Anti-Clerical Campaign of the Third French Republic* (New York: Columbia Univ. Press, 1941); John Eros, "The Positivist Generation of French Republicanism," *Sociological Review* 3 (1955): 255–73; Louis Legrand, *L'Influence du positivisme dans l'oeuvre scolaire de Jules Ferry: les origines de laïcité* (Paris: M. Rivière, 1961).

[56] Quoted in Mayeur, *L'Enseignement secondaire*, 18.

Ferry, Sée, and other like-minded republicans advanced the cause of women's rights beyond what supporters of the Church in 1880 sanctioned. As progressive as they may have looked beside the clerical Right, however, none of these reformers envisaged giving men and women the same rights. Neither in his views on marriage nor in his advocacy of girls' education did Ferry, any more than his supporters, take the individual as the basic social unit in defending women's rights to more instruction. For him as much as for the Right, the family, headed by the father and the husband, remained the building block of French society. To the extent that he gave voice to feminist aspirations, therefore, Ferry limited his concerns to the impact of girls' education on their duties in the home. The state had to educate daughters of the well-to-do not to meet their rights as individuals but to make them better wives and mothers.[57] For decades, in imitation of Rousseau, republicans had claimed that faithful wives and loving mothers set the stage for democratic politics within a male republic.[58] Now proponents of Camille Sée's reform preached a variation on that theme. For republican virtue to flourish in the home required an educated woman.[59]

Hence, even as they championed the "new woman," Ferry's supporters pledged renewed commitment to preserving gendered roles in French society. Schooling would do nothing to alter the nature of the basic tasks that custom and the state assigned to women. In 1882, Octave Gréard, the vice-rector for Paris and chief inspector for the School of Sèvres, underscored this point in a special report on girls' education to the Parisian Academic Council. "Let us beware of seeming to want to change women

[57] For a discussion of "familial feminism" or "relational feminism," see Karen Offen, "Depopulation, Nationalism, and Feminism in Fin-de-siècle France," *American Historical Review* 89, no. 3 (June 1984): 653–55; and Karen Offen, "Defining Feminism: A Comparative Historical Approach," *Signs: Journal of Women in Culture and Society* 14, no. 1 (1988): 119–57.

[58] Mayeur, "La Femme dans la société," in Furet, *Jules Ferry*, 82. For a discussion of Rousseau's views, see Susan Moller Okin, *Women in Western Political Thought* (Princeton: Princeton Univ. Press, 1979), 3–167; Jean Bethke Elshtain, *Public Man, Private Woman* (Princeton: Princeton Univ. Press, 1981), 147–70; Margaret Canovan, "Rousseau's Two Concepts of Citizenship," in *Women in Western Political Philosophy*, ed. Ellen Kennedy and Susan Mendus (New York: St. Martin's Press, 1987), 78–105. Dorinda Outram, *The Body and the French Revolution: Sex, Class and Political Culture* (New Haven: Yale Univ. Press, 1989); idem, "Le Langage Mâle de la Vertu: Women and the Discourse of the French Revolution," in *The Social History of Language*, ed. Peter Burke (Cambridge: Cambridge Univ. Press, 1987), 120–35; Joan Landes, *Women and the Public Sphere in the Age of the French Revolution* (Ithaca: Cornell Univ. Press, 1988).

[59] Sée himself made the point before his fellow deputies: "We must raise the intellectual level of women since, in the spirit of Montesquieu's thought, we want to found the republic on virtue." *Lycées et collèges de jeunes filles*, 64.

into men," he warned. "We have passed the time when people wondered if women had a soul or if it differed from the soul of men. What is undeniable, however, is that neither their destinations nor their natures are the same."[60] Even when the politics of education forced republicans to create a feminine version of a professeur, Camille Sée, the author of the law, did not intend that "lady professeurs" should set a precedent for storming male professions. "I condemn those women who want to be like men," declared this champion of advanced feminine instruction before the deputies he was hoping to persuade.[61] Quite possibly, the majority of Sée's supporters believed the mental aptitudes of the two sexes to be different; but that men's and women's social destinies were and ought to be distinct represented a virtually universal point of view.

The essential point to grasp about these reformers is their insistence on the link between the biological and the social order. A division of social tasks along lines of gender seemed to them to be a rational expression of natural differences in human talents. Far from wanting to collapse the barriers between the sexes, republican school reformers sought deliberately to reinforce them. Henri Marion, an influential spokesman for the Université subsequently maintained that a widening gulf between the tasks of men and those of women was a sign of the progressive rationality of human history. "The more advanced a society's civilization," Marion argued, "the more pronounced the division of labor between men and women becomes."[62] Though far from singular in such pronouncements, no voice spoke with more authority in the early Third Republic on the subject of women's education. Marion's lectures on the psychology of women at the Sorbonne and his position on the permanent board (section permanente) of the Conseil supérieur de l'instruction publique in the Ministry of Education placed him at the epicenter of the whole reform. At his death in 1896, the Ministry of Education named his widow directrice of the School of Sèvres. One can hardly find a more important spokesman for the new republic's goals in educating girls.

Of special interest, therefore, is Marion's idealization of the division of labor represented in French society by the urban middle class. Comparing members of this class with Europe's peasantry, he noted: "In the large

[60] Gréard, L'Enseignement secondaire des filles, 110.

[61] Speech to the Chamber of Deputies on January 20, 1880, in Lycées et collèges de jeunes filles, 192–93.

[62] Henri Marion, La Psychologie des femmes, cours professé pendant plusieurs années à la Sorbonne (Paris: A. Colin, 1900), 28. The precise dates during which Marion gave this course at the Sorbonne were not indicated in this published version. He became a professor at the Sorbonne in 1883 and also taught for fifteen years (1880–1895) at the national Ecole Normale d'Institutrices at Fontenay-aux-Roses.

cities of the great nations of the West where civilization is at its height, gender differentiation is at a maximum. It is infinitely less developed in the poor and backward countryside where men's and women's work is much the same, and their morals, their characters, their manners, even their physical appearances are infinitely less differentiated."[63] This latter situation Marion believed to be a primitive stage of social organization. At the other end of the social scale, he also claimed to see in the convergence of men's and women's lives among the well-to-do and aristocratic rentiers the threat of a historical decay. "If it should happen," he warned his audience at the Sorbonne, "that . . . at the summit of civilization, among the privileged and leisured classes whose lives are almost entirely artificial, the differences between the sexes disappear again, women share the same occupations and sports as men, and men have all the women's softness . . . , instinctively, we view that situation not as a step forward but as a setback—the beginning of disintegration." For Marion social progress could be measured on a continuum along which "virile forms of work become more and more distinct from feminine occupations," and increasingly "women are confined to the home . . . while men reserve for themselves activities outside it."[64]

In many ways, of course, this outlook differed little from the views of spokesmen for the Right. Beginning with the Restauration, monarchists had themselves idealized domestic women beside the image of the virile public man.[65] What marked this rhetoric as distinctive of the Left was Marion's stress on the work women did at home and, above all, on its political implications.[66] Resurrecting the moralizing rhetoric used against the Old Regime, republicans eagerly portrayed the women of the well-to-do as corrupted by a life of luxury and pleasure encouraged by their education. "Is it proper," Paul Broca asked his colleagues in the Senate, "for [a wife], raised in frivolity, to place her ideal in adornment and her happiness in worldly delights?"[67] Certainly the idea of a leisured class of women, devoted to pleasure and self-indulgence, shocked the sensibilities of this middle-class elite qua school reformers. But their more serious concern involved the influence of women's manners on the

[63] Ibid.

[64] Ibid.

[65] Margaret Darrow, "French Noblewomen and the New Domesticity, 1750–1850," *Feminist Studies* 5, no. 1 (1979): 41–64.

[66] In the seventeenth century, the pedagogue Bishop Fénélon drew a similar connection between politics and noblewomen's domestic duties as part of an attack on absolutism, but his political goal was to reassert the power of the old nobility. See Carolyn Lougee, "*Noblesse*, Domesticity, and Agrarian Reform: The Education of Girls by Fenelon and Saint Cyr," *History of Education Quarterly* 14, no. 1 (Spring 1974): 87–114.

[67] Speech on November 20, 1880, in *Lycées et collèges de jeunes filles* (1900), 257.

nation. "In France today less than anywhere and less than ever," Marion claimed, "can we be satisfied with a frivolous and purely decorative education for women from the upper classes of society. The country needs them too much; if they are not serious, their brothers, their husbands, and their sons will not be either; if the women are not up to their tasks and do not act as an example, neither will the men be up to theirs."[68]

For Marion, the ideal women served society and the nation through the moral authority that she exercised within the family. As indoctrinator of the young and inspiration for her spouse, she found her proper place within the social order. In stating this position, Marion merely parroted ideas that dated from Rousseau and had become common currency among republican reformers by the 1860s.[69] Camille Sée himself maintained before the Chamber of Deputies that women created social values. "Whatever one does," Sée argued in defense of secularizing and upgrading girls' instruction, "women determine mores, and it is mores even more than laws that make a people."[70]

The reformers were still more explicit when it came to specifying the essential social task of mothers. Invariably, they placed their emphasis not on women's biological capacity as reproducers but on their socializing role as children's teachers. Thus, Paul Broca in his report on Sée's proposal to the Senate observed, concerning a wife's maternal occupations: "While the man works and struggles in the outside world, the woman raises the children. Just as she suckles their bodies she feeds their minds. She is their first and sometimes their only institutrice; she cultivates their faculties and develops their feelings, tastes, and moral outlook."[71]

If socializing children was the woman's major task, it is no wonder that republicans took the issue of girls' education seriously. For republican reformers were not just moralists and anticlericals; philosophically, they were idealists, convinced that mind ruled over matter and that the moral outlook of a people determined their material success. Though they considered women by nature ill-suited for the public sphere of politics and work, they nonetheless could argue that their role within the family was a crucially important one for civilization. For it was there, within the bosom of the family, that the moral ethos buttressing the social order took its shape.

One can hardly overstate the importance that republicans attached to life within the middle-class family. Yet what these reformers valued in

[68] Marion, *La Psychologie des femmes*, 20.
[69] Auspitz, *The Radical Bourgeoisie*, 38–46.
[70] *Lycées et collèges de jeunes filles*, 60.
[71] Ibid., 256.

such families was not their sentimental aspect. Rather they admired the ability of the family to translate into mutual moral obligations relationships of inequality and power. In so doing, familial life produced a social outlook ideally suited to maintaining an inegalitarian social order in a democratic state. Republicans did not intend to overturn the social order with regard to either social class or women's status.[72] But if relationships of power were not to be secured by force alone, society required some legitimizing credo to support them. "What would become of a society where all unreasonable women were held in check only by the authoritarian resistance of all men?" inquired Marion before a sympathetic audience at the Sorbonne.[73] The answer, he maintained, lay with the principle of duty and responsibility ingrained in members of the bourgeois family. "We must raise women for a completely moral life, that is, for duty and responsibility . . . ; we must raise them in the full sense of the word, not only train them to please and to obey. . . . For there is only one thing that prepares one truly for the moral life and that is principle."[74]

Some historians have traced republicans' obsession with the theme of duty to the influence of Protestantism among their leaders.[75] Though certainly important, the sense of duty on which these men aspired to build a sense of unity in France came from no one sectarian point of view. It emerged from the morally charged relations in the middle-class home where the young learned early, through the chidings of their mothers above all, the self-sacrificing credo of the family's ethos.[76] By taking over future bourgeois mothers' schooling, republicans imagined that they could turn that education in familial duties to the interests of the nation and the state.

Secondary Schooling for Domestic Creatures

The slogan "different but equal" (*l'égalité dans la différence*), coined by an early defender of girls' secondary studies, Ernest Legouvé,[77]

---

[72] Sanford Elwitt argues that the educational reforms of the 1880s reflected a social policy designed to protect the bourgeois order. *The Making of the Third Republic: Class and Politics in France 1868–1884* (Baton Rouge: Louisiana State Univ. Press, 1975), 170–229.

[73] Marion, *La Psychologie des femmes*, 21.

[74] Ibid., 161.

[75] Zeldin, *France 1848–1945*, 1: 627–28 and 2: 154–58.

[76] Lévy, *De mères en filles*. See also B. Smith's description of the exactitude with which some mothers in the industrial bourgeoisie of the Nord kept track on a daily basis of their children's failings. *Ladies*, 64.

[77] Ernest Legouvé taught a course entitled "Histoire morale des femmes" at the Collège de France in the spring of 1848. A book under the same title came out in 1848

expressed precisely the social ideology behind this school reform as well as the reformers' unquestioned patriarchal intentions. For what reformers from Legouvé to Ferry to Sée himself desired was not to duplicate boys' secondary education but to found another system tailored to the social destiny of bourgeois girls and to what they claimed to be the sphere natural to the female of the species. "The schools that we want to found," declared the author of the law, "have as their objective not to tear [women] from their natural vocation but to make them better able to fulfill the duties of a wife, a mother, and a housewife."[78] Only in the rhetoric of these reformers did such a future promise women equality with men. In reality, the goal of this reform was to confine the graduates of girls' secondary schools to tasks defined as feminine because they did not threaten the authority of men. And to achieve that goal, the law of 1880 called for a unique curriculum for girls, separate feminine degrees, and a distinctive school organization for girls' schools.

In most respects, the curriculum that the law approved took up secondary education for girls where institutions for girls in Paris in the 1840s had left it. Once again, feminine studies would focus on modern languages and French literary classics instead of Latin, the core subject in secondary schools for boys.[79] The law called, in addition, for courses in history and a smattering of scientific subjects with an explicit warning

---

(Paris: Sandré), followed by eight more editions. Several other publications concerned with girls' education and their role in the family placed him among the earliest republican defenders of reform: *La Femme en France au XIXe siècle* (Paris: Hetzel, 1873); *Nos Filles et nos fils. Scènes et études de famille*, 9th ed. (Paris: Hetzel, 1881); *La Question des femmes* (Paris: Hetzel, 1881). Both his long-standing interest in improving girls' education and his prestige as a member of the Académie française recommended him to the director of secondary education, Charles Zevort, who created a special position for him at Sèvres as inspector general, director of studies. He also occasionally lectured to Sévriennes in letters. Some of the lectures were published. *Dernier travail, derniers souvenirs. Ecole Normale de Sèvres* (Paris: Hetzel, 1898). See Karen Offen, "Ernest Legouvé and the Doctrine of 'Equality in Difference' for Women: A Case Study of Male Feminism in Nineteenth-Century French Thought," *The Journal of Modern History* 58, no. 2 (June 1986): 452–84.

[78] *Lycées et collèges de jeunes filles*, 191–92.

[79] Article 4 of the law of December 21, 1880 listed the subjects to be taught. *Lycées et collèges de jeunes filles*, 435. The law of December 21, 1880 merely indicated the subjects to be included in a secondary curriculum for girls. It did not establish the topics that each subject would cover, how the curriculum would be organized, or even how many years of study would complete a feminine secondary education. The Conseil supérieur de l'instruction publique and Paul Bert, who took Jules Ferry's place as minister of education in December 1881, decided all these issues. The results appeared in the form of two decrees, one on January 14, 1882, the second on July 28, 1882. The minutes of all meetings of the Conseil supérieur de l'instruction publique leading up to this decree are located in F17 12964, A.N.

that scientific subjects not exceed an elementary level.[80] As for the traditional "feminine" arts, the law reserved a place for them as well, although the emphasis had shifted since the 1840s from the social graces to domestic skills.[81]

The only striking innovation in the new curriculum was the absence of religious education. Even here, however, the change had less substance than might first appear, since in its final version, the law permitted girls to take religious classes should their parents so request. The moral instruction that replaced religious studies in the standard curriculum, in any case, resembled catechism class in key respects. Like classes in religious dogma, the course in ethics taught in girls' secondary schools was intended to avoid all hint of speculation. The point deserves reflection. For just when speculative philosophy had earned a reputation as the "crowning glory" of boys' secondary studies,[82] a doctrinaire program of moral education became the centerpiece of the curriculum for girls. The purpose of that instruction was to teach adolescent girls their social duties as females—first within the family, then within society, and, finally, in the nation-state.[83]

Given the curricular innovations it proposed, not surprisingly the law also provided for uniquely feminine diplomas. Here again, the law reemphasized the homely destiny of bourgeois girls. Whereas boys at graduation had to undergo a national examination (the baccalauréat), girls would take exams administered independently by their own teachers. The advantages were several, according to proponents of the plan. Girls subject to in-house examinations would avoid unseemly public scrutiny,

[80] Clause 6 of article 6 stated that only "the elements" of geometry, chemistry, physics, and natural history would be taught, a cautionary phrase added by the Senate to Sée's original bill. Sée himself was dissatisfied with the ministry's interpretation of this phrase. He considered the science curriculum too heavy and inappropriate for girls. For an early defense of scientific education by one of the first directrices of a lycée, see J. Desparmet-Ruello, *Les Programmes de sciences dans les lycées des jeunes filles: réponse à M. Camille Sée* (Paris, Guillaumin, 1884).

[81] The law of December 21, 1880 included hygiene, domestic economy, and design. Of the "social graces" associated with earlier curricula only needlework and music remained. Dancing had disappeared from the curriculum altogether. In its place we find gymnastics, clearly a product of postwar concern over national health. *Lycées et collèges de jeunes filles*, 461.

[82] Zeldin, *France 1848–1945*, 1: 205–26.

[83] The curriculum for this course was written mainly by Henri Marion with a few changes introduced by the rest of the Conseil supérieur. Marion headed the ministerial commission set up to make recommendations to the Conseil supérieur on the girls' secondary curriculum. His report, entitled "Rapport de M. Marion au nom de la Commission chargée d'examiner le projet d'organisation de l'enseignement secondaire des jeunes filles," December 30, 1881, can be found in F17 12964, A.N.

curb their sense of competition (an unfeminine concern), and suffer less from the mental strain occasioned by exams, believed by some doctors, at least, to be especially dangerous for adolescent girls.[84] Still, the main excuse for school exams and for girls' diplomas was that graduation signaled the end of bourgeois girls' education and a permanent retreat into the home. Unlike the preprofessional training given boys in secondary schools, girls' education would be *désintéressée*, with no objective other than self-improvement.[85] "Preprofessional" training for bourgeois girls would take place inside the home under the guidance of mothers who prepared their daughters in the few years just before their marriage for the social and domestic obligations facing them as future matrons.[86] So seriously did the Conseil supérieur take this maternal premarital training that in carrying out the law, the Ministry of Education shortened the length of girls' secondary studies from seven years to five and organized their studies so that those who so preferred could graduate with a certificate of secondary studies after only three years of instruction.[87] The vast majority of students, reformers thought, would not require diplomas that paved the way to further study or employment. The few who did could use the *diplôme d'études secondaires* to pursue a career in secondary teaching.[88]

The majority of republicans in the National Assembly voted to go even further. Most concluded not only that a feminine secondary education should lead back into the home but also that teenage girls should not leave their families to attend school. Disagreement on this point produced the only instance when a major feature of Sée's proposed new law ran into overwhelming opposition.[89] When Sée suggested that the state found boarding schools (*internats*) for girls, several reformers took ex-

[84] The danger to students' health of overwork was widely discussed both in the legislature and in medical publications from the 1870s through the 1890s. Camille Sée particularly stressed the need to avoid this problem in girls' schools. *Lycées et collèges de jeunes filles* (Paris, 1888), xxix–xxxi.

[85] Mayeur, *L'Enseignement secondaire*, 38–39.

[86] For a good description of this training, see A. Martin-Fugier, *La Bourgeoise. La femme au temps de Paul Bourget* (Paris: Grasset, 1983).

[87] Françoise Mayeur considers that Minister of Education Paul Bert made this decision on his own and that it did not come from the Conseil supérieur. Sée was vigorously opposed. Mayeur, *L'Enseignement secondaire*, 101.

[88] With only a diplôme from a secondary school for girls, a graduate could get a position as an assistant teacher in a girls' secondary school. To be named *chargée de cours* or professeur, though, a teacher would need a professional degree.

[89] The debate began with a widely read attack on boys' lycées entitled *Quelques Mots sur l'instruction publique in France* (Paris: Hachette, 1872), in which Michel Bréal argued that public boarding schools did not offer students the moral guidance that they were assured in the family and that the state should therefore discourage internats.

ception.[90] As one opponent put it to the Senate: "A young man on leaving the collège usually is called upon to live far from his family, at least for several years ... and many reasonable minds believe that life at boarding school prepares him advantageously for this existence. A woman's life, by contrast, is entirely within the family, and it is desirable for a girl to get her education without departing from this salutary setting."[91] On his side, Sée complained that the absence of internats would compromise the institution they were founding.[92] He wondered how without facilities for boarders, girls' secondary schools would survive their competition from the convents.[93] But the appeal to family values, and especially to the crucial role assumed by mothers in their daughters' raising, proved too strong for Sée's pragmatic views.[94] Even Ferry took sides with his opponents.[95] In the tradition of the cours and of maternal education, republicans in the Senate rejected Sée's idea for state-run boarding schools, leaving to local councils the task of organizing such facilities should the need arise.[96]

Behind this controversy lay a fundamental problem for state schools. Parents from the bourgeoisie, indeed, from the entire middle class, imposed on daughters much more than on their sons an exceptionally sheltered life in adolescence. No unmarried girl or even young and single woman, if she valued her good reputation, appeared in public places unaccompanied by a chaperone. Even the social contacts that a young girl might permissibly enjoy were necessarily supervised. So intense was the concern of bourgeois parents that on those grounds alone Broca had opposed an internat. "The government cannot," he warned the Senate, "commit itself to organizing throughout France under a uniform rule ... the individual supervision of every girl and to being itself the guarantor of their morality."[97] The problem was that both convent education and lay pensionnats had been providing that security for years. To compete

[90] Mayeur, *L'Enseignement secondaire*, 29, 39–52.

[91] Paul Broca, Senate, session of November 20, 1880. *Lycées et collèges de jeunes filles*, 268.

[92] Debate in Chamber of Deputies, session of December 15, 1879. Ibid., 218.

[93] *Lycées et collèges de jeunes filles* (1900), 21. This argument appeared in the preface of the first edition and was reprinted in the edition of 1900.

[94] For an excellent analysis of prescriptive maternal education, see Lévy, *De mères en filles*.

[95] Ferry gave a speech to the Senate on the subject of the proposed law on December 10, 1880. Quoted in *Lycées et collèges de jeunes filles*, 410–12.

[96] The Chamber of Deputies voted the revised version of the law during the session of December 16, 1880. Ibid., 420.

[97] Senate, Session of November 20, 1880, quoted in ibid., 268.

with them, public schools for girls, even without boarders, would have to offer comparable guarantees.

Competing with the Image of the Teaching Nun

In the context of that competition Sée's proposal to staff secondary schools for girls with women teachers gained acceptance by the Left. No one questioned placing a directrice at the head of girls' schools, whatever the level of instruction. That had been since Falloux's Law the universal practice. As one observer, Antoine Villemot, subsequently remarked, "It would have been impossible, given public opinion in this country, to place men at the head of girls' schools."[98] He did not accept, however, the need for women teachers, since women had never taught in secondary schools before.[99] Yet no one on the Left protested when Sée, as the reporter for the parliamentary commission for the lower house, declared, "It will be necessary in the first years to give . . . most chairs to men. . . . [but] one by one as women capable of handling the instruction come before us, we will take care to give them preference."[100]

Sée himself advanced two reasons for introducing women into second- why ary teaching. He first invoked the need to find employment for women who, because they lacked a dowry, might not marry. Teaching had traditionally been the only respectable secular occupation for such women from the middle classes, and Sée seemed truly anxious to increase their options now.[101] Contemporary debates in England may well have influenced his views, since in France, where the problem of "surplus" single "ladies" was somewhat less acute, few publicists had taken up the matter.[102] His second reason for preferring women teachers spoke more di-

---

[98] Antoine Villemot, *Etude sur l'organisation, le fonctionnement et les progrès de l'enseignement secondaire des jeunes filles en France de 1879 à 1887*, reprinted in *ESDJF* 1 (1905): 203. This revue appeared biannually. Volumes were not numbered consecutively.

[99] Ibid.

[100] "Proposition de loi sur l'enseignement secondaire des jeunes filles présenteé par M. C. Sée, député," in *Lycées et collèges de jeunes filles*, 61.

[101] Ibid., 162.

[102] For selected documents on the English debate, see Susan Groag Bell and Karen M. Offen, *Women, the Family, and Freedom: The Debate in Documents*, vol. 1, 1750–1880 (Stanford: Stanford Univ. Press, 1983), 392–406, 417–23. In 1851, only 12 percent of the women in France remained definitively single according to Michelle Perrot, "Figures et roles," in *Histoire de la vie privée; de la Revolution à la Grande Guerre*, vol. 4, ed. Michelle Perrot (Paris: Editions de Seuil, 1987), 134. For a breakdown by age group, see Patrice Bourdelais, "Le Démographie et la femme seule," in Farge and Klapisch-Zuber, *Madame ou Mademoiselle?* 58–60. The problems of single women look considerably more acute when viewed from the perspective of all women over fifteen who were sin-

rectly to typically French concerns. Sée insisted on the widely touted view that women as potential mothers possessed a special aptitude for teaching. This argument had long served as the principle rationale for women elementary teachers. The novelty of Sée's position was to stretch its application beyond primary schools to the far more prestigious and intellectually demanding task of secondary teaching.

Yet despite the sweeping nature of that change, the Left showed little interest in probing Sée's or his commission's reasons further. That fact cannot help but raise suspicion since it suggests a different sort of motive altogether operating to shape this consensus. In reality, republicans approved this new profession not because it met a few unfortunate women's needs or even because they saw it as an appropriate application of special female talents. Behind this ready acquiescence lay the rivalry of anticlerics with the convents. Long ago Catholic educators had pioneered the notion that schools had two distinct objectives: one to impart knowledge (*instruction*), the other to give the young a moral outlook which protected them from vice (*éducation*). To outbid convent schools, public girls' schools had to convince prospective clients that they, too, could follow this tradition. That meant competing not only with the reputation of the convent but, in addition, with the image of virtue and commitment of the ubiquitous teaching nun. With all deliberateness, therefore, Sée and his supporters set out to launch a feminine teaching corps that would rival nuns for moral rectitude as teachers while surpassing them as intellectual guides.

The moral reliability of women secondary teachers, in fact, concerned the makers of the law that founded Sèvres far more than did their academic training. Perhaps because the prospect of providing women with advanced degrees made even republican politicians nervous, the bill to found a higher normal school for women hardly dealt at all with the academic side of this proposed new institution. The legislators gladly left entirely to the administration what *normaliennes* might study or how to certify a corps of female teachers. Instead, they focused exclusively on the organizational rules for the school. These included a competitive exam to select students, free tuition for all of those admitted, and a requirement that all students reside at school. Only the last of these provisions prompted any comment.

---

gle (31 percent in 1896) or widowed or divorced (15 percent in 1896), figures reported by Linda L. Clark, "A Battle of the Sexes in a Professional Setting: The Introduction of Inspectrices Primaires, 1889–1914" *French Historical Studies* 16, no. 1 (1989): 102n. 28. The one contemporary who did attempt to publicize the problem of poor single women in France was J.-V. Daubié, *La Femme pauvre au XIXe siècle* (Paris: Guillaumin, 1866).

Since normal schools traditionally housed their students, the decision to do the same at Sèvres ought not to have required an explanation. But to the men considering the law that founded Sèvres, boarding institutions had become suspicious places. Only a few months earlier, the Senate had rejected internats for girls' secondary education on the grounds that daughters needed to be closer to their mothers. In July 1881, legislators might well have reasoned that normaliennes with families near the school similarly would be better off at home. To dissuade them from that view, Camille Sée and Jean-Baptiste Ferrouillat, who presented the bill drawn up by the parliamentary commission to their respective chambers, resorted to appeals familiar to their Catholic rivals. "Day girls might bring habits, ideas, and distractions to the school," Sée warned fellow deputies, "that would be out of keeping with the elevated moral course on which we plan to set it."[103] In a similarly unselfconscious imitation of the Church, Ferrouillat invoked before the Senate a school modeled on the cloister. "It is imperative," he insisted gravely, "to eliminate . . . whatever might alter the character of a retreat that this lay novitiate requires."[104] In a contest with the Church over who could better educate young girls, the state could do no better than to mimic in preparing its own teachers the cloistered life of nuns inside the convent.

Still, competition with the nuns does not alone explain why these reformers insisted on monitoring this new professional education closely. The audacity of the social mission handed over to Sèvres's graduates also seemingly required it. Republicans had committed the republic to bringing into being a "new woman" in girls' secondary schools, and they were perfectly aware of the potential for challenges to male authority should these schools fail to channel their effects. Much depended on the attitudes fostered in girl students by their teachers. For as Sée warned the Chamber of Deputies, "On leaving the Ecole Normale, these girls will take charge of souls (ames) in their turn."[105] A crucial task for this professional school, therefore, was to create an image of the woman teacher that would not detract from feminine domesticity by validating a worldly role for women. "If it is important," Sée observed, "to give future professeurs a broad and solid education, it is at least of equal import to shape their characters and accustom them to an austere and contemplative

[103] "Rapport par C. Sée au nom de la Commission chargée d'examiner la proposition de loi de C. Sée, ayant pour objet la création d'une école normale destinée à preparer des professeurs-femmes pour les écoles secondaires de jeunes filles," Chamber of Deputies, session of May 14, 1881. *Lycées et collèges de jeunes filles*, 443.

[104] "Rapport par M. Ferrouillat, sénateur, au nom de la Commission chargée d'examiner la proposition de loi, adoptée par la Chambre des députés." Ibid., 445.

[105] Ibid.

life."[106] Only a cloistered professional training would insure that the new teachers, mirroring the nuns whom they replaced, would do nothing to upset the gendered social boundaries which republicans approved and which placed bourgeois women inside the home.

The cloistered model of the professional school had yet one more attraction for Sèvres's founders. The men who followed Ferry's lead saw themselves on a historic mission. Thus, in the manner of the Catholic church, they wanted missionaries with whom to trust the cause. To rely simply on academic courses and credentialing exams to field the necessary teachers would have put at risk the cultural revolution that they hoped to launch in France. They needed an institutional setting where young women would prepare themselves at once for a profession and a calling. For what Ferry, Sée, and their supporters desired was more than accredited professionals with traditional social values. They wanted lay women teachers who would discover in their professional training a moralizing mission for the state.[107] To that end, ironically, these anticlerical reformers could imagine no finer vehicle than the cloistered training pioneered and defended by their rivals.

Separate Spheres within the Université

If the example of the Church inspired the ethos of this new profession, its organizational model came entirely from the state, which meant this new profession paralleled the men's profession very closely. Just as for the masculine corps of teachers, the Université certified its women secondary teachers through professional exams. Both men and women teachers competed in more difficult exams called *agrégations* if they hoped for posts as professeurs in lycées. And once credentialed, all teachers received assignments to specific schools from the Ministry of Education, which also paid their salaries, supervised their competence inside the classroom, and decided on demotions and promotions.

Camille Sée anticipated the parallels between the two professions when he first advanced the bill that founded Sèvres. Moreover, a true believer in the principle "égalité dans la différence," he even imagined a completely even-handed treatment by the ministry of the two second-

---

[106] Ibid., 443.

[107] In this respect, the role of Sèvres resembled normal schools for primary teachers, male and female both, more than it did the Ecole Normale Supérieure for men. See, for example, Jean-Noël Luc, "L'Ecole Normale Supérieure de Saint-Cloud: clé de voûte de l'enseignement primaire, 1882–1914," in *The Making of Frenchmen: Current Directions in the History of Education in France, 1679–1979*, ed. Donald N. Baker and Patrick J. Harrigan (Waterloo: Historical Reflections Press, 1980), 415–28.

ary corps. "[Women teachers] will get their credentials just like men and will belong to the teaching corps with the same rights, the same salary, the same retirement, [and] the same conditions for advancement," Sée confidently predicted before his colleagues in the Chamber of Deputies.[108] But in his eagerness to see the idea of separate-but-equal spheres applied to women teachers, he failed to reckon with the ethos of the Université.

Once the rhetoric of the politicians had subsided, the ministry made absolutely clear that women would not have equal rights with men within the Université. In the first place, the law of 1853, which set the terms of men's employment, would not apply to women in the same profession: not to salaries or to sick leaves, not to their retirement, not even to their weekly teaching loads. Second, they would not be treated as full members of the Université, which meant in practice that they had no right to serve in the inspectorate supervising secondary schools or on the Conseil supérieur, the body responsible for advising the minister of education on all educational policy for secondary schools, or on any other academic council. The rationale for this discrimination lay not with differences in sex per se or even in the mores of society. It had its basis in the Université's most fundamental credo.

Since the early nineteenth century, this corporation of teachers had become the principal promoter of the ideal of privilege based on merit in French culture. In pursuit of that ideal, it introduced as early as the 1820s the national exam, or baccalauréat, which boys prepared for in their secondary studies. Success at this exam had since become a prerequisite of higher education. In its own professional ranks, the Université applied a still more rigid code of merit by tying the promotions of its professeurs in boys' lycées to their year and order of success at the agrégation. The problem was that women secondary teachers, like their students who earned girls' diplomas, did not compete for men's professional degrees. By 1883 they had their own teaching credential, the certificat, and competed in their own professorial exam, the women's agrégation. No one denied the need for distinct credentialing exams since women would be teaching in a separate system with its own curriculum and course assignments. But the Université refused to countenance assigning the same value and the same privileges to differing degrees. Given its own traditions, the masculine profession was absolute in its position. As long as girls did not prepare for the baccalauréat, they had no claim to higher learning. And as long as women teachers had

[108] Ibid.

their own credentials, the Université could, with a clear conscience, treat them differently from—and worse than—men.

Within a decade and a half, republican reformers had achieved what they set out to do. They had created an educational system that forged a cultural bond between the worlds of men and women and yet preserved their separate roles. They had established a system of lay secondary schools for girls that sufficiently resembled convent schools to reassure large segments of the public. And they had launched a new female profession that, instead of rivaling men in teaching, existed in a world apart. Certainly republicans had cause for self-congratulation. Observers mostly concluded that they had fashioned a lasting institution and that girls' secondary schools would preserve in perpetuity distinctions between male and female roles in French society. There was, nonetheless, a tension informing this experiment from the outset, a tension between the social ideology of equality in difference to which republicans appealed and the bureaucratic ethos of the state for which *unequal* could only mean "inferior." To keep that tension from rising to explosive levels, much depended on the women sent out to teach in the new schools; and that meant, above all, graduates of the new Ecole Normale Supérieure at Sèvres.

PART I | Fashioning a New Women's Profession

On the occasion of the twenty-fifth anniversary of the opening of the School of Sèvres, Gaston Darboux reminisced about the early classes. "The first class," he recalled, "even the second were rather an ill-assorted lot. One noticed it immediately in their accents and, if you will pardon this intimate detail, in their toilettes."* Intended to amuse his audience of officials, alumnae, and longtime supporters of Sèvres, Darboux's observation unselfconsciously revealed the underlying purpose of the school. What the founders had hoped to shepherd through the School of Sèvres was a group of women who shared the same professional outlook and whose personal behavior once they left the school would fashion an approved professional style for women teachers. Twenty-five years later, the Ministry of Education sponsored the celebration at which Darboux gave his speech partly in order to congratulate Sèvres's founders and their protégées on their success in meeting that objective.

Observers who attributed such importance to the influence of Sèvres had good reasons for defending that opinion. Most of the directrices of the major girls' lycées in France as well as the majority of professeurs in Parisian lycées were former Sévriennes. More important, of the alumnae who had reached

* Quoted by Louise Belugou in her preface to Mme Jules Favre, *La Morale de Plutarque* (Paris: Henry Paulin, 1909), xlix. A professor at the Faculty of Sciences in Paris, Darboux taught mathematics at Sèvres from 1881 to 1917. He gave this speech on the occasion of Sèvres's twenty-fifth anniversary celebration.

43

these coveted posts by 1907, all had graduated in the first ten or eleven classes. Their experience at Sèvres belonged to a single institutional era. The same directrice had welcomed the oldest of them to the school in 1881 and ushered out the youngest in 1895; the same teachers or at least those who most impressed their students had taken part in their professional training; and no reforms either from within the school or from outside it had altered the routines associated with school life during the period of their studies. To the extent that these women shared a common professional outlook, it was easy to conclude that the normal school at Sèvres had chiefly shaped it.

Nevertheless, if Sèvres succeeded in imparting its own ethos to many of its students, the credit lay only partly with the school itself. In the first place, young women who came to the Ecole for training brought values with them from their homes that had prepared them for accepting central aspects of their normal school's credo. Furthermore, once working, they had to modify their conduct, just like colleagues who had not attended Sèvres, to fit prevailing public expectations for women teachers. Finally, as underlings in the bureaucratic world of girls' secondary schools, Sévriennes would have to master a code of conduct in some respects at odds with the elitist outlook nurtured by their training. For all these reasons, the mature professional profile of the generation of alumnae basking in the state's approval in 1907 did not reflect Sèvres's influence alone. The making of this women's profession involved a dynamic and complex process, an interaction among the expectations of the state, the demands of local clienteles, and the attitudes of the women who went into secondary teaching.

2 Profiles of the First Recruits

THE SPEED with which the ministry moved to open Sèvres in part explains why the first class to matriculate would prove so "ill-assorted." Less than four months after the National Assembly had given the ministry a mandate, seventy-three young women gathered in the centers of the eleven academic districts in France to compete for entry to a school that as yet had no curriculum or established term of study.[1] Those who qualified at these exams assembled in Paris two weeks later for oral examinations before a jury of male professors chosen by the Ministry of Education to teach at Sèvres. On the third day of these orals, forty contestants learned that they had won admission to the school.[2] Hastily organized with neither the contestants nor the jury certain of the criteria for selecting winners, this first competition like the one the following year did result in curiously heterogeneous classes.

The hybrid character of Sèvres's initial classes owed as much to the absence of prerequisites for applications as to the hurried inauguration of the school. From 1881 through 1883, any woman between the ages of seventeen and thirty could compete to enter Sèvres.[3] As a result, students in the first three classes varied widely both in age and in their educational achievements.[4] The first of these conditions changed after 1884 when the ministry lowered the maximum age of applicants to twenty-four and raised the minimum age from seventeen to eighteen.[5] But a more homogeneous academic profile for recruits to Sèvres would not emerge until the new secondary schools for girls became the routine avenue for women into secondary teaching.

Meanwhile, Sèvres necessarily admitted students of widely differing schooling and experience. Of the forty women entering Sèvres in 1881, for example, two or three had had advanced instruction under supervision in their homes. A few had taken secondary classes at the Sorbonne

---

[1] Ecole Normale Supérieure de l'enseignement secondaire de jeunes filles, Le Cinquantenaire de l'Ecole de Sèvres 1881–1931 (Paris: Printory, 1932), 128–30.

[2] A list of the victors is located in F17 14189, A.N.

[3] An arrêté (ministerial decree) from Jules Ferry on October 14, 1881 set the age limit of candidates for Sèvres at thirty. Another in April 1882 confirmed this limit. Le Cinquantenaire, 128, 134, 143–44.

[4] Nine of the forty women accepted to Sèvres in 1881 were twenty-three or older.

[5] Arrêté of January 1884. Ibid.

45

or in one of the surviving offshoots of Victor Duruy's experiment with secondary cours. Four could boast of training at a normal school for elementary teachers. But two-thirds had only had a primary education, acquired sometimes at a convent, occasionally at public schools, but far more often in one of the many private pensionnats owned and run by women everywhere in France. Precisely what these Sévriennes might have studied in these varied settings is a matter for anyone's conjecture. Two girls with private instruction had passed the baccalauréat;[6] a few others claimed to have the second degree brevet. But the vast majority had neither diploma nor credential or had only the first-degree brevet for elementary teaching. Apparently, the jury that admitted them to Sèvres made its selection on the basis of some sign of intellectual promise since most candidates, according to their examiners, revealed enormous gaps in their acquired knowledge.[7] But what set the first classes apart from later Sévriennes, above all, was less their ignorance and age than the fact that many already had employment. Fully one-half of the first two entering classes were elementary teachers when they applied to Sèvres. One had even directed a private girls' school for several years.[8]

Why would women who already had a teaching job undertake a grueling competitive exam with the prospect, if successful, of two or three more unsalaried years of training in a boarding school? Almost certainly their motives point to the financial advantages of secondary teaching. Salaries for women primary teachers varied greatly from school to school in this period, but everywhere they tended to be stingy.[9] One Sévrienne from the class of 1881 remembered giving up a mere fifty-six francs a month as an *institutrice-adjointe* in a small town to try her chance at

[6] In 1861, Julie-Victoire Daubié became the first woman allowed to sit for the baccalauréat. Despite her success, the minister of education refused to issue her diploma on the grounds that to do so would "disgrace" his ministry. Statistics on the number of women who repeated Daubié's success over the next two decades are not available. Karen Offen, "The Second Sex and the Baccalauréat in Republican France, 1880–1924," *French Historical Studies* 12, no. 2 (Fall 1983): 270.

[7] The jury's comments on the results of the entrance exams for Sèvres in 1881 and 1882 are located in F17 8808, A.N.

[8] Augustine Frémont (class of 1881) had been the directrice of the Ecole laïque libre in Paris. Dossier personnel, A. Frémont, *correspondance*, F17 22445, A.N.

[9] According to J. Daubié, who examined the conditions under which women school teachers worked in the 1860s, the minimum salary of an institutrice in 1866 was 440 francs per year. In the same year a survey of the *sous-maîtresses* of Paris revealed that some received no salaries, only their room and board, while those who were paid received annual salaries ranging from 100 to 440 francs. J.-V. Daubié, *La Femme pauvre*, 126, 151. See also Daubié, *Des Progrès de l'instruction primaire* (Paris: Imprimerie de Mme Claye, ca. 1862).

Sèvres,[10] and even that amount would have seemed a tidy sum to the several candidates listed as private tutors on their application forms for Sèvres. By comparison, an annual salary of three thousand francs, the amount promised by the Ministry of Education to beginning professeurs in girls' lycées, represented a veritable fortune. No other respectable employment open to women at the time paid so well, and Charles Zévort, as the director of secondary education, urged rectors and inspectors to exploit the issue of salary in tempting women and girls to apply to Sèvres.[11]

The ministry's initial reliance on its own officials to recruit candidates for Sèvres also undoubtedly explains why so many teachers showed up in the first classes.[12] Officials spread the news of Sèvres's creation most easily to the women whose schools they regularly inspected, and teachers in turn must have felt obliged to consider seriously any suggestion regarding their careers offered by their superiors. One primary school teacher who entered the class of 1881, Mathilde Trézaunne, left a poignant account of how she personally arrived at the decision to compete for Sèvres. "Late in October of 1881, the primary inspector of my district informed me that a competition would be held November 2 for the first admissions to the School of Sèvres. He urged me to send my application within three days to meet the deadline. Excited by this unexpected proposal but caught between the desire to accept it and my inability to overcome the difficulties that had forced me to turn down Fontenay,[13] I wept bitterly. Then I went into action."[14] The local *instituteur* located a copy for her of the law creating Sèvres, which left her almost as ignorant as before. Still uncertain what to do, she journeyed to Reims to consult with the departmental inspector there. Once again she met a stern admonishment by a superior to throw her hat into the ring.

[10] Lucie Bérillon (class of 1881). At 56 francs a month her annual salary would have come to 672 francs. *Le Cinquantenaire,* 372.

[11] Circular of October 14, 1881, F17 8808, A.N.

[12] Along with the decree of October 14, 1881 indicating the conditions of admission to Sèvres, the director of secondary education sent a circular that asked each rector to ensure "all possible publicity" for the decree. *Le Cinquantenaire,* 128–29.

[13] Trézaunne refers here to the Ecole Normale Supérieure for primary school teachers established the preceding year at Fontenay-aux-Roses outside of Paris. The women trained at Fontenay were expected to seek positions training other primary school teachers in the new écoles normales for institutrices required after 1880 in each department.

[14] *Le Cinquantenaire,* 130. These recollections were quoted anonymously by Anna Amieux (class of 1889) from a letter she had received from a former Sévrienne. Mayeur established that they belonged to M. Trézaunne, *L'Enseignement secondaire,* 111.

"Mademoiselle, you must not reflect so much about it; don't hesitate; apply."

"But I am sure to fail!"

"In that case, we will be delighted to keep you in our service, but present yourself!"

Normally Trézaunne would have consulted with her family on a decision with such momentous consequences for her future, but she knew that her widowed mother would have "worried" to see her at twenty-eight "give up an established position for an uncertain future," while her brother, whose opinion she respected on such matters, was in the colonies, too far away for rapid consultation. In desperation she turned instead to the mayor of her commune who saw at once the advantages that this change in careers could offer the tearful teacher confronting him in his dining room. He not only urged her to enter the competition but even loaned her enough money to pay her way to Paris for the orals. "Thus, everything," she later wrote, "fell into place. I applied. I qualified at the written exams, then passed the orals. And I entered Sèvres."

The anxiety that Mathilde Trézaunne described was probably not unusual among the girls and women who dared to throw their lot in blindly in the early 1880s with the state's experiment in secondary education. Whether already employed or not, until then they had channeled their ambitions into a narrow scheme of options which ensured that at the very least, they would remain working, if not near their parents' home, at least in the same department. Indeed, at the time they entered Sèvres, nearly all of the students in the first two classes resided with their parents. The decision to enter Sèvres cast all of that in doubt. In accepting a place at Sèvres they had to sign a contract committing them to teach wherever the ministry wanted to appoint them. The entire undertaking had the air of an adventure for which candidates like Mathilde Trézaunne had little warning and no time to prepare.

The same could not be said of girls entering Sèvres at the end of its first decade. By then anyone who aspired to Sèvres had organized her life accordingly, months, even years ahead of time. As early as 1883, last-minute decisions to compete for Sèvres were already out of the question. Published eight months in advance, the topics covered in the annual competition for a place at Sèvres became increasingly detailed and broad in scope. Several lycées added a sixth year of courses to their standard program simply to prepare girls for the entrance exam for Sèvres.[15] Mean-

[15] Article 6 of the law of December 21, 1881 foresaw the possibility that the new secondary schools might add a course in pedagogy. Article 13 indicated that a sixth year of instruction might be added without stipulating its content. Henri Marion made clear

while, as secondary schools for girls multiplied in size and number, more girls learned earlier of this narrow door of opportunity open to anyone with a secondary diplôme. Former Sévriennes with enthusiastic memories of their alma mater pushed their best students in that direction, while inspectors, who periodically attended classes, joined in the search for future teachers. Given this publicity, candidates for Sèvres increased in number every year. Over the same period, openings at the normal school gradually declined because the Ministry of Education refused to admit more Sévriennes than it could place as teachers once they had degrees, and by the end of the 1880s, unfilled posts in girls' secondary schools were rapidly disappearing. Consequently, ten years after the first entrance exam, more than two hundred girls competed for a mere eighteen places available at Sèvres.[16]

As a result, by the end of the first decade, entering students at Sèvres bore a remarkable resemblance to boys aspiring to the *grandes écoles*. All successful candidates had had some secondary schooling, and although Sévriennes came from schools far more dispersed than did the average *normalien* or *polytechnicien*, who typically attended a Parisian lycée, they did tend to come from one of four or five particular schools. Half the successful candidates for Sèvres in 1889 and 1890 had spent at least one year at Fénelon, the oldest of the three girls' lycées operating at the time in Paris.[17] That meant as well that the majority of girls in the classes of 1889 and 1890 had left their parents' home in order to pursue their studies. Just as boys in state schools had discovered, girls in secondary schools had found that the way up the ladder of ambition led from collèges to lycées and from the provinces to Paris. The experience of these younger Sévriennes brought them closer in another way to candidates for grandes écoles: hardly any of them managed to pass the entrance exam for Sèvres on their first try. Of the eighteen successful candidates in 1890, only one had never taken the exam before, while nearly a fourth

---

by 1882 that the purpose of this sixth year would be to "prepare for special schools or careers." *Le Cinquantenaire*, 155. In 1893, thirteen lycées and two collèges each managed to get at least one candidate into Sèvres. By 1904, all the successful candidates came from only five lycées: Besançon, Bordeaux, Fénelon in Paris, Toulouse, and Versailles. Ibid., 155–56.

[16] The number of candidates admitted each year was as follows: 1881, 40 students; 1882, 41 students; 1883, 30 students; 1884, 36 students; 1885, 25 students; 1886, 22 students; 1887, 25 students; 1888, 22 students; 1889, 21 students; 1890, 18 students. Of these women, three would die in the course of their studies; seven others resigned without taking a teaching position. For a list of Sévriennes and their positions throughout their careers see *Le Cinquantenaire*, appendix, v–viv.

[17] The three lycées were Fénelon, founded in 1883; Lycée Racine, founded as Lycée Passy in 1887 and renamed in 1889; and Lycée Molière, founded in 1888.

had failed at least twice already. Chance encounters, last-minute waver-
ings, precipitous decisions—in sum, all the unpremeditated aspects of
the very first Sévriennes' experiences—had disappeared. The new version of the path that led to Sèvres required hard work, careful planning,
and the financial wherewithal for a secondary education in a major urban
center.

The very difficulty of this long and arduous journey helped insure that
the first generation of Sévriennes came overwhelmingly from bourgeois,
middle-class, or petty bourgeois homes. In this respect again, Sévriennes
bore a close resemblance to students of the grandes écoles for men, or at
least to those attending the Ecole Normale Supérieure on the rue d'Ulm.
A collective profile, based on residence and father's occupation, of the
young people who went to Sèvres and the Ecole Normale confirms indisputably that both schools recruited a disproportionate number of their
students from the same social milieus in French society (see table 2.1).
In the first place, sons and daughters of *universitaires* constituted a far
greater percentage of the student bodies of both Sèvres and the Ecole
Normale than did their fathers in the general population. Whether male
or female, children of universitaires showed a similar inclination to follow in their fathers' footsteps. Three other occupational groups followed
a similar pattern: the percentages of primary school teachers, military
officers, and professional men in the general population were much
lower than those of their offspring in the schools' student bodies. Among
Sévriennes a somewhat higher percentage came from military families
than at the Ecole Normale, doubtless because girls could not imitate their
fathers by joining the army or the navy.

By contrast, the occupational groups least likely to send their young to
either Sèvres or the rue d'Ulm were either farmers or independent entrepreneurs in commerce or manufacturing. Farming families, in particular,
rarely had a son or daughter in either of these grandes écoles, an absence
all the more noteworthy since farmers along with small businessmen
formed both the political backbone of the Third Republic and the majority of the *classes moyennes*. The typical father of a Sévrienne or Normalien differed from such men not so much by social class or wealth as by
the fact that he earned a salary and worked for someone else.[18] Three of
every four fathers of a Sévrienne, if not employees of the state, were employees of a private company or firm. Those in the private sector frequently had jobs with one of the quasi-public railroads; almost all the
rest worked either for a bank, an insurance company, or an industrial
enterprise. In other words, they belonged to that white-collar class which

[18] Several of the professional men outside teaching worked for the state.

TABLE 2.1

Social Origins of Sévriennes and Normaliens, 1880s (in percent)

Profession of Father	Approximate Active Male Population (1872)	Sévriennes (1881–1890) N = 173	Normaliens (1880–1889) N = 352
Businessmen	9.2	8.1	17.5
Higher officials	1.0	1.2	5.0
Liberal professions	0.8	9.8	12.5
Commissioned officers	0.2	4.6	2.0
Universitaires	0.1	9.8	16.5
Total bourgeoisie	11.3	33.5	53.5
Other teaching corps	0.5	9.2	8.0
All white collar	4.5	22.5	15.0
Middle, lower officials		9.8	
Other white collar		12.7	
Artisans, shopkeepers	6.7	13.9	7.0
Total *classes moyennes*	11.7	45.6	30.0
Noncommissioned officers	1.1	7.5	—
Skilled labor	19.9	8.1	—
Unskilled labor	6.7	0.0	—
Farmers	35.0	5.2	—
Agricultural workers	14.3	0.0	—
Total *classes populaires*	77.0	20.8	16.5[a]

Sources: For Sévriennes, data based on dossiers personnels, series F17, A.N. For Normaliens, data calculated from Robert J. Smith, *The Ecole Normale Supérieure and the Third Republic* (Albany: State University of New York Press, 1982), p. 34, table 4, and p. 42, table 6. Estimates for the active male population come from Victor Karady, "Normaliens et autres enseignants à la Belle Epoque. Note sur l'origine sociale et la réussite dans une profession intellectuelle," *Revue française de sociologie* 13 (1972): 40–41.

Note: Data in parentheses published by Smith for all classes of Normaliens from 1868 to 1941. A class is identified by its year of entry.

[a] Percentages here and hereafter are all rounded off to the nearest tenth of 1 percent, which explains why the sums do not always total 100 percent.

in France, unlike England and Germany, would not become a cultural pacesetter or a major political force until after the Second World War, but which offered men of talent in the later nineteenth century an avenue for individual advancement.

New men by their occupations, the fathers of Sévriennes and Normaliens also signaled this condition by the way they moved their families up the urban hierarchy over the course of their careers. The records on Sévriennes and Normaliens do not reveal just how many times their families moved; we only know their residence at birth and at the time of their matriculation. Enough emerges, though, from these two bits of information to reveal an image of unmistakably ambitious families. Sévriennes' residential history, in particular, offers a dramatic example of mobility up the urban ladder. Table 2.2 compares the geographic mobility of Sévriennes in the classes of 1881–1890 with the mobility of Normaliens from the classes of 1868–1941. The results suggest a remarkable similarity in the general pattern of mobility between the families of these future male and female teachers, with one notable contrast. The elite of the new women's corps of teachers in the making originated more often from small-town France. At the time these girls were born, almost half (45 percent) their families lived in towns and villages of under five thousand inhabitants. In the year they entered Sèvres, however, less than a quarter still resided in such small communities (23 percent), while over half (56.7 percent) lived in cities of twenty thousand inhabitants or more. Those in Paris had jumped from 13 percent at birth to 20 percent at the time of entry to Sèvres. Moreover, families headed by white-collar employees accounted for the vast majority of residential changes, especially when they involved considerable distance. Only 16 percent of the families with self-employed fathers moved at all in the interim between a daughter's birth and her entrance into Sèvres, and if they did change residence, such families almost always stayed within the same department.[19]

In most instances, the motives behind a change of residence remain obscure. Several families who left Alsace-Lorraine did so presumably as victims of the German annexation. Likewise, the mobility of a family headed by a teacher or a military officer simply registered the conditions of advancement in those occupations. Apart from these examples, though, the silence of our sources drops an impenetrable curtain around the reasons for a family's changing its residence. All we can assume with confidence is that any move from a small community to a city favored the chances of some member of the family on the ladder of success.[20] More important, the necessity of moving must have affected the way that

[19] R. Smith's study gives no indication of how this movement correlated with white-collar status since, regrettably, he ignores this dimension of occupational classification that has proven so fruitful here.

[20] For confirmation of this generalization see William H. Sewell, Jr., *Structure and Mobility: The Men and Women of Marseille, 1820–1870* (New York: Cambridge Univ. Press, 1985), 234–312.

TABLE 2.2
Birthplace and Residence of Sévriennes and Normaliens by City Size (in percent)

	1901 Census	Residence at Birth	Residence at Matriculation
	Sévriennes, 1881–1890[a]		
	N = 202		
Paris/Seine	9.4	12.9	20.1
Over 100,000[b]	4.4	3.5	9.4
20,000–100,000	10.3	20.8	27.2
10,000–20,000	5.1	10.9	11.9
5,000–10,000	6.2	6.9	7.9
Under 5,000	64.6	45.0	23.3
	Normaliens, 1868–1941[a]		
	N = 2983		
Paris/Seine	9.4	20.3	33.0
Over 100,000[b]	4.4	11.0	12.7
20,000–100,000	10.3	20.8	21.2
10,000–20,000	5.1	8.3	7.6
5,000–10,000	6.2	7.9	5.5
Under 5,000	64.6	31.7	20.8

Sources: For Sévriennes data based on dossiers personnels, series F17, A.N. For Normaliens, data calculated from Robert J. Smith, *The Ecole Normale Supérieure and the Third Republic* (Albany: State University of New York Press, 1982), p. 32, table 1.
[a] French professional schools identify classes of students by the year of entry.
[b] Paris/Seine not included.

parents thought about their children's futures. Not themselves deeply rooted in one area, such parents might more easily envisage for their children careers requiring a mobile life-style and even a residence far from home.

Reconstructing the world in which Normaliens and Sévriennes decided on a future in secondary teaching suggests, then, several important clues to that decision. In the first place, the majority came from homes where the patrimony handed down between the generations did not include a family business or even a particular skill. It did not necessarily link the family to a circle of patrons tied to any one locale. Instead, as youngsters these future teachers learned by the example of their fathers the advantages of technical or professional training applicable to the same job anywhere. No doubt they learned as well to see the value of employment in an organization with some opportunity for advancement.

A sizable minority added to this composite of attitudes and expectations a family tradition that placed a special premium on service to the state. When, in addition, a child's intelligence and academic record promised high performance on exams, a career in secondary teaching assumed a certain logic, even if the offspring were a girl.

Nonetheless, in certain important ways the calculations that attracted girls to Sèvres were not the same as those affecting Normaliens, because for the middle-class woman, having a profession at all cast a shadow on her personal life. For a middle-class boy the choice of a career amounted to his entry into manhood. Once employed, he could move on to marriage and a family of his own. By contrast, for a middle-class female, far from marking her entry into adult status (something only marriage could bestow on women), a profession had the principle advantage of providing for her should she never marry. In principle, marriage and employment constituted two socially incompatible conditions, since a woman who continued working once she married would compromise her husband's reputation. It follows that a girl contemplating a career in teaching looked ahead to an ambivalent personal status, financially independent but, unless she married, still officially a *fille.*

Inevitably, such considerations helped to determine who applied to Sèvres and set these students apart from men aiming toward the same profession. In the first place, the fathers of Sévriennes rarely came from the highest strata of their occupational groups. If employees of the state, they were not its high officials. If universitaires, they taught in secondary schools and not the university, while no father in educational administration above the level of academy inspector sent a daughter off to Sèvres. Military officers among the fathers of Sévriennes belonged exclusively to the middle or lower ranks of officers, and the few *négociants* with daughters at Sèvres came exclusively from small towns, which suggests that they enjoyed a modest prosperity at best as wholesale merchants. At both schools, recruitment drew most heavily on the middling echelons of French society, but whereas Sévriennes almost always came from homes strapped financially, sometimes severely, Normaliens might occasionally come from well-off, even socially distinguished families. Only under the most exceptional circumstances would girls from such a milieu end up engaged in paid employment.

Such exceptions did, nonetheless, occasionally arise, and they left their traces on the history of Sèvres's recruitment. Once in a great while, a willful girl, convinced that her future lay in secondary teaching, managed also to persuade her parents, who otherwise would have arranged for her to marry. Marie Bertrand (class of 1884) was one of those who might have married comfortably in her early twenties if she had not insisted on a career in teaching. According to her uncle, the permanent secretary of the Academy of Sciences, Marie developed very early a taste for learning in a library left to her family by her maternal grandfather.[21] At fourteen, she composed a poem about a recently deceased younger brother that so impressed her grieving parents that they had it published, a sign perhaps that her father, too, had certain intellectual predilections. Nonetheless, he resisted the idea that Marie might benefit from any further instruction than what the local nuns could offer in the primary school of Evry. Only after hearing considerable pleading from his daughter did M. Bertrand agree to send her to a convent school at Troyes, the departmental capital. From that point forward, though, Marie's father lost control of her ambition. Her new teachers quickly recognized Marie's talent and their own inability to satisfy this adolescent's curious mind. In a most unorthodox decision, they agreed to let her take courses organized by the municipality at the town hall. Meanwhile, Marie decided on her own to study for the entrance exam for Sèvres. To take the preliminary written exams, however, she had to prevail upon her parents to send her to Dijon, a task that somehow she accomplished. Her success at these exams, "caused more consternation than joy," according to her uncle, "and at first her father refused to let her go to Paris."[22] Indeed, he hesitated so long that Marie arrived in Paris for the orals on the final day of the competition. She came in last in a field of sixteen successful candidates in letters.[23] Even by 1884, it seems, the kind of independent study undertaken by Marie Bertrand barely sufficed to meet the rapidly rising standards of the jury that selected girls for Sèvres.

Ordinarily, therefore, when socially well-connected girls did occasionally turn up at Sèvres, it meant that parents had approved of their career. Otherwise, they would never have acquired the education necessary by the middle eighties for success at these exams. Of the factors that elicited such support, a Protestant background proved especially helpful. Between 12 and 15 percent of the students in the first ten classes came from Protestant homes as compared to the under 2 percent of Protestants in the total population.[24] Quite clearly, respect for learning, traditional to Protestants, facilitated a career in secondary teaching for girls of that faith. Nonetheless, even in such households, consent depended less on parents' liberal views than on the cold logic of necessity. The real expla-

---

[21] Letter to Ernest Legouvé from J. Bertrand, published in *ESDJF* 1 (1889): 145–47.

[22] Ibid., 146.

[23] Ibid., 147.

[24] Since ministerial forms did not report religious affiliation, I have relied for this information on informal references in teachers' dossiers, biographies, and death notices.

nation for why a girl from a respectable, middle-class background had applied to Sèvres often turned up in interviews with ministerial officials. Thus, from the inspector reporting on Emma Remoussin (class of 1883) we learn: "She might have hoped for a brilliant future from the point of view of personal fortune. But her uncle's firm with which her father was associated has declined in recent years, though without going out of business." "This," the inspector's notes concluded, "is what decided Mlle Remoussin to go into secondary teaching."[25] Her case was not exceptional. Several applications from both Protestants and Catholics made reference to a "reversal of fortune" or to parents who had gone "bankrupt" as the motive for a candidacy to Sèvres.

The most common explanation, though, for why a girl who might otherwise have married comfortably and settled down to raising children chose instead to prepare herself for secondary teaching was her father's death. Fully 18 percent of the Sévriennes in the first ten classes had lost their fathers. This rate closely approximates the proportion of families lacking fathers in the total population in 1900, but it was no doubt high for families in the middle classes.[26] Such a loss could devastate a family's financial prospects. The emergence of a life insurance industry still lay years ahead, and even government employees, many of whom by now enjoyed the right to pensions at retirement, could not bequeath that payment to their heirs.[27] The premature death of a father presented the entire family with a crisis of the highest order. To take just one example, Lucie Kuss (class of 1882), a close relative of the last French mayor of Strasbourg and a member of an old Alsatian family, "entered Sèvres in deep mourning for her father whose death," according to a former classmate, "completely changed the orientation of her life."[28] Far fewer girls had already lost their mothers by the time they entered Sèvres,[29] and only 2 percent were orphans.[30] The more characteristic image of these victims of a premature parental death was that of daughters whose father's sudden decease left them without a dowry and with responsibilities toward a widowed mother.

The majority of Sévriennes, of course, still had both their parents living when they came to Sèvres, but they had also worked long and hard

[25] Dossier personnel, correspondance, F17 23993, A.N.

[26] Zeldin reports that six of twenty-one families were incomplete in 1900 with either a mother (two of twenty-one) or a father (four of twenty-one) dead. *France 1848–1945*, 1: 315.

[27] Ibid., 123.

[28] *BAES* (January 1926): 2–5. Also see obituary in *ESDJF* 1 (1925): 193–95.

[29] On this point of information the documents may be incomplete.

[30] Three out of 213.

to get there. Almost always the effort had involved a considerable financial and emotional cost to the entire family. By the mid-eighties, to get a
daughter into Sèvres meant committing a substantial portion of these
families' income toward that goal. Once a girl reached Sèvres, the government picked up the tab for her professional education.[31] But before
then, with scholarships for girls at a premium in secondary schools,[32]
parents generally shouldered all expenses for her education: tuition,
books, uniforms, school supplies, and when a girl lived at school, her
boarding fees. The amounts involved depended on the secondary school
a girl attended and how many years of schooling her success required.[33]
Nevertheless, Marguerite Perrot's conclusion that socially ambitious parents spent from 20 to 35 percent of their annual incomes on the education of their children could easily have applied to parents of Sévriennes,
since many of them had sons to educate as well.[34] A few families even
financed the education of more than one daughter who ended up at Sèvres.

Pauline Grandjean's story (class of 1885) provides an excellent example of the sacrifices forced on families of limited resources whose ambitions for their children centered on a grande école. Early in 1884, Pauline's father, a retired artillery commander at Dôle, learned to his dismay
that his daughter, aged seventeen, would not be eligible to compete for
Sèvres that year without a special dispensation. In an effort to get a
waiver for her age, he described his difficulties in a letter to the Ministry
of Education. "In effect, the pension for an artillery commander who retired before the law of 1878 . . . is notably inadequate to raise and educate two children, the eldest of whom will compete this year for the
Ecole polytechnique for the third time. I have felt obliged to abandon
temporarily our family home, despite the cost to me, so that, in the inter-

[31] Each Sévrienne signed a contract with the state promising in return for her education at Sèvres to teach for ten years. Under an arrêté of April 3, 1882, if she quit early,
she or her parents had to reimburse the government seven hundred francs for each year
spent at Sèvres. The text of this regulation appears in *Le Cinquantenaire*, 134.

[32] Mayeur, *L'Enseignement secondaire*, 184–85.

[33] The law of December 21, 1881 did not fix the tuition for the new schools. This
decision was taken at the local level and depended largely on the cost of living in different places. Sending a daughter to school in Paris meant a far heavier financial burden
on her family, therefore, than leaving her in a provincial school. At the collège at Cahors, the annual fee for a boarding student in her fifth year amounted to 600 francs. At
the collège at Albi or the lycée at Mâcon, the same girl would need 650 francs to pay
her fees. By contrast, in Paris, she could expect to pay 800 francs a year as a *demi-
pensionnaire*, which meant that she only took her lunch at school. Parisian lycées did
not have boarding facilities. Ibid., 183–84.

[34] Marguerite Perrot, *Le Mode de vie des familles bourgeoises, 1873–1953* (Paris:
A. Colin, 1961), 92.

est of their studies, I can provide them with a residence at Besançon."[35] The cost in this case had been a mortgage on his house at Dôle. He could not afford to carry this debt another year, he claimed, while his daughter continued studying at the lycée for girls at Besançon.

Disappointed in his effort to move the ministry, Pauline's father withdrew her the following fall from the lycée so that the family might together return to Dôle and some financial equilibrium. Yet neither father or daughter gave up the primary goal, and she continued her studies at the *cours secondaire* in her hometown. One birthday and one year of intensive study later, Pauline Grandjean entered Sèvres seventh in her class, typical not in the specifics of her past so much as in the collective sacrifice that her preparation represented for her family.

The single-mindedness of this commitment must have deeply marked the characters and attitudes of future Sévriennes. To judge from evaluations of them by directrices and inspectors on their application forms to Sèvres, successful candidates were almost universally hardworking and obedient as students regardless of their social or religious background. Some girls had a "persevering character," others a "persevering will"; several were "serious in character"; and at least one earned the label "a model of docility." When it came to attitudes toward schoolwork, evaluations became still more fulsome. Repeatedly, observers described one or another girl as "very hardworking" or "laborious." More interesting ways of stating the same thing included "energetic," "assiduous," or "dedicated to work"; "an ardent love for study"; and "the habit of working in the most sustained manner." Partly, of course, officials' emphasis on these traits suggests how highly prized they were in public school teachers. All the same, several things weigh in favor of the accuracy of these observations: their confidentiality, the rich variety of the descriptions, and the occasional appearance of a girl who did not fit the mold because she was "not always respectful of her directrice's remonstrances"[36] or had "not yet acquired the qualities of order and perseverance in her work."[37] Resistance by a few girls to the expectations of their parents and their teachers renders more believable the compliance repeatedly acclaimed as characteristic of the rest.

Exactly how their childhood experience produced in so many Sévriennes this combination of social timidity and driving conscience is a theme to which we shall return again. Suffice it to suggest at this point that the effort it took to get to Sèvres offers certain clues. Once the com-

---

[35] Dossier personnel, correspondance, 1884, F17 23893, A.N.

[36] Dossier personnel, Anne Rollet (class of 1884), 1884, F17 24029, A.N.

[37] Dossier personnel, Marie Lardley (class of 1888), 1888, F17 23923, A.N.

petition stiffened and the exam was based on secondary studies, the path to Sèvres became both arduous and costly. Tremendous moral pressure built up on girls at home to justify the hopes and energies expended on them. Pauline Grandjean's father made this filial debt explicit when he remarked in his letter to the ministry that he "was counting on his children to shorten the time" that he would have to be in debt.[38] As much as a sense of obligation, though, a sense of privilege must have weighed upon these girls. Almost all of them could claim to be the first female from their family to attend a secondary school and the only one to get a higher education. Compared to mothers and often even sisters, they possessed extraordinary learning. Indeed, some fathers may have had no more than a primary or advanced primary education, though they were prepared to see in higher education a promising route for ambitious sons and daughters.

The intensity of feeling that this narrow avenue of opportunity inspired in both parents and daughters comes through clearly in this letter to the director of secondary education from the father of a distraught future Sévrienne: "My daughter has just experienced a great disappointment at the competition for the School of Sèvres. Despite the legitimacy of her hopes, given the fact that she had prepared all of the required subjects, including those for the agrégation, and in appearance at least had answered all the exam questions . . . , she was excluded from the list of contenders."[39] "Though badly shaken," he went on to assure the director, "her courage is not broken." Would the director be good enough, therefore, to indicate the subjects on which his daughter had performed badly so that she might resume her preparation for the following year? Perseverance obviously enjoyed the same approval in the home as it received from school officials.

Together these bits and pieces of information create a social profile of these early Sévriennes suggestive of the personal motives and familial pressures that propelled them into secondary teaching. Some we know, like Marie Bertrand, were motivated by strong personal inclination. They included Adrienne Prieur (class of 1884), the daughter of a Parisian butcher who renounced his opposition to her call to teaching in the face of her persistence.[40] Likewise, Berthe Guyot (class of 1884), also the daughter of a merchant without savings, "turned to teaching by vocation more than from necessity." "She cost a lot," an inspector pointed out, "and would have cost [her parents] less had she turned to a different

---

[38] Dossier personnel, correspondance, 1884, F17 23893, A.N.
[39] Archives, E.N.S.
[40] Dossier personnel, correspondance, 1884, F17 23738.

career.''[41] But just like these two girls, the great majority of Sèvres's students, whatever their attitudes toward teaching, prepared themselves for paid employment out of need. With neither dowry nor inheritance to ensure a financially attractive marriage or a comfortable spinsterhood, these girls had to plan for independence while they waited on events. Several could foresee a time when family members would require their material support. Even without the possibility of entering this well-paid, new female profession, most of these girls would have looked ahead to some kind of future paid employment.

What made the choice of secondary teaching different from other feminine options was the prestige attached to this career when men pursued it. That in turn perceptibly affected the way that fathers thought about their daughters' futures. Instead of leaving to their wives the supervision of a daughter's education and plans for work, the normal practice in French homes,[42] fathers took an active hand in guiding girls toward Sèvres. They almost always wrote the letters sent by families to the ministry, while mothers confined their public role to chaperoning daughters for interviews with inspectors who reviewed the candidates for Sèvres. Perhaps this interest on the part of fathers represented a sense of shared identity ordinarily denied to fathers and their daughters. Unlike the vast majority of French families, fathers rather than mothers of future Sévriennes provided these young girls with models for their working lives. Only one in twenty mothers of these girls even held a job.[43] On the other hand, the costs of getting girls to Sèvres just as likely could explain this keen paternal interest in their daughters' future. The position of aspiring Sévriennes in this respect resembled that of sons whose families also paid the price of grooming them for entry to a grande école.

Successful candidates most likely brought to Sèvres mixed feelings about the future they imagined. Some may well have felt a certain disappointment that fate required them to work while the majority of their classmates in secondary schools looked ahead to marriage, children, and domestic comfort. Others must have prized the fact that, apart from their own teachers, only brothers and fathers provided models for their professional ambitions. With their admission into Sèvres, they had earned a

---

[41] Dossier personnel, correspondance, 1884, F17 23604, A.N.

[42] John Shafer, "Family, Class and Young Women: Occupational Expectations in Nineteenth-Century Paris," in *Family and Sexuality in French History*, ed. R. Wheaton and T. K. Hareven (Philadelphia: Univ. of Pennsylvania Press, 1980), 180–96.

[43] Only 5.6 percent of the documents indicate a working mother. Most of these were primary-school teachers; one taught music; one was a *sage-femme* (midwife); and in an exceptional case of upward mobility by a talented scholarship girl, one widowed mother was a maid.

training that many male acquaintances might have envied. Furthermore, in contrast to most working women, they could anticipate a future of financial independence and even the possibility of a social rank determined by their own accomplishments. Some politically aware young Sévriennes may have even seen in secondary teaching an opportunity to advance the cause of women's rights. But whatever social purpose or personal pride they attached to their achievement, few of these young women escaped the bonds of family obligations. Like dutiful sons, they bore the hopes of fathers, mothers, and even sometimes siblings whose security in the years ahead might well depend on their success at Sèvres.

3 | Forging a Sévrienne Tradition

THROWN TOGETHER in an unprecedented educational adventure for which few were well prepared, Sèvres's first students understandably felt disoriented. "We were all quite lost," a member of the class of 1881 confided many years later, "especially those of us who had left schools that they directed or where they had been teaching and directing simultaneously."[1] The physical state in which the first class found the school added to this sense of strangeness. Neither the renovations of the buildings nor the landscaping of the grounds was finished by December 12, 1881, the day the school opened. For a few weeks workmen filled the hallways, while for several months the eighteenth-century gardens retained the unkempt state to which they had reverted after the building was abandoned in the 1870s. Lucie Bérillon (class of 1881) drew a somber picture of her classmates' first reaction to their new abode. "Covered with scaffolding and littered with materials of all kinds, with its long corridors, chalk-white walls, and red tiles, the school seemed . . . cold and gloomy."[2]

That forbidding impression would pass quickly, though, fusing into the quasi-mythical traditions that Sévriennes began to build around their school almost as soon as they arrived. Published accounts of Sèvres's first years suggest an emotional intensity to school life that deeply marked the memories of alumnae.[3] The fact that most of them were young and far from home, some for the first time, certainly encouraged students to romanticize the experiences they shared there. The very elegance of their surroundings, once refurbished, added visual, daily confirmation to their sense of self-importance. Yet, the almost epic quality of school life, confirmed repeatedly in memoirs of alumnae, came above all from the sense of drama imparted to the school by the first directrice and its original corps of idealistic teachers.[4] Together these elements pro-

---

[1] Quoted anonymously by Anna Amieux in *Le Cinquantenaire*, 131.

[2] L. Bérillon, "Souvenirs d'une élève de la première promotion," in *Le Cinquantenaire*, 373.

[3] There are striking similarities between the school traditions developed at Sèvres and those described by Vicinus at Girton College in the same period. *Independent Women*, 121–62.

[4] The sources that best describe the spirit associated with this period of Sèvres's history are Marguerite Aron, *Le Journal d'une Sévrienne* (Paris: Alcan, 1913); Jeanne Ben-

duced for the first Sévriennes an image of themselves not just as special but as somehow heroic, a generation at the frontier of a new world that, at some personal risk, they would have a crucial role in charting and inhabiting.

The original architects of Sèvres, men like Camille Sée and Jules Ferry, shared this vision of the school's initial inmates. In deciding on a place to train them, though, they particularly wanted a location that ensured this vanguard would stay out of public view. Publicity could only hurt a cause whose success depended on stealing softly up on bourgeois mores. Sée first suggested putting the school in the empty national palace of Compiègne, several miles to the north of Paris. Ferry and Charles Zévort, the director of secondary education, rejected that idea because it meant forgoing a faculty of teachers drawn from Paris.[5] Still they, too, saw the advantages of a former royal residence, which permitted a cloistered life for female students while avoiding the reactionary overtones of a converted convent. The final choice of the residence and royal manufactory built at Sèvres by Louis XV for Madame de Maintenon met all the necessary requirements. Laid out along the edge of town and set back from the road, this national monument would easily permit the inconspicuous life-style deemed appropriate by one and all for the new school. Twenty minutes by train from Paris, it also offered access to a ready pool of eminent professors. A further feature in its favor was the fact that renovations to convert the building to a school had already begun. The previous year the ministry had decided to install at Sèvres the normal school for male elementary teachers, later known by its final destination as Saint-Cloud.

For all the advantages of this setting, the school derived its distinctive spirit less from its location than from qualities built into school life by those who lived and worked there. From the day it opened, Sèvres veered dramatically away, in its daily operations, from the pattern of the cloister. At least inside the school, Sèvres proved to be exceptional in a culture where convent schools set the tone for all feminine boarding institutions.[6] Jeanne Michotte (class of 1883), who came to Sèvres from a

---

Aben, "Souvenirs de Sèvres," *La Grande Revue* 42 (May 24, 1907); Belugou, "Madame Jules Favre," xvii–xcvi; and the recollections of former students and teachers included in *Le Cinquantenaire*. A more critical view of school life that, nonetheless, captures the school spirit rather accurately is found in G. Réval, *Les Sévriennes* (Paris: Ollendorf, 1900).

[5] *Le Cinquantenaire*, 123–24.

[6] For a good description of life inside a convent school, see B. Smith, *Ladies*, 165–86. Boarding facilities provided by factory owners and department stores for their female employees in the nineteenth century modeled their regulations on these convent schools as well. See, for example, Louise A. Tilly, "Three Faces of Capitalism: Women

pensionnat "where not a crumb could linger on the dining table," remembered "the discipline" at her new abode to have been "extremely light."[7] A younger Sévrienne (1890) had the same reaction when she got to Sèvres a few years later. "After the suspicious discipline of lycées, one is a bit astonished to find oneself so free."[8] The very appearance of Sèvres's students, who could dress however they liked, provided they showed good taste, implied their unique status.[9]

Uniforms were not the only standard feature of institutional living that this school discarded. An equally permissive rule governed the decoration of girls' rooms. Each student received a bed, wardrobe, dressing table with mirror, table, and one chair. Curtains and a bedspread in a matching flowered chintz completed the decor.[10] But what each Sévrienne added to these basics she alone, within the limits of her budget, had the privilege to decide. Aesthetically, the results, according to one witness, varied greatly. "Some girls, but not many, preserved this original spartan bareness. . . . Others cluttered their rooms with trinkets, filling every corner with little nests of color. A few possessed an evident artistic flair . . . , though these last could be counted on one's fingers."[11]

Nonetheless, for all this liberality, certain aspects of school life shared the rigor and seclusion of other boarding institutions.[12] Up at 6:30 A.M., students looked ahead four days out of seven to a sixteen-hour day of class and study, interrupted only by mealtime, tea, and an hour or so of leisure after dinner. All day Sunday plus Thursday and Saturday afternoons, Sévriennes could plan their time at will and even make a trip to Paris. Yet those returning to the school after dark required chaperones, and on Thursdays, a student had to have explicit authorization from the school's directrice to go to Paris.[13] Just to take a walk in nearby parks required girls to organize themselves into groups of five students or

---

and Work in French Cities," in *French Cities in the Nineteenth Century*, ed. John M. Merriman (New York: Holmes and Meier, 1981), 165–92; Theresa McBride, "A Woman's World: Department Stores and the Evolution of Women's Employment, 1870–1920," *French Historical Studies* 10, no. 4 (1978): 664–83; and the novel by Emile Zola, *Au bonheur des dames* (Paris: Fasquelle, n.d.).

[7] *Le Cinquantenaire*, 365.

[8] Reval, *Les Sévriennes*, 44.

[9] In the circular that accompanied his arrêté of October 14, 1881 announcing the conditions for entrance to Sèvres, Charles Zévort advised rectors to notify potential candidates that no uniforms would be required. The circular is quoted in *Le Cinquantenaire*, 129.

[10] Ben-Aben (class of 1888), "Souvenirs de Sèvres," 647.

[11] Ibid.

[12] Bérillon, "Souvenirs d'une élève," in *Le Cinquantenaire*, 375–76.

[13] Belugou, "Madame Jules Favre," in *Le Cinquantenaire*, 336.

more.[14] As for public outings by the entire school, they almost never happened. Louise Thuillat (class of 1891) remembered only two such excursions during her three years at Sèvres.[15] Behind this guarded life-style lay a conscious effort to preserve at Sèvres the cloistered rule under which young unmarried women of the bourgeoisie lived, even when not confined to convents.

Other aspects of school life that recalled monastic living included a cost-conscious attitude toward physical comfort. Heat was a low priority for the administration in this school where tiled hallways, along with a system of radiators that barely worked in classrooms and existed nowhere else, made winter months an ordeal. One freezing first-year student confided to her diary in the dead of January: "It's cold, cold everywhere; the tiles in the hallways are cold, the mouths of heaters blow cold air; the entire school is cold. We cough, we shiver, we whimper. We look like packages wrapped up to our ears."[16] Three sticks of kindling and as many logs represented the full material extent of daily sympathy doled out to students in their chilly rooms.[17] Still, if an ascetic spirit at times inspired the regulations, that spirit did not by any means inform the school's operations.

The formal rules drawn up for Sèvres by its administrative council under the presidency of Octave Gréard, vice-rector of Paris, frequently did not reflect what actually went on behind its walls. To take just one example, the school's code explicitly required students to refrain from studying in their rooms after the nightly curfew. To insure that they complied, the ministry installed a system of gas jets, all of which went on and off together. However, for this system to succeed completely required strict surveillance on the part of the administration, and from the day the school opened, that was just what Sèvres lacked. To explain this laxity one need look no further than the school's directrice, who refused on principle to police the students in her charge.[18] Almost always, in the

[14] Bérillon, "Souvenirs d'une élève," in *Le Cinquantenaire,* 385.

[15] Ibid., 235.

[16] "Le Journal d'une Sévrienne," *ESDJF* 1 (1901): 51. Published in 1912 as a book under Marguerite Aron's name (class of 1893), this memoir first appeared anonymously as a series of articles in the professional journal founded by Camille Sée. Aron published it in response to the far more critical novel *Les Sévriennes,* written by Gabrielle Logerot (class of 1890), which appeared in 1900 under the pseudonym G. Réval. In 1901 Aron claimed this autobiographical account came directly out of her diary. In the preface for the book in 1912, she disclosed that the Sévriennes in the novel were all fictitious composites of students she had known at Sèvres. Aron, *Le Journal d'une Sévrienne* (Paris: Alcan, 1912), viii–ix.

[17] Bérillon, "Souvenirs d'une élève," in *Le Cinquantenaire,* 376.

[18] Belugou, "Madame Jules Favre," in *Le Cinquantenaire,* 330–47.

absence of a formal rule, this administrator's personal code did not require one; while those that did exist she often decided to ignore. Exasperated by the routine permissiveness that this attitude implied, Octave
Gréard, the man responsible for supervising the administration of the
School of Sèvres, wrote in fury to the minister: "It is regarding discipline
that it is the most difficult to win one's case. It can't be said that no order
at all exists at Sèvres, but there is absolutely no regularity. *All do exactly
what they please.* Time and time again I have protested to the directrice.
She acknowledges my complaints and then ignores them. To get satisfaction, one would have to work at Sèvres, even live there. And even then
it is not certain that what one established one day would not disappear
the next."[19]

Yet, what the vice-rector deplored was precisely what made school
spirit at Sèvres develop quickly. For it encouraged the kind of intense
social life that could give birth immediately to school tradition. The obstacles to solidarity among girls already in their twenties seemed considerable to some observers in the early 1880s. As Paul Dupuy put it: "At
the age when girls . . . enter Sèvres, they are very little given to comrad-
ery, especially when the preoccupations of their work absorb them. . . .
They rarely *tutoient* one another. They nearly always call each other
Mademoiselle. And though I see nothing wrong in this, it would be regrettable if these exterior manners expressed too faithfully a certain indifference between students, a coldness that would unquestionably harm
the spirit of the School."[20] In Dupuy's view, single rooms increased the
dangers of aloofness and ought not, therefore, to be allowed, but his fears
on this account proved groundless. Rather than isolated cells, students'
rooms became, like so much else at Sèvres, a focus of the school's collective life.

If from the street Sèvres looked like an army garrison and on the
ground floor, with its vaulted, musty hallways, a lugubrious convent,
that is where its likeness to less intimate institutions stopped. At every
level of this eighteenth-century royal playground, something of the gaiety of its first occupants endured. Throughout the 1880s, girls awakened
to the sound of bells announcing they had one hour to wash their hands
and face and to dress before the day began.[21] By the early 1890s this bath-

[19] Report by Gréard to the minister, April 4, 1888. F17 14187, A.N.

[20] Paul Dupuy, "L'Ecole Normale de Sèvres," *ESDJF* 2 (1882): 154.

[21] According to official regulations, thirty minutes was allowed for dressing. In another of her efforts to soften the discipline of the school, Mme Favre lengthened the
period to an hour. Bérillon, "Souvenirs d'une élève," in *Le Cinquantenaire*, 375. For
the first several years, washing in the morning was confined to hands and face. Once a

ing routine changed. In the basement, underneath the insalubrious lower hall, the ministry had installed showers. Now each morning, when the bell sounded, students clambered four by four down three flights of stairs for a subterranean shower.[22] Once cleaned and dressed but still often in their slippers, they gathered for an hour or so of study. Sometime between 7:15 and 8:00 A.M. students ambled in to breakfast. Anyone too indisposed to come to breakfast could ask a friend to bring back something for her to eat. The looseness of these proceedings left one inspector sputtering: "One can well imagine the difficulties that such a breakfast poses for the quality of the food, for students' health, for control of the budget, for the regular habits that must be inculcated in future teachers, and even for the running of the school."[23] But like all the protests lodged before it, this one, too, had no effect on changing the relaxed attitude toward formal regulations typical at Sèvres.

At lunch and dinner everyone arrived and ate together in a more systematic manner. But even during these meals, a spontaneous rather than an official order reigned. The school maîtresses always ate together. But students sat at any table they liked, and the directrice did not restrain the gaiety of these gatherings by appearing at them. "Nothing is less regimented or more joyous," one recent graduate wrote,

> than these meals with seventy girls, talking science and literature, fashion and pedagogy, seated around tables of ten, and more or less vaguely divided up by class. From the first-year tables comes the loudest chatter and laughter. . . . Third-year students are more restrained . . . ; the traditions, the tiny details of school life no longer interest them. . . . In general, they leave it to first-year students to organize little pranks against the school's purser . . . or to throw from table to table . . . announcements, collective protests, or petitions . . . sometimes embellished with cartoons . . . which produce a moment of general merriment or of protest manifested in the banging of dining chairs.[24]

After dinner, some students always gathered in an adjoining salon for an hour of ballroom dancing or just relaxing with their friends. "It's a delightful time," one alumna of the school reported. "The room is bare, waxed and glistening, with a few fine prints, a piano and some caned

---

week the girls washed their feet, and every thirty days or so they trekked off to the public showers for a bath.

[22] Ben-Aben "Souvenirs de Sèvres," 647.

[23] "Note pour le Directeur de l'enseignement secondaire," from Le Forestier, Troisième Bureau, May 4, 1887. F17 14187, A.N.

[24] Ben-Aben, "Souvenirs de Sèvres," 643.

chairs, which the janitor lines up along the wall, and every evening Sé-vriennes scatter every which way. It could be the parlor of a convent if it were not so wildly gay."[25]

Located on the second story of the school were the places where the main business of the school went on: the classrooms, the study hall, the office of the school directrice. Here the more serious tone associated with public schools generally held sway. Yet even on this level the presence of a splendid eighteenth-century hall, complete with sculpted recessed cabinets and floor-to-ceiling windowed doors, lightened the atmosphere again. Better perhaps than any other room, this elegant reception hall, which served as the school's library, mingled together the ascetic and lighthearted moods that nostalgic alumnae remembered as permeating the atmosphere at Sèvres. A decade after leaving Sèvres one of them published a collection of reveries and anecdotes that she claimed to have recorded in her diary. She recounts a prank that took place in the library during her first year which perfectly recaptures the style of merriment adopted by the entering class as soon as they arrived. "November 4, — . . . Freshmen, we haven't yet done anything extraordinary! A wager: let's see if we can make tea in the library without anyone's getting caught!"[26]

Teatime was, in fact, a pivotal moment in the communal daily life of Sèvres. Usually students took tea in their rooms, high above the school, huddled in groups of two or more around a fire where they shared hoarded wood and sweets from home. "Often teatime was a truly gigantic, familial love-feast," Jeanne Ben-Aben (class of 1890) recalled, "where immense cakes and magnificent pâtés de foie gras, the precautions of far-sighted mothers for a cherished child, melted like butter under the repeated sallies of a multitude of famished armies."[27] At other times, it was the moment in the day when special friends could be together in an intimate setting. "The most delicious memory that we carried from our rooms," Ben-Aben remembered, "was of reading sessions with one or two others . . . and grave discussions of our futures . . . while the teapot whistled on the brazier."[28]

If one remembers how diverse Sèvres's students were at first, this social life takes on its full importance. On the one hand, it made possible the rapid integration of individuals into the social network of the school. Previous social training based on maintaining social distance was effectively disarmed. On the other hand, it encouraged girls entering Sèvres

[25] Quoted from the novel based on her experience at Sèvres, Reval, *Les Sévriennes*, 56.

[26] Aron, "Le Journal d'une Sévrienne," *ESDJF* 1 (1901): 14.

[27] Ben-Aben, "Souvenirs de Sèvres," 657.

[28] Ibid., 657.

together to identify their school persona with their class. "We were like a little family," Marguerite Aron wrote about her class of 1893. "The promotion[29]—the word sounded already like a rallying cry . . . and we put in its virile, almost military sound a touch of fraternal pride. Long live the freshman class!"[30] The note struck here sounds typical of the younger, smaller classes after 1884. But if bravado thrived particularly among Sèvres's later, younger classes, school spirit developed in them all. And it was this that helped to shape Sèvres's core traditions.

Two different student traditions grew up at Sèvres in its first decade, one spontaneous, satiric, and essentially oral; the other formal and respectful, dutifully recorded in a "Book of Traditions" that successive classes kept for fifty years. The first of these bore a distant resemblance to the "delinquent culture" that characterized boys' secondary schools during the Third Republic.[31] Humor served as the main arm against authority. Those who used the weapon well earned informal designations as class poets since it was as lyricists above all that students liked to parody their world. Typically the objects of their sallies included their professors, school rules, institutional food, and an uncomprehending, hostile public. But self-mockery also tickled students' fancy. Above all, what characterized this humor, though, was its unchurlish tone. Robust, naughty, clever—it reflected the antics not of an alienated group of girls deeply hostile to their elders but of mischievous and basically docile adolescents. The following ballad from the period conveys the tone of this good-natured banter:

> *Ballad of the Bohemian*
>
> *We are the Bohemian*
> *Rebel spirit, nose windward,*
> *Those who scold are no less won,*
> *By her good heart they're lured.*
> *It's she who sings in merriment*
> *Whose reason does not bore;*
> *She is always out in front,*
> *The Bohemian's off to war.*

[29] The French term for a class of students entering a professional school in the same year.

[30] Aron, "Le Journal d'une Sévrienne," *ESDJF* 1 (1901): 11.

[31] For a description of life inside boys' secondary schools in the nineteenth century, see Paul Gerbod, *La Vie quotidienne dans les lycées et collèges au XIXe siècle* (Paris: Presses universitaires de France, 1968). The term "delinquent culture" belongs to Jesse R. Pitts, "Continuity and Change in Bourgeois France," in *In Search of France*, ed. Stanley Hoffman (Cambridge: Harvard Univ. Press, 1963), 235–305.

Her existence is a problem
For the wise and correct gent;
"What madness and what sloth,"
On her disparagement.
She cares not for the present,
The future hardly more;
To the failed exams indifferent,
The Bohemian's off to war.[32]

Another limerick mocked the slander heaped by opponents of educated women on Sèvres:

Where girls' hearts dessicate
and insanity is their fate.[33]

For the most part, though, students at Sèvres could ignore the distant rumblings of a hostile world. More troubling for schoolgirls, to whom feasting represented the favorite social act, was lack of money. Impecuniousness, as the following song suggests, took pride of place among the themes favored in students' lyrics.

That each of us was baptized
By Saint-Poverty
Does not our need disguise
For cream to take with tea.[34]

The second, the deferential set of school traditions nurtured at Sèvres sought another kind of solidarity, based not on rebellion but on a conscious effort to imitate a family. It evolved directly out of precedents set by the first classes, and the essential task of later ones was to preserve what earlier ones began. On the day of a credentialing exam, for instance, freshmen customarily made coffee in their rooms for whichever of the upper classes were to be examined.[35] After breakfast the whole school gathered in the courtyard to wish luck to those departing for Paris and to watch the school directrice give her blessing. "There was something heroic," G. Reval claimed, in her novel about Sèvres, "in the confident smile that for just a moment passed across these poor, strained, feverish faces. . . . That moment was the one when Mme Jule[36] . . . bestowed her kiss. At that instant, she had the proud look of a chieftain who would

---

[32] *Le Cinquantenaire,* 398.
[33] Ibid.
[34] Ibid., 401.
[35] Aron, "Le Journal d'une Sévrienne, *ESDJF* 1 (1901): 116.
[36] A transparent reference to Mme Jules Favre.

give her soul to those about to leave, and it was with beating heart that each girl received her kiss."[37]

Successive classes kept a record of similar rituals, together with notes concerning any innovations, in the "Book of Traditions" until 1936. Of all these formalized occasions, the annual school party in December rapidly assumed the most importance. It started with a spontaneous birthday celebration in Lucie Bérillon's honor (class of 1881) on the day that Sèvres officially opened.[38] The following December, students turned the occasion into a party to honor Sèvres itself. Almost immediately this anniversary became a day for all Sévriennes, past and present, to reaffirm their school ties and for the older students to welcome the new first-year class officially to Sèvres. Responsibility for the occasion, which increased in scale as the number of alumnae grew, fell entirely on second- and third-year students, who spent a frenzied November preparing skits and planning for the annual feast. One second-year student, caught up in the whirlwind, made a list in 1890 of what the task entailed: "Organize the annual school party, make the costumes, create the scenery, learn lines, rehearse, recite, gesture, and on top of it all, study for the certificate exam, all with an activity that could move a world!"[39] Each year when the big day finally came, everyone in Sèvres's immediate entourage made an appearance, everyone, that is, except the male professors. The rule excluding men from this occasion until the 1920s eloquently expressed the core of Sèvres's existence. Sèvres remained at heart a female world closed in on itself. Only little sons of the alumnae broke up the sea of female faces gathered together to celebrate their school. All graduates, of course, received an invitation, and in the early days, those who could not come often telegrammed regrets to the assembled guests. As for first-year students, each of them arrived on the arm of someone from a class above her. At the final moment, with Sèvres's offspring, new and old, gathered together in a single hall, Mme Jules Favre, the school's directrice and the figurative mother of this extended female family, arrived. Her appearance, calculated for dramatic impact, signaled that the party might begin.[40]

Forging a Moral Tradition

Officially, Mme Jules Favre, the administrative head of Sèvres, had a reputation as "not just an excellent directrice" for the normal

---

[37] Reval, *Les Sévriennes*, 159.

[38] *Le Cinquantenaire*, 396.

[39] Aron, *Le Journal d'une Sévrienne* (1912), 53.

[40] See the *Cahiers de traditions: Ecole de Sèvres, 1889–1936* for the details of these events as they were passed down from class to class. Archives, E.N.S.

school at Sèvres but "the very directrice" needed by the fledgling institution.[41] This public adulation notwithstanding, the actual view of her that circulated among insiders at the ministry flattered her far less. Superficially cordial relations actually concealed a deep antipathy between the directrice and several of her superiors, an antipathy born of opposing views on how the School of Sèvres should run. A columnist for *Le Temps*, writing on the occasion of Mme Favre's death, alluded in vague terms to troubled waters. "If it is ever written, the history of her administration risks being the history of an enduring battle with several of her superiors, over important as well as minor issues."[42] In fact, that history never saw the printed page. Official panegyric of Mme Favre proved far too useful to the ministry for those who knew the inside story to expose the colorful details. Her friends admitted later only that twice during her administration, Mme Favre, in a fit of solemn outrage, threatened to resign. On the first occasion, her principal opponent, Vice-Rector Gréard, refused even to transmit her resignation to the minister.[43] But the second time, when the issue touched the organization of the women's agrégation and not just the operations of the school, Gréard called in the minister. This time, members of Sèvres's faculty rose to Mme Favre's defense and lobbied at the ministry on behalf of both her cause and her administration.[44] Their victory on both points confirmed the indispensability of Mme Favre at Sèvres. Ten years after the founding of this higher normal school, its first directrice had herself become an institution.

Who was this woman who one of her admirers declared in 1896 could "only be compared for her philosophical elevation and influence on her students to the great stoic and director of the rue d'Ulm, Ernest Bersot?"[45] By marriage Mme Jules Favre had a pedigree attractive to republicans looking for a name with stature. Jules Favre had excellent political credentials even if his reputation never quite recovered from the unpopular

---

[41] A quote from G. Darboux, in *Le Cinquantenaire*, 125.

[42] From a newspaper column by Henri Michel, quoted by Anna Amieux in *Le Cinquantenaire*, 187–88. A personal letter from P. Blany addressed to "Suzanne" and dated February 3, 1896, in the archives of the Alumnae Association of Sèvres, alluded to the well-known antipathy between the deceased directrice of Sèvres and both her immediate superior, Vice-Rector Octave Gréard, and Ernest Legouvé, who had been appointed director of studies at Sèvres. The letter asked, "Did Mme Jules Favre know before her death of the completely false praise that M. Gréard gave to M. Legouvé whom he called 'the director of Sèvres' and to whom he tried to give, instead of to her, all the credit for the prosperity and intelligent spirit of the School?" Alumnae Association, archives, E.N.S.

[43] Belugou, "Madame Jules Favre," in *Le Cinquantenaire*, 342.

[44] Ibid. The minister of education at the time was Léon Bourgeois.

[45] Paul Sonday, "Mme Jules Favre," *ESDJF* 1 (1896): 79.

Franco-Prussian treaty of 1871, which he negotiated and signed. Equally to the point, his death in January 1880 left his widow free to put her hand to other tasks. These considerations all weighed heavily with Jules Ferry in favor of her appointment. But Mme Favre, now approaching fifty, had qualifications for the job independent of her married name. Her personal history as a single woman included several years of teaching in a private boarding school for girls, which she ended up directing. She could also boast of an exceptional degree of cultivation for a woman of that day. These achievements sprang in turn from less apparent qualities rooted in her familial past.

Born in 1834, the daughter of an Alsatian Lutheran pastor, Julie Velten grew up steeped in views that encouraged her to tie her personal fortunes to a patriot and defender of the Third Republic. It was not just that her family heritage inspired her to see the men of 1848 as heroes. Nor was it only that as a daughter of Alsace, she deeply felt the loss of France's eastern provinces.[46] Julie Velten shared with Jules Favre a moralistic idealism that had been incubated in her Protestant milieu but also resembled the idealism of Radical reformers in the early Third Republic. More even than the similarity of their views, the austerity of their manners drew these two idealists to one another. Emotional detachment combined with a passionate commitment to ideals stamped them as a couple, just as it marked their characters individually. In this arena, too, the experiences of her childhood offer insights into Mme Favre, the woman.

Several incidents remembered from Julie Velten's childhood suggest an extraordinary emphasis on self-reliance in her family. Reminiscing on the past, Mme Favre recalled her mother watching from a window on the second story of their home as she set out alone each day for school, a child of six or seven, armed with just a ruler against the nipping herds of geese that lay ahead. Hardly less intrepid was the solitary trip she remembered making one night across the local cemetery to fetch a Bible, just to prove to her uncle, a Lutheran pastor like her father, that she could do it. But the family cultivated more than personal courage in the young girl. Her uncle together with her father drew this gifted girl toward interests particularly valued in their Protestant culture: music, books, contemplative walks alone or with a companion through the countryside. Her gender had less importance than the fact that, more than others of the Velten offspring, Julie demonstrated a precocious talent. Indeed, her gifts encouraged the girl's father to send her in her teens to a pen-

---

[46] Belugou, "Madame Jules Favre," preface to Mme Jules Favre, *La Morale de Plutarque*, xix. Except where noted otherwise, all biographical material comes from Louise Belugou's account in this preface.

sionnat in Wissembourg where she learned German and quite possibly English and also passed the exam for the brevet supérieur. Yet the taste for learning and moral questions that would mark this woman's life did not begin at boarding school. It emerged, according to a confidante, "in the small corner of her father's study reserved for her among the old books of the library."[47] Anticipated already in this fleeting image from her childhood is the independent-minded, deeply serious woman Julie Velten would become.

Sometime in her late teens, the future directrice of Sèvres entered a career in teaching and accepted a position in a Protestant boarding school for girls in Paris owned and operated by one Mme Frère-Jean. No record explains her motives for the move to Paris, but the decision to work under this particular directrice gave a new orientation to Julie Velten's life. Thirty-eight years her senior, Mme Frère-Jean became not just Velten's employer but also her mentor and her friend. The significance of that development arises from that fact that Mme Frère-Jean belonged to a school of thought from which republican pedagogical reformers would later draw their inspiration. Ever since the sixteenth century, Catholic pedagogical tradition in France had held the view propounded by Counter-Reformation schoolmen that a child's nature was easily corrupted. Accordingly, to preserve the innocence of youth, schools had to supervise their students closely, teach them to obey, and above all seal them off from a corrupting world. In France, Rousseau raised the first major opposition to this pedagogy by insisting that children allowed to develop in a permissive environment in the home would inevitably retain their natural goodness. In the nineteenth century a group of Protestant educators adapted Rousseau's belief in the strength of the individual will to their own deeply religious concern with building moral character.[48] At the Institute évangélique, the pensionnat that Mme Frère-Jean led, this approach inspired an entirely new method of discipline and learning based on developing individual responsibility for one's actions. To secure compliance with school rules, Mme Frère-Jean relied on the moral conscience of her students in a modified honor system. In the classroom, instead of asking students to memorize a set of rules and facts, she taught them by inductive reasoning. "What a child, and even an adult lacks most," she argued, as did others in this reform movement, "is . . . good mental habits. To lead a child to *examine*, *compare*, and *judge* for herself is what the educator should set out to do. The role of the

---

[47] Ibid., xviii.

[48] For the best study of the application of this new Protestant-inspired pedagogy, see Georges Hacquard, *Histoire d'une institution française: L'Ecole alsacienne*, vol. 1, *Naissance d'une école libre, 1871–1891* (Paris: Editions Garnier Frères, 1982).

teacher is not to pour into a child information passively accepted but to awaken her intelligence by a constant appeal to personal effort."[49]

The superficial similarity of this system to the scientific method disappears on close inspection. Far from using this technique to gather knowledge, Mme Frère-Jean used it exclusively to teach a moral lesson. In studying French literature and language, for instance, students examined only one work, the seventeenth-century novel *Télémaque*, from which they were expected to derive empirically all the rules of grammar and good writing. For Mme Frère-Jean it was enough if a girl's intellectual training had contributed to the development of her character. "What is necessary to give birth to and develop," she insisted, in defending this stripped-down course of studies, "is willpower."[50]

It is not hard to imagine what in Mme Frère-Jean's outlook appealed to the young Julie Velten. The absence of constraint in school discipline contrasted sharply with her own experience as the daughter of a domineering mother under whose intolerance she apparently had chafed. By contrast, her new mentor's emphasis on discovery in learning recalled efforts by her father and his brother in her own education to encourage curiosity and self-expression. Nevertheless, the most profound affinity between these women grew out of a shared moral idealism and an intensely felt belief in personal duty. What they actually discussed over seven years of confidences left no published traces. But late in life, Mme Favre had this reflection on their friendship: "When I return to the source of my two great affections, I discover admiration; the more that I admired, the more I loved."[51]

The other "great affection" here referred to was the love she bore as wife for Jules Favre. When they met in 1871, Julie Velten had taken over as directrice of the Institut évangélique, relocated by that time in Versailles. Her future spouse had just signed the Franco-Prussian treaty, by which France exchanged Alsace and part of Lorraine for peace and the republic. Having followed the parliamentary debates at Versailles with great emotion, Julie Velten wrote to Jules Favre to offer her services as a translator.[52] His acceptance of that offer marked the beginning of a friendship that three years later, when she was forty and he a widower of sixty-five, led the two friends into marriage. This union would prove singularly happy. More important, after marriage the Favres continued to enjoy the intellectual companionship that originally had brought them together. "In strict justice," Jules Favre wrote about his wife in the pref-

---

[49] Quoted by Belugou, "Madame Jules Favre,' in *La Morale de Plutarque*, xxii.

[50] Ibid., xxiii.

[51] Ibid., xx.

[52] Sonday, "Mme Jules Favre," *ESDJF* 1 (1896): 78.

ace to one of his last books, "her name ought to be beside mine on all the works to which over the last four years she has so faithfully contributed and for which I found, in her mind and heart, the surest guide."[53] Eighteen months after his death Mme Favre described the same collaboration from her own perspective. "What can I retrace in the happiness of our intimate life in order to make husbands understand what they are missing when they do not initiate a wife into their intellectual work and elevate her thoughts by discussion and by study?"[54] This ideal of marriage had found a place in the debate on Camille Sée's proposal for a system of secondary schools for girls. If in 1881 a mere handful of couples within the republican elite met this marital ideal,[55] it was not without importance that the memory of one such union deeply marked the early life of Sèvres.

For Julie Velten, marriage to Jules Favre both revealed and crystallized her deepest inclinations. On the one hand, it reinforced a sense of social obligation instilled originally by her Protestant upbringing. On the other, it kept her personal reticence intact. Throughout her adult life, this woman balanced precariously between two opposing drives. While by conviction she felt the strongest sort of obligation to make a contribution to society, a massive shyness compounded by her social position as a woman encouraged her to self-effacement. Both Favres, in fact, suffered from such contradictory impulses. Despite his reputation as an orator, Jules Favre, according to his wife, only spoke in public "when it was his duty to overcome his natural reserve."[56] Yet up until his death, duty remained the axis of his life. His wife's own sense of public obligation grew accordingly. Living beside this personally shy but public man of action, "gave Madame Favre," in the view of Henry Lemonnier, "the passionate, almost heroic sense that drove certain of the men of 1848."[57] Nonetheless, if her husband's interests led Mme Favre to define her goals more broadly and to project a new significance on her actions, she never shifted from her early focus. She remained just as before concerned with individual moral growth, which was, she now believed, indispensable for national strength. It was a perfect compromise for a female activist in the Third Republic. Although the import of her action seemed to touch

[53] Quoted from the introduction to Daedliker, *L'Histoire du peuple suisse*, in Belugou "Madame Jules Favre," in *La Morale de Plutarque*, xxxviii.

[54] Quoted in ibid., xxlx.

[55] Zeldin, *France 1848–1945*, 1: 625–28.

[56] Quoted in Belugou, "Madame Jules Favre," in *La Morale de Plutarque*, xxxiii.

[57] Quoted from the "Rapport sur l'Ecole de Sèvres à l'occasion de l'Exposition universelle de 1900," in ibid., xlviii. Henry Lemonnier taught at Sèvres during Mme Favre's administration.

on public life, its application remained the private sphere of conscience. As a woman, there her preeminence enjoyed official sanction.

Her eagerness to serve the Third Republic together with her moralizing outlook made Mme Jules Favre an ideal candidate to take the helm at Sèvres. Though no account of the negotiations surrounding her appointment to the post survives, she clearly fit the profile of a school head that reformers at the Ministry of Education approved. Like Ernest Bersot at the rue d'Ulm, Félix Pécaut at Fontenay, and Ernest Jacoulet at Saint-Cloud, Julie Favre was a Protestant whose preoccupations with moral issues and the cause of the Republic had turned her mind to pedagogical concerns.[58] A number of scholars have remarked on the important role that Protestants played in drawing up the educational reforms known collectively as the Ferry laws.[59] That contribution pales, however, alongside the part that Protestants would take in putting those laws into action.[60] With Julie Favre's selection as directrice of Sèvres, Ferry merely reenacted what would become a common staffing practice in the Third Republic.

Like several fellow Protestants, moreover, this newly widowed woman came to Sèvres as to an apostolic mission. Throughout her fifteen-year administration, Mme Favre spoke repeatedly at Sèvres just as Pécaut would at Fontenay of the "noble struggle" and the great "work" that lay ahead for the graduates of the republic's new style of professional training. In what did this great work consist? What goals did she propound before Sèvres's students? Certainly, Mme Favre staunchly defended improving women's education. She also argued vigorously on occasion for changing women's place in the society of the future.[61] Yet feminist pre-

[58] Ernest Bersot directed the Ecole Normale Supérieure on the rue d'Ulm from 1871 until his death in 1880. Félix Pecaut, a Protestant pastor from the extreme Left of Protestantism whose early-morning lectures to his students became so famous that they were printed in the *Revue pédagogique*, directed Fontenay-aux-Roses from 1882 until his death in 1896, when Jules Steeg, another Protestant, took his place. Ernest Jocolet headed Saint-Cloud for eighteen years. He contributed a memoir recalling his administration to the commemorative book celebrating the twenty-fifth anniversary of the school. Ecole Normale Supérieure d'enseignement primaire de Saint-Cloud, *Livre-Souvenir (1881–1906)* (Paris: Alcide Picard et Kaan, 1906), 17–32.

[59] See Phyliss Stock-Morton, *Moral Education for a Secular Society: The Development of Morale Laïque in Nineteenth-Century France* (New York: State Univ. of New York Press, 1988), especially chap. seven.

[60] For eighteen years, 1878–1896, the Protestant Ferdinand Buisson would occupy the post of director of primary education while his fellow Protestant Elie Rabier held the same post in secondary education from 1889 to 1907. Hacquard, *Histoire d'une institution française*, 147–50.

[61] Her most forthright feminist statement in print appeared in her preface to her translation of Jean Paul Richter, *Sur l'éducation* (Paris, 1886), 31–32. "It does not seem just

occupations did not characterize her thinking overall. On the contrary, the entire thrust of her consuming interest in the future of girls' second- ary studies focused on the individual's duties and not on women's rights. "To do one's duty," she insisted only two years before she died, "is the goal of life." That idea formed the central core of the professional ethos that she set out to spread from Sèvres. Teaching, in her view, provided an opportunity for professionals of the highest moral conscience to pass their personal sense of moral obligation on to young people. "The gift of brains," she told a group of early graduates, "is priceless, but it is through your moral qualities especially that you will contribute to the glorious cause placed in your hands. Educational instruction delivered with talent by a clear mind is a powerful instrument for raising and for- tifying the intelligence, but the example of the free submission to one's duty, however humble, is still stronger in winning hearts and making others love their duty."[62] A nation of individuals each committed to serv- ing others was in her view the recipe for national revival. In this process of rebuilding, Sévriennes would play a central role through the moral influence they would exert in girls' secondary schools over the next gen- eration of women, who in turn, she hoped, would carry that influence back into the home.

Once ensconced at Sèvres, Mme Favre became the prototype of the professional image she demanded of her students. Her formal role in school instruction was not large—two hours a week teaching first-year

---

to us to conclude that women are inferior in creative power before having placed them in conditions equal to men; for man has always had the means to cultivate his natural aptitudes while these means have always been more or less denied to the woman whose task as wife and mother, moreover, rarely permits her to dedicate herself to a profes- sion." Mme Favre then went on to defend the view of women, propounded by some supporters of Sée's law, as intellectual companions to their husbands. Her views on women resembled those defended by John Stuart Mill in *The Subjection of Women* (1869), including his assumption that women's domestic duties would remain un- changed, even if they ventured into the professions. For a critique of Mill's feminism, see Okin, *Women in Western Political Thought*, 197–232.

[62] Quoted in Belugou. "Madame Jules Favre," in *La Morale de Plutarque*, li. The pol- icy of rating moral character in students even higher than academic performance oper- ated also at the progressive Ecole alsacienne in Paris in the 1870s, where a mainly Prot- estant administration, employing a largely Protestant faculty, experimented with many of the pedagogical principles defended by Mme Favre. This school, which included primary and secondary classes and spawned a companion secondary school for girls called the Collège Sévigné (founded in 1880), provided a laboratory for many of the pedagogical innovations later adopted by state schools under the prodding of republi- can reformers. As in state schools, the students at the Ecole alsacienne and the Collège Sévigné came mainly from Catholic families. Hacquard, *Histoire d'une institution fran- çaise.*

how oversee

students civil law. She relied primarily on informal social contacts to gain ascendance over the conscience of the school. This procedure fitted neatly, in any case, with her most cherished pedagogical assumptions, which themselves originated in her Protestant beliefs. Convinced that moral integrity could only grow from principles acquired on one's own, Mme Favre preferred to win disciples in an atmosphere of free discussion. Three institutions of her own design assured her this kind of contact with Sèvres's students. The first gathered Sévriennes who chose to come around the dining table in her private apartment every Wednesday. These get-togethers resembled in seriousness and intent the practice familiar in Protestant homes of Bible readings; but at Sèvres, the intellectual framework for reflection stretched considerably wider. While her young guests knit and listened, Mme Favre would read from any of her favorite thinkers—"often Emerson, often also . . . Epicurus or Marcus Aurelius, sometimes Molière or Corneille."[63] "At some striking passage," one student recalled, "she would stop to ask our viewpoints. She would question girls individually, at random, calling each by name. A discussion would ensue. These were not textual analyses . . . but philosophical and literary conversations." "It was impossible," the same alumna claimed, "not to remember those gatherings warmly, where serious debate mingled freely with the levity . . . of a chat."[64]

To complement these philosophical *soirées*, Mme Favre hosted afternoon teas every other Sunday. Framed in terms familiar to polite society, such occasions offered Sévriennes much more than an exercise in the mundane arts. A different tone from the ordinary party prevailed. "The full-length portrait and bust of Jules Favre, the black dress in honor of the house's dead introduced to this large drawing room something solemn and austere," according to one former guest.[65] From time to time, someone would agree to share some social talent, to sing if she were able, or to recite a poem. But on the whole these parties gave pride of place to instrumental music because for Mme Favre, who played both the piano and the harmonium, "music was a part of life."[66] Indeed, of Beethoven she had made a kind of cult. "Only he," she once wrote to a friend, "can so profoundly move my soul: those sublime melodies . . . are like the echoes of an ideal world and a presentiment of the true life, of the free expression of all the forces buried in the soul."[67] No doubt, for many students these afternoons of balancing tea and cakes through intermina-

---

[63] Ben-Aben, "Souvenirs de Sèvres," 656.
[64] Ibid.
[65] Ibid., 657.
[66] Belugou, "Madame Jules Favre," in *La Morale de Plutarque*, lvi.
[67] Quoted in ibid.

ble concerts seemed insufferably long and stilted. On others, though, "who listened to this grave and beautiful music piously,"[68] the idealism embodied in these occasions left a lasting mark.

The third and best remembered of the three regular occasions devised by Mme Favre to oversee Sèvres's students was her evening salutation, known as *le salut*. The origins of this practice lie hidden in the still-uncharted history of maternal education.[69] Still deeper roots sink into the history of domestic prayer. At Sèvres, however, Mme Favre turned this familial custom into a nightly self-inspection by the entire school. "About 8:15, students began to drift toward the directrice's apartment. . . . Everyone not prevented by some important matter lined up outside Mme Favre's office and waited. When the half hour struck, the closest student knocked timidly. . . . 'Come in,' came the reply. One by one students disappeared into the study cluttered with books, papers, portraits, and memorabilia to receive a handshake."[70] This ritualized good-night implied far more than appearances might suggest, all witnesses agree. "It was not simply a mark of respect by students or on the part of the directrice a sovereign act. It was something else, something like a collective review of conscience at which the daily balance sheet for every student was drawn up."[71] For some girls, "it was a moment . . . to speak in confidence to the directrice."[72] For most, though, it provided an opportunity to discover Mme Favre's opinion of their moral progress. Generally, Mme Favre refrained from a direct rebuke or counsel. Instead, she tried, in line with her own pedagogical convictions, to be a catalyst tor self-examination. "From the very way she pronounced the traditional 'good-night, my child,' her satisfaction or discontent became apparent. As such, the salut was always a moment vaguely dreaded."[73]

Marguerite Aron recounted an experience from her second year at Sèvres that perfectly displays the moral suasion which the directrice could exercise by indirection. One February evening in 1892, Aron confided to her diary: "It snowed today. I was feeling ill. At salut Mme Favre looked at me, shook my hand, and that was all. . . . Yesterday, she only said, 'Well, are you still tired? . . . You must bestir yourself.' This evening I had almost decided to ask her for an extension on my paper."[74] The fol-

[68] Ben-Aben, "Souvenirs de Sèvres," 657.

[69] For an excellent study of the prescriptive literature written during the Second Empire for Catholic mothers, see Lévy, *De mères en filles*.

[70] *Le Cinquantenaire*, 152.

[71] Ben-Aben, "Souvenirs de Sèvres," 655.

[72] Reval, *Les Sévriennes*, 63.

[73] Ben-Aben, "Souvenirs de Sèvres," 655.

[74] Aron, "Le Journal d'une Sévrienne," *ESDJF* 1 (1901): 193.

lowing evening, with the composition finished and turned in, Marguerite reappeared before the school directrice.

> "I've been told you came down to write your paper; that's fine, my child. I think you've gotten a little thinner. Are you eating enough?"
> "Yes, Madame."
> "It seems to me I heard you cough."
> "A little, Madame, but it's nothing."
> "Oh, but it is! You should stay in your room in the morning and not come down to study hall while it's still cold. And take your oil. Good-night, my child, sleep well."[75]

Clearly, Mme Favre used elements associated with maternal training inside middle-class homes to shape her students. Both her language and the ebb and flow of her affection took on a mothering style. What she added to it was her own insistence, Protestant at base but recharged by the force of her conviction, in the necessity for individual moral growth. This factor gave to her rapport with students an impersonal note that on occasion rendered the maternal image quite remote.

[handwritten margin note: ← maternal image]

Students varied in their emotional reactions to Mme Favre; they varied less, however, in assessing her importance. Among her real disciples, the general view was that she created a tradition in her personal image. "From her elevated and powerful personality," the Protestant Louise Belugou (class of 1883) maintained, "emanated very soon a singular atmosphere at Sèvres made up of a sense of duty and responsibility, a regard for individual dignity, and a respect for freedom of opinion and belief— a serene and pervasive atmosphere from which each one took whatever she needed to fight against her failings, to develop her strengths and her ideal, and to get ready for her mission."[76] Not everyone agreed with this evaluation. Gabrielle Logerot (class of 1890) came away from Sèvres fiercely hostile to its "glacial directrice" who, she complained, "does not have the entrails of a mother."[77] Jeanne Michotte (class of 1883), who later became a great admirer of Mme Favre, as a student also apparently judged her harshly.[78] But if Sévriennes did not invariably like her or share her sense of mission, none entirely escaped the influence of the high-minded tone that she, in particular, nurtured at the school. "I did not see at Sèvres," Jeanne Ben-Aben declared, "any artful and sneaky schoolgirls, profiting from the tolerant supervision to do nothing or from the absence of sanctions to do something bad. A sense of duty and indi-

---

[75] Ibid., 193–94.
[76] Le Cinquantenaire, 153.
[77] Reval (pseudonym for Logerot), Les Sévriennes, 31–32.
[78] Le Cinquantenaire, 362.

vidual dignity was like the air one breathed at Sèvres . . . certain petti-
nesses and a certain lack of moral elevation could not survive there, the
spirit of the school opposed it." In Ben-Aben's view, at least, "that spirit
seemed to us incarnate in the person of Madame Jules Favre."[79]

Unquestionably, Mme Favre created at Sèvres a moral ethos that everyone to some degree absorbed and that became the basis of the school's
professional image. In some ways it differed little from the outlook of
monastic teaching orders. Both viewed teaching as a kind of mission;
both preferred a life-style bordering on the austere; and both placed
moral traits above intelligence. Yet to this Catholic model Mme Favre
added a distinctly personal ingredient derived from her own religious
faith. This new component was her belief in the autonomous conscience
as a guide to moral action even in her work. For a school like Sèvres,
moral individualism proved an ideal ethos because there freedom combined with social pressure to create a sense of common moral purpose in
which, to some degree, everyone could share. Once outside this setting,
though, the suitability of such a credo to professional life was not so
certain. It could be a psychic armor against a disapproving world. It
could inspire the confidence in self required to lead a class. It could even
give focus to a life otherwise without a sense of purpose. But it could
also cause a teacher problems. The guarded mutinies that Mme Favre
herself had led against traditionally minded ministerial officials anticipated tensions Sévriennes would experience when as teachers in a bu-
reaucratically controlled profession they too confronted supervisors
whom they judged overbearing and incompetent.

Forging an Intellectual Tradition

A conscious desire to innovate, to turn Sèvres into a laboratory
for the latest ideas in education, affected the intellectual life of the school
in the initial years just as much as it had shaped its moral ethos. This
impulse toward reform had two different inspirations. One came from
the conviction, recast by Jules Ferry and his entourage to lend support to
their political objectives, that class and gender should determine what
individuals learned at school in preparation for their separate tasks in
the republic. Given that assumption, Sévriennes would obviously not receive an education modeled after that for men on the rue d'Ulm.[80] Both
their gender and their options after Sèvres argued for an entirely new
conception of how to train for this profession. That prospect, in turn,

[79] Ben-Aben, "Souvenirs de Sèvres," 654.
[80] Moreover, since the director of secondary education oversaw the School of Sèvres,
it did not enjoy the independence of the school on the rue d'Ulm.

enormously excited the wing of the reform movement that had been calling for a wholesale reassessment of the pedagogical premises of French
education ever since the defeat of France by Prussian armies. In the view
of several of Sèvres's teachers as well as its directrice, a school devoted
exclusively to training secondary teachers, not future scientists or scholars, would constitute an ideal place to introduce to the profession a new
approach to learning as a first momentous step toward French revival.

Two somewhat different ways of feminizing education shaped the curriculum introduced at Sèvres. One involved restricting the content of
courses to a basic level. The most outspoken proponent of this rudimen-
tary approach, Octave Gréard, called it "an education of conclusions and
results";[81] and as president of the administrative council responsible for
Sèvres, he had the power to make his viewpoint count.[82] "Women teachers," Gréard maintained, "have only to provide a sober education, well
stripped down, . . . which brings to light precisely the attitudes, the
ideas, the innovations, the discoveries, the great accomplishments of civilization."[83] To do this well required only a general introduction to any
subject in which they gave instruction. Women secondary teachers could
be generalists, conversant with accepted theories in several fields of
knowledge but without the specialist's capacity either fully to understand or to speculate beyond them.

The modesty of these demands had implications for the breadth of
women teachers' training. With general knowledge of a field sufficient to
master the material taught in girls' schools, women could teach far more
diverse subjects than could men. That in any case was how the Council
on Secondary Education in the ministry reasoned when it designed the
system for certifying women secondary teachers. Either a teacher taught
in the humanities, which included all the history courses in the girls'
curriculum as well as those on French literature and grammar and geography, or she prepared herself in science, which meant math as well as
all the natural sciences. At Sèvres, just as at the Ecole Normale, the ministry divided the curriculum into two separate trajectories, one for letters
and one for science, but whereas normaliens, after passing the *licence* at
the end of their first year, specialized for two years in preparation for one
of the five men's agrégations, Sévriennes kept their generalist perspective, preparing as many subject areas for the agrégation as they did for
the certificat, taken after the second year at Sèvres. Thus, throughout its

[81] Quoted in *Le Cinquantenaire*, 145.
[82] In line with the effort to give Sèvres the status of a pedagogical institution not attached to higher education, it was placed under the jurisdiction of the vice-rector for
Paris who at the time was Octave Gréard.
[83] *Le Cinquantenaire*, 145.

wide & general ✓ curriculum

), ,

three-year program, Sèvres stuck to the principle of breadth in training women teachers.

If to be a professeur and still a "lady" meant that Sévriennes could not develop into experts, it required in addition a proficiency in skills widely expected of a cultivated woman. Of these requirements, the most incongruous with the actual needs of women teachers in the classroom involved a demonstration at the agrégation that they had mastered English or German as a spoken as well as written language. Never would Sévriennes have to give instruction in these subjects since instructors of foreign language at the secondary level were required to have passed the masculine agrégation in that field. Moreover, with no expectation that they would ever undertake research, women professeurs had no other professional need to learn a foreign tongue. All the same, a modern language represented for a woman, just as Latin did for men, the indispensable mark within the bourgeoisie of cultivation, and the ministry expected women teachers to conform to standard images of femininity as much as possible.

Three other subjects that republicans considered necessary to girls' instruction at the secondary level also appeared in Sèvres's curriculum with no presumption that once employed, a Sévrienne would have to teach them. Needlework, the ubiquitous course in girls' finishing schools in nineteenth-century Europe, was also required of Sévriennes, though *2.* dexterity with a needle did not meet a requirement of their professional exams. The same was true of civil law, a course designed to instruct young females in their legal rights and obligations, which students had *3.* to take at Sèvres to complete their civic education. A third area of study peculiar to the preparation of women for secondary teaching came under the general rubric *la morale*. As a course in girls' secondary schools, la morale assumed the place traditionally reserved for religious education in girls' studies. At Sèvres it became two separate courses, one devoted to ethical speculations and the other to the psychology of learning. All *1.* Sèvres's students had to take these courses, and their contents figured in both sections of the women's agrégations. Yet, in actual fact, few *agrégées*, especially in science, would ever have to teach the course on ethics. Like needlework and a modern language, the main rationale for its inclusion in these teachers' training was to reassure the bourgeoisie that women professeurs did not present a threat to the accepted social order.

Although a unique ideal of education, suited just to girls, inspired curricular design at Sèvres, this ideal was not precisely what excited Sèvres's first teachers. Less concerned than Octave Gréard to restrict Sèvres's education intellectually, key members of Sèvres's faculty placed their emphasis instead on the opportunity that this school could offer as a laboratory for pedagogical reform.[84] Handpicked by the ministry from the faculties of the Sorbonne and the best lycées for boys in Paris, these professors, despite their eminence individually, stood at the top of a profession experiencing convulsions of self-doubt. The debacle of 1870 had sent shock waves through the nation's schools as critics claimed that the educational system had failed both morally and technically to ready the French nation for the demands of modern war. Affected deeply by this national reassessment, several men assigned to teach at Sèvres arrived believing that some of the complaints leveled at boys' secondary education could be corrected in girls' schools partly by the creation of a new professional outlook.[85] Comparing this objective to Gréard's preoccupation with how to limit girls' instruction, Louise Belugou (class of 1883) remarked: "The conception of the elite charged with organizing Sèvres . . . was much more lofty. All was far from perfect in the established system. To have the joy of creating, without traditions or routines, meant for them an end to cramming, to the overloading of names and facts, and to the mere appearance of cultivation."[86]

Part of the excitement stirred at Sèvres, of course, derived from the deliberately streamlined version of its studies. Critics of boys' secondary schools complained above all that rote memorization had replaced reflection as the crucial faculty in secondary education. This development they blamed alternately on the baccalauréat exam, the proliferation of scientific knowledge, and the refusal of defenders of classical instruction to sacrifice any of the traditional components of the curriculum in classics even as the ministry introduced additional requirements. The result, according to the critics, was that while boys' secondary studies were cramming students' minds with information, the schools had lost the ability to shape character. The program of studies laid down for Sèvres answered those concerns. By emphasizing basic knowledge and by keeping the first year at Sèvres free of preparation for a professional exam, the ministry had provided an ideal environment, at least for students in the freshman year, for renouncing memorization as the key to learning.

During Sèvres's first decade and a half, this freedom from preparing for a national exam apparently engendered a heady feeling of exhilaration in both professors and their students. Henry Lemonnier recalled years

[84] The first institutions of higher learning for women in England opened also at a time when curricular and organizational reform was under discussion at Oxford and Cambridge, with the result that there, too, women's colleges became laboratories for new ideas. Vicinus, *Independent Women*, 122–24.

[85] The major critique in this regard was made by Bréal, *Quelques Mots sur l'instruction publique in France*.

[86] *Le Cinquantenaire*, 355.

later the excitement of meetings of the faculty where experienced teachers, inspired by the spirit of reform, thrashed out a common view on how to teach their subjects. "We discussed all the big and little problems of instruction and of education with an ardor, sometimes even with a passion, that demonstrated the sincere concern each of us brought to this endeavor."[87] The central message that emerged from these debates called on teachers to encourage independence in Sèvres's students, to get them to evaluate a subject on their own. By 1890 the same injunction would echo through ministerial instructions directed at secondary teachers in all secondary schools, but in the 1880s, the faculty at Sèvres enunciated independently of the ministry what would become the official pedagogy of the Third Republic.

Certainly, at Sèvres, Mme Favre's input bore on these developments. The notion that students should learn to think alone and act on their convictions perfectly summed up her personal credo. Yet the consensus that came out of faculty gatherings was too strong to have proceeded from the influence of any single member. It derived from the belief propagated by the Ligue de l'enseignement as early as the 1860s and spread through the Université in the succeeding decades that a republic could not survive without a massive effort to restructure French political culture through state schools.[88] To be successful, an attack on the authority of traditional elites had to begin with an assault on the habit of blind obedience itself, instilled in children and adolescents in the authoritarian intellectual atmosphere that pervaded the classrooms of schools all over France. The practice of laying out a subject that students duly memorized should give way to another method which led the young to the "right" conclusion through their own participation in the process of reasoning.

In the 1890s this approach to learning would dramatically alter official methods of teaching science, introducing experiments into class instruction, but the reform movement had not made sufficient headway in the 1880s to transform science instruction during the years the first generation spent at Sèvres. It was in letters, as well as in the courses on ethics and pedagogy which all Sévriennes had to take, that teachers made a concerted effort to involve students as active agents in their education.

[87] H. Lemonnier, "L'Ecole de Sèvres depuis sa fondation (1881–1900)," *ESDJF* 2 (1900): 9.

[88] For a full exploration of this interpretation see Auspitz, *The Radical Bourgeoisie*. Although other currents of thought contributed to the principles of education espoused by the Ligue de l'enseignement, it is not without importance that its founder, Jean Macé, was Protestant.

One startled Sévrienne exposed to this new pedagogy for the first time in her life recorded these reactions in her diary.

> *"Sèvres," Mme Favre said last Wednesday, closing her Pascal with an indulgent smile for our responses and reflections, "Sèvres is a republic."*
>
> *What do you think? What do you believe? That is the essence of all interrogations here. Assert yourself, be yourself, that is the essence of almost everyone's advice. It's frightening for a young woman of nineteen years, just yesterday a docile schoolgirl, to open up her soul that way . . . and then she begins to understand that life and books are one; that abstract and impersonal study is sterile and petty; and that the law of progress, even of life, is in the total giving of all our faculties, all our conviction, all our strength to work.*[89]

We can see summed up neatly in this statement how the personally demanding moral credo by which Mme Favre expected Sévriennes to live reinforced the principles governing their instruction. Inevitably, a great number of young women would emerge from such a charged environment, where all those in authority preached the same ideals, marked for life by the experience.

In concrete terms, this effort "to shape the hearts and minds of students," as Lemonnier put it,[90] boiled down at Sèvres to three objectives. The first involved an effort by their teachers to impart to Sévriennes a style of argument fixed in academic practice. The president of the jury for the women's agrégation in letters, Eugène Manuel, described the general method this way: "Find the key ideas, link them, grade them, establish subtle differences between them, choose appropriate examples, avoid digressions, observe carefully, reason correctly, and conclude well."[91] "To succeed," he added, "is a delicate and superior art, the triumph of all classical education" and no different, in other words, from what boys in secondary schools trained long years to do.

The second and novel ingredient in this educational package encouraged students to gather evidence for their arguments on their own. "In my view," Mme Favre announced to a faculty meeting in 1883, apparently with the full agreement of her listeners, "what girls entering Sèvres . . . should find, together with a . . . library, is guidance and time for the

---

[89] Aron, "Le Journal d'une Sévrienne," *ESDJF* 1 (1901): 49–50.

[90] *Le Cinquantenaire*, 202.

[91] "Rapport sur le concours d'agrégation pour l'enseignement secondaire des jeunes filles (lettres)," *ESDJF* 2 (1885): 267.

only truly profitable work: individual study."[92] Girls wrote papers regularly, therefore, on subjects not discussed in class. They also prepared lectures, written ostensibly for secondary students but delivered before their classmates and their teachers. This exercise taxed not only their ingenuity but their courage as well, because teachers followed these performances with oral evaluations; these, if disapproving, might well include an acid comment well designed to humiliate its victim.[93] In working up their own creations, Sévriennes had before them the examples of the esoteric lectures given by their professors, which became the trademark of Sèvres's education in these years. Mme Cotton-Feytis, an assistant teacher (maîtresse-adjointe) at Sèvres, pointed out some decades later in describing Sèvres's instruction that because the ministry had not set the topics to be covered in Sèvres's classes precisely, "a professor could choose a subject freely, take it as far as students' comprehension would permit, and draw out appropriate conclusions." According to her, this practice aroused in students a "taste for studies freely treated outside of and often above the level of all programs,"[94] which in the end explains why education at Sèvres would not remain at the elementary level favored by Octave Gréard at the school's inception. It also suggests why graduates, once teaching, would sometimes have considerable difficulty translating the education that they received at Sèvres into a form sufficiently elementary to satisfy inspectors in their classes.

The third concrete objective of Sèvres's instruction was to impart, wherever possible, a deeply moral resonance to academic life. The initial effort in this area came directly from the ministry itself, which looked for the same high-mindedness in teachers as it had sought in choosing a directrice. Idealism, it would seem, counted easily as much as brilliance in getting tapped to teach at Sèvres. In this regard, it is of some importance that one of the faculty who left the deepest mark on students' memories was Joseph Fabre—author, senator, professor of the courses on ethics and psychology until the death of Mme Favre, and, like her, a Protestant.[95] Fabre, too, earned his place at Sèvres and in the hearts of former students through his commitment to a moral vision. The friendship between the philosopher and the directrice, which the affinity between their moral outlooks fostered, constitutes a minor theme in the history of

[92] Procès verbaux des réunions de professeurs, 1882–1885. See notes for January 17, 1883. Archives, E.N.S.

[93] A realistic account of such a presentation and the embarrassing aftermath appears in Reval, Les Sévriennes, 49–54.

[94] Le Cinquantenaire, 216.

[95] I thank Steven Hause for this crucial bit of information about Fabre's religious background.

Mme Favre's administration. Separately and together these two figures moved through the halls of Sèvres as they floated later through the memories of Sèvres's alumnae in a vivid image of the school's most compelling message.

If Joseph Fabre drew his philosophical inspiration from Immanuel Kant, while Mme Favre looked to the ancient Stoics, they shared the same belief in the cumulative effect on the advance of civilization of individuals' heroic actions in the service of ideals. Both also worshiped a dead hero. Just as Mme Favre kept the memory of her husband Jules alive in the sanctuary of her study, Fabre devoted most of his adult life to turning the memory of Joan of Arc's achievements into a secular, patriotic cult. As a teacher, Fabre took every opportunity in lectures and assignments to give Sèvres's students a moral lesson in heroism. A glimpse of his technique appeared in the professional journal founded by Camille Sée for women secondary teachers, *L'Enseignement secondaire des jeunes filles*, in the form of an essay written by a first-year student on ethics. The theme, suggested by her teacher, read as follows: "Those who always love do not have time to grumble or be miserable."[96] The Sévrienne whose reflections on this subject merited publication began her essay this way: "To learn to live well, doubtless we must rely on strong principles. But that is not enough. We must also carry in ourselves the passion of a noble sentiment."[97] One can scarcely imagine an answer more likely to enchant her teacher or more closely modeled after the prevailing ethos of the higher normal school at Sèvres.

If the moral message of this instruction stands out clearly, its pedagogical objective may well not. What, after all, justified in the eyes of those in charge at Sèvres a year of humanistic studies and self-exploration in a school for training women teachers? Why should one-third of this instruction go simply to the pursuit of self-development? One can easily imagine courses more directly applicable to future teaching duties. Indeed, given the government's eagerness to fill girls' schools with teachers, an extra year to cultivate "the heart and mind" of students seems a luxury in the 1880s that the state could ill afford. Yet between this training and the task of teaching there existed a total consistency of theory. It derived from the importance that the Catholic tradition of schooling gave to teachers as models for the young. Revitalized by humanists in the sixteenth century, by 1881 the idea that teachers should be models for their students enjoyed the combined approval of popular and professional opinion, even if critics of boys' schools at the time believed some teach-

[96] *ESDJF* 1 (1893): 97.
[97] "Copie de Mlle E. M., elève de 1ère année." Ibid.

ers to be failing in that task. If, therefore, Sèvres's faculty urged students to seek their own ideals, they acted in keeping with accepted precepts of their craft as much as in response to new ideas for pedagogical reform.

Ultimately, however, the old ideal of teachers who displayed their learning in virtuoso performances before an admiring class severely hindered efforts to develop intellectual self-assertion in Sèvres's students. Not surprisingly, given the poverty of their prior education, the first Sévriennes turned their teachers into heros. By the end of the decade, in order to maintain the same awe-filled attitude in students who had already completed a lycée education, teachers simply raised the level of instruction. Thus, throughout the period of Mme Favre's administration, "professors had the prestige of gods," as a character in a novel on the school succinctly put it.[98] Apparently, the men who taught at Sèvres believed that an informal tone permeated teaching there. Classes at Sèvres seemed intimate, Henry Lemonnier claimed, to a faculty used to lecture halls and a sea of faces elsewhere.[99] But for Sévriennes themselves, classrooms seemed like theaters for the genius of their teachers. Remembering the experience, Jeanne Ben-Aben (class of 1888) gushed about H. Chantavoine's lectures on French literature: "They were a joy. He himself was an artist, a poet quivering with sensibility and wit. . . . To hear him was an intellectual feast."[100] Of another of her former professors, Marcel Dubois, she wrote, "He was the inventor of a new method in geography, brilliant in its logic . . . [which] he displayed with stirring, irresistible passion."[101] Even zoology, according to Marie Picot (class of 1882), a student in science, provided hours of high drama with Edmond Perrier: "His scientific doctrine . . . so fired us up that sometimes we were left [with] pens dangling in the air, while following the path of Evolution. . . . All our teachers were distinguished . . . , but none of them, apart from Joseph Fabre and Edmond Perrier, excited an enthusiasm that exploded in spontaneous applause . . . as soon as one or the other teacher left the room, our eminent directrice, Mme Jules Favre, on his arm."[102] These brilliant showmen figured as "the only males at Sèvres six days out of seven,"[103] which naturally added yet another dimension of excitement to encounters designed by consummate performers to thrill their listeners.

Confronted with this display of talent, Sévriennes apparently felt

[98] Reval, *Les Sévriennes,* 49.
[99] Lemonnier, "L'Ecole de Sèvres depuis sa fondation (1881–1900)," 9.
[100] *Le Cinquantenaire,* 230.
[101] Ibid.
[102] Dr. M. Phisalex-Picot, "Edmond Perrier et sa doctrine scientifique," *BAES* (January 1922): 8.
[103] Reval, *Les Sévriennes,* 49.

deeply the inadequacy of their academic preparation. One of those who
came to Sèvres in 1881 remembered her own and her classmates' utter
dismay when, fresh from a triumphal entry into Sèvres, they went to
their first lecture. "The first class with . . . M. Darmesteter revealed to us
our profound ignorance of grammar; it was more or less the same with
all the others. We had everything to learn and, what was worse, to un-
learn in order to become initiates to the true life of thought and personal
reflection."[104] Louise Belugou, a student from 1882 to 1885 and then maîtresse-adjointe at Sèvres from 1886 to 1891, claimed the shock of recognition proved equally severe for later classes. In her experience, "The
first year at Sèvres was always a crisis of modesty."[105] The shock for
some, apparently, was too great ever to overcome. One young woman
who had gone to Sèvres imagining she would one day be a poet never
recovered from the bruising her self-image received there. "The flick
from the candlesnuffer worked," she bitterly recalled half a century
later.[106] Another distinguished Sévrienne, Anna Amieux, agreed. First a
student (class of 1889) and later the directrice of the school herself,
Amieux concluded that the chasm between Sévriennes' expectations and
their experience—a chasm that opened suddenly for first-year students—
explained "why Sèvres did not become like the rue d'Ulm a seedbed of
writers and of scholars."[107]

Such memories, however richly they depict the feelings faculty inspired, tell only half the story. They neglect the multiple layers of past
personal experience that had prepared these girls to accept tight limits
on their egos. Their very demeanor in the classroom shows how completely most of them had already internalized a modest definition of their
talents. The submissiveness that school directrices and inspectors almost
uniformly noted in candidates for Sèvres remained a feature of their outward behavior after they arrived. "We were very docile students," Gabrielle Duponchel (class of 1884) remembered about her classmates in an
observation supported by all the other evidence from the period. The
contrast with Normaliens could hardly be more striking. Rowdy as a
group, individually articulate and committed, students at the Ecole Normale had a reputation for intellectual self-assertion that affected more
than scholarly debates.[108] Beginning as early as midcentury, any major

---

[104] "Marie Deschamps, née Lefèvre," *BTAES* (March 1902): 42. This is an anonymous
death notice written by a classmate.
[105] *Le Cinquantenaire*, 226.
[106] Quoted anonymously by Anna Amieux. Ibid., 226.
[107] Ibid.
[108] See for instance Robert J. Smith, "Normaliens of the Rue d'Ulm: An Elite of the

fracas in the public life of France produced an echo in this grande
école;[109] by comparison, at Sèvres, where the one memorable calamity of
1896 would be the death of Mme Favre, even such ferocious battles as
the Dreyfus Affair did not produce a ripple. Yet as Duponchel herself
remarked, the habit of docility ingrained in Sévriennes as adolescents
"was a danger, if after three years [at Sèvres], they were to become teachers." A major purpose, therefore, of the effort by the faculty and Mme
Favre alike to force Sèvres's students to have and to defend opinions was
precisely to ensure that they could one day teach.

The first external measure of the school's success came at the certificat
exam after the second year and the agrégation at the end of the third year.
As it turned out, intellectual modesty did not prevent Sèvres's students
from performing well on these occasions; in fact, given the concern of
juries in this period to encourage an intellectual style appropriate to
women, restraint in putting forward one's opinion might improve one's
chances. The president of the jury for the women's agrégation in letters,
Eugène Manuel, cautioned candidates in 1885 to avoid emphatic judgments in their historical compositions since "modesty in one's opinions
is one of the most desirable forms of modesty in women."[110] In addition,
Manuel found abstract reasoning offensive in a female's answers. In his
report on the agrégation in letters of 1888, he described the jury's viewpoint:

> We never ask candidates to go against their nature and to forgo the
> simplest notions. . . . Occasionally . . . they are persuaded that they
> must depart from life and enter into science. . . . The more educated
> our agrégées become, however, . . . the more they will distrust set for-
> mulas and the ambitious terminology that they sometimes borrow
> from contemporary history and philosophy. . . . Were they tempted to
> give in to such abstract ideas, not only would it not suit their minds,
> which are delicate and finely nuanced, but their voices either.[111]

In brief, like Octave Gréard, Manuel believed that differences between
the sexes required a bifurcation in the kinds of knowledge male and female teachers ought to have. The world of discrete experiences and the
emotions belonged to women; the world of abstract categories and ideas
pertained to men. For women to approach topics in literature, history,

---

Third Republic" (unpublished manuscript, 1976), 145; and the testimonials of former
students in *Le Centenaire de l'ecole normale 1795–1895* (Paris: Hachette, 1895), 539.

[109] R. Smith, *The Ecole Normale Supérieure*, 79–103.

[110] "Rapport du concours d'agrégation de jeunes filles (lettres)," *ESDJF* 2 (1885): 275.

[111] "Rapport sur le concours pour l'enseignement des jeunes filles (lettres)," *ESDJF* 1
(1888): 139–41.

and philosophy, therefore, in the manner of the other sex involved a distortion of their nature and, in Manuel's view, a breach of taste.

Still, modesty had its limits even for women. A candidate whose modest measure of her own abilities led her to waffle on moral issues struck Manuel as a traitor to her sex. The possibility that female modesty might turn into a defense of relativism horrified him even more. "A female skeptic," he wrote of the exam on ethics, "would be a monster of a peculiar sort."[112] Apparently, no such candidate had yet appeared before the jury by 1888, but Manuel did regret that the reserve which he approved in candidates on other subjects on the agrégation also showed up in the exam on ethics. "Not that candidates lacked convictions," he noted reassuringly, "but their conclusions were perhaps a little timid. . . . At moments one missed that tone of authority which on questions of morality . . . is the product of experience and age."[113] On issues of morality, in other words, he expected female teachers to assert the claim to expertise that the entire republican establishment and increasingly the Catholic Right as well were ready to accord to women in the family.[114]

As it turned out, those who favored using different standards in judging male and female candidates for secondary teaching lost considerable ground at the women's agrégation in the 1890s, due in large part to the influence of Sèvres. Part of the explanation lies in what was happening in girls' secondary schools, where the arrival of alumnae of Sèvres played an important role in raising the level of instruction. Then, as graduates of secondary schools came to Sèvres better prepared, teachers there responded by demanding more of students. All the same, this alone does not explain why Sèvres's faculty pushed early for a professional training closer to that obtaining in the male profession. As noted earlier, these men were not primarily motivated by the vision of a unique ideal for girls' secondary studies; rather, their intention was to improve on practices in boys' schools. Almost immediately, the peculiar slant that this perspective gave to their approach to Sèvres became apparent in the faculty's proposals. No sooner had the ministry decided in 1883 to limit the women's agrégations to two, one in letters and one in science, than the faculty at Sèvres requested five.[115] Anything less, they argued, would sacrifice the competence that specialized professional training assured in secondary schools for boys. However, a special commission named by

[112] Ibid., 279.
[113] Ibid.
[114] For developments within Catholic thought on this matter see Mayeur, *L'Education des jeunes filles*, 45–67.
[115] *Procès verbaux des reunions*, archives, E.N.S.

the Conseil supérieur in 1886 to study their proposals promptly rejected them. "They would distort [dénaturer]," the final report declared, "the character that is desired for the new education."[116]

In reality, the crux of the problem lay elsewhere. As first set up, the women's agrégations "denatured" not girls' secondary instruction but the curriculum designed for training female teachers at Sèvres. Without greater specialization at the agrégation, Sévriennes would have to study the same material in their third year at the school as they had already covered the year before in preparation for the certificat exams. Boredom was not the only issue. Those with the interests of the school at heart recognized that Sévriennes' chances of success at these concours would rise as the exams increased in difficulty. As matters stood, anyone who acquired the certificat could with a bit more work hope for success at the agrégation. A third year at Sèvres did not necessarily insure a decisive edge. Not that Sévriennes failed to dominate these contests. Of the women credentialed between 1881 and 1887, 60 percent of the certifiées and 78 percent of the agrégées had gone to Sèvres.[117] Still, the rate of failures on the first try was high and growing.[118] More serious, critics of the cost of operating Sèvres used these results to argue that this higher normal school served no necessary function and could, therefore, close down without endangering the profession. Advocates at Sèvres of several agrégations, meanwhile, had another gripe about the system. In the 1890s, men still taught in the upper grades of girls' lycées in Paris. The ministry could justify its policy of placing male agrégés in these highly coveted posts as long as female agrégées had nonspecialized degrees. Mme Favre felt the injustice keenly,[119] and it was she who, as pressure built at Sèvres for change, issued an ultimatum to the ministry. Sometime in 1891 she threatened to resign if the ministry again refused to budge,[120] and though existing records are silent on the particulars of the negotiations, the results speak for themselves. In 1894, four women's agrégations came into being: one in literature, one in history and geography, one in mathematics, and one in the natural sciences. If these fields of specialization still represented a uniquely feminine curriculum for

---

[116] Quoted in Paul Dupuy, "L'Etat actuel de l'enseignement secondaire des jeunes filles d'après une publication récente," ESDJF 1 (1887): 16.

[117] Calculated from figures given in "Extrait du rapport au président de la république relatif à l'enseignement secondaire," ESDJF 1 (1890): 66.

[118] Between 1881 and 1887, 23 percent failed the certificat on the first try, 66 percent were dismissed at the agrégation on the first try. As the number of places in girls' schools declined after 1888, failures became still more common. Paul Dupuy, "L'Etat actuel," 201–3.

[119] See her note to the director of secondary education in F17 9154, A.N.

[120] Le Cinquantenaire, 342.

women teachers, women agrégées had nonetheless edged closer to the men's profession.

Yet even as the level of instruction rose at Sèvres, school traditions remained intact. Neither the directrice nor the faculty changed their basic educational goals. Both believed that the essential role of women teachers was pedagogic, which meant to transfer knowledge, not to make additions to it. Sèvres kept its original focus on secondary education. Likewise, the idealism that inspired those who taught there remained, throughout Mme Favre's administration, Sèvres's characteristic mark. Far from the Sorbonne, Sévriennes ignored the scientific spirit that was overtaking the humanities at the Ecole Normale in the 1890s.[121] Sèvres remained, instead, a vanguard for those within the classical tradition who hoped to reinvigorate the moral impact of such studies. As a movement, this reform went far beyond girls' education in the Third Republic, but because of limits placed on girls' futures, it would have, largely through the influence that Sèvres's alumnae gained in girls' secondary schools, its greatest impact there.

The social training Sévriennes received differed from that of Normaliens easily as much as did their intellectual training. Both grandes écoles succeeded in creating in their students an elitist ethos, a sense of belonging to a privileged group. At Sèvres, however, this elitist image had decided limits, for it did not imply an active public life. The very structure of daily school life taught Sévriennes to seek recognition unself-consciously only in the enclosure of those venerable halls. While in the 1890s the Ecole Normale deliberately threw off the cloistered model of the past,[122] Sèvres remained a closed community, a cross between the cloister and the home. Even while at school, Normaliens, lectured as they were on the frontiers of knowledge and encouraged to pursue research, learned to see themselves in relation to the outside world. By contrast, Sévriennes who truly imbibed the message taught at Sèvres focused on developing the self. Of course, behind this goal lay the idea that by training the hearts and minds of bourgeois daughters, Sévriennes would make a vital contribution to the nation. For Mme Favre, the task that lay ahead for Sèvres's alumnae amounted to a national mission. Nevertheless, the arena in which these future teachers would advance the cause of civilization promised, if not anonymity, to shade their contributions modestly from the public's eye.

Nothing captures the essence of this period in Sèvres's history better

[121] R. Smith, *The Ecole Normale Supérieure*, 56–78.

[122] This new policy at the rue d'Ulm came in with the appointment of Georges Perrot as director of the school (1883–1904) and of Paul Dupuy as dean of students (*surveillant général*) (1885–1934). R. Smith, "Normaliens of the Rue d'Ulm," 148.

than the episode that marked its closing: the death and funeral of Mme Jules Favre. All the basic elements were there: the driving sense of duty, the solidarity, and the self-effacement in the public sphere. As always, in these final days, Mme Favre showed herself to be the model of her own ideal. Up until three days before she died on January 31, 1896, she carried on her tasks as usual. No one but the directrice knew for sure the end was near. In preparation, over the preceding month, she sent out twelve or thirteen letters a day to former students, who had no inkling "it would be their last."[123] On the final morning, Mme Favre invited to her bedroom the four alumnae whom she had handpicked to return as maîtresses-adjointes to the school, "but she did not permit them to discuss her health; she talked instead about the school, the welfare of the family members at her bedside, and the fatigue of Anna, her faithful maid."[124]

Her death, when it finally came, sparked a burst of loyalty in Sévriennes all over France. Twenty-six girls' schools sent wreaths or flowers for her funeral.[125] Telegrams and flowers flooded in from individual teachers for whom her death meant a deep personal loss. Several made a special trip to Paris to attend her funeral,[126] a ceremony of which one observer wrote: "The casket was followed by emotional teachers and by tearful girls, and nothing but sobs and praises could be heard in the procession. For one last time it brought together in a single unanimous feeling the great family of Sèvres that she had founded."[127] With three hundred of her students already placed in secondary schools and another seventy-five at Sèvres, Mme Favre quite likely claimed in 1896 more far-flung disciples than any other woman outside Catholic orders in France. Yet at the special service in her memory held at Sèvres, not one of her devotees spoke. Directrices and teachers, maîtresses-adjointes and students listened silently while one male dignitary after another rose to address the assembled mourners: Gréard spoke for the ministry, Lemonnier for Sèvres's teachers, Chantavoine for past and present students, and Joseph Fabre in the name of all her personal friends.[128] It was an ironic though fitting tribute to this new female profession and to the public image that the founders of Sèvres created for it.

[123] Belugou, "Madame Favre," in *La Morale de Plutarque*, xclv.
[124] *BTAES* (February 1896): 1.
[125] *Cahiers de traditions, 1889–1936*, archives, E.N.S.
[126] *BTAES* (1896): 11.
[127] Sonday, "Mme Jules Favre," 83.
[128] *Cahiers de traditions*, archives, E.N.S.

Young Teachers in a Fledgling Profession

TWENTY-SIX YEARS OLD, fresh from Sèvres and a disappointment at the agrégation, Augustine Frémont (class of 1881) waited through the summer of 1884 at her parents' home in La Chapelle in the department of the Seine-et-Oise for news of her appointment.[1] She had left at the Ministry of Education a list of her preferences for schools—Amiens, Rouen, Le Havre—all lycées, all a short distance by train from home, and each a stepping-stone to Paris. Since the agrégation, though, doubt must have eroded her earlier confident hopes for a choice initial post followed by a swift promotion up to Paris. Yet the full extent of her misfortune took her completely by surprise. Ignoring her requests, her youth, and her parents' wishes, the ministry appointed Mlle Frémont in September to the collège of Agen in the far southwest of France, over six hundred kilometers from home. The news, in her own words, left her "horrified."[2] Protestations at the ministry proved ineffectual, and a few days after the letter announcing her appointment reached her, she left La Chapelle alone for a part of France where she knew no one and which she probably had never even seen.

Frémont's experience captures in its most anguishing dimensions a dilemma that plagued this new feminine profession from the outset. The family and the state had competing claims upon young women teachers. Parents expected to keep unmarried daughters close to the paternal home, while the Ministry of Education presumed, in operating a system of schools organized both hierarchically and nationwide, the geographical mobility of its teaching personnel.[3] That presumption had its roots in the experience of the men's profession where, at least in theory, personal ambition took precedence over competing obligations to the family. In mapping out careers, male teachers expected to adjust the claims of families to the necessities of professional success, and those adopting such a strategy counted on community approval for their actions. The first

---

[1] Frémont finally succeeded at the agrégation in 1888 on her fourth attempt. Dossier personnel, notes, F17 22445, A.N.

[2] Ibid., correspondance, 1884.

[3] In this respect, teaching in secondary schools for girls presented problems different from those encountered by primary school teachers who, though often posted out of their hometowns, at least could count on working in their home departments.

generation of Sévriennes faced a very different set of social expectations. Neither they nor their families, in the vast majority of cases, envisaged the start of their careers as entailing a rupture with their families. The communities to which Sévriennes came as teachers proved no more ready to approve of such a rupture; indeed, they viewed with considerable suspicion a young woman arriving among them unaccompanied by her family.

seen as suspicious

The story of Sévriennes as transitional figures in a social world moving toward a new, accepted representation of the female truly begins here. It does not date from their professional training. On the contrary, the architects of life at Sèvres had deliberately sought to mask the innovations introduced in women's education there by presenting to the world a familiar image of a boarding school for girls, tucked away from public life and modeled after relations in the family. With the appointment of Sévriennes to secondary schools scattered sparsely and widely across France, the facade that had hidden the silent revolution in progress at Sèvres fell suddenly away. Sévriennes as teachers stood exposed as harbingers of change, whose presence in the community and activities in their schools brought into question accepted notions of femininity.

The First Appointment

In its main details, the story of Augustine Frémont's appointment to Agen resembles closely that of most alumnae of her generation. Only a handful of Sèvres's students managed to start their careers teaching in or near their parents' homes, though nearly all of them solicited for such locations. Realistically, the ministry could do little to accommodate requests for posts near families. Too many Sévriennes came from the same areas of France, namely, Paris, the East, the Lyonnais, the Southeast and to a lesser extent southwestern France. Generally speaking, the first lycées and collèges for girls sprang up in the same places, but no town or city apart from Paris opened more than one secondary school for girls. That by itself severely limited the number of positions in any one locale. Even more discouraging, only twelve of the fifty-one departments hosting girls' collèges or lycées by 1896 had more than one such school.[4] Given the small size of faculties in girls' schools, that meant three-fourths of these fifty-one departments had something under eight secondary teaching posts available to women. No wonder novice teachers so often met with frustration in their efforts to get home.

not near women or families

realistic problems

[4] By 1900, forty-one lycées and twenty-nine collèges had opened. Mayeur, *L'Enseignement secondaire*, 162.

Sometimes disappointed teachers could overcome the problem by accepting positions in cours secondaires, which were rehabilitated after 1880 because they offered local councils the least expensive form of secondary schooling.[5] But for Sévriennes, this solution to familial needs brought with it other drawbacks. In the first place, the legal regime under which the personnel of cours secondaires worked was not the law of 1880, but Victor Duruy's circular of 1867. Faculty did not enjoy, therefore, all the benefits of secondary teaching elsewhere. Women teachers could generally expect the same remuneration in cours secondaires as in a collège, but the pension plan for public secondary teachers did not include them. Moreover, working conditions often involved more than the ordinary hardships. Physically, the setting for these cours left much to be desired, since they operated in buildings used for other functions. In addition, women teachers sometimes found themselves outnumbered by part-time and therefore more cheaply employed colleagues from boys' schools with whom social inhibitions made it difficult to form a friendship. For all these reasons, teaching in a cours secondaire represented for most Sévriennes an option of truly last resort.

Yet the absence of good posts was not the only worry facing homesick teachers. They also had to qualify professionally for schools located near their parents' homes. Initially, that did not pose insurmountable problems. Desperate for women with any secondary training, the director of secondary education willingly appointed Sévriennes with only their certificat as chargées de cours in girls' lycées.[6] However, as competition stiffened for the most desirable posts, the ministry tightened its requirements. Increasingly, the best a certifiée could hope for was appointment to a collège or a cours, while even agrégées found their options narrowing as the supply of women who had passed the agrégation grew. In imitation of the men's profession, the practice rapidly developed of placing agrégées in schools in the order of their ranking at the agrégation. Agrégées at the lower end of the list of those who qualified each year had to wait for an appointment until those above them found a place. Furthermore, after 1888, the ministry decided not to appoint beginning teachers to Parisian lycées, no matter how brilliantly they performed at the agré-

[5] In theory, these cours secondaires performed a trial function to see if the community could support a collège or a lycée. However, many lingered on for years in a kind of institutional limbo.

[6] According to a decree dated September 13, 1883, which established the salaries of teachers and directrices, only agrégées could get appointments as professeurs in lycées; if a teacher with just the certificat was named to a lycée, she took the title chargée de cours. In a collège, a certifiée had the title professeur. Mayeur, *L'Enseignement secondaire*, 277–79.

gation or how great their private need.[7] In view of all these developments, the calamity that befell Augustine Frémont in 1884, rather than an isolated mishap, was emblematic of this new profession's dangers for young teachers.

Whatever its other drawbacks, secondary teaching initially appeared at least to guarantee a livelihood for Sèvres's alumnae. But by 1889, when secondary schools for girls had stopped expanding, even that assurance came in question. The problem dated back to 1880 and republicans' decision to establish a system of girls' secondary schooling in advance of popular demand. At first the absence of strong public interest mattered little to the politicians. Both in 1881 and again in 1884 the legislature set aside substantial sums for the creation of new schools.[8] Likewise, in many towns and cities where Radicals held sway, municipal councils came up with their share of the funding.[9] By the end of the decade, though, ardor at the local level flagged, and the rate of new creations slowed dramatically.[10] The main problem was the lack of clientele. In the eyes of even sympathetic councils, public demand for girls' secondary schools often remained too weak to justify the cost of funding a new collège or lycée, while sympathy for secondary schools for bourgeois daughters disappeared completely wherever socialists took over local councils. Since the Catholic Right remained as implacably opposed as ever to the "Godless schools" of the republic, few new secondary schools for girls were to be glimpsed on any French horizon in the 1890s.[11]

This fact threw far more into doubt for freshly minted Sévriennes than where in France the ministry might choose to send them. By 1889, some recent graduates found themselves in late September without a job at all. Science teachers suffered most from the dearth of positions, a reflection, in all likelihood, of decisions taken at the ministry and at local levels as

[7] Dossier personnel, Isabelle Delêtre (class of 1883), correspondance, 1893, F17 22580, A.N. Amélie Gandon (class of 1888), who failed the agrégation in 1891, tried to get a temporary position teaching primary classes in a Parisian lycée, ostensibly so that she could prepare for the next year's agrégation. However, even one-year appointments met resistance in the Ministry of Education because, as the director of secondary education complained in 1891, "Experience shows that once they get a foot in Paris, agrégées do everything possible to stay there and escape the application of the rule." Dossier personnel, A. Gandon, correspondance, 1891, F17 23915, A.N.

[8] Mayeur, *L'Enseignement secondaire*, 164–65.

[9] Mayeur discusses the contribution of the state and municipalities to this effort. Ibid., 162–64.

[10] Between 1882 and 1887, forty-four collèges and lycées opened, while only fourteen more were founded in the next eleven years. Sée, *Lycées et collèges de jeunes filles* (1900), vi–viii.

[11] Mayeur, *L'Enseignement secondaire*, 163–66.

well to cut expenses by limiting courses for which there was less public interest.[12] Science teachers were not the only victims of the retrenchment of the 1890s, though. All women secondary teachers, even those in letters, began receiving their appointments on a temporary basis after 1890. Given the uncertainty of public attitudes toward girls' secondary education, the Ministry of Education did not intend to obligate itself to teachers for whom it might not at sometime in the future have positions. Thus, within a decade of Sèvres's opening, graduates could not count on the very thing that had attracted them to Sèvres: a guaranteed career in secondary teaching.

Quite clearly, those left temporarily without a job felt that they had been unjustly treated. One of them, a certifiée who had not succeeded at the agrégation, was so enraged that she penned a veiled protest to the director of secondary education, dropping momentarily the docile tone normally adopted by Sévriennes in their letters. "When I entered Sèvres, I was convinced that after three years of work, I would have a job which would make me independent. All of my classmates have already been placed."[13] Another victim, Marie Lefèvre (class of 1886), went considerably further by calling into question the ministry's policy of limiting the number of agrégées each year, while it continued to hire men to teach in girls' lycées. "Will only agrégées be named after this?" she queried, in a provocative note to the chair of the jury for the scientific agrégation. "I fear that is the case since, among my classmates, only the four agrégées have so far been placed. . . . I know that there were only a few girls' lycées and collèges with openings this year. But . . . in a great many of them . . . there are still men teachers who have posts that could be given

[12] In response to the problem, from 1891 to 1907 Sèvres admitted fewer students specialized in science than in letters, while at the women's agrégations, juries drastically reduced the numbers of scientifiques passed. This solved the problem of an excess of teachers for two or three years down the line. In the interim, though, trained teachers outnumbered openings in girls' secondary schools. As it turned out, during the critical period from 1889 to 1891, the ministry managed to place most Sévriennes within four or five months of the beginning of the academic year. All the same, the status of a few scientifiques remained in doubt for several years, either because they worked as substitutes for secondary teachers on temporary leaves or because, while waiting for a better post to open, they took positions as teaching aides (répétitrices) or as elementary teachers in secondary schools. The practice in boys' secondary schools of offering elementary education in order to insure recruitment for the higher grades spread quickly to the new secondary schools for girls.

[13] Dossier personnel, Marie-Louise Heymès (class of 1887), correspondance, 1891, F17 24000, A.N. Heymès had to wait a year before the ministry finally appointed her as a répétitrice in a lycée and another fourteen years until she finally got a chair in a collège.

men over women ✓✓

to us."[14] She thus protested not only her personal mistreatment but also the larger, officially approved injustice of preferring men to women for teaching older girls in the best lycées.

Students of Sèvres were not the only ones who deemed the state obliged to find postions for the women it had trained. Mme Favre held the same view of the obligations that the state incurred toward Sèvres's alumnae.[15] Thus, when Henriette Gonel (class of 1887), who got her first appointment not in September but in January, asked the ministry for three months in back pay, the directrice of Sèvres wrote a letter supporting her request.[16] The ministry on its side not only refused to reimburse Gonel; it held so little brief with the underlying premise of the request that no one even bothered to reply to Mme Favre's appeal.

no help to transport ✓

Sévriennes faced another test of their forbearance if the ministry assigned them to a post on the other side of France with no provisions for their transportation. The first two classes received no financial help at all. Whatever the distance between their homes and their new posts, beginning teachers bore the costs alone. They did not even benefit from lowered tariffs on the trains, a surprise for some Sévriennes formerly employed in elementary teaching who had enjoyed such discounts. Recognizing the hardship that this policy could cause, the ministry decided after 1885 to offer women coming out of Sèvres a stipend of one hundred francs toward the expense of getting to their posts. Anything over that amount, however, itinerant teachers had to pay themselves.

Several women felt the pinch severely.[17] Surely the cruelest case involved the hapless Marie Lefèvre (class of 1886), who had already suffered from the shortage of posts for science teachers. Things did not immediately improve for her when in November 1889 she was finally named to the collège at Saint-Quentin. Two days after she arrived, the ministry reassigned her to a school at Abbeville, located 120 kilometers away. No sooner had she reached Abbeville, to which she had immediately proceeded, than she found a telegram announcing still another change of post. This time her destination was the collège at Moulins, 450 kilometers to the south, where she was to replace a teacher temporarily

[14] Dossier personnel, correpondance, 1889, F17 14220, A.N.

[15] See her letter to the director of secondary education of April 16, 1891 in which she complains that men are holding posts in girls' schools which could go to Sévriennes. F17 14191, A.N. Mme Favre's decision to force the issue of upgrading the women's agrégation had its origins in this crisis over the shortage of professorial posts.

[16] Dossier personnel, correspondance, 1891, F17 23919, A.N.

[17] A number of Sévriennes requested reimbursements. Several complained that the expense of traveling and settling in surpassed their budgets, especially since a teacher's first month's salary went directly into her pension. She only began receiving money in her second month of work.

on leave. Already convinced that the ministry had reneged on its promise to employ her permanently, Marie Lefèvre was equally persuaded, now, that the ministry ought to share her traveling costs. Unfortunately, she had no more luck in winning officials to her view in this affair than she had had on the earlier occasion. Her supervisor at the collège in Moulins, where Lefèvre finally got a temporary post, expressed his irritation with this "partisan of the right to work" who "does not neglect her material interest."[18]

As in the earlier confrontation, Marie Lefèvre had fallen victim to a situation that would strain relations between individuals in this new profession and the ministry for decades. Unlike men in secondary teaching, women teachers had no professional statute. They could not appeal to any regulatory piece of legislation that defined their rights as members of a bureaucratized profession, and the government was reluctant to provide them with one for fear of increased costs. That hesitation itself reflected the larger problem of a legislature that, though generous in its policy toward founding girls' collèges and lycées, proved exceptionally parsimonious when it came to funding their daily operations.[19] Continually strapped for funds, the ministry tried to limit its financial obligations to women teachers. Sometimes officials treated particularly hardpressed teachers generously, but the ministry avoided any action that gave women teachers as a group a legal claim to anything beyond their basic salary and their pensions.

Despite this discriminatory treatment, Sévriennes would prove over the first two decades after Sée's reforms, both collectively and individually, remarkably willing to accept their peripheral position and the inequities associated with it. What protests did appear in their official files, like those already mentioned, took distinctly muted forms. Rarely did they amount to more than a single outburst followed by the victim's stoic silence. No doubt, in part this diffidence originated in their professional training. Girls schooled at Sèvres had prepared for teaching in an atmosphere of high idealism where duties and not rights constituted the professional watchword. Yet their self-effacing public manner surely stemmed as well from a realistic view of their position both as underlings in a bureaucratized profession and as women whose conduct, once deemed unseemly, could jeopardize not just their careers but even their social reputations.

The real trauma of the journey to these teachers' first positions lay not

---

[18] Dossier personnel, notes, 1890, F17 14220, A.N.

[19] For figures on the funds budgeted for girls' secondary education, see Mayeur, *L'Enseignement secondaire*, 166.

in the rupture with their families, the uncertainty surrounding some appointments, or even the possibility of unforeseen expenses. It derived from the sudden exposure of these youthful teachers to a social and professional setting remarkable above all for its multiple constraints. Taking leave of Sèvres meant more than parting with a second family. Sévriennes also left behind a world where self-defining personalities thrived and everything conspired to push the timid into taking strong positions. At Sèvres, many of the usual taboos that bourgeois mores placed on girls' conversations or entertainment in the name of female modesty did not apply. At least as an ideal, life there consisted of an open forum, while even the delights of Paris had been within their reach. The contrast with the world into which they would enter as teachers could hardly have been sharper. Much of bourgeois France was unprepared to offer women secondary teachers license either to express themselves or to pursue their interests in the manner of a Mme Favre. Small provincial towns would prove especially hostile, with Catholic strongholds the most inhospitable of all. Even in provincial cities, the threat of gossip placed serious constraints on teachers' lives. More insidious were the attitudes of school officials who sought, in their capacity as *chefs* and as guardians of the reputations of their schools, to reproduce in these emancipated women the image of modest, self-effacing femininity approved in bourgeois homes. Most Sévriennes, under the dual pressure of community and school, would eventually adopt the self-denying style of life required of them. Some went further still and made adjustments in the deepest reaches of their psyches.

The Creation of the Model Teacher

The real creation of the model teacher in this new female profession happened not at Sèvres under Mme Favre's inspirational guidance but in the communities and schools to which Sévriennes came as young and inexperienced teachers, eager to win approval for their schools and themselves. They had prepared at Sèvres to "pioneer the future" by "fashioning . . . the soul of the new woman."[20] Yet once out in the field, Sévriennes quickly learned the limits that the public and official France imposed on them as innovators. However much they may have looked ahead at Sèvres to the prospect of their personal independence, emancipation was not what entry into teaching meant.

The task ahead was much more problematic. It required each of them

---

[20] Berthe Israël-Wahl, "Mes Débuts dans l'enseignement en 1888," in *Le Cinquantenaire*, 385.

to integrate into a coherent professional image two inconsistent models
of behavior, one drawn from bourgeois expectations for womanly demeanor, the other based on standards of performance admired in the secondary teacher. Their success in bringing these conflicting norms together would eventually constitute the triumph of this generation, for in
the process, they managed to invent new parameters of feminine conduct
accepted by the bourgeoisie. But this achievment should not minimize
the difficulty of what these women undertook nor conceal the cost exacted from them.

Certainly, Sévriennes themselves were well aware of the sufferings of
those buffeted by conflicting expectations. As the diaspora began,
alarming tales of fledgling teachers' first encounters with the prejudices
of provincial and especially small-town France circulated widely
through Sèvres's far-flung "family." Finding rental lodging presented the
most immediate problem. The trouble sprang not so much from shortages
of rooms as from a woman's need for safe accommodations. A rooming
house too near the haunts of single men or with a sleazy reputation
threatened to embroil a young and single female teacher's name in invid-
ious gossip. Berthe Wahl (class of 1885) was cautioned on her arrival at
Lyon not to take a room at a particular hotel even though two, much
older, single colleagues lived there.[21] In the opinion of the rector who
gave her the advice, her colleagues' presence had no bearing on Wahl's
case. At thirty-two, Mlle Wahl should recognize that the appearance of
too much independence could occasion talk and compromise her reputation. In an even less auspicious start, Marguerite Aron (class of 1893)
spent her first night at Niort barricaded behind her bedroom door after
one of the male guests of her hotel tried to force an entry.[22] Frantic, the
next day she managed to locate what seemed a proper room in the home
of an elderly spinster. On returning to the hotel to get her things, however, she found a note from her directrice warning: "Don't rent from Mlle
Linon. The officers' mess is in the next-door restaurant; there might be
talk."[23] It took eight more days of grueling search before Aron turned up
respectable lodging in the quiet, inconspicuous residence of two spinster
sisters who made a living sewing ladies' boots at home.

Public scrutiny did not abate once a young professeur solved her housing problem. Self-appointed guardians of local morals continued to observe and comment on her social habits, especially in small towns.
"There would be a scandal," Marguerite Caron recalled years later, "if a

[21] Ibid., 385–86.
[22] Aron, *Le Journal d'une Sévrienne* (1912), 123.
[23] Ibid., 126.

teacher appeared [alone] on the promenade. There would be a scandal if, wishing to enjoy the natural surroundings, she took a walk in the fields or woods or if she went for a bike ride or to the skating rink, where she might run into an officer from the garrison."[24] Only in the larger cities where anonymity and changing manners permitted far more freedom could single, unaccompanied women entertain themselves in public without risking their reputations. For young women who had been exposed to Mme Favre's rapturous accounts of foreign travel and hiking in the Alps, or who had profited for three years from the freedom permitted by her to explore Paris alone, bowing to such constraints did not come easily. Yet the pressure to do so was almost irresistible, mainly because those who called them to account had charge of their careers.

Sévriennes' memoirs as well as their official dossiers amply testify to the concern of school administrators for the probity of teachers' private lives. One teacher wrote bitingly years later, "We were subjected to a tight surveillance—which closely resembled spying—and we were the object of reports that bordered on denunciations."[25] Any member of the school administration, from school directrices to academy inspectors to rectors up to the roving inspector generals, might submit such a report. For most the issue was the same: did the behavior of a teacher jeopardize the effort to attract the bourgeoisie to the republic's schools? A favorable answer to that question in some milieus required single female teachers, albeit residing in the community, to adopt a life-style patterned after nuns. Marguerite Aron (class of 1893), commenting on this expectation in her memoirs, wrote: "The old ecclesiastical traditions weighed upon us. This tradition—in its original asceticism—wanted the education of the young entrusted to men and women living apart from their time, ignorant of its vices."[26]

It was not just the provincial bourgeoisie who expected women teachers to project this old ideal. In a striking recognition of the influence of nuns, the Ministry of Education itself urged teachers to adopt a severely simple form of dress. No formal rules guided teachers in this practice, but inspectors made clear the preferences of the administration for the plain black dress, minimally adorned, and for hair pulled back and off the neck into a sensible chignon.[27] "*Quakeresse*" was how Berthe Wahl described this "obligatory" code of dress. Early in her career, Mlle Wahl was called to order on the subject by the inspector of the academy of

[24] Quoted from Marguerite Caron (class of 1887), in Henriette Wurmser-Dégouy, *Trois Éducatrices modernes* (Paris: Presses universitaires de France, 1930), 50.

[25] Israël-Wahl, "Mes Débuts," in *Le Cinquantenaire*, 386–87.

[26] Aron, *Le Journal d'une Sévrienne* (1912), 233.

[27] Wurmser-Dégouy, *Trois Éducatrices modernes*, 50.

Lyon. Dressed fashionably in the usual navy blue suit worn by young middle-class women in the 1890s, with her hemline just above the ankle and a Russian-style blouse complete with sailor collar, Wahl had also swept her hair up into a modish style known as "Catalan." Out of doors, she wore a light, white veil. However correct by current standards for the young bourgeoise, "this way of dressing," she learned from her inspector, "did not in any way suit the gravity of my functions. Eager not to compromise the lycée in my person, I had to raise my neckline, create an old lady's chignon, and, above all, lengthen my skirt and eliminate my veil, which from afar, it seemed, looked like 'a layer of powder.' "[28]

This hasty adjustment to the standards imposed by cautious supervisors saved Berthe Wahl from any disciplinary action. Less fortunate, Pauline Robert-Bérard (class of 1881), who on graduation served for two years as maîtresse-adjointe at Sèvres and then was named directrice of a provincial lycée, never got a second chance. This ill-starred woman apparently "adored traveling," and "in order to undertake a dangerously steep climb during her vacation," she donned a "touring outfit," which in the vocabulary of the day meant pants. When news of the event reached the gossipmongers of her town, rumor spread that the new girls' lycée had "a George Sand" for its directrice. "This term of supreme disdain necessitated the gravest of administrative measures and the least justified," according to Wahl, who claimed that word of the affair shook Sévriennes throughout the secondary system.[29]

This episode reveals not only the puritanical public image that this new profession acquired but also and more important, the power of the administration to impose it. At least in theory, over any teacher who resisted a superior's warnings to conform hung the Damoclean sword of reassignment, and when pressed, the ministry did not hesitate to use it. More often, though, a teacher who ignored the advice of her superiors simply forfeited her chances for advancement.

What officials constituted the adminsitrative hierarchy under which these teachers worked? On the lowest rung stood the directrice of the school. Her authority had the most significant daily impact on a teacher's life, since she made up the academic schedule, oversaw instruction, and supervised the general operations of the school. Each year she also evaluated teachers' contributions to the school in secret reports that she passed up the bureaucratic ladder. Above the school directrice came officials of the "academy," or academic district. Each academy, of which

---

[28] Israël-Wahl, "Mes Débuts," in *Le Cinquantenaire*, 387.

[29] Ibid., 384. Not only did this unfortunate directrice lose her post, but the ministry also placed her back in teaching. Dossier personnel, Pauline Robert-Bérard (married name Colas), F17 23825, A.N.

there were sixteen at this time in France, possessed a rector at its head and under him an academy inspector. Sometime during each year, both the rector and inspector visited the schools in their district. They, too, prepared reports on teachers that, along with those of the directrices, went to the ministry to become part of a teacher's personnel file. Any special request by a teacher, whether for a leave of absence, a change of post, or some special remuneration, went first to her directrice and then to the rector, who in turn forwarded his recommendation on the matter to the ministry.[30]

Alongside but separate from this hierarchy of administrators stretching from the school to the ministry ran a system of roving supervisors called inspector generals. These officials, all of whom were men, visited every collège and lycée theoretically once a year and reported directly to the ministry. Their opinions of a teacher mattered more than any others in the ministerial decisions affecting her career. In the first place, the ministry attached the most importance to their evaluations of a teacher's actions in the classroom, and second, these four men, two for science and two for the humanities, sat with the rectors and the director of secondary education on the ministerial council, which each August decided on promotions and demotions for the following year. In sum, the opinions of inspector generals mattered above all others in determining what the model teacher in this new profession ought to be, as well as who among the early crop of teachers fit it.

During the inaugural years of girls' secondary education, what qualities made up the ideal teacher in the opinion of this coterie of chefs? Respectability clearly figured high among them; but disarming the suspicions of an apprehensive public constituted only one aspect of a successful teacher's duties and a preliminary part at that. To impress inspectors favorably, teachers had also to perform well in the classroom. That in turn required talents that had little to do with those admired in teachers in their social lives. Indeed, the qualities respected by inspectors in these two arenas were not merely different; they stood in fundamental opposition to each other. Socially, teachers were expected to affect a style somewhere between that of the self-effacing nun and that of the modest bourgeois maiden. Yet to win approval as instructors, they

[30] At the ministry itself, many of the day-to-day personnel decisions fell to a section called the Fifth Bureau, but the director of secondary education essentially ran the operation. From his office issued all of the special orders affecting individual teacher's lives. The minister of education rarely intervened on issues other than the formulation of new policies. The only direct access permitted teachers to the ministry came through personal interviews in Paris either with the director or, failing that, with an officer in the Fifth Bureau.

had to demonstrate their mastery of material and authority over students under the critical eye of an inspector in the classroom. On the face of it, the personality traits that made for success in one sphere raised a natural barrier to performing with distinction in the other. From the outset in this new profession, then, young women teachers suffered not only from severe restrictions on their personal freedom. They endured the strain as well of an inherently unstable model of success.

These contradictions originated in the Université's determination to preserve in girls' secondary education the same criteria of excellence in teaching as those applied in boys' schools. Inspectors, who themselves were former teachers and whose duties of evaluation extended to boys' schools, did not revise their notion of good teaching for these female classes. At least in their assessment of instructional methods, they automatically applied a single set of standards in both settings. Clearly, the Ministry of Education intended them to do so, as witnessed by the fact that every year the pedagogical instructions which accompanied the official syllabi for secondary courses were virtually identical for the boys' and girls' systems.

Inspectors started with the premise that secondary teaching, whether undertaken by a man or a woman, required originality in teachers.[31] Although women professeurs generally lacked the erudition of a male professeur, they, too, had to demonstrate a talent for recasting in a personal manner any topic on the official syllabus. Those who mastered the technique received reports like this one on Marie Jablonska Crussaire (class of 1882): "a superior mind with personality and imagination"[32]—or this one for Berthe Israël-Wahl (class of 1885): "self-assured and lively," "possesses a rare clarity of thought, good judgment and inventiveness."[33] Adelaïde Saladin (class of 1889), in one inspector general's view, had "all the essential qualities of a teacher: learning, judgment, a quick mind, a strong personality." Moreover, she spoke "easily and with a penetrating voice that commands attention."[34] Once in a great while, the performance of a Sévrienne so delighted an inspector that he rated it above what he had seen in boys' schools. Anna Amieux (class of 1889), after a particularly successful presentation, won this remark from an inspector general: "The third-year class that I saw is better than all classes at the

---

[31] Gabrielle Logerot (class of 1891), under her pen name G. Réval, described the exhausting efforts made by the young heroine of her novel about a girls' secondary school "to say nothing that did not represent her own opinion" in her classes. *Un Lycée de jeunes filles* (Paris: Ollendorf, 1902) 96.

[32] Dossier personnel, notes, 1887, F17 23906, A.N.

[33] Dossier personnel, notes, 1891, F17 22677, A.N.

[34] Dossier personnel, notes, 1900, F17 23955, A.N.

same level which I inspected this year, not only in the girls' lycées but even in the lycées for boys."[35]

Such high praise presupposed a Cartesian simplicity of exposition, essential in any lesson approved by these inspectors no matter where they heard it. The best lectures they described as "rigorous and simple";[36] or they might commend a teacher's "clear ideas, vividly presented and perfectly ordered."[37] What they detested in the classroom was a discursive style. One inspector, irked by Germaine Lacroix's (class of 1887) inability "to distinguish the essential from details," concluded his critique with the gratuitous blanket censure that this failing was "a general vice in our secondary schools for girls."[38] Clearly, these inspectors intended to make no allowances either for the encyclopedic training given women teachers or for the popular notion that women could not reason in abstractions.

Both of these requirements, originality and clarity of exposition, belonged to the old ideal of teaching in French schools: the master lecture. Yet lecturing as the main method of instruction suffered an eclipse in secondary schools under the Third Republic. In hopes of teaching independent thinking, republican pedagogical reformers preached a more active form of education that would involve the students in reaching conclusions with the teacher. By the early 1890s, this pedagogical objective, which had to some extent inspired instruction at the School of Sèvres, began to make its way into secondary schools. Official guidelines issued from the Ministry of Education for secondary teachers proposed new methods that encouraged the participation of students in the learning process.[39] To judge from the reports of school inspectors, in the initial years of this reform, it seemed enough if women teachers managed to combine "an excellent expository method" with "frequent interrogations."[40] By the turn of the century, though, inspectors would insist that good technique required teachers to engage their students actively in the process of intellectual discovery by stimulating them to apply inductive reasoning in the classroom.

Thus far, the ideal against which school inspectors measured the performance of women teachers resembled what they looked for in men

[35] Dossier personnel, notes, 1901, F17 24471, A.N.

[36] Dossier personnel, Marie Melet, notes, 1892, F17 23698, A.N.

[37] Dossier personnel, Blanche Guillaume, notes, 1895, F17 23350, A.N.

[38] Dossier personnel, notes, 1897, F17 24148, A.N.

[39] The first of these instructions bearing the imprint of the new pedagogy appeared in 1890. Ministère de l'instruction publique, "Enseignement secondaire, instructions et règlements, année 1890." *Bulletin administratif du Ministère de l'instruction publique,* supplement au no. 922. Later versions appeared under the title "Instructions concernant les programmes de l'enseignement secondaire (garçons et jeunes filles)."

[40] Dossier personnel, Marthe Honnet, notes, 1892, F17 24075, A.N.

teachers. When it came to how a woman teacher disciplined her class, though, the parallels between the model images in the two professions lapsed. In principle, all public schools, those for boys as well as girls, shared the same ideal in the decades before the First World War. Discipline did not mean forcing students to submit to school authorities out of fear of punishment but depended rather on instilling in students a sense of moral obligation. Only girls' schools, however, made a serious effort to put this program into practice. While boys' schools maintained a disciplinary council and a whole roster of graded penalties to keep the boys in line, girls' schools did away with organized discipline altogether. A student's worst offense could result in her dismissal, her least in a bad grade. Between these extremes, little more than a written notice home threatened disobedient or disrespectful girls.[41] Underlying the design of the whole system lay the assumption that women teachers could and would establish personal moral ascendancy over students. Accordingly, official expectations for the mode of discipline in girls' classrooms veered dramatically away from the supercilious and sarcastic manner commonly adopted by male teachers. In girls' schools, inspectors disapproved of methods of control based on hostility or intimidation. They frowned on teachers who used sarcasm or anger to control their classes and instead voiced strong approval for teachers with a maternal manner. One of many Sévriennes whose discipline inside the classroom won the praise of her inspectors was described as "gentle in her tone but firm."[42] Another had "no need to punish."[43] The students of still another, according to an overjoyed inspector, pursued "their daily work as much from interest in their studies as from desire to gain the approval of a teacher whom they love and whose authority they respect."[44] The very frequency of such remarks suggests the weight that inspectors gave to the rapport of teachers with their students as well as their insistence that a maternal style set the tone of those relations.

For many teachers fresh from Sèvres, sometimes just a few years older than their students, the mastery over people and materials that this professional ideal implied must have seemed an extremely, even excessively, tall order. Still, youthfulness and inexperience were not at the heart of their dilemma. The deeper problem of this profession for women teachers derived from contradictory models of success. Inspectors asked them, on the one hand, to demonstrate the intellectual and personal authority of professeurs within the men's profession, albeit with significant

[41] Mayeur, *L'Enseignement secondaire*, 180–81.
[42] Dossier personnel, Marthe Honnet, notes, 1896, F17 24075, A.N.
[43] Dossier personnel, Anna Duros, notes, 1901, F17 23299, A.N.
[44] Dossier personnel, Lucie Ravaire, notes, 1893, F17 23949, A.N.

adaptations. On the other hand, in their social and administrative contacts, women teachers were to model themselves after the diffident image of the respectable bourgeois maiden. For a woman to conform to both ideals at once posed difficulties. A teacher with the modest, self-deprecating manner approved of in young women might well discover the self-assurance that inspectors sought in good teachers beyond her powers. Likewise, a decisive woman whose self-confidence made her an excellent instructor might easily offend inspectors if she carried her professional aplomb within the classroom over to relations with her chefs.

Shyness, far more common than unbecoming boldness, posed the most serious problem of adjustment for young Sévriennes. Crippled, one suspects, by an upbringing that valued such a trait in them as adolescent girls, several teachers suffered from excessive shyness in the classroom, at least when an inspector came to watch them. Berthe Bastoul (class of 1886), for instance, could not at her debut master either her materials or her fears when she conducted classes. All of her superiors believed in her intelligence, but her "visible inexperience and nervous body movements" meant that students easily slipped out of her control.[45] Armande André (class of 1884), whose classes even in her seventh year of teaching an inspector still found "slow and boring," only needed, according to her school directrice, "to learn to be less shy."[46] Zéa Claris's (class of 1882) case best exemplifies, perhaps, the quandary of the modest woman turned secondary teacher. "She is intelligent, hardworking, and dedicated," one report on her intoned. "But due to her natural timidity, which is slowly disappearing, she cannot impose her teaching with all the authority that her professional merit deserves. A person both honorable and discrete. Her conduct and her dress are beyond reproach."[47] In her manner a model of feminine comportment, Claris struggled only half successfully to adapt her modest style to a task that also called for confidence in making intellectual judgments.

Those teachers for whom assertiveness came naturally risked displeasing their inspectors, too. Then the problem did not involve authority over students, but insubordination toward their male superiors. At all levels of the educational hierarchy, officials routinely expected docility from their teachers. Partly, this reflected the traditions of bureaucratic life. The good functionary, by definition, knew his place and accepted orders from above without a murmur. But the Ministry of Education enlarged on this tradition when it came to supervising women secondary

[45] Dossier personnel, notes, 1894 (see also 1895–1896), F17 23969, A.N.
[46] Dossier personnel, notes, 1894, F17 23178, A.N.
[47] Dossier personnel, notes, 1889, F17 22608, A.N.

teachers. An assertive female teacher shocked inspectors' sensibilities, not just because such conduct threatened the bureaucratic principle of hierarchical command. Equally important, by challenging a male supe- rior, she defied social mores that demanded modesty in women.

Occasional confrontations with independent-minded women teachers left a trail of bitter comments in Sévriennes' dossiers. Sometimes inspectors reluctant to write a seriously unfavorable report merely alluded to the shock of such encounters. "One is a bit startled by her aplomb," was the guarded comment of an inspector who met Jeanne François (class of 1885) for the first time.[48] More often, though, inspectors lashed out firmly at this alarming insubordination from a female teacher. Of Anne Rollet (class of 1884) one inspector wrote, "She is intelligent but has too high an opinion of herself."[49] Another observer found Gabrielle Chavance (class of 1888) "pretentious, immodest, and lacking tact."[50] Other reports made the connection with unfeminine conduct more explicit. A report on Alice Duprat (class of 1889) found her "too dogmatic and self-confident for a young woman."[51] No comment, however, captures more precisely the dichotomous social images that young women teachers somehow had to bring together than this attack on Clotilde Maréchal (class of 1883) by an inspector general: "The professeur in her is too apparent, the woman not enough."[52]

These negative examples serve only to enrich the portrait of a woman who, like Marie Cotton (class of 1886), exactly fit the mold of the ideal teacher. Almost from the start, Cotton managed to combine in perfect equilibrium the qualities of mind and person needed in the classroom with the personal reserve required of the female functionary. In her second year of teaching at the lycée of Bourg, the inspector of the academy found Cotton "truly gifted for teaching science . . . [and] lucid in her demonstrations." "Both serious and affable in character," he continued, "she combines modesty with learning." A year later an inspector general confirmed this first assessment on all counts: "Precise, careful, systematic, clear and penetrating in her elocution, very dignified in her appearance. Excellent impression." The directrice alerted the ministry the same year to her "keen interest in her students" and the academy inspector reaffirmed his assessment of her as a "teacher of very high caliber and very great modesty." Four years later, an inspector general noted that "she made her students participate in class" and suggested that "she

---

[48] Dossier personnel, notes, 1894, F17 24036, A.N.

[49] Dossier personnel, correspondance, 1892, F17 24029, A.N.

[50] Dossier personnel, notes, 1895, F17 23980, A.N.

[51] Dossier personnel, notes, 1892, F17 23600, A.N.

[52] Dossier personnel, notes, 1888, F17 22453, A.N.

would cut a good figure in Paris."[53] For family reasons, Cotton could not accept a post in Paris for another decade,[54] but in 1898 the director of secondary education proved the high esteem in which her supervisors held her by making Marie Cotton the first Sévrienne to sit on a jury for the women's agrégation.[55]

The apparent ease with which this young teacher of mathematics could incarnate the ideal of her profession should not obscure the difficulties faced by others. Her advantages were in any case substantial. The daughter of a mathematics professeur at the boys' lycée of Bourg, Cotton lived at home where she enjoyed not only the protection and companionship of family life but in addition a ready mentor to guide her through her first uncertain efforts as a teacher. Little wonder if given such support, "she arrived early at a singular intellectual maturity," as her inspector put it. Other Sévriennes, neither so fortunate in their living arrangements nor as favored in their family background, would find the first few years of teaching exhausting, both physically and emotionally, in the extreme.

The Overburdened Teacher

In her final year at Sèvres, Marguerite Aron (class of 1892) received a warning of the ordeal just ahead in a letter from a friend already teaching. "Since the honor of becoming agrégée," her friend confided, "I have never worked so hard; I do not recognize myself, and if I did not find on the notebooks of my students a caricature of my nose, I would doubt my own identity."[56] These musings from the pen of one of the elite of the new feminine teaching corps might have served to characterize the experience of any of her colleagues. For most of them, teaching in girls' secondary schools turned out to be exceptionally demanding. The fatigue that she describes typifies what teachers writing lectures and organizing class materials for the first time ordinarily encounter. But among young teachers in girls' secondary schools the sense of crisis conveyed in this remark diminished very little as these professionals moved beyond the first fatiguing year or two of teaching. If anything, the strain of carrying on their routine duties grew. Something more than the usual stress associated with beginning teaching afflicted young women in this new profession.

The first public admission of something gone amiss appeared in the

[53] Dossier personnel, notes, 1890, 1891, 1895, F17 23581, A.N.
[54] In 1899, her father had his leg amputated. Ibid.
[55] Ibid., 1898.
[56] Aron, Le Journal d'une Sévrienne (1912), 59–60.

professional journal *Revue universitaire* in 1895. A young woman professeur who had not attended Sèvres published an article complaining
that teachers in girls' secondary schools were dangerously overworked
and falling ill at an unprecedented rate.[57] M. Dugard, as she signed herself, blamed her colleagues' plight on an overloaded teaching schedule.
The essential problem, she argued, was that in an effort to create a program which protected adolescent girls from overwork, the ministry had
created a monstrosity from the point of view of women teachers.

In the first place, teachers in girls' secondary schools had too many
class preparations every week in far too many subjects. Official regulations required teachers in letters to teach sixteen hours a week and those
in science to teach fifteen, one hour less to make up for the time spent
looking after scientific collections and equipment. The same rules applied in theory to their counterparts in boys' schools, except for those in
Paris where the elevated level of instruction required greater effort for
any single class.[58] Nonetheless, this rough equivalence of hours spent in
class did not reflect the same amount of work for men and women secondary teachers. Classes in boys' schools lasted one hour and a half,
which meant that teachers had between eight and ten different preparations to do a week. In girls' schools, by contrast—where, in order to ease
the strain on students, the Conseil supérieur had shortened class periods
to an hour—sixteen hours of class a week meant for teachers sixteen different classes to prepare.

Had the system permitted women, like men, to specialize in their
teaching fields, it would have been less onerous. Instead, a woman
teacher who had passed the certificat exam in letters could be asked to
teach any of the courses in humanities in the girls' curriculum: French
grammar; the history of grammar; Greek, Latin, or French literature (the
first two in translation); composition; diction; geography; general history;
the history of civilization; psychology; ethics; even an introductory
course on civil law. Meanwhile, a colleague certified in science might
teach math, geometry, algebra, cosmology, geology, botany, zoology,
physics, chemistry, hygiene, or domestic economy. The goal of keeping
scholars out of girls' instruction had resulted in producing sorely overtaxed generalists. Still worse, in Dugard's view, than the extraordinary

[57] M. Dugard, "Du surmenage des femmes professeurs," *RU* 1 (1895): 107–38. Without
revealing the actual figures, she claimed that records on teachers' sick leaves, compiled
by the Ministry of Education, showed that women secondary teachers fell ill far more
frequently than male secondary teachers. Ibid., 107.

[58] In the lycées of the Seine and Seine-et-Oise, the number of hours required of men
professeurs fell to between twelve and fourteen depending on their speciality. Ibid.,
132.

mental dispersion that an ordinary schedule required of teachers was the possibility that a teacher's course assignments might change from one year to the next in accordance with shifts of personnel within her school.[59]

Dugard's next complaint was that the ministry expected women professeurs to teach at all levels of secondary education. Since the ages of students in secondary courses ranged from twelve to seventeen, this meant that teaching in a girls' school required multiple approaches to a subject, a fact which added greatly to the burdens of instruction.[60] Here again, pedagogical considerations had come before the interests of the teaching staff. A main objective of the architects of the republic's secondary schools had been to rival the moralizing impact of Catholic schools on girls. The course on ethics, called la morale, represented one facet of this multisided effort. The style of life required of women teachers formed another. A third component involved turning the teachers in girls' schools into monitors of the maturation process. Teachers who taught classes at several levels of instruction could oversee the personal development of their students not through a single year but over as many as five years of their adolescence.[61] Thus they could truly act as arbiters of students' moral growth. In other words, inspectors' preference for teachers who developed personal influence over students belonged to a much broader strategy of discipline in girls' schools whereby a teacher, once established as a kind of mentor, could exercise that role throughout a student's schooling.

In drawing up this list of grievances, Dugard did not question the distinctive goals of feminine instruction. Any such suggestion would have struck a sharply discordant note in the chorus of approving voices heard in all professional journals at the time. She merely called on the administration to reduce the hours that students spent in classes or increase the feminine teaching corps.[62] Either solution would have permitted a reduction in the teaching load for individual teachers, thereby solving, in Dugard's view, the major cause of overwork in the profession.

In fact, the strain under which these teachers labored did not derive from the teaching schedule only. Other pressures, both in and outside school, plagued Sévriennes at the start of their careers. For many of them, the problems began with knowing what to teach. A lack of textbooks and teaching manuals in their fields immensely complicated their endeavor. Many relied at first on notes from Sèvres, despite complaints of their

[59] Ibid., 134.
[60] Ibid., 135.
[61] Mayeur, *L'Enseignement secondaire*, 90–96.
[62] Dugard, "Du surmenage," 137.

unsuitability by school inspectors.[63] Efforts to strike out alone did not necessarily fare much better. Here, the danger was that following her own interests, a teacher might select materials that transgressed the narrow boundaries deemed appropriate for girls. In surveying French literature, for example, which the official syllabus centered on the seventeenth-century classics, Gabrielle Minotte (class of 1889) chose to include nineteenth-century authors whom she liked. Her choices irritated an inspector general, who complained, "Mlle Minotte tends like a good number of her colleagues in other lycées to pick texts that are too modern and to accept certain authors' names which ought to be excluded."[64] Another Sévrienne, Cécile Prouyanne (class of 1885), stumbled repeatedly in choosing themes and exercises for her classes because of her insensitivity to what her supervisors judged improper. Once she asked her students to explain the meaning of Alfred de Musset's comment "the only good thing left to me in this world is to have cried a few times." An exasperated inspector general sputtered, "How can a teacher give such a subject to girls fourteen to sixteen years old? Is it reasonable?" Another time, this same ingenuous teacher told her students "to underline the *socialist ideas* in Pascal." "One must not forget," her inspector general ponderously cautioned, "the moral influence all education must have." The final confrontation came over Prouyanne's choice for a dictation in French grammar of a passage from Laharpe that denied the existence of God and used the words *libertine* and *fan*, conjuring up at least in the mind of her directrice a godless world of reprobates and coquettes. Shocked and furious, the directrice urged the rector to arrange for Mlle Prouyanne's immediate transfer elsewhere.[65]

Preparing for a weekly battery of classes did not complete the intellectual tasks of many overburdened teachers. Six of every ten Sévriennes had begun teaching as mere certifiées, after failing at the agrégation. Those who profited in the 1880s from the abundance of positions to get appointed to a lycée faced the prospect, by the 1890s, of demotion to a collège unless they became agrégée.[66] As for those languishing in out-of-the-way places in a secondary cours or collège, a triumph at the agrégation offered the only certain way to change their fortunes. Any certifiée anxious not to compromise her future, therefore, had to study for the agrégation as well as meet her obligations in the classroom.

[63] Dossier personnel, Valentine Mesnard, notes, 1887, F17 23434, A.N.

[64] Dossier personnel, notes, 1895, F17 24398, A.N.

[65] Dossier personnel, notes, 1893, 1895, F17 23721, A.N.

[66] Apparently, some directrices resented the presence of such teachers because their status as mere certifiées detracted from the reputation of their schools. Réval, *Un Lycée de jeunes filles*, 19.

For half these women, the difficulties of the task ultimately surpassed their energies or talents. Partly this reflected changes in the standards of the competition. As openings in girls' schools dwindled, the ministry radically reduced the number of candidates rewarded with success, thereby raising the level of the competition. In addition, the creation in 1894 of four agrégations instead of two disadvantaged older Sévriennes, who had trained for the less specialized exams. Still, the major obstacles for Sévriennes preparing in the provinces were lack of time and lack of intellectual resources. Susanne Pénard (class of 1881) who pleaded desperately in 1893 for a position in a lycée near her family, reminded her superiors of a plight she shared with all her colleagues. "I've hardly time to work toward the agrégation; class preparation and correcting homework absorbs almost all a teacher's life."[67] Claire Poisson (class of 1884), who also wanted a position near her family, attributed her repeated failures at the agrégation to the intellectual backwater where she worked. "At Louhans, there is not a single resource on which I can depend: neither an agrégée who might guide me nor a library."[68] In recognition of such hardships, the ministry decided in 1894 to admit to Sèvres for an additional year of training teachers recommended by their rectors and inspectors.[69] Four Sévriennes from the first ten classes benefited from this extraordinary measure; of these, three did in the end achieve their goal. The rest of the successes depended on dogged persistence by teachers who, in a few cases, sat for the exam five or six years in a row.

Nonetheless, the enormous energy and time that Sévriennes as young professionals devoted to their work reflected more than the difficulties of the tasks assigned them. In truth, many of them found little else to do. Separated from their families, most young women teachers fell quickly into a singularly isolated and secluded style of life. Financial considerations played some role in the simplicity of their existence. It seems, to judge from sketchy evidence, that Sévriennes without financial obligations to their families had little problem budgeting on salaries of three thousand francs a year for agrégées and twenty-five hundred for certifiées.[70] Not that such amounts permitted many luxuries. Berthe Israël-Wahl claimed, for instance, that the modesty of beginning teachers' sal-

[67] Dossier personnel, correspondance, 1895, F17 22696, A.N.

[68] Dossier personnel, correspondance, 1891, F17 23685, A.N.

[69] Anna Amieux, "L'Ecole Normale de professeurs-femmes (1881–1931)," in *Le Cinquantenaire*, 163–65.

[70] An anonymous Sévrienne writing for the Alumnae Association bulletin claimed that fifteen hundred francs sufficed in small towns to meet expenses for the bare essentials. "Notes de lecture. Le jeune professeur en province (J. J. Weiss)," *BMAES* 29 (1890): 10.

aries prevented them from hiring a cleaning woman, something their counterparts in boys' schools took for granted on their higher salaries.[71] On the other hand, many Sévriennes did have financial obligations to their families, which reduced their incomes so considerably that they often tutored students privately on the side. The heroine of the novel *Un Lycée de jeunes filles*, by the Sévrienne Gabrielle Logerot, fit the second type, a fact to which her wardrobe of two dresses, one an "everyday dress in back serge" and the other for special occasions, eloquently testified.[72] So stretched were Marie Fleuret's funds that she worried about whether she could pay her way to Paris for the orals of the agrégation should she pass the written exams.[73] If lack of money was a factor in depriving some young teachers of an active private life, however, encultured attitudes raised still greater obstacles.

What truly handicapped these women was not a lack of funds for entertaining outings but a remarkable inability to make friends. Neither in the communities where they lived nor even among colleagues from their schools did young Sévriennes socialize with ease. Part of the explanation lies of course in the proverbial hostility of French provincial towns toward interlopers, an outlook documented by Lawrence Wiley for two communities in France into the 1950s and found by Paul Gerbod to have marginalized the mobile corps of male teachers in the nineteenth century as well.[74] But women teachers suffered from a far more crippling social disability in their efforts to find friends. The middle classes organized the social world of women around the family, and most Sévriennes in their first teaching positions had left their relatives behind.

The Lonely Teacher

Apparently, the frequency of social invitations for young women teachers varied greatly from one place to another. As a single woman Berthe Wahl found Roanne a veritable social desert: "Apart from housework and teaching, not a break, not a distraction! . . . young professeurs were invited nowhere."[75] Even the families of the men professeurs refused their hospitality to women teachers. Writing anonymously for

[71] Israël-Wahl, "Mes Débuts," in *Le Cinquantenaire*, 383.

[72] Réval, *Un Lycée de jeunes filles*, 62. The novel also includes a breakdown of the heroine's monthly budget: 70 francs room and board, 25 francs toiletries and upkeep, 5 francs cleaning, 10 francs unforeseen expenses, 90 francs sent to her family in Montbéliard.

[73] Ibid., 108.

[74] Gerbod, *La Condition universitaire*.

[75] Israël-Wahl, "Mes Débuts," in *Le Cinquantenaire*, 383.

the alumnae bulletin, another Sévrienne drew a very different picture
based on her experience elsewhere: "The welcome extended to a professeur in society is always honorable and eager. She never lacks for invitations." Yet this hospitality offered no advantage to a teacher, since she
endured on such occasions a scrutiny of every gesture. "Our dress and
conversation must always be a masterpiece of taste, tact, and dignity
without a trace of pedantry or arrogance," she claimed and then concluded mournfully, "Oh! how hard it is to play one's role in a mondain
setting and how exhausting to be observed so closely." Her advice to
colleagues "not by nature social" was "not to cultivate the trait" and to
those with a sociable nature "to give into it as little as possible."[76]

Both of these accounts share common features with yet a third description left by Marguerite Aron of her experience at Arras as a young
teacher. While no one invited her personally to their home, Aron's directrice expected her to attend the annual garrison ball and to visit the
homes of all local officials once a year on New Year's Day. The bleakness
of such occasions for a lonely teacher comes through clearly in this dev-
astating sketch of her impressions. "I sat down awkwardly in those still
salons. I listened to loquacious old ladies complain about their maids,
their gas lamps, today's generation of young girls. I saw silent husbands
make a sign to wives after five minutes that it was time to continue on
their round of visits. In all those exchanges of greetings and compli-
ments, not a sign of real cordiality shone through."[77] Such ritual gatherings did not produce new friendships for young teachers, nor was that
the purpose of these obligatory outings. Formal visits functioned to display relationships in these small social worlds, not to redefine them.

All the same, the hesitation that prevented Sévriennes from making
close, new friends did not result from the reluctance of local people only.
A personal reserve, which many of them shared, made it difficult to grasp
with warmth even an extended helping hand. Such was the case for the
young teacher described in a letter published in Camille Sée's professional journal for girls' secondary education by one Mme Clément-Baumann. The letter portrayed the teacher as "pretty, refined, courageous,
and moody," a young professional "who drags herself without a murmur
to her lycée, returns exhausted to her tiny, freezing, and solitary lodging,
where she slaves over her papers until she drops, eats little, and worries
about her elderly father, her four brothers, and her career." Further, it
seems she was frequently ill. Her would-be benefactor, Clément-Baumann, a graduate of the girls' lycée, reported: "I have sent the doctor to

[76] "Quelques Reflexions sur le professeur," 38 (April–May 1890): 2–3.
[77] Aron, Le Journal d'une Sévrienne (1912), 145.

her. I have gotten her to look after herself a bit. I invite her to the house as often as I can. But to really care for her . . . I have no power. For her I am only a stranger."[78]

The conclusion to this account of generosity is astonishing. Why was it that this young teacher so obviously in need of friends kept such a careful guard on her affections? What made her persist in viewing the other woman as a "stranger" despite so many acts of kindness? If friendship could not take root in such a setting, how could this young teacher develop any friends at all? Significantly, Mme Clément-Baumann showed no particular surprise at the younger woman's reaction. She seemed to take for granted her marginal position in this woman's life, a response that in itself reveals much about the cultural attitudes of the society in which they moved.

The difficulty that many of these women seemed to have in making friends would also shape their attitudes toward colleagues. Rarely did the sisterly atmosphere that reigned at Sèvres infuse exchanges between staff members at girls' secondary schools. One inspector, used to the more congenial, offhand manners of men teachers, criticized the new corps of women teachers for their indifference and formality toward each other. "What I reproach in our women professeurs . . . is their desire to have the least possible contact with each other. They treat each other like strangers."[79] What he had unsuspectingly tripped over was a major fault line in the social mores shaping male and female friendships in the middle classes. Whereas male friendships typically developed in arenas separate from the home and family—the school, the workplace, cafés, or through political organizations—women's social contacts normally evolved outward from their families. Lacking that familial context, young women professeurs felt deeply constrained in their emotional lives.

At Sèvres, students had overcome the cultural inhibitions isolating them from one another, partly because they lived at school and also because of Mme Favre's concerted efforts to create an atmosphere of sharing. In girls' secondary schools the task was far less simple. Not only did secondary teachers sleep at home, they took their meals there, too. In stark contrast to Sèvres, which functioned as a home as well as a workplace, girls' secondary schools gave their professeurs no place to mingle private and professional life together.[80] Even when teachers had time to

---

[78] "De Mme Clément-Baumann à Mme X . . . Shanghai," *ESDJF* 2 (1904): 196.

[79] Dossier personnel, Madeleine Sébastien, notes, 1892, F17 23505, A.N.

[80] This absence of sociability presents a striking contrast to faculty relations in women's colleges in the United States and in girls' boarding schools in England where teachers lived at school. Compare Glazer and Slater, *Unequal Colleagues*, and Vicinus, *Independent Women*.

chat between their classes, the administration generally provided no locale for them to gather. The faculty lounge did not yet exist in public
schools. Frustrated by the lack of common turf and fresh from Sèvres,
where a completely different attitude had reigned, Marguerite Aron exploded in her diary: "Private interest, good sense, the spirit of solidarity,
they all defend the notion 'one for all.' The administration replies 'everyone in their homes.' You are a teacher? You go read in the library. . . .
Except for the tiny vestibule that is their privileged terrain, nowhere do
teachers feel at home."[81]

Faced with similar conditions in boys' secondary schools, men professeurs had in cafés and sometimes through their clubs an alternative place
to meet informally with acquaintances and friends. Women had no such
public place to get together since except in metropolitian centers cafés
were off-limits for respectable single women. Partly for that reason, secondary school teachers would not develop any organizational life until,
under a new generation of directrices, their schools began to offer them
a forum. Meanwhile, left to entertain their colleagues in tiny apartments
or more often in furnished rooms, teachers rarely issued invitations.

The rare exception to this pattern might develop when two Sévriennes
who had known each other at Sèvres ended up in the same school. That
happened far less frequently than one might at first imagine. Most often
Sévriennes on the same faculty had not crossed paths at Sèvres. In such
cases, each viewed the other as a stranger, no more accessible than any
other colleague. Of course, when classmates from Sèvres did end up together, friendship blossomed often into intimacy. In the lonely worlds to
which this new profession led, Sévriennes turned in open affection to
the one person in the school and community with whom they shared
some roots. A few elected even to reside together. Often, though, Sévriennes did not share lodging with another teacher, whatever the material advantages might have been. Perhaps a deep sense of privacy or a
fear based on sexual taboos, which even Sèvres had fostered with its single bedrooms, played a role here. Marguerite Aron and her best friend
from Sèvres, though placed in the same school, never considered keeping house together. "Yvonne loves her room," she wrote, "and is getting
used to the smell of wood. . . . my own place I like too. We run into each
other several times a day, but hours go by when we don't see each other
even though we live next door. We keep to ourselves out of respect for
each other, and perhaps when we do meet, we enjoy it more."[82]

Few Sévriennes at the start of their careers enjoyed the reassuring

[81] *Le Journal d'une Sévrienne* (1912), 208–9.
[82] Ibid. 192–93.

friendship of a woman like themselves with whom to share the burdens of this new profession. Most faced alone the professional and private pressures exerted by the originality of their position both as teachers and as independent single women. Inevitably, no two cases exactly replicated each other. The points of greatest tension varied with the personal resources of individuals and the peculiarities of the schools and towns in which they worked. Some suffered most from their relations with superiors. Others simply found the daily tasks of teaching too demanding. Still others felt tormented above all by the solitude that propriety or their own reserve imposed upon them. Young women teachers differed also in the ways they came to grips with this new world, with both its opportunities and its limitations. But in one respect the vast majority responded uniformly. Almost all of them fought hard to get appointments near their families. Ready to claim the right of women to an education, committed to the concept of the female professeur, they nevertheless stuck close to the traditional image of the woman deeply rooted in the family. That reaffirmation would not only set the contours of their own lives; it would shape the profile of the schools and the profession that this generation of Sévriennes pioneered.

5 Young Teachers and Their Families

OF ALL REQUESTS that Sévriennes made as young professionals, none resonates more persistently through their official dossiers than the plea for posts near home. To rejoin
their families became for the majority of these women a fiercely pursued
objective. But Sévriennes did not rely only on personal resources to
achieve their goal. Whole families contributed to the task. Parents, siblings, occasionally grandparents or aunts became a party to the collective
effort. Surprisingly perhaps, the purpose of such planning was not
merely or often even primarily to end the isolation from which so many
young and single Sévriennes suffered. By locating near their families,
Sévriennes hoped above all to fulfill long-standing duties in the family.
Incontestably, the proximity of kin eased the loneliness of a socially marginalized existence. Yet the picture of Sévriennes' obligations, once they
were united with their families, suggests extraordinary additional burdens on these women. Rather than providing a safe haven from professional pressures, in the end family life simply piled more responsibilities
on their already overladen plates.

Stratagems for Reuniting Families

Some families of Sévriennes had clearly anticipated the fissure
that a daughter's entry into secondary teaching might open in the family
circle. Others just as obviously had not. But even those prepared for such
a rupture never envisaged, before the fiat from the ministry arrived, an
appointment that placed a daughter so far away from home that she
could not make regular visits. In a sense that optimism was natural. Every family could name at least one, sometimes two or three secondary
schools close to the parental home or within reach by an easy train ride.
Parents and Sévriennes alike readily imagined such schools as their
likely destination, especially as the ministry habitually requested that
candidates for the agrégations list their preferred locations. Such requests, delivered by Sévriennes in person either to the chairman of the
jury at the agrégation or in a personal interview at the ministry, typically
received a sympathetic hearing. Hidden from view, of course, was the
secret bargaining that went on within the ministry among inspectors, rectors, the director of secondary education, and his minister in the annual

reshuffling of posts. Ignorant of the quid pro quo this entailed, Sévriennes and their relations relied on the paternalism of the state to protect the integrity of the family.

This confidence in officials' good intentions only added to the shock of disappointment that many Sévriennes experienced on learning of their first appointment. But once disabused of their initial hopes, families did not cave in to the inevitable, as they might have with a son, by letting the logic of developing careers take precedence over proximity to the family. Instead, they fought tenaciously, with a battery of weapons, to bring these young professional women back into the family fold.

In planning a campaign for their reunion, Sévriennes and their families had two strategies from which to choose. Either members of the family would come to share a teacher's exile or a daughter would seek a job closer to her parents' home. During the early phase of Sévriennes' careers, only a minority could effectively pursue the first of these alternatives because fathers were not at liberty to move around, and that in most cases immobilized their wives. Occasionally, of course, a father would die prematurely, and his widow gathered her resources and went to join her working daughter, accompanied sometimes by other, younger children. Three Sévriennes at least were reunited with entire families in this unexpected way.[1] In other cases, fathers accepted the temporary absence of their wives who wanted to look after lonely daughters. Such arrangements worked reasonably well for mothers with no dependent children, when the distance between the homes was not too great. Emma Appy's (class of 1881) mother, for example, left her husband, a proprietor at Lacoste, to join their only daughter in Montpellier, fifty kilometers away. But when the ministry reappointed Emma to Rouen, the family faced an impossible dilemma. At first Emma refused to go, warning her superiors, "Papa would never agree to my departure for Rouen alone or to a separation from his wife and daughter of over eleven hundred kilometers."[2] In the end, the two women reluctantly acquiesced in the administration's will. Ten months later, though, both were back home in Lacoste, Mme Appy to tend her husband and Emma, who had quit her job, to wait for a more satisfactory post.

Precisely because of the inherent instability of such solutions, most families relied on relatives other than a teacher's parents to recreate a family life for young and single women far from home. Among the various kin called into service figured grandparents, aunts, and Sévriennes'

---

[1] See, for example, the dossiers personnels of Henriette Gonel, F17 23919 and of Amélie Revert, F17 23796, A.N.

[2] Dossier personnel, Emma Appy (married name Chauvin), correspondance, 1885, F17 23253, A.N.

unmarried siblings. Augustine Frémont, for instance, whose pitiful story opened chapter 4, avoided the worst consequences of her appointment to Agen when her grandparents agreed to join her there.[3] Both Cécile Clair (class of 1885) and Louise Masson (class of 1887) escaped the hardships of living alone in distant places when their aunts decided to set up housekeeping with them.[4] But the most common remedy for the hardship of separation from the family was for siblings to share the homes of lonely sisters. Sometimes this meant that a school-aged youngster could take advantage of a sister's presence near a lycée to pursue an education. In other cases, a Sévrienne welcomed an older, nonworking maiden sister to her home. The most frequent combination in these households involved two single sisters, both of whom had been to Sèvres and gotten posts together. Sévrienne sisters, a permanent feature of Sèvres's recruitment in this period, made their first appearance in the class of 1881 when Louise Ménassier and her older sister Marguerite entered Sèvres together. A few years later the Fourcade sisters repeated the Ménassiers' feat by passing the entrance exam in the same year. More commonly, however, two sisters went through Sèvres in different classes.[5] Once teaching, invariably they requested posts in the same school so that they could live together. Indeed, Adèle Fourcade claimed that her older sister had "only gone to Sèvres to avoid a separation."[6] By dint of all these varied efforts, just over a quarter of those Sévriennes living far from home had someone from their families with them for a portion of their early years of work.[7]

The majority of Sévriennes could not depend on such solutions to the loneliness they faced as young professionals. Too few of them had relatives at liberty to move around, even on a temporary basis. Most families turned their minds instead to getting posts for daughters close to home. This goal also frequently occasioned energetic efforts by several members of the family. The major burden fell, of course, on Sévriennes themselves who, in order to get the ear of the administration, had first to impress superiors as professionals. Most believed, however, that to rely on formal

[3] Dossier personnel, Augustine Frémont, correspondance, 1885, F17 22445, A.N.

[4] Dossier personnel, Cécile Clair (married name Grenier), correspondance, 1892, F17 24073, and dossier personnel, Marguerite Caron, reference to Louise Masson's aunt in correspondance, 1890, F17 24126, A.N.

[5] Charlotte Verdeilhan entered Sèvres in 1881; her sister Marthe came three years later (class of 1884). Louise Belugou, who came to Sèvres in 1882, was followed six years later by her sister Sophie (class of 1888). Aline Martin (class of 1885) followed in the footsteps of Berthe Martin (class of 1884). Louise Masson (class of 1887) preceded her sister Hélène (class of 1890) by two years. Both Marthe Honnet (class of 1887) and Camille Malou (class of 1890) had sisters at Sèvres in the 1890s.

[6] Dossier personnel, Adèle Fourcade, correspondance, 1887, F17 23985, A.N.

[7] This percentage covers only the first decade of each Sévrienne's career.

channels for the fulfillment of their dreams risked disappointment for the family in the end. To swing decisions in the ministry in their favor, therefore, over half of Sèvres's alumnae and their families turned for help to influential outside patrons.

Patronage

Patronage had played a central role in filling government offices in France for centuries. Under the Third Republic, despite official pronouncements to the contrary, it still functioned alongside and in some ministries in place of the official merit system of promotion. The Ministry of Education boasted a better reputation in that regard than most other branches of the government, partly because by profession the teachers who ran the Université valued impartiality and wanted to protect the excellence of their schools. In addition, the resistance to political appointments grew out of the system of competitive credentialing exams that publicly established real differences in talent. For the ministry openly to have disregarded rankings established at these juried competitions in handing out positions certainly would have invited serious protests from within the Université and perhaps even from the general public.

Occasions nonetheless arose when the professional merits of candidates for the same position differed very slightly. In such cases, special pleadings, independent of professional qualifications, could affect decisions taken at the ministry. Precisely for that reason, Sévriennes and their families often wrote at length to ministerial officials explaining the specifics of their personal problems, especially those imposed on all concerned by the separation of women teachers from their families. Many families imagined that to ensure a sympathetic hearing for such personal tales of woe required an influential patron from outside the ministry. Several hundred notes and letters in the dossiers of young teachers testify to the strength of that conviction.

This correspondence, which richly documents the importance attached to family by these women teachers, illuminates as well the limits and patterns of their contacts with the national republican elite. Not everyone had access to politically influential circles, and of those who did, not all drew patrons from the same arenas. An examination of the identity of patrons, therefore, yields important clues to the social world in which Sévriennes and their families moved. As students, some of these young teachers made useful allies independently of their families. In particular, Mme Favre, Joseph Fabre, Henry Lemonnier, and Ernest Legouvé proved willing later to write letters on behalf of young alumnae who experienced personal problems. For the most part, though, young women teachers relied on the good connections of their families for their patrons.

Few enjoyed the influential contacts of an Alice Duprat (class of 1889) whose great-uncle had served as deputy and ambassador (*ministre plénipotentiaire*) to Chile and whose father, before his untimely death, had been subprefect in the southern town of Pau.[8] For Duprat doors to prominent members of the republican elite would open easily. Indeed, her mother, in an effort to obtain for her a coveted post at Sèvres as an assistant teacher, planned to mount on her behalf a veritable "campaign" at Pau, as Duprat herself would characterize it. "I learned from my mother," she wrote to the director of secondary education, "that she had already secured the support . . . of M. Barthou, who is our compatriot and a schooltime friend of my brother's. . . . She also planned to approach M. Monod who is her doctor and a family friend, and M. Mennier who knows my stepfather."[9] Meanwhile, Duprat approached a family friend in Paris with ties to the secretary of the director of secondary education.[10] Unfortunately for this well-connected Sévrienne, her family's strategy backfired when the director warned her that such brazen politicking compromised her chances. "For posts of this sort more even than for others, it is indispensable that the administration of Sèvres and the central administration preserve their absolute freedom to choose. . . . I can only urge Mlle Duprat to modify . . . , in the future, the ardor and impatience of her proceedings [*démarches*]."[11] Though the principle defended here applied throughout the period to the most coveted posts in this profes-

[8] She explained in a letter to the director of secondary education in 1893 that her father had died when she was eighteen, and until that time she had not expected to have to work to make her living. Dossier personnel, Alice Duprat, correspondance, F17 23600, A.N.

[9] Ibid. Duprat's motive for seeking assignment to Sèvres differs from the familiar one of seeking to locate near her family. On leaving Sèvres, she had the great good fortune of being named to Montauban, a short distance from her family at Pau and a post that in her own words "gratifies to the highest degree my family's wishes and my own." Five years later, she explained in asking for sick leave over the summer that because of her mother's recent remarriage, she was financially on her own, which suggests that for Alice Duprat, the protection of the family ended early and under unique circumstances.

[10] She also claimed to have had Henri Marion as a "protector" before his recent death and that his widow, appointed to succeed Mme Favre as directrice of Sèvres, would welcome her appointment to Sèvres. Insisting on her great-uncle's eminence in republican political circles, she further reminded the director, "It is worth something after all, to come from the republican race, even if in my quality as a woman I am not permitted to have an opinion." Ibid.

[11] Ibid.

sion, no other Sévrienne received a similar reprimand, doubtless in large part because few if any had Duprat's connections.

On the face of it, the social strata from which Sèvres's students came made personal contacts between their families and the highest echelons of the republican elite unlikely. Just under half (44 percent), in fact, enlisted no patrons at all, apart from those at Sèvres. Most of the rest had only one or at best two spokesmen on their behalf. All the same, this poverty of contacts did not exclude some highly influential people, including on occasion ministers. To explain such contacts requires a careful reconstruction of the patronage system as it revolved around male members of the family, for it was men who in the first instance forged the links between families and patrons with influence in the national arena. Almost always, fathers determined the parameters of Sévriennes' connections in the first stage of their careers. Once married, a Sévrienne could, of course, exploit as well the contacts of her husband. Alternatively, a brother or an uncle would intercede on her behalf. Women, on the other hand, though sometimes intermediaries like Mme Duprat, could only manipulate the contacts of their men. Differences among Sévriennes in the use of patrons, therefore, invariably mirrored differences in the working and leisured milieus of male kin.

On the basis of this assumption, the evidence of Sévriennes' experience suggests that in the modest social ranks from which their families came, only the professional middle class—here defined to cover all employees of the state as well as members of the liberal professions—found access to republican patronage relatively easy. By contrast, families from the commercial middle class of small merchants, small manufacturers, and private employees had few points of contact with the national republican elite. The stastical evidence is compelling: three-fifths of the families without patrons came from the commercial sector, while three-fourths of the recorded patrons acted on behalf of professional families.[12] The disparity comes into better focus with a reconstruction of the methods by which families from these different occupational milieus tapped their patrons.

For the professional class, contacts made at work offered families the most usual avenues for seeking patrons in the national elite. Still, such

---

[12] The only families considered are those for whom the occupation of the father or husband is known. Fathers of Sévriennes were nearly evenly divided between these two sectors of the middle class, though Sévriennes more often married into professional families. Even if we arbitrarily assign to a commercial status all families seeking patrons whose occupations were not stated, two-thirds of the patronage is still reserved to professionals. This analysis is based exclusively on data drawn from the first ten years of Sévriennes' careers.

families tended to be resourceful in forging useful ties to influential patrons. Frequently they enlisted the assistance of friends, relatives, and local politicians to put pressure on the Ministry of Education on a Sévrienne's behalf. Just which of these connections proved most useful varied slightly by occupational group.

Public employees relied most heavily for their patrons on connections made at work. In return for long and loyal service, they could expect even high officials in their branch of the administration to write letters in support of wives and daughters in another. Exceptional service from a father or brother might even win the backing of a minister, as was the case for Suzanne Palaa's (class of 1883) father, head clerk in the Ministry of Transport with the title *chevalier d'honneur* and forty years of working at the ministry to his credit.[13] Men within the Université itself benefited from the advantage of direct professional ties with officials under whom their wives or daughters also worked. Quite naturally, they too viewed superiors as potential patrons for their families. Primary school teachers, by contrast, who worked under different inspectors and whose professional contacts tended to be local, relied on politicians far more often for support.

Outside this group of privileged state employees, no single avenue of influence superseded others. Families with connections to the liberal professions tended to exploit multiple patrons, some based on work, some on school ties and other friendships, some on well-placed relatives. Although this pattern was especially typical for doctors, lawyers, and journalists, it not infrequently characterized the approach of the rest of the professional bourgeoisie. Such families got access to the national republican elite in a variety of ways and with a certain ease.

In striking contrast, commercial families, at the modest levels from which most Sévriennes came, found neither work, kin, nor ties of friendship ready sources of useful conduits to the Ministry of Education. As small, independent merchants or employees in the private sector, they lacked the routine interaction with official France that professionals and civil servants experienced on a daily basis. Nor did the picture alter when their social and kinship ties came into play. Not a single commercial family had direct access to some official in the Ministry of Education, while only two could call on high officials in other ministries for support. Sometimes they turned to people on the fringes of official life such as editors of papers,[14] rabbis or pastors,[15] even an occasional well-

[13] Dossier personnel, Suzanne Palaa, correspondance, 1888, F17 22559, A.N.

[14] Dossier personnel, Estelle Schwob, correspondance, 1891, F17 23957, A.N.

[15] See the dossiers personnels of Amélie Bacharach (married name Wallich), corres-

known employer.[16] Mainly, though, they sought the help of legislators
from their local areas. Deputies proved relatively easy to approach, as
they represented small, single-member constituencies. Several commercial families even managed to elicit more than the perfunctory support
of their local deputy for a teacher. Senators, by contrast, who were
elected under a two-tiered system for an entire department, served as
patrons for commercially oriented families far more rarely, unless a father happened, as in the case of Marie Salvat (class of 1884), to be a sen-
atorial elector.[17] Nevertheless, even the relative success of commercial
families in mobilizing deputies paled by comparison with the success of
families in the free professions or with fathers working for the state.
Twice as many deputies and two and a half times more senators wrote
letters of support for teachers from professional families than for those
whose fathers worked in commerce. Only in midcareer, when Sévriennes
in their capacity as established teachers could themselves approach such
politicians, did this imbalance in the record of their patrons disappear.

So marked a contrast almost certainly handicapped women from families in commerce, if patronage had any part in school appointments. The
relative success of either group in getting posts near home can serve to
measure, therefore, whether patronage, in fact, influenced ministerial decisions. Françoise Mayeur has argued that political influence had little
impact on assignments to the most prestigious posts in girls' secondary
schools.[18] If the measure becomes appointments close to home, the conclusion holds as well. Statistically no difference emerged in the rates of
success that professional and commercial families achieved in getting
daughters placed in schools near their homes. For this massive effort to
succeed depended entirely, therefore, on the willingness of ministerial
officials to weigh family interests in the balance when awarding posts.

The Attitude of the Administration

In fact, appeals for help in reuniting young women teachers
with their families won considerable sympathy from high officials in the
early years of this new feminine profession. E. Legouvé confirmed this
when he wrote to Rabier, the director of secondary education in 1892,
regarding Gabrielle Minotte (class of 1889), "I know how much you favor

---

pondance, 1891, F17 24034, and of Hélène Leypold (married name Séry), correspondance, 1890, F17 23801, A.N.

[16] Dossier personnel, Gabrielle Chavance, correspondance, 1891, F17 23980, A.N.

[17] Dossier personnel, Marie Salvat (married name Durand), correspondance, 1888,
F17 22272, A.N.

[18] Mayeur, *L'Enseignement secondaire*, 310–35.

leaving young teachers with their parents or at least close by, realizing the benefits both the women and their teaching derive from this arrangement."[19] A fatherly interest in these teachers' welfare may have inspired official thinking, as Legouvé's words suggest. Yet paternalism, though it certainly played a part, does not alone explain officials' sensitivity to familial concerns. More important, female teachers could improve their public image if they resided near or, even better, with their families. From the administration's point of view, the main beneficiaries of a policy aimed at placing teachers with their families were not so much these women as the cause and the schools that they served. A note in 1887 from a subordinate in the ministry to Zévort, Rabier's predecessor as director, made the point plainly, apropos of the Ménassier sisters' efforts to get posts together: "Young women abandoned to themselves are socially isolated and sometimes the object of malevolent gossip. If the administration wants to increase the dignity and prestige of girls' secondary education, an innovation disparaged in certain towns, it must encourage and facilitate the uniting of families so that teachers can live more sociably and comfortably as well as improve their social standing."[20] To the extent that the first generation of Sévriennes succeeded in adapting their profession to familial needs, their achievement owes a great deal to the politics of girls' education in the early Third Republic.

As policy, however, official willingness to promote family reunions in handing out appointments had decided limits. Rarely did it override professional considerations when the ministry made its annual selections. Teachers with a compelling personal need for any particular post had to have the requisite credentials. Without the certificat, for example, Sévriennes often could not get posts as secondary teachers even in cours secondaires, while a certifiée found it difficult to get a position in a lycée. Moreover, only the most talented of the provincial secondary teachers who aspired to Paris had any realistic hope. Besieged by requests for Paris from young women teachers, the rector at Le Havre fumed furiously in 1896, "If it was enough to invoke family reasons for a call to Paris, hardly a teacher would be left in the provinces."[21] He was wrong about the exclusive pull of Paris for young teachers eager to locate near their families, but his disgust with those who hoped that the administration

[19] Dossier personnel, Gabrielle Minotte, correspondance, 1892, F17 24398, A.N. Charles Zévort was director of secondary education for all but one year between the Loi Camille Sée and 1887. His successor, George Morel, lasted only two years. Elie Rabier took over in 1889. Mayeur, L'Enseignement secondaire, 306–7.

[20] Dossier personnel, Marguerite Ménassier, correspondance, 1887, F17 22507, A.N.

[21] Dossier personnel, Marie Boué (class of 1889), notes, 1896, F17 24046, A.N.

would place family claims above professional merit reflects official thinking on the matter.

For many teachers avid to get home, much depended, therefore, on their ability to prove themselves professionally. The pathetic record of occasional teachers who attempted the agrégation five, six, even seven years in a row almost always belongs to this wider story of Sévriennes' relationship to family. Repeated failures meant for the unhappy victim more than a professional loss of face. Often it involved a blow for the entire family.[22] Of course, success at the agrégation did not guarantee teachers a reunion with their families either. Agrégée or not, all teachers faced the possibility that the school for which they qualified near home had no position open on the faculty.

Confronted by such problems, Sévriennes generally resigned themselves to what they hoped would be a temporary exile with stoic patience. A few resolute souls, however, took the extraordinary step of giving up prestigious positions some distance from their homes for inferior ones in schools closer to the family.[23] Lucie Ravaire (class of 1884), for example, forfeited the salary and title of professeur at the lycée of Tournon, located four hundred kilometers from her parents, to become a less important teacher in the collège at Auxerre, thirty kilometers from home.[24] Marie Cotton (class of 1886), who came in first at the agrégation in science in 1889 and whose illustrious career would lead eventually to Paris, started out at her own request teaching in the cours secondaires of Bourg to avoid a separation from her father.[25] Elizabeth Butiaux (class of 1881) and Marie Bouet (class of 1883), both Parisians, accepted posts as elementary teachers in lycées in Paris rather than accept professorial appointments in provincial schools away from home.[26]

Surely for some Sévriennes, loneliness explains this single-minded effort to reconstitute the family circle. Especially in the first year or so of teaching, when teachers keenly felt the strangeness of their new surroundings, fear of isolation drove certain of them back into the nest. That

[22] Good examples of such personal tragedies can be found in the dossiers personnels of the following Sévriennes: Marie Aulon (class of 1886), F17 22464; Sophie Belugou, F17 23562; Marie Brunaud, F17 23676; Louise Trouplin (married name Butot), F17 23573, A.N.

[23] An identifiable 8 percent of Sèvres's alumnae made this sacrifice for their families at the outset of their careers. The number would be larger if it included opportunities forgone later on in Sévriennes' careers or those of married teachers.

[24] Her parents lived in the nearby town of Champlost. Dossier personnel, Lucie Ravaire, F17 23949, A.N.

[25] Dossier personnel, Marie Cotton, correspondance, 1889, F17 23581, A.N.

[26] Dossier personnel, Elizabeth Butiaux, notes, 1887, F17 22556, and dossier personnel, Marie Bouet (married name Segand) correspondance, 1891, F17 22637, A.N.

was how Estelle Schwob (class of 1887) justified her offer to teach elementary classes if she could stay in Paris with her family: "Everywhere else I would be alone," she wrote to the director of secondary education. "This motive supersedes all others."[27]

Yet to judge from what most suppliants wrote to their superiors, more of them returned to families out of duty. Behind Sévriennes' reluctance to leave home and their anguish once they did so lay a deep concern to carry out their obligations to the family. Repeatedly, in their requests for transfers home, single women stressed the tasks that it behooved them as daughters to perform. Oldest, youngest, only child—it did not seem to matter; all were equally obliged to help their families. Elder daughters felt responsible for siblings still in school; only daughters suffered over parents left alone; and any daughter with ill and aging parents worried if events prevented her from being at their side. Earlier we noted the importance of familial ties in Sévriennes' affections. But if family constituted the sentimental focus of their lives, filial duty acted as the pivot of their moral conscience.

Two major responsibilities that Sévriennes undertook within their families emerge in sharp relief from their appeals for new appointments. Financial assistance figured as the most pervasive, though not necessarily the most important one. In 1891 Mme Favre, who sustained a lively correspondence with alumnae and knew a great deal about their private lives, declared in a letter to the ministry, "Most of them must support their families."[28] Few records of the actual terms of this assistance survive. All the same, evidence of this assistance, based on the testimony of Sévriennes and their families, crops up repeatedly in correspondence with the ministry.

Many Sévriennes who lived apart from parents unquestionably sent a portion of their income home. There is, of course, no way of knowing how much of what young teachers made went to their families. The heroine of *Un Lycée de jeunes filles* by Gabrielle Logerot (class of 1890) allocated nearly half her salary to her family, or ninety francs from a monthly income of two hundred.[29] That amount may well exaggerate the sacrifice that teachers ordinarily made for families, but in certain families, Sévriennes away from home undoubtedly relinquished more. A case in point involves Marie Gasnault (class of 1889) whose family became entirely dependent on her when her father, a primary school teacher,

---

[27] Dossier personnel, Estelle Schwob, correspondance, 1890, F17 23957, A.N.

[28] In a note to Rabier, Mme Favre warned that this situation would prevent those who had not yet passed the agrégation from returninng to Sèvres for another year of work. F17 14191, A.N.

[29] Réval, *Un Lycée de jeunes filles*, 62.

died in 1892. In a letter to the ministry, she declared herself to be "at twenty-four . . . the sole support of a family composed of my mother and two brothers."[30] Unfortunately, Gasnault was also a victim of the shortage of posts for science teachers in the 1890s. Unable to get a position in secondary teaching, for four years she had to shoulder those responsibilities on an elementary teacher's salary of eighteen hundred francs at Guéret, 250 kilometers from home. Similarly, Cécilia Terrène (class of 1890), a certifiée in letters, who lacked the credentials for a position in the lycée near her parents' home, supported them for a year from the other side of France on a collège teacher's salary.[31] In explaining her obligations and desire to get home, Terrène noted that she was her parents' "only daughter."[32]

Sévriennes residing with their families would also generally contribute at least a portion of their salaries to the household. A father's letters occasionally referred to such arrangements in requesting his daughter's transfer to a post close to home. When the Fourcade sisters applied for positions in their hometown, their father pointed out to their superiors, "Here I could reestablish their health, and they could lighten my financial burdens."[33] Likewise, Marthe Dugland's (class of 1881) father insisted in appealing for her appointment to the local collège, "Marthe's presence is almost a necessity, all the more since we still have a daughter in school and must carefully manage our resources."[34] If Sévriennes living at home contributed to the family income in a subsidiary way, however, once family members came to live with them, these young working women functioned financially as heads of households.

Except in cases where two Sévrienne sisters lived together, siblings almost always moved into sisters' households as dependents. Suzanne Pénard (class of 1881), for example, the eldest daughter in a family of ten children, supported one or another of her siblings all her working life. Pénard's uncle, an official in the prefecture of the Seine, first documented her financial service to the family when in her second year of teaching, she was demoted from a lycée close to home to a collège 150 kilometers away because she failed the agrégation. "This news," according to her uncle, "devastated her along with her parents." He explained the reason for his brother and sister-in-law's dismay: "[They] cannot

[30] Dossier personnel, Marie Gasnault, correspondance, 1892, F17 23995, A.N.

[31] Dossier personnel, Cécilia Terrène (married name Lafleur), correspondance, 1894, F17 24386, A.N.

[32] Ibid.

[33] Dossier personnel, Adèle Fourcade (married name David) correspondance, 1886, F17 23876, A.N.

[34] Dossier personnel, Marthe Dugland, correspondance, 1890, F17 22612, A.N.

without anguish contemplate their daughter . . . separated from the family at an age when she may still feel the need of the moral support of the latter. Moreover, my niece contributes, to the extent economizing on her salary permits, to my brother's expenses. . . . Notably, she has taken financial responsibility for her sister who is a day student at the lycée of Moulins . . . and who will be forced to follow [Suzanne] to Châlon-sur-Saône in order to continue her studies."[35] Eleven years later, Pénard took in two school-aged sisters to help out her family after her appointment as a chargée de cours in a lycée nearer home. Finally, at her father's death, she welcomed a blind sister to her hearth. This sister would still be living with Pénard when she retired in 1924.[36]

The heaviest financial burden fell on the teacher whose father's early death sent his widow to her working daughter's home. That happened to Marguerite Aron when in 1900 her father died, leaving her mother with young children still to raise. "That catastrophe changed my life from top to bottom," Aron recalled in 1920. "To meet my unexpected duties as head of the family, I had to find some source of income in addition to my salary."[37] She appealed to Camille Sée, who offered to pay her for writing articles for L'Enseignement secondaire des jeunes filles with the result that Le Journal d'une Sévrienne, Aron's autobiographical novel, first appeared in that professional journal.

The second major theme in petitions to the ministry for immediate transfers home stressed the need for working, single daughters to tend to an ailing parent. If families in good health could do without their daughters for a few years while they waited patiently for their turn to move homeward, whenever illness struck, all concerned dropped their customary reticence in the overriding interest of getting daughters home. Cécilia Terrène, for example, once she got a post two hundred kilometers from her parents, limited herself to periodic requests for Agen where her parents lived. But when her mother's health collapsed, financial assistance and occasional weekends home would not suffice to meet her filial obligations. Obviously distraught, she pleaded in a letter to her academy inspector, "My mother's health is deteriorating daily and to have me close at hand would be for her an enormous consolation."[38] Meanwhile, her directrice confirmed the seriousness of the problem and the lengths to which Terrène had gone already to attend her mother: "only daughter—mother gravely ill—no hope for a cure. Installing a sick person in a

[35] Dossier personnel, Suzanne Pénard, correspondance, 1885, F17 22696, A.N.

[36] Ibid.

[37] M. Aron, "Intimité: le directeur de la Revue chez lui," ESDJF 1 (1919): 32.

[38] Dossier personnel, Cécilia Terrène (married name Lafleur), correspondance, 1899, F17 24386, A.N.

village far from her customary haunts . . . is not easy. I know that Mlle Terrène has tried and without success. It is therefore desirable for her, for the mother, and for her father, already along in age, that this professeur be brought closer to her family."[39] Although Terrène did not get the coveted appointment, both inspector and directrice approved of her plan to let her mother's health determine the course of her career. Their views in that regard merely echoed those of many teachers' parents. When Marthe Dugland requested her transfer from the collège where she taught away from home to the cours secondaire in her hometown, professionally a clear demotion, her father adamantly supported her intentions. "I fervently desire that her wish, which is my own, be taken seriously into consideration," he wrote his local deputy, for as he explained, "her mother is often ill, [and] I am myself infirm and unable to work."[40]

Working daughters, in other words, offered parents more than another material resource. They were expected to provide emotional and physical support as the aging process took its toll on parents' health. This was not a novel invention by families of women in this new profession. Ernest Legouvé, in his book on the moral history of women, first published in 1849 and republished several times thereafter, summed up the popular wisdom of the day when he declared the duty of a daughter toward old and infirm parents to be to "station herself at their bedside . . . like a daughter now turned mother."[41] Sons, by contrast, had no obligations in this arena since "men don't know how to console," as Legouvé put it.[42] Sévriennes gave every indication that they concurred with that conventional assumption. In her appeal for a reassignment for her daughter, the ailing mother of Angèle Bourgoignon (class of 1887) put the matter plainly: "My son is too absorbed in his work to be much help and anyway he doesn't take to nursing."[43] Obviously, her son's indifference did not shock this mother. On the contrary, his absorption in his work struck her as entirely natural, something officials in the ministry would also understand. Contrastingly, she just as naturally assumed that Angèle's priorities were different from her brother's and would meet with ministerial approval. In both of those assumptions, she proved right. What strikes us now in perusing such appeals is how traditional the social values of Sévriennes remained despite the novelty of their lives as professeurs. To their critics, they epitomized the cultural phenomenon known

[handwritten marginal note: women meant to console]

[39] Ibid.

[40] Personnel dossier, Marthe Dugland, correspondance, 1890, F17 22612, A.N.

[41] Legouvé, *Histoire morale des femmes*, 23.

[42] Ibid.

[43] Dossier personnel, Angèle Bourgoignon (married name Séverin), correspondance, 1890, F17 24108, A.N.

as the "new woman"—single, careerist, the vanguard of a social revolution that threatened to undermine the family. In fact, far from threatening
the integrity of the family, Sévriennes demonstrated time and time again
their commitment to exploiting their opportunities in the interest of familial concerns.

Not surprisingly, given the sympathetic attitude of the administration,
this persistence generally paid off. Seven out of ten (72.5 percent) Sévriennes managed as young professionals to spend at least a part of their
first ten years of teaching in schools close enough to home for them to
visit parents, at the very least, several times a year. Of these, one-third
(33.3 percent) actually lived with parents for part of their first decade
teaching. Another quarter (24.5 percent) worked at schools within one
hundred kilometers of home. Fifteen percent more had positions between one hundred and two hundred kilometers of their hometowns, a
distance that, if not conducive to reunions on the weekends, did allow
for periodic visits. The price of this success, of course, was high mobility.
Only one in ten (11 percent) remained in the same school throughout the
first ten years of her career, while the average Sévrienne changed posts
three times (2.8), a figure that underestimates the actual frequency of re-
locations for those who moved at all since it includes the stationary
teachers. What the numbers suggest about these teachers' lives is their
readiness to add the hardship of regular uprootings to the burdens of
teaching and looking after family members. Numerous petitions to the
administration for financial help in moving, which it regularly turned
down,[44] bear witness to their economic hardship. The more intangible
difficulties represented by adjusting to new places, different people, and
altered teaching schedules, if rarely mentioned, are no less easy to imagine.

Marriage and the Founding of Another Family

For a great many Sévriennes, simply to rejoin their families did
not represent their fondest hope for personal fulfillment; they dreamed
instead of motherhood and marriage. One of these romantics in a moment of exceptional candor wrote to the director of secondary education,
"Our students are agreeable and not at all pedantic; happier than we,
they will make adorable mothers, both well-educated and kind."[45] That
maternal image must have had considerable appeal for women teachers
of this generation when spinsterhood had so few advantages to offer. As

[44] The state refused to bear the cost of moving functionaries who had requested reappointments.

[45] Dossier personnel, Adrienne Dreuilhe, correspondance, 1894, F17 23756, A.N.

single women, even if they did succeed in moving close to parents, Sévriennes would still find their liberty restricted and the opportunities for
socializing few. Unlike England, where roughly 15 percent of the female
population never married and visibly peopled the elite's social world,[46]
the somewhat fewer single women in France often disappeared into a
convent. The resulting rarity of so-called *vieilles filles* necessarily marginalized such women socially and made them to their own minds, no
doubt, more conspicuous as well. Add to that the enormous value attached to motherhood by both the Catholic church and republican ideologues, and one can easily imagine the importance that individual Sévriennes might have placed on getting married.

Marguerite Aron maintained that certain teachers among her colleagues considered any marriage preferable to remaining single: "They
tire of this equivocal condition, which is neither that of a *jeune fille* nor
of a *femme*, neither entirely independent, nor completely cloistered; a
fixed idea, a monomania for marriage, any marriage, marriage for the sake
of marriage, germinates in their otherwise enlightened and often superior
minds."[47] For the sake of the most banal forms of domesticity, Aron
claimed, such women married whomever they could interest, even if it
meant accepting manifestly inferior men. "Mademoiselle X., at thirty-
eight, marries a traveling salesman of twenty-seven. Mademoiselle Z.
adds her salary of thirty-five hundred francs to the eighteen hundred
francs of a man in training for the *économat* [the administration of school
maintenance] and second clarinet in the musical *union*. After school,
they do their marketing together, and every Thursday and Sunday they
promenade their baby along the main street in his little carriage. *Bébé*
too well-behaved, Mama too pale."[48]

Certainly the rate of marriage and the age of brides suggest that finding
suitors did not come easily to the first Sévriennes. Only 40 percent of
them married, and those who did so took their vows on average at age
twenty-eight, late by contemporary standards.[49] Actually, the obstacles
to marriage are hard to document precisely. The absence of a dowry,
which had pushed so many of them into secondary teaching in the first
place, presumably remained the main impediment once Sévriennes began to work.[50] Teachers' salaries represented a poor substitute since their

[46] Tilly and Scott, *Women, Work and Family*, 92.
[47] Aron, *Le Journal d'une Sévrienne* (1912), 234.
[48] Ibid.
[49] Twenty-eight was both the average and median age of Sévriennes who married.
Thirty percent of Sévriennes married in the first ten years of teaching; another 10 percent married after that.
[50] G. Réval, *La Grande Parade des Sévriennes* (Paris: Fayard, 1933), 305.

utility to the household depended on their continuing to work, something bourgeois propriety disapproved. Aron also suggested that the education which Sévriennes received intimidated men with similar social
backgrounds and that the horror of "bluestockings" within the provincial
bourgeoisie encouraged men to keep their distance. Quite likely it made
the woman professeur a frequent butt of men's salacious jokes. Yet another major problem for these teachers was the lack of opportunities to
meet men in the first place. As a rule, middle-class women relied on
families for an introduction to eligible bachelors, a practice that could
only handicap a mobile corps of female teachers on the marriage market.

Nonetheless, despite the difficulties, just under half (49.3 percent) of
the Sévriennes who married met their spouses while living far from
home (more than two hundred kilometers). Two-thirds of these did not
even have a member of their families living with them when their romances started. This suggests, of course, that already by the 1890s the
rules of courtship had considerably loosened in provincial France, permitting men and women who put a high value on respectability to find
spouses on their own initiative. Precisely how they managed did not ordinarily become a part of a Sévrienne's official record. But occasionally
a bride-to-be, in announcing her good fortune to superiors, described the
circumstances that had led to her engagement. The Protestant Hélène
Leypold (class of 1881), for instance, reported that she had met her fiancé, the son of a deceased local pastor, through her Protestant connections in Toulouse. Apparently his mother, who sympathized with the
cause of girls' secondary education, entertained women professeurs from
the new lycée.[51] Clara Marsat (class of 1888) and Natalie Georges (class
of 1883) met and married brothers of Sévriennes with whom they were
colleagues for a time.[52] Similarly, Jeanne Ochs (class of 1889) fell in love
with the brother of her first directrice.[53] In the case of others, more reti-
cent about their private lives, the general pattern of their courtships can
be glimpsed through the occupations of the men they married. Over half
(53 percent) of Sévriennes who married while away from home found
husbands from within their own profession.[54] These romances must have
come about quite naturally, partly owing to the interest that the faculties

[51] Dossier personnel, Hélène Leypold (married name Séry), correspondance, 1887,
F17 23801, A.N.

[52] Personnel dossiers of Clara Marsat (married name Poirot), correspondance, 1899,
F17 24098, and Natalie Georges (married name Beuque), correspondance, 1894, F17
22602, A.N.

[53] Dossier personnel, Jeanne Ochs (married name Madeuf), correspondance, 1898, F17
23414, A.N.

[54] My assumption is that when the occupation of the husband is not reported by any
source, he was not a teacher.

of local schools had for each other, partly because, until early in this century, some girls' schools continued to hire occasional teachers from the local boys' collège or lycée.[55] More than common professional interests drew Sévriennes far from home to other teachers, though. More often than not, the men, too, because they worked within an even more mobile profession than the women, would have been outsiders. Once on friendly terms, quite possibly teachers of both sexes found that independence from their families eased the way for them to fall in love and marry.

By comparison, chance meetings between a teacher and a local man that blossomed into romance could encounter serious resistance from the suitor's family. Lois Delluc (class of 1881) nearly lost her job at the lycée of Bordeaux when an outraged mother, well known to the rector, called for her immediate transfer to prevent a marriage with her son.[56] Since the rector took the mother's side, the lovers had no choice but to renounce their plans, with the result that Delluc never married.[57] A few years later at Grenoble, Marguerite Rakowska (class of 1881) begged the ministry for a post in Paris to avoid a similar disappointment when her fiancé's Protestant family opposed his marriage to a Catholic.[58] This time the administration proved more understanding. Rakowska got her reappointment, and the lovers, both with jobs in Paris, married without his family's interference. Meanwhile, one of Delluc's and Rakowska's classmates at Sèvres, Pauline Robert-Bérand (class of 1881), looked as if she had beaten the odds when she fell in love with a local man at Niort whose mother favored their betrothal. Astounded at her luck, Robert-Bérand wrote exuberantly to the director, "I am overjoyed to inform you that I shall marry in early August with the complete approval of my fiancé's mother."[59] But perhaps in this case maternal generosity bordered on relief, since this Sévrienne's suitor was an unemployed poet, younger than herself, whom she would support for eighteen years until, in 1905, she finally kicked him out.[60]

Less is known about the Sévriennes who married while living in or close to their parental home. In the only cases when a romance mentioned in a teacher's dossier did not lead to marriage, the apparent obstacle was a teacher's failure to secure a post in the place where her fiancé

---

[55] In Parisian lycées, this policy continued into the interwar period, much to the disgruntlement of women agrégées. See chap. 9.

[56] Dossier personnel, correspondance, 1891, F17 23830, A.N.

[57] Her consolation was to keep her job.

[58] Dossier personnel, correspondance, 1889, F17 23223, A.N.

[59] Dossier personnel, Pauline Robert-Bérand (married name Colas), correspondance, 1887, F17 23825, A.N.

[60] Ibid.

worked.[61] That fact alone suggests that these particular lovers met each other through their families, for if the man lived somewhere else, neither work nor proximity in their daily lives could have brought the two together. Other evidence also points to the conclusion that families played a crucial part in finding partners for daughters living near their parents. To judge only by the occupations of their husbands, teachers close to home had access to a much broader social circle than those who lived away. Only 17 percent of Sévriennes residing in proximity to their families married other teachers; in other words, four out of five husbands of such women pursued another line of work. Evidently, Sévriennes whose lives revolved around their families relied less for their male friendships on their own professional contacts than on the social world created by their families.

Still, if suitors for Sévriennes were difficult to find, rarely did those who married choose a spouse as indiscriminately as Marguerite Aron's cruel vignettes, mocking matronly colleagues, would imply. On the contrary, marriage for Sévriennes almost always involved a remarkable rise in social status from more humble social origins associated with their families. A comparison between the occupations of their husbands and those of fathers at the time that girls entered Sèvres leaves no doubt on this account. This discovery in turn reveals something about the social prestige of the new feminine profession. Already by the 1880s and 1890s, women were beginning to propel themselves upward on the social ladder, in the same manner as men, through success in public schools and professional training. Three out of five (59.4 percent) Sévriennes went to the altar with men of higher social rank than their fathers.[62] Nearly a third (31.9 percent) married men of roughly the same social standing. Only a few cases of downward mobility confirm that Aron's sketches had some basis in reality. More precisely, four (8.5 percent) Sévriennes married beneath their social origins, if we take fathers' occupation as the baseline. If the baseline is defined as the professional status of the Sévrienne herself, twice as many (eight cases or 17 percent) slipped down the social scale at marriage. Thus, Claire Poisson (class of 1884), a professeur in the collège of Louhans, who at thirty-three married an elementary school teacher, may represent the kind of teacher to whom Aron's harsh words refer.[63] So may her classmate Marie Salvat, who at thirty-

[61] See the dossiers personnels of Berthe Wahl (married name Israël), correspondance, 1894–1895, F17 22677, and Alice Duprat, correspondance, 1894, F17 23600, A.N. Wahl eventually married another man.

[62] These figures are based on the forty-seven cases in which we know the occupation of both the husband and the father. The total number of marriages was eighty-three.

[63] Dossier personnel, Claire Poisson (married name Dodille), correspondance, 1896, F17 23685, A.N.

nine became the wife of a notary's clerk at Toulouse where she herself had been for several years a lycée professeur.[64] These exceptions notwithstanding, the very rarity of such matches indicates a strong resistance to them. Perhaps, as Aron implies regarding her own decision not to marry,[65] the majority of Sévriennes took their social achievements far too seriously to risk them on what they judged to be a misalliance.

All the same, if matrimony did not generally mean a drop in social status, it frequently involved a major sacrifice for teachers. One-third (32 percent) of the Sévriennes who married simply gave up their careers, making no plans, barring unforeseen disaster, to return. Just why any particular Sévrienne resigned rarely entered into the official record, but indirect evidence offers some important clues to the pattern of decisions on this matter. Marriage to another educator almost ensured that a Sévrienne would never give up working; whereas those who married outside their profession had a fifty-fifty chance of leaving, either immediately after marriage or once they fulfilled their ten-year contract (see table 5.1.).

Though certainly a factor in some of these decisions, financial considerations cannot have been the only issue. Had this been the case, women married to teachers would presumably have left the profession later, as their husbands' salaries rose. In fact, all but five of the twenty-seven women who married other teachers made a commitment to their careers that even motherhood would not reverse.[66] More likely than financial

TABLE 5.1
Impact of Marriage on Career Plans

Husbands' Profession	Wife Left Career	Wife Continued Career	Total
Teachers	5 (14.5%)	28 (84.5%)	33 (47.1%)
Other	18 (48.6%)	19 (51.4%)	37 (52.9%)
Total	23 (32.9%)	47 (67.1%)	70 (100%)

Sources: Tabulated from dossiers personnels, series F17, A.N.
Note: This table includes only those marriages for which the occupation of the husband is known.

[64] Dossier personnel, Marie Salvat, F17 22272, A.N.

[65] Aron, *Journal d'une Sévrienne* (1912), 234–35.

[66] Of the five who left, two quit because they could not get posts together with their husbands (Marguerite Rey [married name Roche], F17 23496, and Jeanne Mosnier-Chapelle [married name Letellier], F17 23406, A.N.). Two others fell ill. The obituary for Marie Grouhel (class of 1882) recounts that she had found in the practice of her profession "a real vocation." Nevertheless, "she married very quickly after leaving Sèvres and

calculations, what this behavior highlights in these academic households are real differences in the attitudes of husbands toward their spouses' work. Men who were themselves in education could more easily sympathize with a wife's ambition or simply her devotion to her teaching, as well as take a certain pride in her achievements. In contrast, men in other occupations more readily adhered to the common bourgeois view of working wives as a dishonor for the principal provider or as women who neglected their domestic duties.

Assuming that a common professional outlook accounts in part for the behavior of academic couples, what explains the fact that half the women who did not marry teachers also continued their careers? Part of the answer this time seems to lie less with the attitude of husbands than in the professional commitment of their wives. Three indexes measure this commitment. In the first place, the more years a Sévrienne had worked, the likelier was her decision to continue her career once she married. While the median term of service for women who quit their jobs at marriage was four years, of those who stayed in the profession, half had worked eight years or more before they married. Second, Sévriennes who dropped out of teaching typically held lower professional credentials than those who kept on working after marriage. As table 5.2 shows, two-thirds (69 percent) of the agrégées marrying outside the profession remained committed to their work, while all those who had failed to pass the certificat exam resigned immediately. The exceptions themselves confirm the rule, since of the six agrégées who gave up their careers to

TABLE 5.2
Impact of Credentials on Working after Marriage (Women Who Married Outside of their Profession)

	Agrégée	Admissible[a]	Certifiée	Non-certifiée	Total
Left career	7(39%)	3(17%)	5(28%)	3(17%)	18
Continued career	13(69%)	3(16%)	3(16%)	0	19
Total	20	6	8	3	37

Sources: Tabulated from dossiers personnels, series F17, A.N.
[a] This term refers to contestants whose written exams were good enough to permit them to compete in the orals of the agrégation.

quit the Université, her husband having insisted that she stop teaching for her health. At first she consented rather willingly. . . . But as soon as she returned to Paris, the taste for teaching revived in her, and she gave lectures on literature in private cours." M. Tiart-Badeuf and J. Lochert, "Marie Petit-Grouhel," BAES (1938): 13–14.

marry, two moved to cities without schools in which to teach, and two apparently did not enjoy the classroom from the outset.

A third and final measure of professional commitment is the fact that Sévriennes already in prestigious posts at marriage left them behind far more reluctantly than women on the lower rungs of the profession. All directrices and a large majority (64 percent) of the professeurs and chargées de cours in lycées chose to continue working after marriage, whereas Sévriennes at the bottom of the professional ladder—teachers in collèges, institutrices primaires, and répétitrices—more often (69 percent) preferred domestic life to working (see table 5.3). Without explaining why, Françoise Mayeur discovered that resignations peaked for Sévriennes who married between 1885 and 1895, then fell to 20 percent until the outbreak of war, when they would drop dramatically.[67] A graph of Sévriennes' professional opportunities during this period would follow more or less the same configuration. That in turn suggests that for some Sévriennes, at least, domesticity offered an alternative to inferior positions when, from the late 1880s to the middle 1890s, there were so few jobs to go around. Disappointed in their professional ambitions, they could retreat with dignity and relief into the home.

The Home as Refuge?

As a refuge for women who continued working, though, family life offered a rather more ambiguous promise. The domestic ideology of

TABLE 5.3
Professional Achievements and the Decision Whether or Not to Work after Marriage (Women Who Married outside their Profession)

	Dir.	Teacher Lycée	Teacher Coll. or Cours	M.R.	I.P.	Total
Left career	0	8(44%)	6(34%)	2(11%)	2(11%)	18
Continued career	2(11%)	14(73%)	1(5%)	1(5%)	1(5%)	19
Total	2	22	7	3	3	37

Sources: Tabulated from dossiers personnels, series F17, A.N.
Note: Dir. = directrice of a lycée, collège, or cours secondaire
Teacher Lycée = professeur or chargée de cours
Teacher Coll. or Cours = professeur or chargée de cours
M.R. = maitresse répétitrice
I.P. = institutrice primaire

[67] Mayeur, *L'Enseignement secondaire*, 258–63.

Europe's middle classes depicted the home as a haven for husbands, where they could restore their nerves in calm refinement amid a caring family. As Sévriennes rapidly discovered, since women were responsible both in theory and in practice for the creation of this shelter, family life did not give working wives and daughters the same chance for repose. Companionship, diversions, even healthier eating habits than those of solitary colleagues might well improve the quality of life for women who married or rejoined their parents. But in exchange for those improvements, they had to figure on a substantial increase in their own, unpaid domestic labor. On that score, the appeals of countless letters to the ministry leave no doubt. Daughters expected to resume the filial duties of tending parents and younger siblings if they lived at home. As for teachers who married and had children, they incurred still heavier obligations. Painting the grimmest sort of consequences of motherhood and marriage, Gabrielle Logerot described a teacher in her novel *Un Lycée de jeunes filles* who, after giving birth to four children, simply worked herself to death.

Yet family life did hold out the possibility to women teachers of a sort of refuge different from that offered men because it gave such women an arena other than the school, and roles apart from teaching, on which to build their sense of self-esteem. Unlike men, for whom achievement in professional life set the stage for their success as sons and fathers, women did not need to excel professionally to gain recognition of their worth as wives and daughters. That made it possible for Sévriennes to use their domestic obligations as a shield against the pressures of their work. Daughters who managed to get posts close to their homes might quickly find that from their parents' point of view, they had accomplished all they needed to professionally. Indeed, Jeanne Ben-Aben (class of 1888) complained about the problem, "If [a woman professeur] is single and has the good luck to live with her parents, they always consider her their little girl and do not have the same respect at all for her work, for her profession, as they would . . . for a son who was a professeur."[68] Understandably, that indifference might frustrate an ambitious woman. Yet other women, unhappy in their work, might find that it offered an escape from career pressures. Instead of flailing themselves in pursuit of professional approval, they could simply increase the time that they allotted to the home. Their families would certainly not resist and might indeed encourage such a shift. Likewise, a female teacher who married and had children might find it easy to subordinate her prepara-

[68] Jeanne P. Crouzet-Ben-Aben, "Le Surménage du personnel féminin," *RU* 1 (1910): 421.

tion for the classroom to what she deemed more pressing needs at home. Given the values placed on the domestic roles of women, the social risks of such a choice, at least, were slight.

Lucie Baltzinger's (class of 1887) response to marriage provides a case in point. Baltzinger had some reason to privilege her domestic over her professional duties when at thirty she married a simple postal clerk. Her career up to that point had gone extremely badly. A victim like many other science teachers of the scarcity of posts in the 1890s, she was a mere institutrice primaire, albeit in a lycée, when she met her husband. Almost immediately she lost interest in her teaching, a fact that both her directrice and inspectors blamed on her domestic life. Yet following her early death in 1902, her obituary notice in Sèvres's alumnae bulletin treated her domestic efforts with deep respect. "To really understand this simple, delicate, and loving spirit," wrote a fellow Sévrienne, "one had to see her in her home. She was born for obscure devotions and peaceful family joys. Her warm, vivacious wit and especially her unfailing selflessness explain the great tenderness with which her loved ones encircled her."[69] Those loved ones included, together with her husband, elderly parents whom Baltzinger had supported since Sèvres and a sister who came to live with her once she had married.[70] Quite obviously, Lucie Baltzinger Serre distinguished herself in the traditional realm of female action and self-sacrifice, and that entitled her to homage even from her former colleagues.

Up to a point, the Ministry of Education shared that view of female teachers' family obligations. From the outset, the administration made the family duties of its women secondary teachers a factor in handing out new posts. Zévort and Rabier, as already noted, favored reuniting women teachers with their parents; their administrations proved no less accommodating with regard to marriage. The ministry not only approved of marriage; if two teachers who married showed a little patience, officials made serious and usually successful efforts to find them dual posts.[71] Even motherhood had the ministry's official blessing. It guaran-

[69] *BTAES* (January 1901): 1.

[70] Dossier personnel, Lucie Baltzinger (married name Serres), correspondance, F17 13516, A.N.

[71] It sometimes took several years for the ministry to come up with a combination of jobs acceptable to both the husband and wife. See, for example, the dossiers personnels of Léa Camourtères (married name Bérard), F17 23670; Julie Fougères (married name Scarabin), F17 23876; Pauline Grandjean (married name Blanc), F17 23893; Marie Lardley (married name Jaudel), F17 23923; Marguerite Ménassier (married name Rey), F17 22507; and Aline Pechin (married name Girbal), F17 23695, A.N. For an analysis of a similar official attitude toward marriage among primary school teachers, see Leslie Page

teed to women teachers one month of paid maternity leave and permitted pregnant teachers to work right up to term. In an administration dedicated to rooting clerics out of girls' education, pregnancy itself invited no false prudery from school officials. Indeed, inspectors actually delighted in reporting on the dedication of particular teachers to their homely tasks. One academy inspector went so far as to announce in praising the maternal virtues of a teacher that in addition to keeping up her classes, she had managed to nurse her infant child.[72]

Official sympathy, however, did not extend to teachers like Lucie Baltzinger who sacrificed their professional obligations to the demands of private life. On the contrary, the reports of a directrice or school inspector who perceived a teacher as having made that choice could be brutally acerbic on the subject. Adrienne Prieur (class of 1884), for instance, who in her third year of marriage appeared to an inspector general "to rely too much on her experience" in the classroom and to be teaching solely "from the book" had also, as he caustically described it, "taken on the airs and manners of a provincial bourgeois matron."[73] Even women simply overwhelmed by the weight of dual burdens in their homes and school could expect severe reports from their superiors, who typically judged any shortfall in their performance, intentional or not, to represent a dereliction of professional duty. Thus, Cécilia Terrène (class of 1890) would win high praise from her superiors for supporting first her grandfather and then her ailing parents in her twenties, while her teaching was steadily improving. But when a late marriage, two babies, one of them deformed, and her own bad health distracted her from teaching, her directrice changed her tune. "This professeur," she complained in her annual report, "is too absorbed and depressed by the preoccupations of her private life."[74]

Meanwhile, from Sèvres, until her death in 1894, Mme Favre delivered a similar message to her scattered flock of former students. Repeatedly, she expressed her own support of teachers with heavy family obligations by her willingness to write the ministry on their behalf. She, too, held familial duty in the highest possible regard, and though she herself had never had a child, her enthusiasm for motherhood shines through her personal correspondence. On one occasion, she wrote to an alumna who

Moch, "Government Policy and Women's Experience: The Case of Teachers in France," *Feminist Studies* 14, no. 2 (Summer 1988): 301–24.

[72] Dossier personnel, Adèle Fourcade (married name David), notes, F17 23985, A.N.

[73] Dossier personnel, Adrienne Prieur (married name Besairie), notes, 1897, F17 23738, A.N.

[74] Dossier personnel, Cécilia Terrène (married name Lafleur), notes, 1903, F17 24386, A.N.

had recently given birth: "What a valiant little wife! And how proud your husband must be of you. What a fine little mother you will be when your son returns from the wet-nurse!"[75] If Mme Favre affirmed the importance of the family, however, she never wavered from her view of Sévriennes' professional obligations as a sacred duty. Indeed, in her eyes the two compartments of these professional women's lives, the family and the school, had equal claims upon their moral conscience. Moreover, she expected Sévriennes to show a skeptical public, used to nuns in the role of teacher, that however difficult the task, women could combine professional careers and family obligations without neglecting either one. Her views received the clearest possible statement in the following excerpt from a letter to another former student. "I wonder how you are managing to reconcile your duties as a teacher with those of a mother. You know that I am counting on the students at Sèvres to solve this problem, which seems to me a serious one."[76]

In sum, the image of success held up for Sèvres's alumnae encompassed more than excellence in the classroom, docility toward superiors, and circumspection in their private lives. Everyone whose opinion on their behavior mattered—officials, friends, and, above all, relatives and kin—also expected these young professional women to adopt an attitude of selfless dedication to the family. Those responsible for girls' secondary schools saw that obligation as deriving from the larger charge entrusted to this pioneering generation: to win the public over to advanced, secularized instruction for bourgeois girls. For their part, families in most cases reversed that order of priorities and envisioned the professional lives of working wives and daughters as an extension of their familial duties. Parents depended on their single, working daughters to support and nurture disabled or dependent family members. Husbands, though ambitious sometimes for their wives' careers, saw them also in traditional domestic roles as homemakers and mothers. As different as these tasks might be from what inspectors and directrices required of Sévriennes in schools, they had one thing in common. Everywhere the model of behavior pressed upon these women called for self-abnegation. That very fact, of course, created the likelihood within this generation of a collective vision of themselves as heroic figures. But it prepared the way as well for some deeply painful struggles as these young professionals discovered the boundaries of their lives.

[75] Quoted in Belugou, "Madame Favre," in *La Morale de Plutarque*, 87. The practice of using wet nurses was still common among working women with some means in nineteenth-century France. See George Sussman, *Selling Mothers' Milk: The Wet-Nursing Business in France, 1715–1914* (Urbana: Univ. of Illinois Press, 1982).

[76] Ibid.

Victim, Rebel, or Martyr?
Images of the Young Teacher

AT THIRTY-THREE, Valentine Pasquier (class of 1888), a professeur of science at the collège of Avignon, may have had
more disappointments to look back on than most of Sèvres's
alumnae, but the chagrins and frustrations of her still-young life followed a familiar enough pattern.[1] Disappointed three years in a row in
her efforts to get accepted into Sèvres, in 1888 she finally entered the
school convinced that she had earned through her hard work a bright
career in teaching. Her widowed mother, who "made numerous sacrifices for her daughter's education," shared this confidence and with it
the belief that her daughter would provide for her in her old age. Unfortunately, after leaving Sèvres in 1891 without passing the agrégation,
Pasquier, like some other science teachers, could not get a job in secondary teaching. Instead, she settled for a live-in post as maîtresse répétitrice, which meant her mother could not come to join her.

Four years passed in this unsatisfactory way before Pasquier got a promotion into teaching. Yet even then, bad luck seemed to track her, since
her new position as a collège professeur paid seven hundred francs less
than the twenty-five hundred that municipalities customarily gave beginning teachers.[2] After two years of protesting this injustice, she secured
two temporary appointments in succession, each in different parts of
France. Angered by such callous disregard for her concerns, Pasquier
wrote to the director of secondary education: "In fairness, I cannot be
sent each year from one end of France to the other . . . neither my health
nor my finances permit me so many moves." Moreover, until she got a
"permanent position," she could not take her septuagenarian mother
with her.

Once installed at the second of these posts, Pasquier recovered, for a
short time, something of her earlier trust in her professional future. Her
students liked her, her directrice and inspectors reported favorably on

---

[1] Dossier personnel, F17 23459, A.N.

[2] Ordinarily, when municipalities negotiated with the Ministry of Education to establish a municipal collège, they agreed to pay the faculty according to the official salary
scale. However, in the case of Vic-en-Bigorre, the municipality refused this condition.
This is the only instance I came across in the dossiers of Sévriennes in which municipalities did not pay their collège teachers the going rate.

her teaching, and from temporary, the status of her appointment changed to provisional. Then in her third year of teaching, without warning or any possibility of redress, her course assignments were completely changed. Instead of five math classes, Pasquier's directrice asked her to teach physics and natural science to all six levels in the school. By Christmas, she was sick with flu and had to discontinue teaching. A few weeks later, while at home alone and "in a fit of feverish delirium," according to her doctor, Valentine Pasquier put a bullet through her head.[3]

ANOTHER SÉVRIENNE, Valentine Besnard (class of 1882), managed a very different but in some ways equally violent escape from teaching, though here again mystery veils the conscious or unconscious feelings of rebellion that impelled her. We simply know that sometime in her sixth year of teaching Besnard went quite unexpectedly insane.[4] Her doctor described her condition as "mental derangement characterized by melancholic delirium with notions of grandeur." Certainly Besnard, whom the ministry had sent the year before, in disgrace, to a new school, had objective reasons for experiencing depression, for her reappointment not only injured her professionally, but it also deprived her of a lively social world of friends and family.

Several years before, Besnard's career had gotten off to a slow start when she failed the certificat exam and the ministry made her a maîtresse répétitrice. After she passed the certificat exam, however, she achieved her heart's desire: a professorship in the collège closest to her parents' home. Delighted with her fate, Besnard apparently worked very hard at teaching.[5] On the other hand, since she had no desire to leave her collège for a lycée, she saw no reason to study for the agrégation. Instead, she spent her free time socializing, a choice of which both her directrice and academy inspector strongly disapproved. In the end, they managed to convince the rector that this teacher's refusal to prepare for the agrégation and to lead a less active social life amounted to insubordination.

In punishment and over her anguished objections, the ministry reassigned Besnard to another collège, several hundred kilometers from home. There, according to her new directrice, the chastened Besnard, "living absolutely without social relations, worked throughout the winter toward the agrégation." By springtime she was diagnosed insane.

[3] The rector reported the doctor's theory that Pasquier committed suicide while delirious from fever.

[4] Dossier personnel, Valentine Besnard, F17 23207, A.N.

[5] The inspectors who visited her classes generally approved of what they heard and saw, and according to the directrice, she had a good reputation among the students.

Upon her entry into the asylum where her family placed her, Besnard's doctor sounded an optimistic note: "This malady, which originated recently, appears curable to us." In fact, Valentine Besnard never returned to teaching, and when she died in 1912, she may well have been an inmate of the asylum still.

A THIRD SÉVRIENNE, even more obviously in revolt against conditions pressed on her by teaching in this new profession, refused to accept a humiliating demotion; instead she forced the ministry to dismiss her. Ironically, this ultimate sanction could not have been imposed on a more brilliant teacher. Juliette Delaprez's (class of 1884) dossier brims with recognition for her talents.[6] First at the agrégation in science in 1887, she gave, according to the chairman of the jury, "the best oral presentation in physics and natural history since the women's agrégation began." In 1890 her academy inspector described her as "remarkably gifted," while her rector found her "absolutely the mistress of her subject." The following year the inspector general responsible for her last inspection was "very impressed by her qualities as a professeur."

Alongside praise for her ability as a teacher, critical remarks appeared on Delaprez's independent manners, a defect that some of her superiors attributed to her being Swiss. Thus, her first rector, in assessing her debut at the lycée of Rouen warned, "[She] has the initiative of a young woman raised in Switzerland; one could even imagine her American; that is a praiseworthy frame of mind, but at Rouen, where everything which is new alarms, it would better to temper Mlle Delaprez's ardor." On bad terms with her directrice at Rouen, she managed nonetheless to get appointed to the lycée of her choice at Nice. Within a year her uninhibited style had strained relations there with all her local chefs as well as certain parents. The directrice found that "her conduct and language diverged from good taste and accepted usage." The academy inspector described her as "an eccentric whose upbringing appears deficient." And the inspector general, who for his own part found her "conduct . . . irreproachable," concluded that "she has in her manner a certain independence that seems to have displeased some local families." All three recommended her appointment elsewhere.

Unfortunately, the only post open at the time in science was at Caen in a cours secondaire, hardly the sort of place an agrégée expected to be sent. Horrified at what appeared to her to be an unmerited and totally unexpected humiliation, Delaprez resisted, first by defending her behav-

[6] F17 23276, A.N.

ior, then by pretending to be sick, and finally by refusing to show up. For as she explained in a letter to the ministry, "having done nothing wrong, I could not accept a post that would pass in the general opinion for a punishment and, consequently, a merited demotion." Hoping for a better position in the future, she assured the ministry, "I will wait patiently . . . , and I will try to find at Marseille some sort of work to support myself and not be a burden to anyone." In a fury, the director of secondary education responded by explaining her reappointment as the result of "problems with the directrice at Nice," her "willful disdain for certain proprieties," and her "unwillingness to take the counsel of her critics." He then declared her in a "state of inactivity as a disciplinary measure." The next year, with no explanation to be found either in her dossier or in the alumnae bulletin at Sèvres, Juliette Delaprez was dead. A victim of bad health? an accident? or perhaps another suicide? Once again, as in the case of Valentine Pasquier, the records shroud the death of a young Sévrienne in mystery.

IN SOME WAYS these three cases veer dramatically from the typical experience of the first generation of Sévriennes as young teachers. Neither suicide nor madness represented a common response to the hardships that these women faced as young professionals. No other dossiers leave the impression that suicide might explain an early death. Moreover, although stress clearly prompted emotional and physical disorders, sometimes even bizarre behavior, no other teacher lost control of her psyche so completely that a doctor declared her to have gone insane. Even instances in which a single woman voluntarily cut short her career for reasons other than a pending marriage or bad health proved exceptionally rare, probably because those who hated what they did either could not afford to quit or found the alternatives hardly more inviting.[7] Yet if the cases recounted here illustrate extreme reactions, they highlight all the better the pressures under which other teachers like them labored. Nothing in the adversities that these three teachers confronted sets them apart from former schoolmates.

Unquestionably, teachers in the early years of their professional lives

[7] I discovered only four cases of Sévriennes who, though unmarried, left teaching voluntarily: Louise Bouvard (class of 1886), Gabrielle De Burrine (class of 1886), Alice Grombach (class of 1884), and Louise Roussel (class of 1884). De Burrine and Grombach ostensibly had more pressing duties to perform at home. After her mother died, De Burrine did, in fact, return to teaching in order to support her father and younger brother. See dossier personnel, Gabrielle De Burrine, F17 23744, A.N., and obituary notice for Alice Grombach by A. Dreuilhe, *BAES* (1924): 4–5.

suffered in one way or another from the pressures elaborated on in the previous two chapters. Hardly a dossier fails to give some sign of friction or distress in these young women's lives; a sizable number report some major crisis. Thus, the response of Sévriennes individually to the multiple expectations placed upon them forms the subject of the next phase of this study. This topic offers more than biographical interest, for Sévriennes' own notions of success as well as their reactions to the demands of families and superiors measure the extent to which they belonged to a distinctive professional culture. On the fringes of possible response lay insanity, resigning from the corps, or suicide. Arguably such solutions, however exceptional, represent extensions of behavior rather typical of young teachers in this generation. Insanity, if understood to represent the complete collapse of an overtaxed psyche, falls within the general pattern of a generation plagued by nervous ailments. Resigning to avoid humiliation was a rebellious gesture different only in its rashness from many others made by Sévriennes with injured pride. Even suicide fits into the professional profile of this generation if understood to be a radical expression of self-denial. Out of the effort to interpret the evidence of conflict and stress in teachers' dossiers, we can piece together the image of this female profession in the making.

The Ailing Teacher

Of all the bits of evidence pointing to distress among young teachers, the most pervasive and convincing concern their state of health. In a veritable litany, requests for sick leaves lasting from two weeks to as much as a year echo through the correspondence in their dossiers. Augustine Frémont (class of 1881) could not continue teaching after three years: "a nervous affliction combined with cerebral anemia," requiring twelve months' rest, sent her ailing to her bed.[8] After only four months of teaching, Marie Lardley (class of 1888) developed "chronic bronchitis."[9] The remainder of the year she spent in Paris, convalescing in her parents' home. At thirty-two, Marie Delbosc (class of 1889) suffered from "acute depression, nervousness, headaches, and exhaustion" and asked for five months off. When a facial tic developed and her eyes began to fail, the leave of absence lengthened into years.[10] It would be easy to multiply such examples. Clearly, illness stalked these teachers, even in the bloom of young adulthood: 40 percent had serious health

[8] Dossier personnel, Augustine Frémont, correspondance, 1887, F17 22445, A.N.

[9] Dossier personnel, Marie Lardley (married name Jaudel), correspondance, 1892, F17 23923, A.N.

[10] Dossier personnel, Marie Delbosc, correspondance, 1901, F17 23277, A.N.

problems in their first ten years of teaching; by midcareer the rate would rise to 60. Ten Sévriennes would die before they even got that far.

Most often this medical history records chronic rather than acute disorders. Teachers certainly caught occasional flus and colds or childhood diseases that they had escaped when young, but that fact rarely finds its way into the record. Typically, the ailments diagnosed by doctors in the medical statements that accompanied applications for a leave were of long duration and had recently entered an exacerbated state. Since doctors did not always provide a diagnosis in their reports or agree on common labels for the same complaints, the only way to compare one illness with another is to group afflicted teachers according to their symptoms. The result, displayed in table 6.1, reveals a pathology characteristic of the whole profession. Women teachers in the early stages of their careers suffered mainly from nervous disorders, anemia, and infections of their lungs and throat. Brief indispositions showed up infrequently in personnel reports because for short-term absences, teachers avoided taking leaves. Instead of officially requesting time off work, they preferred, whenever possible, to rely on colleagues to pick up classes for them.[11]

[handwritten margin note: ✓ most common]

TABLE 6.1
Teachers' Illnesses in Early Career

Complaint	Cases	Percent of Total
Nervous disorders (neurasthenia[a])	21	22.3
Anemia (chloro-anemia, cerebral anemia)[a]	19	20.2
Persistent chest and throat ailments	17	18.1
Failing eyesight	4	4.2
Rheumatism and arthritis	4	4.2
Diseased organs: kidney, heart, liver	4	4.2
Tumor	1	1.1
Acute diseases	3	3.2
Unknown	21	22.3
Total	94[b]	99.8[c]

Sources: Tabulated from dossiers personnels, series F17, A.N.

[a] When a diagnosis did accompany a list of symptoms of this sort, these were the diseases named.

[b] Teachers whose illnesses involved different types of symptoms will be recorded more than once. The total number of teachers who took sick leaves during their first ten years of teaching was eighty-four out of the two hundred teachers who remained in teaching at least four years after leaving Sèvres.

[c] This figure does not reach 100 percent as a result of rounding off numbers.

[11] Sometimes, a woman married to another secondary teacher even had her husband take her place.

Sick leave did not count toward retirement before 1897, which made it financially unattractive in the long run.[12] More important, those who took it had no assurance of a salary while on leave. As a matter of practice, the ministry usually gave female secondary teachers one month off at full pay and two months at half their salary whenever they fell seriously ill. Exceptionally, a teacher ill beyond three months might receive half salary for two more months.[13] If the ministry or the directrice of a school ran short of funds to pay for her replacement, however, an ailing teacher had to cover those expenses from her salary even in the first month of her leave.[14] In this respect the personnel of girls' schools suffered a serious disadvantage by comparison with faculty in boys' collèges and lycées. Under the decree of 1853, which applied to the men's profession only, a teacher had no obligation to pay the salary of the teacher who replaced him.[15] Moreover, he could count on fifteen days at full pay as a legal right and up to three months at full pay and three more at half pay with ministerial permission. Indeed, for male teachers a full year of leave with salary was not out of the question.[16] Matched against that standard, the conditions imposed on ailing women teachers who requested leaves appear at once draconian and capricious. Sévriennes with nothing but their salaries for support or with financial obligations to their families could ill afford to take time off under such terms.

Nevertheless, by the middle of the 1890s the incidence of medical leaves for women teachers surpassed the rates of absence for male teachers. The ministry never published the relevant statistics. But Dugard, who claimed to have examined official tables comparing requests for leaves by men and women professeurs, made the difference between them the basis of her article on overwork within the feminine profession.[17] Concern over the health of women teachers grew sufficiently at

[12] By the decree of July 1897, the ministry changed this practice and made the time spent on a paid sick leave count toward a teacher's years of service. Dossier personnel, Pauline Grandjean (married name Blanc), correspondance, 1904, F17 23893, A.N. For an example of the lasting impact of the earlier practice on a teacher's income, see the dossier personnel of Adrienne Prieur (married name Besairie), correspondance, F17 23738, A.N.

[13] The ministry generally refused to pay the summer salary of any woman teacher who missed July, the last month of the school year. Indeed, at its parsimonious worst, it would not permit a teacher who had taken off before July to return to work in the final weeks of school precisely to avoid paying her a summer salary.

[14] So little remained sometimes after such deductions that one husband complained it did not even cover his wife's medical bills. See the dossier personnel of Marie Friedlowska (married name Jouennes d'Esgrigny), correspondance, 1892, F17 23608, A.N.

[15] Decree of November 8, 1853.

[16] Mayeur, *L'Enseignement secondaire*, 292n.1.

[17] Dugard, "Du surménage," 129.

Sèvres by the turn of the century to affect the ministry's procedures for recruiting students. Beginning in the later 1890s, medical examinations, which had always been a part of screening candidates for Sèvres, would receive additional consideration by the jury deciding who should have a place at Sèvres.

One might expect this medical history to have spread the view among observers that women's procreative organs made them physically and emotionally incapable of withstanding the demands of this profession. That, after all, represented the prevailing medical opinion throughout the nineteenth century, and opponents of Camille Sée's two laws had repeatedly declared that the mind and body of the female did not suit her naturally for intellectual work. Nonetheless, those closest to the problem—teachers, their doctors, and their immediate superiors—invariably sought other explanations. A running record of their views accumulated around the numerous appeals for sick leaves that appear in teachers' files. Doctors writing medical excuses frequently noted the causes of the ailments they described. Teachers or patrons supporting their appeals often appended to a request for sick leave an account of how and when their illnesses began. As a request for sick leave moved up the administrative ladder, directrices and rectors added their opinions on the supplicant's state of health. Taken together, these observations clearly suggest the medical frame of reference of those closest to the problem. Invariably, those who offered an explanation attributed the maladies besetting teachers to the stress that they were under in their work or in their homes or to the adverse effects of an insalubrious climate. Throughout the references to nervous diseases, anemia, or throat and lung infections in these dossiers, not one observer laid the blame for teachers' aliments on their gender.

Among the varied explanations found in teachers' dossiers for their ailments, overwork easily outnumbered all the others. When Louise Beuque (class of 1881) fell ill in her second year of teaching, first with "dyspepsia," then with "anemia, complicated by very violent neuralgia," her doctor reported her a victim of "an excess of work over the last three years." The patient concurred with that opinion, attributing her problems to a "state of health already compromised by my work at Sèvres [and] gravely altered by the fatigue of my first two years of teaching."[18] Likewise, Anne Massen (class of 1887), who avoided an official leave of absence, suffered from chronically bad health as a young teacher, a situation that her academy inspector blamed on overwork. Indeed, she risked "cerebral anemia," in her inspector's view, if she continued in her

---

[18] Dossier personnel, Louise Beuque, correspondance, 1885, F17 23671, A.N.

"ardor [and] enthusiasm for teaching" to sacrifice herself so unstintingly for students.[19] As for Louise Bruneau (class of 1886), who had to take a year off in her thirteenth year of teaching, her directrice described her to the rector as "sick because she worked with too much ardor for her students," while her doctor diagnosed her to be "suffering from neurasthenia as a result of too much work."[20]

Sometimes, though, observers of health problems among teachers saw in a specific case of illness the effects of private anguish on a teacher's body. Julie Esménard, for instance, blamed her ill health in her second year of teaching on loneliness. "My health suffers very much from the isolated state to which I have been reduced," she informed the minister in her formal request for a position near her siblings' home.[21] Likewise, when at age thirty-three Henriette Gonel (class of 1887) collapsed with what her doctor diagnosed as "anemia," her rector in a letter to the minister identified the tragedies that had destroyed her health: "Already deeply shaken by the long illness and death of her sister, Mlle Gonel has just lost her youngest nephew." Meanwhile at the ministry, an intramural note revealed that having paid all the expenses for the two funerals, Gonel had fallen "into a state of grave material and moral distress."[22] In another case of illness linked to emotional upset, Clara Marsat Poirot (class of 1888) attributed an extremely painful case of rheumatism in her second year of marriage to the anguish she experienced living separated from her husband because they could not get two teaching posts together.[23]

The only other explanation for a teacher's ailments that cropped up occasionally in dossiers implicated the ill effects of weather. Wet and cold climates proved especially noxious to the health of teachers, but hot, dry, or windy environments caused difficulties, too; the types of climate teachers found particularly harmful depended in most cases on

[19] Dossier personnel, Anne Massen, notes, 1896, F17 24087, A.N.

[20] Dossier personnel, Louise Bruneau, correspondance, 1901, F17 23976, A.N.

[21] An orphan, Esménard had been raised by her sister and brother-in-law in Marseille. At the time of her complaint, she was teaching at Tournon. Dossier personnel, correspondance, F17 23991, 1892, A.N.

[22] Because Gonel taught in the Academy of Paris, her rector's formal title was vice-rector. Dossier personnel, Henriette Gonel (married name Bohren), correspondance, 1898, F17 23919, A.N.

[23] This explanation appeared in a letter from a deputy who petitioned the minister of education on behalf of the separated couple. Marsat married the brother of Berthe Poirot (class of 1891), a Sévrienne with whom she taught, which explains why, at the time she married, she and her new husband had teaching posts in different towns. Dossier personnel, Clara Marsat (married name Poirot), correspondance, 1901, F17 24098, A.N.

what they had been used to.[24] Some teachers actually claimed that they could not adapt to climates radically different from the one in which they grew up. Thus, Mathilde Rouxel (class of 1888) refused in midcareer to take a post offered to her at Laval because, as she explained, "In the west of France, I feel isolated, painfully out of my element, and I am constantly sick, the climate being completely pernicious for me."[25] Born in Châteauroux, raised at Pau, she apparently had suffered greatly during six years as a répétitrice at Lorient.[26] Marie Lépine (class of 1886), a southerner by upbringing, felt the same way about the climate she encountered at Reims. Acknowledging the general problem, one of the deputies from the Landes, a fellow southerner, wrote a sympathetic note on behalf of her request to leave: "Mlle Lépine, having just spent a harsh winter in Reims, whose climate does not suit young women from the Midi, . . . suffered severely."[27] But not all problems stemming from climate originated in a sense of being out of one's natural element. Marguerite Lejeune's request to leave Paris for the Midi on medical grounds stands out as one exception since she grew up in an even harsher climate at Cherbourg.[28]

Interpreting the implications of such medical excuses can, of course, be tricky since those who made them had specific goals in mind. Invariably, the principal objective for a teacher was to win approval at the ministry. Those requesting lenient financial terms for leaves of absence clearly strengthened their position if overwork explained an illness. Failing that excuse, as ailing teachers surely understood, exceptional service in the exercise of family duties could also strike a sympathetic chord. As for complaints about unhealthy climates, when voiced by teachers aching to get closer to their families—arguably, such medical excuses represent transparent efforts to get a transfer to a school near home. One might even anticipate in this regard a certain complicity between teachers and their doctors or between teachers and immediate superiors won over to their cause. All the same, even if a degree of calculation shaped some medical reports, for the complicity of teachers, doctors, and superiors to take the form it did required more than recognition that such

[24] Although most complaints focused on the bad climate of the North, Northwest, and central France, Anne Rollet Saussotte (class of 1884), who grew up in the Southeast at Dôle and Grenoble, complained that the excessive heat of Algeria as well as the rain and cold of Guéret had ruined her health. Dossier personnel, Anne Rollet (married name Saussotte), correspondance, 1891, F17 24029.

[25] Dossier personnel, Mathilde Rouxel (class of 1888), correspondance, F17 23954, 1910, A.N.

[26] Ibid., 1896, 1899.

[27] Dossier personnel, Marie Lépine, correspondance, 1893, F17 23856, A.N.

[28] Dossier personnel, Marguerite Lejeune, F17 22953, A.N.

excuses would earn approval at the ministry. To be convincing, explanations for an ailing teacher's troubles had to correspond to a pathology at once familiar and accepted in this professional milieu. By the 1890s, French medical science had developed just the kind of diagnostic model that ensured teachers' ability to attribute a multiplicity of symptoms to emotional stress, especially stress arising from their work, and to get away with it.

Neurasthenia and the Woman Professeur

Ever since the eighteenth century, French medicine had associated illness with the fatigue of intellectual work.[29] In the early Third Republic, during the national debate touched off by Michel Bréal's critique of boys' lycées, that medical tradition enjoyed a popular revival. The main complaint of Bréal and his supporters was that secondary students suffered physically and emotionally from overwork. Surménage, they claimed, had become the scourge of public secondary education and threatened to destroy the health of the republic's future leaders before they even reached their prime. By the later 1880s, physicians had identified in neurasthenia the illness to which the style of life in secondary schools gave rise. As a consequence of this debate, the idea of neurasthenia, which its American inventor George M. Beard attributed to modern urban life, would merge in France with long-held medical suspicions of the damaging effects of mental strain.[30]

However, as French doctors' interest in the illness grew, so did the range of social groups that they identified as likely victims of this modern epidemic. At the outset, Dr. Lagneau, the physician who in 1886 first sounded the alarm before the Academy of Medicine, proclaimed schoolboys to be most seriously affected. He laid the blame on "mental fatigue, sedentary habits, and poor hygiene."[31] J. M. Charcot agreed with Lagneau on the group at greatest risk, but he attributed the nervous disorders rampant among schoolboys to the Université's intensely competitive national exams. "At the age of sixteen, seventeen, or eighteen, when beginning a career involves passing exams like the baccalauréat or those which are required for admission to special schools," Charcot warned,

---

[29] Daniel Roche, "L'Intellectuel au travail," *Annales (économies, sociétés, civilisations)* 37, no. 3 (1982): 465–80.

[30] George M. Beard, *A Practical Treatise on Nervous Exhaustion (Neurasthenia)* (New York: W. Wood, 1905). Beard first published on the subject in 1869.

[31] Quoted in Dr. Jadwiga Szejko, *L'Influence de l'éducation sur le développement de la neurasthénie* (Lyon: A. Rey, 1902), 56. The next year the Academy of Medicine decided to form a commission to study the question.

"neurasthenia becomes widespread, raging fiercely and tenaciously."[32] Other physicians, though, focused on the pathology of neurasthenia among young men who had gone through this rite of passage and were engaged in launching a career. In their epidemiological models, neurasthenia germinated above all in those milieus where ambition and mental exertion jointly ruled. Ferdinand Levillain made professional life the foremost crucible for neurasthenic victims.[33] Another leading expert on the subject, L. Bouveret, considered any occupation that demanded "considerable intellectual work" and provoked "long-lasting and intense moral preoccupations" capable of producing the condition. In contrast, among occupational groups not subject to such concerns, such as "bureaucrats and civil servants, people who have few worries concerning the result of the business that they handle, whose future is more or less assured, and whose tasks are limited and well defined," Bouveret maintained, "neurasthenia is extremely rare."[34] Ambition, in other words, and its darker side, the fear of failure, counted for as much in neurasthenic disorders as excessive mental effort.

← fear of failure

This broadening of the epidemiological model to embrace emotional worries permitted French physicians to identify as neurasthenics even certain of their middle-class female patients who, though not engaged in intellectual work, did occasionally suffer deep anxiety. The affection and responsibility that bound women to their families meant that they, too, inhabited a world of high expectations and uncertain outcomes. According to Dr. Bouveret, pregnant women and mothers of infants, who faced "the nightly vigils, the care, the worries caused by the new baby's illnesses" were particularly likely to develop neurasthenia.[35] But other preoccupations linked to private traumas might precipitate a neurasthenic crisis. "Neurasthenia frequently develops in the wake of prolonged grief, a sudden reversal of fortune, thwarted projects, unhappy love affairs," A. Mathieu claimed. "The illness or death of close relatives, a spouse, or one's children often has an influence of this sort."[36] Men as well as women, of course, could suffer from any of these shocks or disappointments with the same effect.

The only difference between the sexes in the pattern of the malady, according to most experts, was its greater frequency in men.[37] "This un-

---

[32] J. M. Charcot, preface, in *La Neurasthénie: maladie de Beard*, by Dr. Ferdinand Levillain (Paris: A. Maloine, 1891), x.

[33] Ibid., 38–39.

[34] Dr. L. Bouveret, *La Neurasthénie: épuisement nerveux* (Paris: Baillière, 1891), 24.

[35] Ibid., 23.

[36] Dr. A. Mathieu, *Neurasthénie (épuisement nerveux)* (Paris: J. Rueff, 1892), 5.

[37] The one discordant voice that I encountered on this subject belonged to Dr. Emile

equal distribution of the illness . . . cannot be explained by a special pre-disposition of the masculine sex," A. Proust and G. Ballet maintained. Rather, it reflected "the preponderant influence of obsessive work, wor-ries, excesses of all sorts, which are the consequences of a more active and militant role of the man in the struggle for existence."[38] For women to experience similar levels of nervous exhaustion merely required their exposure to the same pressures as those which middle-class men con-fronted in their work.

Thus, when young women teachers arrived in doctors' offices drawn and pale, complaining of sleeplessness, headaches, gastritis, even ar-thritic, aching joints, a ready explanation lay at hand. They were simply the casualties of a profession widely recognized to be pernicious to good health and were probably suffering the effects of neurasthenia. That di-agnosis was all the easier to reach because the ailments recognized as symptomatic of the disorder were so varied.[39] Indeed, since hypochon-dria was itself a symptom, the complaints of neurasthenics had no pre-determined limits. Consequently, when doctors attributed the sufferings of women teachers to excessive work, they made their diagnosis on the basis of prevailing medical opinion. They did not deliberately intend thereby to get the best terms possible for patients requesting sick leave. Likewise, when they complained that separation from a husband, social isolation, or caring for a dying relative had made them sick, teachers spoke from within a culture that recognized such explanations to be medically valid. They did not, in other words, have to invent medical excuses designed to gain approval at the ministry for the duties they per-formed. Doctors, school officials, as well as Sévriennes themselves rec-ognized the possibility that the faithful execution of a teacher's multi-

---

Laurent, who claimed that neurasthenia attacked people from the ages of twenty-five to fifty and especially women. Contradictorily, he also claimed that "it hits particularly those engaged in intellectual work, but no profession is safe." He further noted that Jews and Slavs were the most likely victims. This sociological grab bag suggests a re-actionary political outlook. In any case, it stands far outside the mainstream of medical opinion in the mid-1890s. Dr. Emile Laurent, *La Neurasthénie et son traitement vade-mecum du médecin praticien* (Paris: A. Maloine, 1895), 7.

[38] A. Proust and G. Ballet, *L'Hygiène du neurasthénique* (Paris: Masson, 1897), 13.

[39] Specialists agreed that symptomatically the disease varied, even dramatically, from one patient to another. For as exhaustive a list of symptoms as I found in the extensive literature on the subject, see Dr. Ferdinand Levillain, *La Neurasthénie: maladie de Beard* (Paris: A. Maloine, 1891). M. Huchard, the first French physician to give a learned description of "Beard's malady," particularly emphasized the links between neurasthenia and arthritis, according to Mathieu, *Neurasthénie*, 12. See also Dr. R. Vi-gouroux, *Neurasthénie et arthritisme* (Paris: A. Maloine, 1893); and Szejko, *L'Influence*, 24–25, 44–45.

sided duties to her school and family might well result in a serious deterioration of her health.

That perception could hardly fail to shape the way these women conceptualized their plight as young professionals. They might see themselves as hapless victims of unjust demands. Alternatively, they could imagine themselves as martyrs, whose personal tribulations paled when placed beside the interests of those they loved or served. Which of these responses they, in fact, adopted belongs to the much larger story of sacrifice and defiance that framed the life experience of this generation of teachers. For in the early years, at least, poor health was only one of many ways in which Sévriennes sensed themselves under permanent siege. Mistrusted by the public, peripheral in the Université, these pioneers of their profession felt beset from every side. Inevitably, their reactions differed, but the episodes in teachers' dossiers that reveal their struggles create a collective portrait all the same. The image of this generation wears two faces. One—proud, sometimes stormily resentful—depicts a teacher determined to stand her ground against incursions on her rights. The other—also often proud, though obsequious or plaintive on occasion—reveals a woman self-consciously posed in abnegation. Precisely how these faces alternated in the lives of this professional generation, as its members moved from young adulthood through middle age toward their retirement, now becomes a central focus of this study.

The Rebellious Teacher

In their medical petitions and requests for transfers, Sévriennes presented themselves to the administration as hardworking functionaries, dutiful servants of familial interests, and humble supplicants subject to a benevolent paternalism. Based solely on reports by their superiors, however, what stands out about this generation's early years in teaching is the image of the rebellious teacher. Certainly not every Sévrienne behaved defiantly toward the administration as a young professional. At most a quarter of their dossiers cite an instance of insubordination. Nevertheless, even that number assumes importance when compared to administrators' highly favorable impressions of these women a decade after their initiation into teaching. The timing of the rebelliousness is significant since the resentments underlying it grew largely out of individual teachers' pride in newly acquired professional credentials. Indeed, most of the young Sévriennes involved in confrontations had recently experienced the heady triumph of a successful showing at the feminine agrégation.

Inevitably, women who entered teaching with the dual title of Sévrienne and agrégée believed their talents superior. Repeated successes at professional exams and competitions offered in their own eyes indisputable proof of their exceptional ability to teach. That self-assessment, which the best students at Sèvres carried with them to their teaching posts, let many of them in for a surprise. Anticipating only admiration from inspectors, instead these luminaries from the tiny world of Sèvres often got critiques from supervisors prompt to offer their advice. For their part, rectors and inspectors, whose age, experience, and patronizing attitudes toward the feminine profession led them to expect these teachers' deference, resented deeply any sign of disrespect. Even worse were interventions by a school directrice who insisted on her rights to oversee her teachers but often lacked, in the view of her Sévrienne subordinates, the requisite professional credentials. In the conflicts and animosities to which these differing expectations unavoidably gave rise, an atmosphere of tension settled over girls' secondary schools. This embattled phase did not last long in the history of the institution, but its consequences were disastrous for the careers of occasional Sévriennes. More important for the generation as a whole, from the countless little episodes of friction as well as from major confrontations, Sévriennes would soon construct a lore around their early years of teaching in which they portrayed themselves as hapless victims.

The reproaches leveled by inspectors and rectors at young teachers leave little doubt about the nature of the conflict. The academy inspector at the collège of Auxerre fumed in two different reports on Lucie Ravaire (class of 1884), "[This professeur] has difficulty conforming to the regulations: nature a bit capricious, very inclined toward independence"; "[she] refuses to make her mind up to prepare an outline or a summary, turns a deaf ear to advice."[40] In a similar explosion, an infuriated rector at Nice reported concerning Ravaire's classmate and fellow agrégée Marthe Verdheillan, "[She] relies on what she calls her dossier de Sèvres to avoid paying any attention to unfavorable observations."[41] An inspector general reviewing teachers at Auxerre two years before Ravaire arrived took umbrage at Natalie Georges's (class of 1883) indifference to his counsel, which he defined as an instance of the more general problem of self-important Sévriennes. "She spoils her qualities with a confidence and self-satisfaction that we have met too often among students of . . . Sèvres."[42] Meanwhile, at Lyon, Marie Lacharrière's (class of 1881) rector wrote scathingly of her professional pretensions, "[She] thinks that she

[40] Dossier personnel, Lucie Ravaire, notes, 1890 and 1891, F17 23949, A.N.

[41] Dossier personnel, Marthe Verdeilhan, notes, 1888, F17 23806, A.N.

[42] Dossier personnel, Natalie Georges (married name Beuque), notes, 1887/88, F17 22602, A.N.

is capable of teaching the most difficult subjects and is surprised an agrégée is not completely equal in all respects with an agrégé."[43]

Clearly, the lack of modesty in certain Sévriennes shocked their male
inspectors not just because they found it graceless in a woman but even
more because it demonstrated, in these officials' view, an unjustified
pride in their achievements. Rectors and inspectors, who had themselves
come from the ranks of secondary teaching but boasted masculine degrees, refused to treat the titles earned by women teachers with the same
respect. As for the women, confirmed in their ability by the opinion of
the various juries that had admitted them to Sèvres, awarded them the
certificat of secondary teaching, and finally crowned them with honor at
the agrégation, they believed themselves to be completely competent in
their own professional sphere. More than symbolic gestures were involved here. The real struggle pitting rebellious Sévriennes against their
rectors and inspectors focused on control of the classroom. Beneath all
these conflicts lay a basic disagreement over the amount of freedom from
supervision to which their proven excellence entitled agrégées.

Sévriennes did not invent the tug-of-war between secondary teachers
and an administration determined to get control of the classroom
through the influence and power of its inspectors. That contest had its
roots in a long-standing conflict between the centralizing goals of the
state and the pedagogical assumptions operating in secondary eduction.
On its side, the Ministry of Education had envisioned since Napoleonic
days a schooling system closely supervised from Paris and synchronized
in a kind of military lockstep. To that end, the ministry laid down a single schedule of classes for the entire system of public secondary schools,
determined a set syllabus for every course, and required every secondary
student who aspired to a university education to sit for the national exam
called the baccalauréat. One of the major tasks of school inspectors was
to see that every teacher conformed to the decrees regulating this academic program. With these objectives, the teaching profession had no
apparent quarrel. Indeed, when teachers gained complete control of the
governing board of the Université after 1880, the principle of centraliza-
tion remained inviolate. On the other hand, throughout the nineteenth
century, the profession stressed the role of personal genius and creative
individuality in successful teaching.[44] That tenet had given men in the
profession considerable leverage against inspectors and especially
against interference in their teaching methods. As long as the profession
continued to treat teaching not as a science with rules that could be

[43] Dossier personnel, Marie Lacharrière, notes, 1885, F17 22930, A.N.

[44] Zeldin, France 1848–1945, 2: 312–13.

taught but rather as an art which only the truly gifted person ever mastered, teachers at the top of their profession felt protected from the pedagogical zeal of their inspectors.[45]

It was not surprising that something of that professional outlook invaded girls' secondary schools with the arrival of teachers who, after three years of study at Sèvres, had topped their previous achievements with a triumph at the agrégation. Throughout the 1880s, this traditional view of teaching had prevailed at Sèvres. No course on pedagogy figured in the school's curriculum, nor was there any practice teaching apart from preparing lessons for delivery to one's classmates. Instead, the school encouraged students, especially those in letters, to read widely, reflect on what they read, and in so doing fashion an intellectual personality of their own. The ideal materialized for students in the classes of the school's most memorable teachers. As for Sévriennes who passed the agrégation, they had done so precisely because they managed to impart to their responses originality and force. Understandably, with such a background, these women came to teaching convinced that they did and ought to have authority over what happened in their classrooms.

All the same, if the defiance of young teachers occasionally brought the wrath of rectors and inspectors down upon them, it did not result in any serious damage to their futures. The evidence in this regard seems quite conclusive. Of the four women cited as examples, Lucie Ravaire became a maîtresse répétitrice at Sèvres;[46] Marthe Verdheillan exchanged her post at Nice for another at Marseille, the largest girls' lycée in southeastern France;[47] while Marie Lacharrière got a promotion up from teaching to the directorate of a new lycée.[48] Only Natalie Georges experienced a temporary setback in her professional advancement, but this reversal in her fortunes resulted not from clashes with inspectors over pedagogy but from a far more dangerous collision with her school directrice.[49] Moreover, to win such favors, none of these women appears to have adopted an obsequious manner in dealing with inspectors. They simply succeeded in convincing their superiors of their real ability as teachers. In a profession steeped in the ethos of merit and reverent toward the virtuoso teacher, inspectors and rectors in the end always supported the

---

[45] In the 1890s, as we shall see in chap. 8, republican pedagogues began an effort that would prove only partially successful to change that perception of the act of teaching and to give their own inspectors more authority over teachers' techniques in the classroom.

[46] Dossier personnel, Lucie Ravaire, F17 23949, A.N.

[47] Dossier personnel, Marthe Verdeilhan, F17 23806, A.N.

[48] Dossier personnel, Marie Lacharrière, F17 22930, A.N.

[49] Dossier personnel, Natalie Georges, F17 22602, A.N.

advancement of a woman of undeniable talent in the classroom, as long as her behavior outside class did not give rise to any serious offense.

Rather more hazardous for their careers were the clashes that many Sévriennes had with a directrice. Indeed, most of the turbulence documented in teachers' dossiers for the founding period of girls' secondary schools, rather than involving male inspectors, grew out of conflicts of this sort. Two factors in particular explain these frequent confrontations. In the first place, directrices of girls' secondary schools had far more authority over teachers than principals exercised over faculty in boys' schools.[50] That in itself caused friction between Sévriennes and their school heads. The second and more serious problem, however, lay in the kind of women selected to head the new girls' schools. In order to fill these posts with women who could insure student recruitment, the ministry did not look to the youthful graduates of Sèvres. Those in charge of these appointments turned instead to older women, who sometimes possessed at most a brevet supérieur as a professional credential.[51] Their appeal for the administration lay in their ability to dispel the fears of local families who either knew of them by reputation or considered long experience in primary instruction to be a guarantee of competence and morals.[52] While parents may have felt secure with such women at the head of the new schools, Sévriennes, and especially the most talented of them, frequently did not. Their presence in secondary schools for girls set the stage for several years of intermittent sparring between resentful teachers, on one side, and, on the other, directrices threatened by the challenge to their authority from better-qualified subordinates, who themselves sometimes aspired to administrative posts.[53]

Merely imposing their authority raised serious problems for several of these first directrices. Sometimes they complained about the attitudes of insubordinate teachers in their own evaluations. More often, though, they reserved their most acerbic comments for oral interviews with rectors and inspectors who would repeat the denunciation in their own reports. Thus, we learn from the academy inspector that Louise Roussiez's (class of 1885) directrice at Reims found "her closed to all advice [and]

[50] For a discussion of the duties of directrices see chap. 7. See also Mayeur, *L'Enseignement secondaire,* 175–78.

[51] In 1887, of the twenty directrices of lycées, seven had only primary teaching credentials, four had masculine degrees, either the baccalauréat or the licence, one had the certificate of secondary education for girls, and eight were agrégées. In the twenty-three collèges during the same year, seventeen directrices had only primary credentials; of these, three had just the brevet élémentaire. Of the remaining six, there were two bachelières, two certifiées, and two agrégées. Ibid., 177 and 177n.6.

[52] Ibid., 176–77.

[53] Israël-Wahl, "Mes Débuts," in *Le Cinquantenaire,* 383.

infatuated with herself."[54] Likewise, the academy inspector at Saint Etienne described Madeleine Sébastien Rudler (class of 1887) thus: "Polite with the directrice but accepts her observations with poor grace and a long face."[55] Another academy inspector actually witnessed the disdain lavished by Gabrielle Chavance (class of 1888) on the head of her collège at Vitry-le-François: "Contradicted every assertion of Madame the directrice in a shocking manner in class and in front of me. She appeared very surprised when I rebuked her."[56] As for Marie Meynier (class of 1886), when an inspector general learned from her directrice at Tarbes that she had refused to teach a class in physics because she preferred a course in natural history, he not only attacked what he described as her "caprice" but also noted the endemic nature of the problem: "In collèges and too often in lycées, women teachers do not consider themselves subject to any regulations."[57]

As long as teachers worked hard and possessed the proper credentials for their posts, a muted resistance to a school directrice confined to school affairs did not ordinarily jeopardize their futures. Indeed, male superiors might even protect young teachers from the calumnies of a directrice if they considered them unjust. Caroline Balansa's (class of 1888) rector, for example, sprang to her defense when the directrice at Toulouse accused her of incompetence in managing a large class and of "subversive ideas to which she is very much attached." Brushing these remarks aside, the rector gave his own version of Balansa's merits: "The subversive ideas!! of which Madame the directrice speaks . . . are simply . . . a somewhat exalted manner of feeling certain things . . . remarkable moral outlook and personality. Not yet experienced in teaching."[58] In another school, Louise Langard Bréjoux (class of 1890) even found defenders after her directrice convinced the rector that this ailing mother of two young children was essentially lazy. While the rector insisted that Bréjoux was "mainly responsible for the problems with her directrice," the academy inspector suggested that the "directrice may sometimes have been tactless."[59] A few years later, when Bréjoux applied for an administrative post herself, she pleaded her version of events at the ministry to great effect. A sympathetic interviewer there recorded his reactions in an

---

[54] Dossier personnel, Louise Roussiez, notes, 1899, F17 23502, A.N.

[55] Dossier personnel, Madeleine Sébastien (married name Rudler), notes, 1899, F17 23505, A.N.

[56] Dossier personnel, Gabrielle Chavance, notes, 1899, F17 23980, A.N.

[57] Dossier personnel, Marie Meynier, notes, 1892, F17 23727, A.N.

[58] Dossier personnel, Caroline Balansa, notes, 1894, F17 23188, A.N.

[59] Dossier personnel, Louise Langard (married name Bréjoux), notes, 1899, F17 14236, A.N.

intramural note: "Complains bitterly of receiving bad reports from her directrice as a personal vendetta. After her explanations, I am ready to believe that considerable truth resides in her complaints."[60]

Nevertheless, alienating the directrice of the school was always risky for a teacher who hoped either to stay in her position or to use it as a stepping-stone to someplace better. The importance that the ministry attached to the position of directrice in girls' schools gave her assessment of a teacher's impact on her school's reputation considerable weight in personnel decisions taken at the ministry. If she convinced her superiors that the continued presence of a teacher undermined either her own authority or the good name of the school in any serious way, that would be enough to get the teacher transferred. Two categories of offense that particularly alarmed the ministry would account for the majority of reappointments forced on Sévriennes as young professionals. The more serious involved behavior in a teacher's private life that threatened to compromise the reputation of the school. Yet disgruntled Sévriennes whose antipathy for a directrice factionalized a school's staff constituted, in the eyes of the administration, nearly as serious a danger.

Among the teachers sacked for scandalous behavior in their private lives, almost none lost their jobs without a warning. Gabrielle Logerot (class of 1890) received a letter from her directrice at Niort advising her that her friendship with a widowed military officer had excited local gossip and asking if they planned to marry.[61] Though Logerot lived with her mother at Niort, the couple had been seen together at La Rochelle, Poitiers, and Paris without the mother. Logerot wrote back that she had taken several trips with M. de la Forterie but that there would be no wedding since he had promised his first wife that he would not remarry. Unwilling to break off the affair and powerless to get assigned to Paris where it might have gone unnoticed, Logerot had to resign from teaching.[62] However, she went on to write three novels based on her own trials and aimed at tearing the experience of her generation loose from the idealistic mission preached at Sèvres. In its place, she intended to present what she judged to be a daily ordeal of injustice visited on young women teachers.

Cécile Clair shared with Logerot the view that the administration had no right to interfere in teachers' private lives. Named to Bourg when she left Sèvres, which put her close to home, she personally wrote to the director of secondary education to thank him for the post. Within two

---

[60] Ibid., notes, 1907.

[61] Dossier personnel, Gabrielle Logerot, correspondance, 1896, F17 23411, A.N.

[62] The plot of her novel *Les Sévriennes*, written under the name of G. Reval, was obviously drawn from this ill-starred romance.

years, however, her directrice sent a letter up the hierarchical ladder asking for her transfer. "By her eccentric dress, her attitude at the theater and concerts, Mlle Clair has given rise to suppositions of the most wounding sort for her dignity. . . . To the advice that I have offered her on several occasions she has responded by insisting on her absolute independence outside of the lycée. This false conception of her duty has lost her the respect and confidence of local families." Called in by the rector, Clair reiterated the position she had taken with her school directrice, pointing out that "she had not taken vows and was not therefore a nun" and that "once finished with her class, she was free to live as she liked."[63] The rector called on the ministry to deliver her "a lesson," which it promptly did by transferring her to Brest, on the other side of France from Lyon, her parents' home.

As it turned out, Cécile Clair took quite some time to profit from the warning. Enraged by others' efforts to control her personal life, she kept up her verbal sallies with officials and even tried to kill the aunt who joined her in her exile. Interviewed by her directrice, Clair responded to appeals to "her sense of duty, love of family, and self-esteem" with a threat to take her own life. The shocked directrice concluded that the intelligence of this young agrégée had "developed at the expense of her character and heart."[64] For its part, the ministry decided to transfer her again, this time to Montauban in the far southwest of France. Received there by a directrice whom she liked, Clair sent a letter of contrition to the director of secondary education in which she promised to try to find "the moral equilibrium" that had eluded her thus far.[65] Scandals continued nonetheless to dog this young teacher. A "natural coquette," according to her new directrice, Clair received a love note from a local pharmacist two years after her arrival. To the dismay of her superiors, the discouraging letter that she mailed him in reply "made the rounds of all the local cafés."[66] Sheltered by her directrice, Clair this time managed to avoid another banishment, but four years later her luck ran out when a woman friend, jealous over Clair's close ties with her eighteen-year-old nephew, accused her of immoral conduct. The most an official inquiry found against her was a certain indiscretion. Nonetheless, she became a laughingstock as snatches of the brouhaha reached local gossips. Disgraced and transferred once again, this time to Chambéry in southeastern France, Clair's tribulations ended when she met and married a teacher at

[63] Dossier personnel, Cécile Clair (married name Grenier), correspondance, 1890, F17 23073, A.N.

[64] Ibid., correspondance, March 25, 1892, report by the directrice of Brest.

[65] Ibid., correspondance, letter of April 22, 1892.

[66] Ibid., correspondance, letter from the rector to the director, August 16, 1894.

the local boys' lycée. Subsequently, this now-respectable matron's resistance to the demands that her directrice made upon her took the muted form of making family life her first priority.

Not taken to extremes, this last sort of defiance teachers could risk without inviting serious reprisals. Directrices would grumble, rectors and inspectors would occasionally issue warnings, but as long as teachers performed their ordinary duties more or less routinely, a lack of zeal would not generally jeopardize their jobs. Such tolerance did not apply, however, to women who, opposed to the demands of a directrice, found allies among the other personnel. The second major way in which heads of schools rid themselves of a rebellious teacher was to claim that she had factionalized the staff. As in the case of public scandal, ministerial officials proved particularly sensitive to charges of this nature brought by a directrice against a hostile teacher. Even if an official inquiry showed that the directrice was herself at fault, provided a general mutiny did not cast doubt on her ability to lead, she almost always emerged from factional fights triumphant. The reason was that officials, though tolerant of the lone delinquent, feared the consequences of school cliques. Both offended the principle of hierarchical command, an ideal that the state worked hard to impose on public teachers; but while an obstinate teacher only made relations with the directrice disagreeable, factions menaced the operations of a school. That called, in the administration's view, for drastic actions.

Such actions, waged against Sévriennes accused by a directrice of fomenting divisiveness among her staff, left a trail of anguish in young teachers' dossiers. Sometimes the Sévrienne herself escaped a transfer, but her accomplice in resistance disappeared. Both Marie Aulon (class of 1886) and Bertha Bastoul (class of 1886) watched helplessly as a close friend experienced the disgrace of a forced transfer meant as a warning to each of them as well.[67] Others, singled out as the most serious troublemakers, were themselves the first to be displaced. Louise Beuque (class of 1881), for instance, whom her rector described as the "kingpin in the dissension in the lycée" at Lons-le-Saunier, found herself demoted to a collège, while her friend, the vice-directrice of the boarding school, escaped with just a warning.[68] The same destiny awaited Emilie Bardenat (class of 1889) at Saint-Quentin when she became the central figure in the staff's resentful reaction against a new directrice of the lycée. Bereaved over her mother's recent death, rejected the same year at the agré-

[67] Dossier personnel, Marie Aulon, notes, 1898, F17 22464; dossier personnel, Berthe Bastoul, notes, 1898, F17 23969, A.N.
[68] Dossier personnel, Louise Beuque, notes, 1897, F17 23671, A.N.

gation on her fifth attempt, Bardenat apparently found the loss of the special status that her friendship with the previous directrice had afforded simply too much for her pride to take. The ministry delivered the final blow. In retribution for her attacks on the directrice, it decided to reassign her to a collège.[69]

Sometimes the ministry dealt with factionalism by reassigning more than one of the offending parties, a measure that occasionally caught two Sévriennes up in a single disciplinary action. Two sets of friends to whom this happened—one from the class of 1886, Eugénie Lecocq and Emma Gascuel, the other from the class of 1887, Josephine Wable and Madeleine Sébastien—had requested posts together as soon as they left Sèvres.[70] In both cases, the tightness of their bond of friendship itself created problems with a school directrice. Lecocq and Gascuel managed to alienate their directrice at Tournon within a year of their arrival by their inseparability and cool manners. Alerted to that fact, the academy inspector complained about Lecocq: "Very much under the influence of Gascuel for whom she is like a double: same knowledge, same cold manner in teaching, same indifference toward the interests of the school." "For her own and for the school's sake," the rector concluded, "she must be separated from Gascuel."[71] Within a year, the director of secondary education reassigned Lecocq to a new school, and he arranged the same fate for her friend Emma one year later. Josephine Wable and Madeleine Sébastien's friendship led them down a remarkably similar path. Less lucky in their first attempt to teach together, it took a year for these two classmates to end up in the same school, but once happily ensconced at Brest, they encountered the same hostility from their directrice, who, as in the other case, begrudged the exclusiveness of their interests and affections. Within a few months, the rancor of the school's directrice showed up in her evaluations when she described Sébastien's teaching as cold and dry. "This dryness," she continued, "appears also in her relations with colleagues. Sees only Mlle Wable to whom she is extremely tied."[72] In full sympathy with the directrice and unbeknownst to the two friends, the academy inspector sent a critical report to the rector. The

[69] Dossier personnel, Emilie Bardenat, notes and correspondance, 1891–92, F17 23888, A.N.

[70] Dossier personnel, Emma Gascuel, correspondance, 1889, F17 23376; dossier personnel, Madeleine Sébastien (married name Rudler), correspondance, 1890, F17 23505; dossier personnel, Josephine Wable (married name Michot), correspondance, 1890, F17 22583, A.N.

[71] Dossier personnel, Eugénie Lecocq, notes, 1891, F17 23394, A.N.

[72] Dossier personnel, Madeleine Sébastien (married name Rudler), notes, 1892, F17 23888, A.N.

following summer both young women got reassigned to different schools, much to their astonishment and sorrow.[73]

These were not isolated episodes. All but one pair of friends from Sèvres who applied for positions together ran into trouble along the way from a directrice hostile to their intimacy.[74] That fact should come as no surprise under the circumstances. On both sides of such conflicts, the chance of injury quite naturally increased when a directrice without the agrégation confronted teachers whose friendship had its roots in their elite professional training. Moreover, as in the incidents already cited, all such confrontations ended up with teachers' reappointments. A directrice faced with what she perceived as hostile teachers did not even require justice on her side to get them out.

This describes the case of Louise Beuque (class of 1881) and Natalie Georges (class of 1883), whose academy inspector himself absolved them of wrongdoing, even as he recommended their replacement.[75] Together at Auxerre, where Beuque had asked to come in order to join her fellow Sévrienne, the friends almost immediately antagonized their new directrice, especially Georges, who as an agrégée apparently took little note of her directrice's pedagogical convictions. Recognizing the problem, the academy inspector noted, "Mlle Georges would do better under a directrice *plus autorisée* than Mlle Colin," by which he surely meant one with more credentials.[76] Relations became so tense that Beuque and Georges avoided school as much as possible, a response for which the academy inspector himself could hardly blame them. Angered by their arrogance and disrespect for her authority, Mlle Colin's fury began to take a malevolent turn. To the academy inspector she complained that gossips were spreading rumors in the town about the nature of these teachers' intimacy. The local inspector, who had his ear to the ground for scandal also, repeated the accusation to his superiors but himself denied the charge. "I have personally heard no other testimony unfavorable to the accused," he wrote to the rector. Nonetheless, he did concede the necessity, in the interest of the lycée, for sending one or both of the offending Sévriennes away. "Mlle Beuque and Mlle Georges cannot be left at Aux-

[73] Dossier personnel, Josephine Wable (married name Michot), correspondance, 1892, F17 22583, A.N.

[74] The exception was the friendship between Marguerite Caron (class of 1887) and Louise Masson (class of 1887). After five years together at the collège of La Fère, Caron took over the directorate, and when she left, her friend Louise succeeded her. Dossier personnel, M. Caron, F17 24126, and dossier personnel, L. Masson, F17 23861, A.N.

[75] Dossier personnel, Natalie Georges (married name Beuque), F17 22602, and Louise Beuque, F17 23671, A.N.

[76] Dossier personnel, Natalie Georges, correspondance, 1889, F17 22602, A.N.

erre another year under the direction of Mlle Colin. It would mean the return of difficulties, a struggle without reprieve, an uninterrupted series of grievances that would become a source of comment and gossip throughout the town and would do the greatest damage to the school."[77]

For the victims of such reprisals, the lesson in obedience proved a harsh one, especially if as a result of changing schools, they lost a post that had put them close to home. Very few would need like Cécile Clair a second demonstration of the risks of fomenting trouble for a school directrice or of parading their disdain for local mores. Yet for every Sévrienne like Cécile Clair who fought the demands of her profession or who like Gabrielle Logerot mocked the sacrifices it required, several others accepted the burdens of their job with no sign of conscious discontent. Repeatedly in their reports, inspectors and directrices reported on the conscientiousness of individual Sévriennes as teachers. Even in the early years, perhaps two-thirds of them appeared to be "devoted," even "zealous" to superiors. The proportion of teachers who fit this image grew as they moved into midcareer; some even developed an exalted version of it, adopting in the performance of their daily tasks an almost missionary spirit. Of these apostolic types inspectors frequently would write, "She has a high sense of duty" or "She has the faith" or, most typically of all, "She has the sacred fire." Such language was not uncommon in the early Third Republic. Republicans endowed their schools with a historic mission to replace the outdated intellectual leadership of organized religion with a civic-minded, secular outlook, and they envisioned teachers as proselytizers in charge of that conversion. An inflated rhetoric of service pervaded the discourse of the entire educational establishment after 1880. However, within the women's corps of secondary teachers, this rhetoric of sacrifice gained a special hold on the conscience of an entire generation. Not just dedicated functionaries, woman secondary teachers proclaimed themselves heroic figures. Not just overworked, they donned the mantle of the martyr who if called to do so would die in the exercise of her profession. And in crystallizing this image of their professional generation, alumnae from the first ten classes trained at Sèvres would lead the way.

The Heroic Teacher

The question of salaries—absurdly low as ours were—left us completely indifferent: a harsh and perhaps solitary life, the absence of distractions, the struggle against injustice, these were things that

---

[77] Ibid.

concerned us little! Had we not the most beautiful of tasks to accom-
plish! On top of the grandeur and the beauty of our role as educators,
we felt that we must be the pioneers of the future, that it belonged to
us to mold, to create the soul of the new woman.[78]

This portrait of her classmates conjured up by Berthe Israël-Wahl
(class of 1885) some forty years after the Ministry of Education first scattered them across France does not do justice to the variety of actual responses. Nonetheless, it very precisely captures the persona that Sévriennes in the founding years of their profession created for themselves.
For a quarter century, at least, from the pages of Sèvres's Alumnae Association's bulletin, the same image of the woman secondary teacher
emerged: young, idealistic, indifferent to the personal deprivations she
encountered in carrying out her educational mission. It was an image of
the Sévrienne that the school's first directrice heartily approved. And to
her deep satisfaction, even prior to her death a substantial minority of
Sèvres's first graduates fit the ideal closely.

Mme Favre's credo, with its combination of stoic moralism and missionary zeal, appealed to Sévriennes for several reasons. In the first
place, it offered lonely teachers a psychological defense against the pain
of their marginal existence in unfamiliar places. Instead of social misfits,
they could see themselves as pioneers, and that in turn invested their
lives with meaning, even as they faced hostility or indifference from
their neighbors. But less defensive reasons for identifying with their
work emerged from their experience also. Given the exceptional nature
of their training, Sévriennes were bound to have a deep respect and even
reverence for the transforming opportunities of education. The substantial changes wrought by advanced instruction in their own lives could
hardly fail to make large numbers of them converts to the cause of higher
learning for women and believers in the importance of their charge.

That commitment, in turn, encouraged a deep devotion to their students. For some Sévriennes, at least, the real key to their zealous dedication lay in their delight in teaching. Marguerite Caron (class of 1887),
in a moving reconstruction of her generation's lonely isolation, recalled
in 1931 the importance that many of them attached to students.

The only satisfaction, the only pleasure for these women on the mar-
gin of society was in class, where youngsters, amazed at learning, at
their initiation into poetry and science, seduced by a wonderful les-
son or by readings that were beautiful and morally uplifting, re-
turned in their affection for their lonely teacher the delights to which

[78] Israël-Wahl, "Mes Débuts," *Le Cinquantenaire,* 384–85.

*she introduced them. Conscious of her moral and social role, adoring
her profession, she knew how to be happy at a time when her earn-
ings were 197 francs, 90 centimes per month in a town of three thousand souls.*[79]

Remembering back to this idyllic time before the war, Marguerite Caron
called it "the golden age of the well-mannered student for whom the
teacher was a superior being."[80] Nothing in the personnel reports disputes the accuracy of this recollection. Rather, the image that emerges of
experienced teachers is of women more often loved than not, whose dignity in the eyes of students was hardly every questioned.

To a large extent, the prestige of women teachers grew naturally out of
the morally charged atmosphere of girls' schools. Hardly any school activity did not in some way drive a lesson home; the course in morals
constituted only the most explicit of these forums. All instruction aimed
to inculcate certain habits that officials associated with probity. These
included such mundane traits as neatness, promptness, diligence, a clear
and modulated voice, and a modest manner. But it also meant establish-
ing in students a pattern of reflection that made idealism a mental habit.
Not surprisingly, teachers responsible for such indoctrination became in
turn the beneficiaries of the climate it produced. As one student wrote of
Louise Ménassier at her death in 1901:

> *We made a cult of her out of passionate attachment and respect . . .
> and the thought that she would disapprove very often kept us from
> doing something wrong. . . . She never told us anything that she did
> not believe or which did not stimulate our minds or awaken our
> imagination and our feelings. So intensely did she love the beautiful
> and the good which history revealed to us . . . that we always left her
> class with an immense regret not to have known Montcalm or Pericles
> or not to have lived in the time of early Christianity. She gave us the
> vision of and desire for perfection! We were convinced that she had
> no faults.*[81]

Possibly, as this tribute would suggest, the stature of these teachers depended less on the moral order that they sought so earnestly to impose
than on their own example of commitment.

Sèvres doubtless encouraged an exalted sense of duty among many of
its progeny, but three years of professional training cannot alone account
for years of selfless dedication by alumnae. More likely, Sévriennes im-

---

[79] Quoted in Wurmser-Dégouy, *Trois Éducatrices modernes*, 50.

[80] Ibid., 58.

[81] Quoted in obituary for Louise Ménassier, *BTAES* (November 1901): 7–8.

bibed the stoic and idealistic message taught at Sèvres to the same extent that they had learned to value duty elsewhere. Sévriennes themselves had a clear notion of the origins of this driving sense of obligation. It derived in the first instance from the ethos of responsibility that permeated so many of their homes. Henriette Wurmser-Dégouy would write of Anna Amieux (class of 1889), who eventually matured into a model woman educator of the Sévrienne ideal: "Goodness, duty, she had learned them both at home, in that dear family house whose memory has remained a gentle spot in life. . . . In that invigorating atmosphere where she grew up, surrounded by the farsighted and courageous love of excellent parents, inspired by her duties as the eldest daughter, she understood at an early age the enriching value of effort, work, and selflessness."[82]

Nor were Sévriennes' homes atypical in the exchange suggested here of love for self-denying conduct. There is a curious irony about the Marxist-inspired critique of republican social doctrine in the Third Republic.[83] Critics on the Left perceive this "bourgeois" culture, loosely labeled, as mean-minded, grasping, and self-serving, a product of capitalist greed. Yet the rhetoric that saturated public speeches, private correspondence, and pedagogy made sacrificing self the centerpiece of life. Reading it, one senses a kind of routine heroism that many people from their own experience recognized as real. In fact, sacrifice provided the only possible working ethos for the average middle-class family. A corporate group that segregated tasks by sex, dedicated surplus to setting up the young, and expected children to look after aging parents voluntarily had to rely heavily on moral conscience. No levels of the middle class escaped this underpinning altogether. Even in the wealthiest homes, love and duty were inextricably related in a system of values designed to protect the family's wealth and social standing.[84] Still, the social strata to which intrafamily solidarity arguably meant the most by century's end were the ones from which Sèvres's students mainly came: the struggling middle and lower middle classes.

To explore the cultural outlook of the class from which they came does not entirely trace the roots of this self-sacrificing spirit among Sévriennes. In the vast majority of families, religious culture played an equally central role in giving middle-class girls a sense of duty early. A

---

[82] Wurmser-Dégouy, *Trois Éducatrices modernes*, 90.

[83] See, for example, Elwitt, *The Making of the Third Republic*.

[84] See Adeline Daumard, *La Bourgeoisie parisienne de 1815 à 1848* (Paris: S.E.V.P.E.N., 1963); B. Smith, *Ladies*. Though Smith does not interpret her evidence in this manner, the strategies for marriage among the textile families of the Nord and the relationship between parents and children that she describes bear out this point.

disproportionate number of Sévriennes, among them Anna Amieux herself, came from Protestant families where appeals to conscience saturated daily life for both men and women. In Catholic families, throughout the nineteenth century, women far more than men felt the weight of
a religious training. Girls more often had religious schooling; women
more often went to church.[85] Whether students at Sèvres in its first decade participated in the religious culture of other Catholic women of
their class is hard to know for certain.[86] Religious life at Sèvres was carried on discreetly, with the same tolerance of diversity as Mme Favre
sought to realize in intellectual matters.[87] Nonetheless, if creeds were a
purely private matter at Sèvres, the moral discourse and images attached
to Christianity flourished. Whether in the Protestant form of self-examination or the Catholic form of abnegation, the model of the teacher held
up to Sévriennes for emulation played to values that they had learned in
church.

The cumulative effect of this multiple layering of duties might turn
some Sévriennes into rebels. More often it prepared them to be martyrs.
The life and in particular the death of Berthe Ceccaldi (class of 1888)
provide an archetype of the Sévrienne schooled in self-denying service.
Orphaned while at Sèvres, Ceccaldi took over full responsibility for her
emotionally ill and only sister as soon as she could work. Then, two
years into teaching, she contracted a fatal kidney ailment. The disease
took six years to destroy her. "Each morning," during her long illness,
according to the president of Sèvres's Alumnae Association, "she was
brought by car to the lycée where she spent most of the day reclining,
getting up only to give her classes. Yet throughout these years of suffering, her letters were not resigned but thankful—serious, gay, amusing
even, and always matter-of-fact."[88] Belugou then went on to list what she
believed to be the shaping influences on this heroic fellow teacher. "Her
strength of heart, her simple valor, she first learned in her paternal
home. . . . Even more she owed them to her Faith. . . . But in her simple
courage there is also something of the School that she loved so much. 'A
Stoic who was also a Christian could not have done better' was the observation of the academy inspector at her graveside. For us at Sèvres, that
brings back other memories."[89]

---

[85] See Lévy, *De mères en filles*, and B. Smith, *Ladies*.

[86] A few, at least, arrived at Sèvres militant in their secularizing spirit (see chap. 12).
A couple of others would court trouble later on, compromising the reputations of their
schools by associating too closely with a hostile Catholic circle in their towns.

[87] Mme Favre arranged regular weekly outings for her students to attend the services
of their faith.

[88] Louise Belugou, "Assemblée Générale," *BTAES* (November 1900): 4–5.

[89] Ibid., 5.

In the Sévrienne tradition, such deaths expressed the ideal of what a graduate ought to be. Obituaries in the school paper dwelt on sacrifices that dying teachers made to meet their duties. To families they were an irreplaceable comfort and support; to students they gave up the last days they spent on their feet; and to everyone they turned a face of calm acceptance. Only 5 percent of Sèvres's young teachers were dead by 1901.[90] Many others, though, suffered from ailments that they believed were due to teaching. To the extent that these women shared a professional image, therefore, it was one of teachers as martyrs. Far from resisting this collective self-appraisal, the average teacher voluntarily enhanced it. Throughout the period, women teachers corrected students' papers with so close an eye that even inspectors found their scrupulousness excessive.[91] Yet efforts to get them to shorten their comments and lighten their work load foundered on teachers' own professional consciences. Such commitment reflects a real conviction about the value of the education that the state had offered girls. It also shows, however, a way of thinking to which teachers had become accustomed. For Sévriennes, like other daughters of the middle class in this generation, were raised to think in terms of moral obligations toward the social world around them. The family was the original focus of this ethos. The Church applied it to the needy. Sèvres linked this sense of duty to professional service, while the state assigned it to itself. By the time they entered teaching, therefore, teachers had multiple claims upon their conscience. Perhaps because as daughters they kept their filial obligations active, perhaps because as women they were closer to the Church, this esprit de corps retained a resonance for women teachers long after men in the profession were ready to renounce it.

[90] A list of the graduates who had died appeared in *BTAES* (November 1901).
[91] Crouzet-Ben-Aben, "Le Surménage," 416–17.

A Generation and an
Institution Come of Age

The two decades of the Belle Epoque through World
War I turned out to be triumphal years for the first
generation of teachers trained at Sèvres. Those who
stayed in teaching found the adulation that many
had already known within the classroom now accompanied by community acceptance, while those
promoted into the administration assumed a task
considerably altered by a new enthusiasm for girls'
secondary studies among the middle classes, including the bourgeoisie. With even the Catholic church
promoting secondary education in its schools after
1900, directrices could devote their efforts aggressively to realizing their own ideal of schooling for
the modern girl in collèges and lycées. The major
claim that the first Sévriennes can legitimately make
on our attention lies in their accomplishments during these critically important years for girls' schooling.

For us, the major question surrounding these
achievements is the extent to which the cultural images of femininity that this generation pioneered reinforced the notion of separate spheres for men and
women as republicans had hoped or if, instead,
these women moved girls' secondary schools, intentionally or not, in an androgynous direction. One
way to explore the question is to examine the paths
by which Sévriennes as individuals climbed to posts
of influence. To the extent that their ambitions followed the direction of the men in their profession,

181

Sévriennes were moving toward an androgynous model of the career woman. To the degree that opportunities or motives among these women diverged from those of men, Sèvres's first alumnae opened up new vistas within a cultural field still defined as female. Yet personal histories of professional advancement reveal only one part of the story. Sévriennes had a crucial role to play as well in fleshing out a cultural image of the educated woman inside their schools, especially once they entered the administration. An examination of their pedagogical intentions as directrices offers a second way, therefore, to measure the impact of this generation on the changing images of women emanating from their schools. As the official architects of bourgeois feminine culture, directrices faced no easy task after the turn of the century. Assigned to the defense of the traditional moral and social goals of girls' secondary schooling, they had to reconcile those goals with new pressures from their students for professional training and from the administration for a more active engagement by women with the world around them. The war offered an unprecedented opportunity to display to the community what they had crafted by way of a new feminine culture. Yet if the war brought honor to Sévriennes as heads of schools, it also threatened to destroy their lifetime work by revealing the instability of the image of femininity that they had worked so hard to build.

7 Professional Ambition in a Feminine Key

FROM THE OUTSET, the pathways open for advancement to the woman professeur cast this profession into a distinctly feminine mold. Women secondary teachers, unlike their counterparts in boys' schools, could not become inspectors, nor could they aspire to a position in research or university teaching. Ministerial practice forced them to choose instead between two other options. Either they remained in secondary teaching or they moved into an administrative post as directrice. Whichever route a woman took, it led away from the experience of the ambitious and talented male professeur. A second feature of this career structure that distinguished it from the men's encouraged women teachers to spend their professional lives working in a single institution. Inspired by a concern first voiced by Camille Sée that women teachers "not be nomads like the other functionaries in teaching," the ministry did not rank girls' collèges and lycées outside Paris.[1] Teachers received, therefore, the same salaries in all provincial schools, which meant they lacked a financial incentive to move around. Once given an appointment commensurate with her degrees, a woman teacher could remain in the same school permanently, while the ministry moved her up the ladder of promotions. Together, these official measures projected a distinctive ideal of the female professeur—confined to a secluded feminine world, tied to one community, and limited in her professional ambitions.

The actual profile that the first Sévriennes developed of themselves deviated in some important ways from that projected schema. As young teachers, Sévriennes eager to locate near their families had pursued a highly peripatetic life, contrary to the administration's hopes. On the other hand, they had also evidenced only modest professional ambition, placing the interests of the family above all other considerations in their pleas for one or another post. In midcareer that pattern shifted. Ambition raised its head, replacing family as the first concern of Sévriennes who importuned their superiors for better posts. Important contrasts emerged, moreover, in the way that teachers and directrices responded to their opportunities. While teachers became more self-assertive, directrices

[1] "Proposition de loi de Camille Sée," *Lycées et collèges de jeunes filles*, 61.

183

aligned themselves with the official ideal by becoming ever more self-denying and committed to their schools. This difference marks the beginning of a significant bifurcation in the pattern of expectations between teachers and directrices who came from Sèvres. Whereas the former looked increasingly toward Paris, with its cosmopolitan, exciting intellectual life, and came to see themselves as members of a larger professional world, directrices devoted their attention to their schools and to upholding an image of them to the community as uniquely feminine institutions.

Ambition Rears Its Head

Something important changed in the requests for new appointments made by Sévriennes in their thirties. Rarely did they any longer plead for posts in out-of-the-way places in order to rejoin their families. To all appearances, Sévriennes in midcareer shifted their primary focus from familial needs to professional ambition. All the same, that new concern did not announce a volte-face in these women's values, transforming them from dutiful wives and daughters into self-seeking individualists. The reasons they expressed suggest, instead, the opening of a new phase in their domestic obligations that freed them from the need to stay at home. Fathers retired, parents died, siblings left the familial nest. All such shifts in the domestic lives of teachers now enabled them to move, often with a dependent parent or other family member at their side.

Thus, Anna Amieux (class of 1889), who placed second at the agrégation in 1892 and since then had been teaching at Roanne because it was the nearest open post close to her family in Lyon, in 1897 asked her rector to advance her candidacy for Paris. That year her father had retired as *chef de section* for the Lyon-Marseille railroad. A post in Paris, she informed the rector, "would permit me to live with my parents, who would join me, help my brothers, who are pursuing their studies in law and medicine, one of whom is already in Paris, and provide me with the resources to work."[2]

The story line revealed in Anna Amieux's file paralleled the early stage of Jeanne François's (class of 1885) career. François also passed the agrégation on taking leave of Sèvres in 1888 but had to take a post in the small subprefecture of Charleville because its location served familial interests.[3] By 1899, François convinced her parents that a move to Paris would benefit them all. She would escape the trials of a provincial back-

[2] Dossier personnel, correspondance, 1897, F17 24471, A.N.
[3] Dossier personnel, correspondance, 1897, F17 24036, A.N.

water where, as she complained to an inspector general, "relations are difficult . . . and the resources . . . mediocre." Furthermore, her father, who suffered from "a serious infection of the bone," could find a better doctor in the capital.

Still another teacher, Marie Nirascou (class of 1886), gained her freedom to move about at will only after both her parents died. For her that meant even more years of treading water professionally than Amieux and François had to wait. In other ways, however, Nirascou's history resembles theirs. She, too, passed the agrégation in good standing, placing second in 1889. That triumph earned her an immediate post at Reims, ordinarily a stepping-stone to Paris. But instead of moving up the ladder promptly, Nirascou remained at Reims for sixteen years to meet "overarching family duties."[4] Not until 1905 was she free of filial obligations and able to submit her candidacy for Paris.

While pointing up the link between ambition and the family, each of these examples also underscores the role of Paris as a pole of attraction. Several factors account for this appeal. For women raised there, family ties remained the most important pull, but for others, a post in Paris fulfilled more individual aims. Unquestionably, one of them was recognition. Prestige drew talent to the capital just as surely in the women's corps as in the men's profession. Many women also craved, as Anna Amieux and Jeanne François did, the rich resources available there to them as teachers.[5] Equally important for this beleaguered generation, Paris promised an escape for single women teachers from the malevolent gossip typical of provincial towns. In the cosmopolitan atmosphere of Paris, they discovered both a life enriched by cultural refinement and the anonymity needed to enjoy it. Above all, what teaching in the capital offered women was a location at the very hub of their profession. With five Parisian lycées (Fénélon, Molière, Jules Ferry, Victor Duruy, and Lamartine), another at Versailles, and Sèvres only twenty minutes away, Paris clustered enough teachers in one place to create the first community in this profession not defined by Sèvres's scattered alumnae. Inhibited earlier by the taboos hedging women's roles in public spaces, Sévriennes either hid their talents away in individual schools, or if they dared to share their expertise in publications, their names did not appear under their work. Especially in Paris, that habit gradually disappeared. Once teachers had a professional community to speak to, more and more of them would find the confidence to do so.

[4] Dossier personnel, correspondance, 1904, F17 23715, A.N.

[5] Rather more discreetly, Anna Amieux described herself in her request for Paris as "absolutely deprived of intellectual resources and unable to renew my scientific knowledge." Dossier personnel, correspondance, 1897, F17 24471, A.N.

journals

Signs of this development proliferated after 1900. One of the most noticeable was the new readiness of Sévriennes to send signed articles to professional journals like Camille Sée's *Revue de l'enseignement secondaire des jeunes filles* and Sèvres's alumnae bulletin. The lively interest that from the beginning they evidenced in teaching would manifest itself in a variety of publications. To meet the great need for such materials, some wrote textbooks for girls' secondary studies. Others joined in the pedagogical debates that raged in Camille Sée's review. Still others published memoirs or biographies of key figures in the founding years of girls' secondary education. In 1901, *Le Journal d'une Sévrienne*, by Marguerite Aron, first appeared in serial version in Camille Sée's *Revue*, a landmark of the new openness in this profession.[6]

Scholarship to travel

Meanwhile, in another example of the broadening opportunities for teachers in Parisian schools, Anna Amieux and Jeanne François took advantage of their contacts and professional reputations to get scholarships for traveling abroad.[7] Amieux visited Scotland, England, and the United States in 1906 with Pierrette Sapy (class of 1892); Jeanne François won a scholarship to travel around the world in 1912.[8] Another of their colleagues, Camille Tollemer (class of 1884), got a three-year leave of absence in 1911 to teach at the French Institute in Russia.[9] These women reaped the benefits of success in this profession individually. After 1904, others focused on uniting their efforts to raise the rewards of teaching for the whole profession. Beginning in Paris and in imitation of the men's profession, women teachers founded professional associations called *amicales* to defend, at the ministry, the interests of women teachers.[10]

Quite obviously, a teaching post in Paris opened doors barely ajar in most provincial schools. In light of that, the competition among Sévriennes to secure one of these coveted positions promised to be fierce. Only a small minority could realistically entertain the hope of a promotion up to Paris. Since all the schools in the Paris region were lycées, agrégées alone could expect appointments. Furthermore, the year they passed the agrégation and the rank that they obtained all figured into when and if they got selected. Forced to wait patiently in the provinces

---

[6] Aron did not actually get a post in Paris until 1908. But from Reims, where she taught from 1901 to 1908, it was an easy train ride to Paris where she had family. Dossier personnel, F17 24282, A.N.

[7] The Bourse Albert Kahn "autour du monde" was made available to Sévriennes in 1900. Sapy, who at the time was maîtresse-adjointe at Sèvres, was the first beneficiary.

[8] Dossier personnel, Anna Amieux, notes, 1906–1907, F17 24471, A.N. Dossier personnel, Jeanne François (married name Antoine), notes, 1912–1913, F17 24036, A.N.

[9] Dossier personnel, Camille Tollemer, notes, 1911, F17 23730, A.N.

[10] See chap. 10.

for their turn, dedicated teachers convinced of their professional talent felt badly treated and said so if another Sévrienne with fewer years of service or one who had passed the agrégation more recently got there first.[11] Still, even having all the right credentials in her pocket did not cinch a teacher's case unless her rector and an inspector general pressed her candidacy in the committee controlling these appointments.

Largely owing to this last requirement, teachers from petty bourgeois and working-class families suffered a decided disadvantage in the struggle for Parisian posts.[12] At the agrégation, Sévriennes who came from humble social backgrounds appeared in no way disadvantaged by comparison with classmates raised in middle-class environments. In fact, the daughters of manual workers, on the whole, outperformed white-collar and professional workers at these competitive exams. Though superficially surprising, these results actually conform to findings by two French sociologists, Pierre Bourdieu and Jean-Claude Passeron, who have studied the contemporary process of selection through national exams in France within a class analysis. Given their conclusions, one would expect a girl from the working classes who made her way up to the agrégation to possess exceptional talent, far more in fact, than the average middle-class student. Otherwise, she would never have been able to overcome the cultural obstacles excluding the vast majority of other girls like her (see table 7.1).[13]

When the measure of success shifts, however, from the agrégation to the classroom and to the qualitative judgments made by school inspectors, the social profile of high achievers changes drastically. Daughters of manual laborers immediately drop from first to fifth place, while those whose fathers worked in the liberal professions, education, railroads, and commerce move up in that order to the first through fourth positions.[14] Within each occupational category, the higher the social status of

[11] See, for example, dossier, personnel Angèle Coustols, correspondance, 1907, F17 24187, A.N.

[12] The experience of Sévriennes in this regard confirms contemporary studies by Pierre Bourdieu and Jean-Claude Passeron, who argue for the importance of familial culture in determining success within the Université. *Reproduction in Education, Society and Culture*, trans. Richard Nice (London: Sage Publications, 1977), 141–76.

[13] Ibid., 74, 116, 119, 122, 130.

[14] These calculations are necessarily somewhat imprecise since they represent an effort to tabulate qualitative remarks by inspectors commenting on the performance of young teachers during their first decade of teaching. Sévriennes were grouped into two categories of performance. Those whose inspectors were consistently enthusiastic about their talents as teachers, whatever the criteria they used, fell into one group. Those whose reviews by school inspectors were either mixed or consistently unfavorable, again regardless of the criteria applied, were placed in another category. I then used

TABLE 7.1
Sévriennes' Performance at the Agrégation

Fathers' Occupation[a]	Number Succeeding	Rate of Success[b]
Manual labor	16	75%
Liberal professions	14	71%
Railroad	10	70%
Education	35	63%
Civil service	27	59%
Unknown	36	56%
Military	18	55%
Commerce	45	51%
Agriculture	9	33%
Total	210	

Sources: Tabulated from dossiers personnels, series F17, A.N.
[a] The occupational groups are arranged in rank order based on rates of success by daughters from those categories.
[b] These figures represent the percentage of all Sévriennes with fathers in a given occupational group who competed successfully at the agrégation.

the father, the better his daughter's chances of achieving instant recognition as a teacher. Over time, this correlation between social origin and professional performance eroded. Teachers from industrial and artisan families regained by midcareer some of the ground that they had lost when measured for their brilliance as young teachers. Nonetheless, as a group they would never again achieve the ascendancy over former classmates promised by the results of their exams.

The explanation seems to lie in the cultural style that women from more privileged social backgrounds possessed as part of their familial inheritance. Verbally agile teachers with an easy social grace had the best chance of winning strong endorsement from inspectors, and these attributes turned up most often among women from families where that social style thrived—to wit, the urban middle class. Marie Lardley (class of 1888), for example, the daughter of a Parisian doctor, already possessed at twenty-six, in her admiring inspector's view, "vivacity, charm, spirit, a very sure literary sense, and great finesse in her analyses."[15] The same mastery of the rules governing refined manners came easily to Clothilde Maréchal, whose father was a justice of the peace. "She speaks well,"

these groups to establish a rate of success for girls from different social backgrounds in the same manner as I had for the agrégation.

[15] Dossier personnel, Marie Lardley (married name Jaudel), notes, 1896, F17 23923, A.N.

one inspector wrote, "even elegantly. Remarkable results."[16] Both these women came from professional families where a high premium on learning and elegant expression doubtless figured prominently in their upbringing. Even in commercial families, though, where education may have carried somewhat less prestige, daughters of prosperous merchants typically had the mental, verbal, and social skills that inspectors sought in the most admired teachers. Thus, on various occasions, different inspectors characterized Blanche Guillaume (class of 1889), the daughter of wholesaler in grain, as "articulate," well-groomed without coquetry," possessing "great clarity and firmness of ideas."[17] Families of middle-level bureaucrats also generally passed along to daughters skills that served them well in this profession. Anna Amieux represents a stellar case of just this cultural transfer. One inspector general found her "lively, intelligent," possessing, together with a lucid mind, "great simplicity" and "ease." Another noted her "agreeable voice, correct language, attractive appearance," as well as self-assurance.[18] She combined, in her biographer's opinion, intellectual self-assurance with the social graces of a woman of the world.[19] The fusion of the two in a single teacher guaranteed her successful candidature for Paris.

Such glowing comments contrast sharply with those reserved for several Sévriennes of lower social origins who, despite stunning successes at the agrégation, shone less brightly in the eyes of their inspectors in the classroom. Though Marie Renard (class of 1883) ranked seventh at the agrégation, this daughter of a cloth dyer, according to two different school inspectors, lacked "distinction in her manners and her language" and had "a certain regrettable 'laisser-aller' in her attire."[20] In much the same way, Valentine Guilloux (class of 1886) followed a brilliant performance at the agrégation with a lackluster beginning as a teacher. The daughter of a widowed domestic servant, Guilloux had a personal style that unfavorably impressed her rector. "She goes to class like a worker with no taste for what is just to her a mechanical chore," he complained in his report.[21] His very choice of words alluded to a class distinction that he quite likely intentionally evoked. Even Louise Bruneau (class of 1886), whom her directrice at Versailles considered "original, open-minded, and one of the liveliest and most interesting teachers in the school," worked for seven years to hear that praise. Before then, various

[16] Dossier personnel, Clothilde Maréchal (class of 1883), notes, 1887, F17 23581, A.N.
[17] Dossier personnel, Blanche Guillaume, notes, F17 23350, A.N.
[18] Dossier personnel, Anna Amieux, notes, 1897, 1898, F17 24471, A.N.
[19] Wurmser-Dégouy, Trois Éducatrices modernes, 89.
[20] Dossier personnel, Marie Renard, notes, 1887, 1893, F17 23644, A.N.
[21] Dossier personnel, Valentine Guilloux, notes, 1891, F17 23194, A.N.

inspectors complained about her: "A nasal voice, cold and monotone"; "Her teaching smacks of textbooks"; "More vigor than finesse"; "Lacks originality and accepts ready-made opinions easily."[22] Ranked first at the agrégation in letters in 1889, this daughter of a carpenter relied on sheer determination to accomplish what other agrégées claimed immediately as a birthright.

Of course, not all women whose social background might have barred the way to Paris failed to get there. Some like Louise Bruneau overcame initial handicaps by dint of their intelligence and dedication. Others threw careers in secondary teaching away in order to fulfill their more important goal of reaching Paris. Among the latter figured several natives of the city raised in humble families. Elisa Culot (class of 1886)— "timid," "a peasant in appearance," and, for all that, agrégée—after nine years of asking for a post as professeur in Paris, where her father was an agent of the city's tolls, agreed instead to teach in elementary classes. Pauline Giraud (class of 1882), "puny, sad, reserved, with few resources" and the daughter of a school teacher, followed the same route to Paris. Gabrielle Gonzalles (class of 1886) whose "learning" an inspector characterized as "very ordinary" went into school management and became a *surveillante générale* in a Parisian lycée in order to return to Paris, where her father made his living as a joiner.[23] All three women got to Paris by adjusting their ambitions downward, a decision that, though disappointing, represented an acceptable alternative to the less tolerable prospect of an entire career in some provincial school.

Not every Sévrienne viewed that likelihood with trepidation. After the peregrinations of their early years, most teachers had either settled near their families, brought a relative to their homes, or simply found a school that in some other way fulfilled essential needs. For those who stayed in teaching, the road that stretched ahead held few surprises.[24] A majority would spend their entire midcareer in a single school. Many remained in the same spot until retirement. To the extent that these women felt

[22] Dossier personnel, Louise Bruneau, notes, F17 23976, A.N.

[23] Dossiers personnels, Elisa Culot, notes, F17 24131; Pauline Giraud, notes, F17 22617; Gabrielle Gonzalès, notes, F17 23340, A.N.

[24] Statistically, the most striking new development in the career patterns of middle-aged teachers was that as a group, they became less mobile. While young, Sévriennes could expect on average to work in three different schools over a ten-year period. (The statistical rate was 2.82.) During the second decade of their careers, the average rate of transfer from one school to another dropped to 0.94 per teacher. Indeed, this figure overestimates the actual mobility of experienced teachers. For fully 50 percent of the teachers in the sample remained in the same institution for the entire ten years, compared to a mere 11 percent who stayed put over the first decade they were working. As teachers grew older, this tendency to settle down became still more pronounced.

ambition now, it focused mainly on their professional reputation in the small arena of the school and among the generations of students who passed through it.

Directrices: The Other Option

Another road lay open, though, for those who did not go to Paris but for whom teaching in the provinces worked a hardship. They could aspire to become the directrice of a school. As an alternative to teaching, that option had certain obvious attractions. Agrégées might envision administering a lycée, if not at first then later on in their careers. Those with only the certificat always began in collèges or cours secondaires, but even certifiées, if exceptionally successful in administering a collège or if their collège itself was upgraded into a lycée, could hope for a promotion to that post.[25] Financially, the move could prove highly advantageous, especially for women who became directrices of lycées (see table 7.2). More important, though, than pecuniary gains, teachers who entered the administration experienced an immediate increase in their powers. One would expect that prospect to hold considerable appeal for women trained to see themselves as an elite and frustrated by the multiple constraints imposed upon them. Whether personally ambitious or

TABLE 7.2
Salaries of Teachers and Directrices by Class, Decree of 1904 (in francs)

	Directrice Lycée[a]	Directrice Collège	Prof. Lycée[b]	Prof. Collège, Chargée de Cours Lycée
1st	6000.00	4000.00	4200.00	3400.00
2nd	5700.00	3700.00	3900.00	3200.00
3rd	5400.00	3400.00	3600.00	3000.00
4th	5100.00	3100.00	3400.00	2800.00
5th	4800.00	2800.00	3200.00	2600.00
6th	4400.00	2600.00	3000.00	2500.00

Source: *L'Enseignement secondaire des jeunes filles* 1 (1904): 42–43.
[a] The directrice of a lycée who was agrégée received an indemnity of 500 francs added onto this base salary. Directrices in Paris received an additional 500 francs.
[b] Lycée professors in Paris received an additional 500 francs.

[25] This possibility was not foreseen under the terms of the decree of September 13, 1883. Mayeur, *L'Enseignement secondaire*, 288.

simply disgruntled over their position as subalterns, teachers stood to profit greatly from selecting this avenue of advancement.

All the same, the appeal of a directorate was neither general in the profession nor shared equally by women from different social backgrounds. Once again, as in requests for Paris, familial considerations played a crucial part in shaping Sévriennes' ambitions. In fact, some women in their middle years turned toward administration largely to accommodate their family duties. This was particularly true for married women with young children. Because directrices lived as well as worked at school, mothers often discovered in administration an ideal way to meet their homely duties while advancing their careers. Thus, Amélie Gonnet (class of 1888), pregnant in her second year of marriage, immediately requested an administrative post. The ministry obligingly appointed her directrice of the collège of Laon where her husband also found a post at the local boys' lycée. So well did this arrangement fit the Gonnets' private needs that the next year, in addition to their baby, they had Amélie's mother and father living with them.[26] Similarly, after her second child, Cécilia Terrène Lafleur (class of 1890) asked her rector for assistance in getting a post as directrice so as to lighten her domestic burdens. She, too, eventually found a position where her husband, a lieutenant in the army, could find work.[27] Marie Lefèvre Samuel (class of 1886), on the other hand, only succeeded in getting a promotion into the administration as a widow with four small children to support. Before then, the ministry ignored her annual requests for a post as directrice partly because she had not passed the agrégation but even more because her husband, a professeur, like herself, in a collège, reputedly "frequented cafés."[28] Ironically his death, which left his wife grieving and financially at risk, cleared the way at last for her to get the only kind of post in this profession easily managed by a working mother.[29]

Single teachers, too, often justified shifting into the administration purely on familial grounds. When Léonie Allégret (class of 1882) could not get back to Lyon where her ailing parents lived, she decided a directorate would resolve her problem since she could then create a home

[26] Dossier personnel, Amélie Gandon (married name Gonnet), correspondance and notes, 1895–1897, F17 23915, A.N.

[27] Dossier personnel, Cécilia Terrène (married name Lafleur), correspondance, 1904, F17 24386, A.N.

[28] Dossier personnel, Marie Lefèvre (married name Samuel), notes, 1896, F17 24220, A.N.

[29] For letters testifying to the campaign waged on her behalf by certain of her former classmates as well as teachers at Sèvres, see ibid., correspondance, 1900–1901.

where she could tend them while she worked.[30] Likewise, Caroline Humiecka (class of 1889), asked for a position as directrice for her father's sake because she could not get to Paris where he lived. "My father, who has no other children," she explained in a letter to the ministry, "finds himself in a state of singular isolation. . . . He has no family; I can even say that he has hardly any friends; sixty-seven years old, he has been sick ever since my mother died. He has no money and has consequently had to work three years beyond the age of retirement."[31] The remedy for his situation was for him to come to live with her wherever she got a post as a directrice. Alexandrine Vautier (class of 1888) and Suzanne Pénard (class of 1881), on the other hand, both asked for a directorate to look after widowed mothers and dependent sisters.[32]

Some teachers chose to switch from teaching into the administration not so much to care for others in their family as to protect their own precarious health from erosion by further teaching. Several Sévriennes accompanied their requests for a directrice's post with warnings from their doctors. Marie Huet (class of 1882), who suffered from chronic laryngitis, asked to exchange a post at the Lycée Fénélon in Paris for that of directrice at a provincial school because her doctor had ordered her to give up teaching. Marie Delbosc (class of 1889), on leave from teaching for five years after being diagnosed as neurasthenic, returned in 1905 convinced that she could not survive the ordeal of the classroom. Instead, she asked for a position as directrice.[33] Even without specific ailments, teachers sometimes alluded to exhaustion as the reason for requests to leave instruction. "Teaching quickly saps professors who give themselves to it with all their heart," Marie Lacharrière (class of 1881) announced in her appeal for an administrative post. "My energy declines and I begin to yearn for a post a bit less tiring."[34]

[margin annotation: ← protect own health]

Nonetheless, the indirect appeal of this alternative to teaching—a chance to care for loved ones or to spare one's health—does not alone

---

[30] Dossier personnel, Léonie Allégret, correspondance, 1886, F17 22599, A.N. Finding her too young for this position, her rector advised instead that she be reappointed to Lyon. That transfer put off her promotion into the administration for another three years.

[31] Dossier personnel, Caroline Humiecka (married name Farand), correspondance, 1902, F17 24498, A.N.

[32] Dossier personnel, Alexandrine Vautier, correspondance, 1907, F17 24172; dossier personnel, Suzanne Pénard, correspondance, 1904, F17 22696, A.N.

[33] Dossier personnel, Marie Huet, correspondance, 1888, 1905, F17 22448, A.N. Reluctant to entrust a school to a virtual unknown, the ministry did acquiesce in her demand after she had taught for two more years. See notes, 1907. Dossier personnel, Marie Delbosc, correspondance, 1905, F17 23277, A.N.

[34] Dossier personnel, Marie Lacharrière, correspondance, 1887, F17 22930, A.N.

account for its attraction. Half the women seeking a directorate submitted their requests without referring to either their family duties or their own exhaustion. They simply asked for the post because it represented a promotion. Even those who dressed up their applications in an array of private motives undoubtedly also sometimes acted from ambition. The social profile of the women who tried to shift from teaching into school administration, in any case, belies the kind of random pattern familial or medical considerations would produce. Instead, a consistent preference for administration over teaching showed up in Sévriennes from certain backgrounds. Daughters of civil servants and railroad employees demonstrated far more interest in becoming heads of schools than did those whose fathers belonged to the Université, the liberal professions, or the world of entrepreneurial commerce.[35] The correlation between religious background and the choice of this professional option was even stronger. Teachers from Protestant families entered the administration at nearly twice the rate of other Sévriennes.

Making sense of the effect of fathers' occupations on ambition presents more difficulties than explaining the role of religion in shaping Sévriennes' career goals. For example, one might attribute the preference for teaching exhibited by universitaires' daughters to prejudices learned at home, since in the male profession the best secondary teachers moved to the major lycées, into the inspectoral service, or even, with more advanced degrees, to higher education. To become headmaster of a school represented a professional dead end.[36] Likewise, one might interpret the preference for administrative careers among daughters of civil servants and railroad employees, as well as the distaste for such jobs among those raised by men within the free professions or in small commerce, as reflections of attitudes nurtured in the home. Arguably, daughters of liberal professionals and commercial entrepreneurs valued the relative autonomy associated with secondary teaching; whereas women raised by fathers entrenched in bureaucratic organizations saw the benefits of moving up the hierarchy of command. Yet such hypothetical reconstructions of professional motivation begin to break down when we introduce the fact that daughters of universitaires and liberal professionals got promoted quickly into the most prestigious teaching posts. Their relative

[35] Two of every five Sévriennes in the former category put in requests to change career direction, and three-quarters of those candidates mentioned neither medical nor familial motives in their applications. By contrast, fewer than one in five daughters of commercial families or of universitaires and one in ten with fathers in the liberal professions ever considered administration as an option, while two-thirds of those who did so justified their decision on grounds of health or family duties.

[36] Vincent, "Les Professeurs du second degré," 47–73.

disinterest in administration may simply be a function of high rates of success in pursuing their ambitions through the classroom.

Religion, on the other hand, had an undeniably compelling impact on Sévriennes' ambitions. Already greatly overrepresented in Sèvres's student body, where they were six to seven times as numerous as in the general population, Protestants increased their visibility by at least one-third at the helm of secondary schools.[37] To be precise, 21 percent of the directrices considered in this study shared a Protestant upbringing. Sèvres's graduates merely replicated, in this regard, a widespread tendency in the profession. By 1895, one out of every four girls' secondary schools had a Protestant directrice.[38] That early grip on girls' education only strengthened over time as the first recruits from Sèvres took control of the best-known schools within the girls' system. In the 1920s, Protestants from the first generation of Sévriennes would enjoy a virtual monopoly of directorates in Paris, while from 1906 until 1935, two Protestant protégées of Mme Favre's would successively administer their alma mater.[39] Far from a unique example of nondiscrimination in a Catholic nation, Mme Favre's appointment in 1881 would usher in a golden age of Protestant influence on girls' secondary education.

Among the factors that might account for the presence of so many Protestant directrices, preferential treatment by the Ministry of Education presents one possibility, particularly as a Protestant, Elie Rabier, served as director of secondary education from 1889 to 1907. Mme Favre herself may have had some impact on the trend, for though she refused on principle to lobby at the ministry for such promotions, she did encourage those whom she thought suited to the task.[40] Nonetheless, nothing in the personnel dossiers hints that sectarian preference hid behind the facade of impartiality that the ministry erected around its appointments.[41]

[37] Protestants made up from 12 to 15 percent of the first ten classes of Sévriennes.

[38] Mayeur, *L'Enseignement secondaire*, 365.

[39] Louise Belugou (class of 1882), directrice of Sèvres 1906–1919; Anna Amieux (class of 1889), directrice of Sèvres 1919–1935.

[40] These included Lucie Kuss (class of 1882), Louise Belugou (class of 1882), and probably Léonie Allégret (class of 1882), three Protestants all destined for illustrious careers in the administration. Belugou came back to Sèvres with Mme Favre's blessing as a maîtresse-adjointe from 1886–1891. From there she went directly to Le Havre as directrice of the girls' lycée. Mme Favre wrote one of her rare letters of support to help Allégret get a post teaching in Lyon in 1885. When the latter asked for a position as a directrice in 1887, she mentioned a position as maîtress-adjointe at Sèvres as a possible alternative, which suggests a close relationship with her former directrice. Dossier personnel, Lucie Kuss, correspondance, 1897, F17 22621; dossier personnel of Léonie Allégret, correspondance, 1885, 1887, F17 22599, A.N.

[41] This is Françoise Mayeur's conclusion, too. Mayeur, *L'Enseignement secondaire*, 308n.14.

Rather, the impression those records do impart is of Protestant women whose personal values, interests, and aptitudes closely matched what ministerial officials looked for in directrices.

The varied nature of the tasks assigned to heads of the new schools certainly called for a multiplicity of talents.[42] Unlike headmasters of boys' lycées, directrices administered their schools without a censeur (assistant headmaster), which meant that all the school's paperwork fell to them alone. Aided only by a bursar (économe), they kept the school's accounts, handled all official correspondence, and organized the archives and the library. It fell as well to the directrice to see that everyone within the school observed the regulations. Twice a month she reported to the rector on the situation in her school. Every trimester she reviewed the moral conduct of girls with scholarships whose social background placed them under some suspicion. At the end of the year, she submitted the school's accounts to the administrative board for the academy, the conseil d'académie.[43]

In addition to administrative functions, a directrice retained an active pedagogical role within the school, again a contrast with the head of a boys' school. An arrêté of 1884 ordered directrices to hold monthly meetings with the faculty to consider discipline and school instruction.[44] This procedure made her personally responsible for any measures taken against delinquent students. It also meant that with her faculty's cooperation, a persuasive school head might shape the pedagogical goals of her school.[45] This arrêté noted further that a directrice would not necessarily give up her teaching duties altogether. In fact, most of them did not.

It was also understood that a directrice managed the public relations for her school. Indeed, good communication with the world outside the school could matter even more for a directrice than for the typical headmaster, since a directrice could not expect a school to fill up automatically every year with daughters of the well-to-do. She had to actively recruit them. Her rapport with municipal officials had serious implications for her school as well. The very existence of a cours secondaire

[42] An arrêté of July 24, 1884 outlined the powers and obligations of a directrice of a collège or lycée. For a complete description of these duties see ibid., 175–79.

[43] Although like a proviseur, the directrice of a girls' lycée reported on the material conditions of her school to an advisory board made up of local notables, she alone presided over the administration of her school. Ibid., 177.

[44] Ibid.

[45] This influence was often felt particularly in the elementary-level classes, since teachers often owed their appointments to such posts to the recommendation of the school directrice. Beholden to the school directrice, these women might more easily accept her guidance on such matters. Ibid., 176.

hinged on the municipality's continuing willingness to support it, while a collège would collapse if a hostile municipality refused to renew its ten-year contract. Moreover, any directrice who hoped to get her school upgraded to a collège or a lycée or who simply wanted better buildings depended largely on support in the community. In many places, boarding facilities attached to girls' secondary schools drew the directrice further into municipal affairs. Under the law of 1880, the state refused to take responsibility for boarding schools but left municipalities free to institute them. Almost everywhere outside of Paris, student residences grew up beside the new girls' secondary schools. Sometimes a local woman ran them, but elsewhere municipal officials asked the school's directrice to do it. For all these reasons a directrice, even though she lived inside her school, necessarily engaged herself actively with the community where she worked.

Given the multiple audiences to which she had to play, a school directrice needed above all to command respect, and this greatly affected whom the ministry selected. Normally women in their twenties were not considered old enough to lead a school. Plainness and even a lack of social sophistication, on the other hand, did not handicap a candidate. In provincial settings where more rustic social forms obtained, grand manners might even mar a school head's reputation. As for picking leaders for the great lycées, the ministry looked for women whose integrity even more than social manners imparted dignity to their personal demeanor. *Distinction* was the inspectors' usual term for this attribute, in origin a quality of mind, which had the potential for transforming even gauche and physically unattractive women into imposing representatives of their schools. Léonie Allégret (class of 1882) had neither looks nor social background in her favor. Described as ugly by one inspector general,[46] this daughter of impoverished artisans[47] eventually rose to the top of her profession to direct a Parisian lycée. Already at age thirty she possessed the characteristic mark of a "directrice d'élite." "Her face . . . lights up when she talks about her students, their education, their future, about her collaborators, their teaching, about the great work, so delicate and so important, to which she is entirely devoted. She is universally respected at Guéret and in the region and is completely worthy and capable of directing a Parisian lycée."[48]

This flattering account of Allégret as a young directrice points up a second mark of excellence in this profession. A good directrice felt a gen-

[46] Dossier personnel, Léonie Allégret, notes, 1888, F17 22599, A.N. Also see report by chairman of the jury that awarded her the agrégation, notes, 1884.

[47] Wurmser-Dégouy, *Trois Éducatrices modernes,* 13.

[48] Dossier personnel, Léonie Allégret, correspondance, 1894, F17 22599, A.N.

uine enthusiasm for the task of educating girls. Even more than in a teacher, professional zeal in a school head gratified inspectors, since her fervor could potentially inspire a school's entire staff. Yet Allégret's credentials went beyond her authoritative bearing and professional commitment to include a style of relating to her students lauded by her superiors as maternal. "She governs this large establishment, which she founded and which she profoundly loves, with a rare firmness and an almost maternal gentleness," enthused a rector over her management of the lycée of Guéret. "She is not content to supervise the functioning of the academic program," reported the academy inspector; "she actively concerns herself with the moral education and physical development of the girls."[49] Allégret's solicitude for the well-being of her students and her interest in their moral education rounded out a portrait of a school directrice deemed the best the Third Republic had to offer. Several Sévriennes in addition to Léonie Allégret measured up to these high standards. Many of them, moreover, came as she did from a Protestant milieu.

Not all Protestants who entered the administration bore the stamp of natural leaders. Lucie Kuss, for instance, eventually a major star in the firmament of Protestant directrices, showed little sign as a young woman of the magnetism characteristic of the better heads of schools. Personally reserved, she lacked the warmth that promised a maternal style of administration. Indeed, in 1887, when she first requested a directorate, an inspector general expressed strong reservations. "She is good enough to teach in Paris but not for a *direction*. Prestige, authority, and worldly experience would be most likely missing should she get such a position." Sure enough, at Besançon where Kuss became directrice the following year, her rector reported, "I have advised her to live a less isolated existence, to put herself as often as possible in contact with students' families, to take numerous measures to establish an exact, vigilant, and maternal discipline, and to develop even in a day school the familial life necessary for students' moral education and for the affectionate sympathies of the entire staff."[50]

Still, if at first the reserve of this young Protestant limited her impact, intelligence and dedication to the task eventually pulled her through. At Besançon, she turned her school within nine years into a major lycée, despite an initially indifferent climate of opinion. As a reward for her achievement, in 1895 the ministry sent her on to Paris where she made her slow adjustment to the style of leadership expected in girls' second-

[49] Dossier personnel, Léonie Allégret, correspondance, 1894, and notes, 1890, F17 22599, A.N.

[50] Dossier personnel, Lucie Kuss, notes, 1887, 1889, F17 22621, A.N.

ary schools. Put off at first by the reticence of Kuss's manner, the vice-rector at Paris complained, "Carries her reserve a bit far sometimes and does not always know how to establish her authority." Yet he also recognized that "with her application and diligence" she would "develop quickly." Within a couple of years, reports by various of her inspectors proved this prediction right. "An excellent directrice who pays the closest attention to every detail of the school's activities" was how one inspector general described her in 1898; she was "equally preoccupied with the moral and intellectual progress of each child . . . as with their dress and manners." Two years later, another of her superiors exulted, "Respected and loved by both her staff and students, there is no question that under the leadership of Mlle Kuss the Lycée Victor Hugo will prosper and grow increasingly appreciated."[51]

Such praise was not uncommon in the dossiers of Protestant directrices. After studying inspectors' portraits of these women, one might well conclude that a Protestant upbringing afforded an outstanding preparation for this post, for it appeared to have produced young women with a predilection for hard work, the initiative of born administrators, and, most characteristic of all, a driving sense of pedagogical mission. The memory of Mme Favre rises irrepressibly to join the images evoked by inspectors' sketches of these distinguished Protestant school heads. All of them avowed a deep commitment not just to advancing feminine instruction but also and especially to using that education for purposes of moral growth. In the spirit of Mme Favre, women like Léonie Allégret and Lucie Kuss believed deeply in the moral purposes that inspired the pedagogical reformers of the early Third Republic, men who, in answer to the republican dilemma of how to offer moral training without religion, fastened on the hope of cultivating a sense of individual moral responsibility in each student. Much of the credit for the initial formulation of this program in the 1870s belonged to Protestant reformers.[52] Not surprisingly, their educational objectives struck a strong responsive chord in women from the same religious culture. The particular concern of Protestants with building character doubtlessly explains why so many women of this faith applied for positions as directrices. Likewise, this commitment to moral education earned high marks with rectors and inspectors. In the earnestness of their pedagogical convictions, not in favoritism by a Protestant director, lies the real key to the prominence of Protestants as heads of girls' secondary schools.

[51] Ibid., notes, 1896, 1898, 1900.

[52] According to Mayeur, Protestants dominated the Société pour l'étude des questions de l'enseignement secondaire, which articulated the principles underlying the new republican pedagogy. *L'Enseignement secondaire*, 365.

Neither "distinction," nor a sense of mission, nor maternal sentiments, however, were limited to Protestant heads of schools. Officials found some version of these qualities in all directrices of whom they approved, and surprisingly many Sévriennes figured in that favored category. Given the almost accidental way in which several of these women took up administrative work, this record of official satisfaction seems on the face of it remarkable. Indeed, only four of the seventy-one women who became directrices over the course of their careers left their posts involuntarily as victims of ministerial displeasure.[53] The vast majority of Sévriennes, once they shifted out of teaching, finished their professional careers as heads of schools.

The stability of this professional corps owes much to attitudes within the ministry. Both the difficulties of the founding years and the great diversity among girls' secondary schools encouraged a certain official tolerance for women who clearly flopped in any particular administrative setting. A transfer to another post could often be arranged without demotion. Moreover, Sévriennes in administration benefited from the support that rectors and inspectors generally extended to directrices faced with insubordination from their teachers. Still, the willingness of rectors and inspectors to recommend such lenient treatment depended largely on their perception that a woman took her educational task to heart.

Few Sévriennes failed to meet that minimum criterion as a school directrice. In some ways, their behavior replicates the dedication typical of Sévriennes in teaching. Many of the reasons that underlie the selfless attitude of teachers also operated at the level of administration. Yet for directrices the sense of personal responsibility to a corporate effort was necessarily different. They did not endure that odd disjuncture between the dignity and respect accorded teachers in the classroom and the mild contempt to which their profession and often their unmarried state exposed them in the outer world. Wherever they went, inside their schools or out in the community, directrices projected an aura of authority and

---

[53] Three proved to be inept as directrices. Dossier personnel, Léontine Martellière, notes, 1891–1895, F17 22307; dossier personnel, Marie Camus (married name Poirier), notes, 1921, F17 24098; dossier personnel, Marie Huet, correspondance and notes, 1901–1904, F17 22448, A.N. The husband of the fourth risked the reputation of the school through his political activities. Dossier personnel, Léa Camourtères (married name Bérard), notes, 1892, F17 23670, A.N. Two others returned to teaching when their husbands' jobs required them to move. Dossier personnel, Marguerite Ménassier (married name Rey), correspondance, 1905–1906, F17 22507; dossier personnel, Natalie Georges (married name Beuque), correspondance and notes, 1913, F17 22602, A.N. Mayeur found a much higher rate of forced resignations when studying the entire administrative corps. Mayeur, *L'Enseignement secondaire*, 324.

prestige embodied in a title that women had held throughout the century. Unsurprisingly, these women did not, like teachers, represent themselves as martyrs. Heroic they could be as they tried against tremendous odds to win acceptance for girls' secondary schools; but they did not appear, either to themselves or to contemporaries, as sacrificial figures. Their medical history, in any case, would not support that image any longer. Though often sickly at the time they entered the administration, Sévriennes rarely fell seriously ill as directrices. Their record of good health relative to teachers' certainly paralleled and may well have reflected a dramatic difference in the emotional texture of these two groups of educators' lives.

The picture that emerges from official reports portrays a corps of women deeply engaged emotionally in the running of their schools. That loyalty arose in part from the enormous authority handed a directrice and the identification with her school that it encouraged. Directrices not only felt proprietary about their schools, many would perceive the schools they led as extensions of themselves. As much as any factor, this accounts for the commitment recognized as nearly universal by inspectors in this new administrative corps. Just as potent, though, in attaching directrices to their schools was the image fostered by the ministry of the school as a family. The maternal manner that inspectors looked for in a good directrice belonged to the pervasive familial idiom encouraged in girls' secondary schools. The same ideal inspired teachers' obligations to treat their students gently in the classroom, but the responsibilities placed on teachers for the creation of this ethos paled beside the obligations of the school directrice. Metaphorically, the entire system depended on the generative and nurturant qualities of the school directrice, represented as a kind of mother to her school.

That conception of their role was likely to appeal to women for whom familial ties and nurturing had always figured at the center of their personal concerns. Spinsters clearly relished the occasion that administration offered to found a family of their own, for they pursued their task with single-minded zeal. Even married women, however, some of whom would languish in one school for years, earnestly performed a labor that magnified their maternal role several hundredfold as every year another entering class renewed the ranks of students to be mothered. It is this aspect of directing to which Sévriennes as a group acclimatized most readily and most completely. Superiors sometimes complained that a directrice failed to keep her books, was tactless with officials, or could not impose her will upon her staff. But no Sévrienne who remained in the administration was ever faulted for showing insufficient interest in her students. That fact alone might have insured that girls' schools would adopt a tone different from that of boys' schools. In addition, though, the professional stature that Sévriennes, once promoted into the administration, would bring to the position of directrice guaranteed that they would stamp this view of feminine education on their schools.

position like a mother ... feminine in nature

8 Shaping Girls' Schools in the Belle Epoque

THE HISTORY of girls' schools during the quarter century of this generation's institutional ascendance does not present a static face. By the time Sévriennes replaced the first generation of directrices, sometime in the middle of the 1890s, girls' collèges and lycées had begun to recruit regularly within the middle classes.[1] To oversee this growth while upgrading the social clientele as much as possible became the driving ambition of these new Sévrienne directrices. Much of the story of their efforts and struggles in the Belle Epoque amplifies that theme. Yet in order to assure the expansion of their schools, these administrators had to make girls' secondary schools attractive to prospective clients. By itself, that obligation guaranteed an institutional evolution in this period, since the demands of girls attending collèges and lycées underwent important changes. Added to this public pressure, though, were other calls for innovations from pedagogical reformers and from a new generation of republican ideologues inspired by the social theory known as "solidarism." However cautiously, Sévriennes responsive to this movement set out to transform girls' secondary schools from unobtrusive institutions modeled on the cloister into institutions open to the social and intellectual currents of their time.

One aspect of school life remained the same throughout these changes, though. Sévriennes brought to the role of directrice differing versions of the same institutional ideal. In the spirit of Sèvres's own example, the school that they imagined formed a moral community, binding students, teachers, and directrice together in a kind of family. The perfect realization of that vision turned directrices and teachers into allies in a common mission whose object was the carefully guided intellectual and moral maturation of each student. Ideally, the entire faculty stood behind their school head in a common willingness to sacrifice their personal interests in selfless dedication to the cause. Nowhere did a school live up to that

---

[1] "Tableau du personnel des lycées et collèges de jeunes filles, par ordre d'ancienneté," *ESDFJ* 2 (1900): 49–83. Fifty-six percent of all lycées had Sévriennes at their heads in 1900, including all but six of the largest schools: Racine and Fénélon in Paris, Toulouse, Lyon, Bordeaux, and Amiens. Five of these would acquire a Sévrienne at their helm within a decade.

exemplary image wholly, but the very effort to implant this ideal as a collective goal placed a characteristic imprint on schools led by Sévriennes throughout the Belle Epoque.

The Model School for Whom?

Sévriennes who took charge of girls' secondary schools in the later 1890s inherited an institution already middle-class in its recruitment.[2] Frequented earlier by girls from the petty bourgeois and even working-class milieu, sometime between 1892 and 1898, these schools jettisoned the lowest of their social elements and began to recruit primarily from the middle classes. That achievement notwithstanding, at the turn of the century girls' collèges and lycées remained small in size and limited in appeal for both the Catholic elite of landed and military families and the upper levels of the professional classes. They had not succeeded in attracting the real clientele for which republicans had designed these feminine secondary schools: the bourgeoisie. Instead, the girls who filled their classes came from the families of small businessmen and those obliged to send their children to state schools: public teachers and middle-level functionaries. Rather than serving the old bourgeois elite, girls' secondary schools had become, in sum, a pole of attraction for Gambetta's *nouvelles couches*.[3]

Under a new generation of mainly Sévrienne directrices, girls' schools would make a major effort to expand recruitment to the upper classes. That attempt achieved only marginal success before the First World War. All the same, the very effort of appealing to the socially conservative and well-to-do bourgeois, while holding on to daughters of shopkeepers and government employees, placed heads of schools in a quandary. Each group wanted different things from feminine education; and directrices, spurred on by the desire to expand recruitment, had to meet the needs of both. The resulting institutions fulfilled the fondest dream of their republican creators for an educational system that rivaled the moralizing claims of convent schools while outbidding them in the quality of their instruction. Yet the effect of recruiting broadly from the middle classes transformed the social objectives of girls' collèges and lycées, edging them away from schooling for homemaking only toward the professional concerns of secondary schools for boys. At the time, however, directrices, utterly devoted to their schools, failed to recognize the corrosive

[2] Mayeur, *L'Enseignement secondaire*, 192–95.

[3] Ibid., 192–96. "Situation sociale des parents des élèves présentée le 15 octobre 1899 par académies," F17 14185, A.N.

impact of this alteration on the institution whose creation constituted their life's work.

The Ideal School: A Moral Community

Whatever motives or talents brought a woman into the administration, responsibility for the popular success of her own school turned a directrice into a recruiter. It was she who gave her school a profile and a personality in local settings. Happily, a precise record of just how Sévriennes as directrices wished their schools to appear found its way into a collection of school prospectuses gathered by Camille Sée for the international exhibition of 1900.[4] Personally prepared by each headmistress, these documents inscribe in their own words what Sévriennes promised parents for their girls. Most themes strike the reader as entirely predictable, especially on the subject of morality, but the treatment of the academic side of school offers some surprises. Although composed by some of the best-educated women in France, these brochures give short shrift to academic subjects. It was almost as if directrices, addressing the preoccupations of the bourgeoisie, sought to hide the real originality of their schools in hopes of reassuring parents that the traditional concerns of feminine education would be met.

All began with a physical description of the school. Directrices had three concerns in this regard: the attractiveness of their school, its relative seclusion, and its salubrious condition. Marie Prouhet (class of 1886), for instance, dwelt on the isolation of the beautiful setting for her school at Guéret. "At the extreme southern end of town, atop a hill . . . and facing a magnificent panorama," read her brochure, "the school is completely isolated from the nearby streets by fields and vast gardens planted with trees." By insisting on the almost cloistered setting of her lycée, Prouhet clearly meant to reassure protective parents of its moral safety.[5] The beauty of the view spoke to another equally traditional bourgeois expectation, namely, that an education in preparation for domestic life developed aesthetic sensibilities. Striking a more modern note in keeping with the national alarm over the depopulation crisis and the need for better health,[6] Prouhet also noted that the hygiene in her school was "exceptional." Everywhere the picture painted by these brochures was the same. Whenever, without straining credibility, directrices could praise the beauty of their schools, they did so; a sequestered setting al-

---

[4] He included these prospectuses in the much expanded seventh and last version of *Lycées et collèges de jeunes filles*, exposition edition (1900).

[5] Ibid., 1106.

[6] Karen Offen, "Depopulation," 648–76.

ways got top billing; and school heads consistently guaranteed the sanitation of their dwellings. In some cases, the concern expressed by a directrice for good hygiene went beyond just keeping students well. Hélène Leypold Séry (class of 1881) promised at Saumer "a great many games and frequent recreation," which would "maintain students in good health and high spirits."[7] Her perfectly ordered school, like several others, would not only keep the girls healthy but make them happy too.

In striking contrast to prolix remarks about the physical conditions of their schools, directrices allocated remarkably little space in these prospectuses to describing class instruction. To the extent that they referred at all to academics, they usually repeated the standard pedagogical defense of secondary education. "The object of this school," Jeanne Rith (class of 1881) intoned at Besançon, "is to give students solid information, but, more important, to develop their judgment, to elevate their thoughts, and to accustom them to thinking."[8] Like Rith, most directrices neglected to mention exactly what substantive topics girls would reflect upon. They sought instead to reassure interested parents that this education would in no way undercut the subordinate intellectual role assumed by women in contemporary life. "Our instruction . . . does not aim to produce scholars," promised Marie Grun (class of 1882), "but, instead, sensible women whose minds are open and whose characters are sufficiently firm for them to fulfill their roles in the family and society honorably."[9] With that remark, Grun intended to soothe fears that secondary schools for girls aimed to change the social order. The main task of this education, as represented by these school heads, remained the customary one of turning girls into morally reliable women for their duties in the home.

Overall, directrices waxed particularly eloquent on the theme of moral education. Jeanne Rith enthused, "The first rule of this establishment is to inspire in students self-respect, a love of duty, and devotion to the family and the nation; to turn them into serious women; and to prepare them to become good mothers of families."[10] Marie Prouhet confirmed this orientation at Guéret: "Building character holds an important place in the preoccupations of the directrice, the professors, and the maîtresses."[11] To make sure that students did not abuse their independence, Marie Grun vowed personally to inspect every book that entered her lycée at Charleville and every letter which left it, a practice common in

[7] *Lycées et collèges de jeunes filles*, (1900), 1141.
[8] Ibid., 1108.
[9] Ibid., 1099.
[10] Ibid., 1108.
[11] Ibid., 1103.

Catholic boarding schools. Inspired for her part by the discipline of Sèvres and her Protestant upbringing, Hélène Leypold Séry pledged to rely
instead on the restraints imposed by conscience. "Maîtresses live among
the students and seek to inspire in them rectitude and goodness," with
the result, she claimed, that at the lycée of Saumur, "girls are led into
obedience to the rules through affection and respect."[12]

Reading these prospectuses, one can hardly miss the way they weave
together traditional expectations for girls' schools with newer pedagogical objectives preached at Sèvres. The older themes reflect the absolute
insistence of the bourgeosie on the moral reliability of schools where
they sent their daughters. Mothers placing daughters in a pensionnat typically entrusted them specifically to the directrice as the authority who
personally guaranteed the morality of her school. Sévriennes designed
these brochures, therefore, to present themselves as scrupulously attentive to the moral safety of their schools. At the same time, these adver-
tisements announce a central theme from the pedagogy taught at Sèvres:
the development of a reflective conscience. Certainly the focus on the
moral impact of their schools arose for many women from their own pedagogical convictions. Several, inspired by their religious training, had requested an administrative post out of personal interest in the moral side
of schooling. But Sévriennes had also learned in their professional education to cast their intellectual endeavors in a moralizing light. If these
prospectuses appear in retrospect unusually skewed toward the moral
issues of instruction, they merely echo the message taught at Sèvres.

The Model School Implemented

The inspiration of their alma mater becomes still clearer when
we turn from the goals of directrices as enunciated in prospectuses to
their modes of implementing them. Free to teach whatever they wished,
most heads of schools chose the course called la morale, designed to instruct third-year students in their social duties. In itself the subject seems
well suited to a school head. For someone trained at Sèvres, its special
interest lay in the method of instruction urged on teachers. Conceived by
its inventors as the core of girls' studies, la morale did not require a formal manner of delivery. The official teaching manual called for an intimate, conversational approach in class to maximize the teacher's personal impact. Treated in this way, such a course perfectly matched the
image of a directrice projected by prospectuses. But it equally recalled
the maternal, moralizing style that Mme Favre had assumed at Sèvres in

[12] Ibid., 1141.

turning novices into teachers. Her example proved exceptionally powerful. As her protégées took the helm of schools all over France, two
traits came to characterize girls' collèges and lycées. One was their leaders' strong commitment to moralizing girls' studies; the other, their eagerness for a maternal intimacy with students.

The small size of girls' secondary schools at the turn of the century
greatly facilitated efforts by directrices to personalize the atmosphere
within them. Opportunities increased wherever local councils attached
a pensionnat to a collège or a lycée, an almost universal practice outside
Paris, since a familial atmosphere could develop far more easily in
schools where students were continuously present. By 1898 one-quarter
of the girls enrolled in collèges and lycées boarded at school, and at least
as many more took lunch there or stayed a couple of hours after school
to study.[13] For directrices who aspired to exercise a lasting moral influence on their students, this development could only ease the way. Dor-
mitories, which in boys' lycées filled massive halls lined with several
rows of beds, in girls' schools often slept fewer than twenty-five. In these
conditions, directrices could usually arrange to enhance their schools
with a few individualized creature comforts. Older boarders usually had
partitions between their beds and curtained doorways to insure their privacy, while in study halls, directrices sometimes managed to replace the
standard student bench with chairs.[14]

Still, the main method for personalizing the experience of students in
girls' school was the individual attention that directrices as well as
teachers devoted to them. All administrative heads made it a practice to
learn the names of students, something of their family background, and
as much as possible about their character and progress. When girls dis-
obeyed, they excused themselves to the directrice and received their
punishment from her. When they excelled at school, the directrice announced the fact before their classmates, either during trimester reports
or at the annual prize ceremony at graduation. Moreover, should a girl
fall ill, arrangements for her care were handled by the school head in
loco parentis.[15]

A school gathering became another popular tool used by administrators to impart a homey air to school life. In smaller schools, invitations
to dinner, weekly parties, and even nightly salutations in the manner of

[13] Calculated from officially compiled figures found in Ministère de l'instruction publique, "Lycées et collèges des jeunes filles, population scolaire au 5 novembre de 1892
à 1898 inclus," F17 14185, A.N.

[14] *Lycées et collèges de jeunes filles* (1900), 1128–29.

[15] One directrice, Amélie Duporge (class of 1888), even took in a student dying of
diphtheria whose parents had temporarily left the country. Dossier personnel, notes,
1908, F17 23589, A.N.

Mme Favre were not unusual. Yet even in larger schools, Sévriennes found ways to use collective gatherings in an intimate, familial way. Each morning in her lycée at Versailles, for instance, Léonie Allégret began the school day with an assembly in which she presented her "enfants" with a homily. "She would talk with them familiarly about all manner of subjects," her biographer recounted: "an anecdote, a birthday, an incident from the previous evening, a moral idea—one by one, these ideas would inspire her conversations. Their form was intimate and lively, their tone simple and friendly, with no big words or eloquent effects . . . but always with the profound accent of her conviction."[16] Everywhere, directrices made room for school parties. The usual schedule included a Christmas and a springtime celebration. On such occasions, students performed a play or concert; sometimes the school chorus sang. But whatever the performance, girls spent a great many weeks in preparation, weeks when a spirit of belonging shaped their mutual activities.

Ideally, teachers, too, joined this social side of school events. In this regard, Sévriennes as heads of schools proved no less demanding on their colleagues than their predecessors. Given the missionary zeal of some alumnae, they may even have increased the moral pressure placed on teachers. If so, they also met with less resistance. Lucie Kuss, for one, left a moving reminiscence of her staff's collective efforts at the Lycée Victor Hugo in Paris.[17] Speaking to her former students, she recalled in 1921 with clear nostalgia, "We worked together for you in an absolute union: we gave all our ardor, all our intelligence, and all our devotion." She then detailed the goals that she had shared with a faculty composed almost entirely of Sévriennes from the early classes. "Certainly your teachers tried to teach you all the wonderful things that you expected from your lycée education. But above all, they forced themselves to develop your intelligence and your judgment, to teach you to reflect, to give you a taste for work and intellectual integrity, to turn you into cultivated young women, simple and modest. We wanted you courageous, sincere and good, smiling and gay, ready to fulfill your duty." It was not enough for this directrice and her staff to offer intellectual and moral guidance, according to Lucie Kuss. Together they worked to introduce a spirit of belonging. "We tried to imbue those lessons with our warm affection, to make the school welcoming for you, a place for joyous reunions so that much later you would return with pleasure to your lycée which had become for you a second family."[18]

---

[16] Wurmser-Dégouy, *Trois Éducatrices modernes*, 26.

[17] She administered this school from 1895 to 1913.

[18] "Le 25e anniversaire du Lycée Victor Hugo; discours de Mlle L. Kuss," *ESDJF* 2 (1921): 31.

Familial metaphors turned up repeatedly in the language circulating in and around these institutions in the Belle Epoque. Directrices addressed their students as "my children"; inspectors spoke in praise of "maternal" school heads; and alumnae associations made up of former students, as Camille Sée once neatly put it, "formed the family of a lycée or a collège."[19] Efforts to develop such perceptions of a school community were not invented for girls' secondary schools. Catholic schools adopted the same metaphors in schooling boys as well as girls.[20] Sèvres had used familial images to wonderful effect. So had normal schools for women primary teachers, even before the Third Republic.[21] But for lycées, modeled since Napoleon's time after the army and the barracks, this represented an important new departure.

The difference was clearly perceptible to school inspectors who in 1899/1900 undertook an official inquest into the state of secondary education throughout the nation. Summarizing the results of the reports by his subordinates on boys' schools in his region, the rector of Caen concluded: "It is indisputable that nowhere or almost nowhere do teachers participate in the life of their schools. Very few spend any time at all with students outside class. . . . The monthly meetings of professeurs, from which so much was hoped, . . . do not even occur in the larger establishments, and nowhere do they have any appreciable influence on the course of studies."[22] The inspector for the Seine-Inférieure confirmed this lack of solidarity among répétiteurs in Paris. "Preoccupied, above all, by their own studies and their future success, these young men have little interest in their work. . . . The directors of Lakanal and Michelet are severely critical of their répétiteurs, who are for the most part tactless, unrestrained, and impertinent, and whenever possible, avoid doing work so as to increase the time available for earning money on the side."[23] At the same meeting of the council of the Academy of Paris, the report on girls' schools read as follows: "Almost everywhere there reigns perfect understanding between directrices and staff on how to coordinate intellectual and moral guidance in order to inspire in students the spirit of solidarity that is indispensable to an education in common. . . . I am

[19] *Lycées et collèges de jeunes filles* (1900), xxxiii.

[20] For an analysis of this phenomenon in boys' Catholic secondary schools, see John W. Padberg, *Colleges in Controversy; The Jesuit Schools in France from Revival to Suppression, 1815–1880* (Cambridge: Harvard Univ. Press, 1969).

[21] Quartararo, "The *Ecoles Normales Primaires d'Institutrices*," 162–251.

[22] Rapports annuels sur la situation de l'enseignement secondaire 1899/1900. Académie de Caen, conseil académique, "L'Enseignement dans l'académie de Caen de 1898 à 1899 pour les établissements publics," F17 6829, A.N.

[23] Académie de Paris, conseil académique, "Rapport de M. Hémon, lycées de garçons (Seine), juin 1900," F17 6829, A.N.

struck by the unanimity that prevails and by the desire of everyone to help each other. Examples of individualism and narrow self-absorption are the rare exceptions."[24]

Reports to academic councils elsewhere in France repeated similar findings. Of the girls' collège at Alais in the Midi, an inspector at Montpellier could write, "Monthly meetings of the professeurs take place regularly and the strongest spirit of solidarity pervades them."[25] To the far west, at Brest, the inspector of the Finistère reported, "The directrice has succeeded in uniting the personnel in a spirit of solidarity that has powerfully contributed to the prosperity and good name of this lycée."[26] In the east, at Lons-le-Saunier, an inspector repeated the same story. "The attitude of the staff is very satisfactory. Relations of cordial sympathy and esteem exist among the teachers and between the teachers and their administrative head."[27]

The overwhelming impression left by these reports is that a new mood had entered girls' schools, transforming routine life within them. Not every school exuded harmony. Some directrices were less adept than others,[28] and there were always teachers who refused to pursue collective goals. Nevertheless, the evidence attesting to ongoing sparring is scattered and infrequent.[29] Even a cursory glance at teachers' dossiers turns up a striking change of tone in staff relations. Tales of feuds between directrices and teachers no longer fill reports by school inspectors. Hardly ever because of a dispute with a directrice would a teacher now expect to lose her job. By 1900 the factionalism that had plagued young teachers' lives was in decline. In its place, a new esprit de corps had taken hold in girls' secondary schools.

The atmosphere of good will apparently extended to students in these lycées and collèges for girls as well. In school after school, inspectors for

[24] Académie de Paris, conseil académique, "Rapport sur les lycées et collèges de jeunes filles de l'académie, session de juin 1900," F17 6829, A.N.

[25] Académie de Montpellier, conseil académique, "Rapport sur la situation de l'enseignement secondaire public dans le département du Gard, mai 1900," F17 6829, A.N.

[26] Académie de Rennes, inspecteur académique de Finistère, "Rapport 1900, lycée Brest," F17 6829, A.N.

[27] Académie de Besançon, conseil académique, "Rapport sur la situation de l'enseignement secondaire du Jura en 1900," F17 6829, A.N.

[28] Women like Marthe Dugland at Castres (class of 1881) and Jeanne Mehl at Le Mans (class of 1887), though sharing the educational aspirations of Léonie Allégret and Lucie Kuss, lacked the tact or personal charm required to galvanize their staffs. Dossier personnel, Marthe Dugland, F17 22612, and Jeanne Mehl, F17 24013, A.N.

[29] The main exception to this otherwise peaceable new era were disputes between directrices of schools and women appointed by municipalities to head a municipal internat. See, for example, dossier personnel, Julie Esménard, notes, 1911, F17 23991, A.N.

the inquest of 1899/1900 found students docile, receptive, and, to all appearances, happy in their schools. At Lons-le-Saunier, the inspector wrote: "Girls are attached to the lycée and to their teachers. They work from preference and sometimes with ardor, and it is truly rare for a serious delinquency to occur."[30] At Bourg, the inspector found: "Students are docile, well-disposed, and generally well brought up. They also want to bring honor to their school. The notions of morality and proper behavior that they receive in several intimate gatherings seem to have a good effect on them. . . . The desire to please their teachers is enough to maintain their good behavior and hard work."[31] Even in the large lycée at Bordeaux, the inspector reported that discipline was easy and students' spirits high.

> The only punishment in use is a two-hour detention and very often it goes begging. If, from time to time, two or three students do receive this punishment, it is for some silliness, some negligence, or a little laziness, never for lack of docility. It is an excellent tradition established in this lycée to rely on students' feelings of delicacy and self-respect and to replace the fear of punishment with the fear, no less effective, of displeasing one's teacher and of diminishing oneself in one's own eyes.[32]

Reports of this unique atmosphere in girls' schools do not vanish after 1900. Fourteen years later and two months before the outbreak of war, the inspector for the Academy of Paris presented to his academic council confirmation that the promise of this personalized instruction had borne fruit.

> In this lively education girls take a real delight. The proof is in a fact for which one would find with difficulty an equivalent in boys' schools. It is not rare for girls to return to the lycée to play on Thursday afternoons and on all other holidays! It is true that nothing is neglected to make them love their school; artwork and images of good taste multiply around them; the most ingenious methods are used to keep that charming sign of well-being on their faces: gaiety. There, as in the family, they are enveloped in a climate of affection.[33]

[30] Ibid.

[31] Académie de Lyon, inspecteur académique de l'Ain, "Rapport en 1900, lycée de jeunes filles de Bourg," F17 6829, A.N.

[32] Académie de Bordeaux, "Rapport d'ensemble sur la situation de l'enseignement public, 31 décembre 1899," F17 6829, A.N.

[33] J. Combarieu, "L'Enseignement secondaire des jeunes filles pendant la guerre: Académie de Paris. Rapport présenté au Conseil académique (Extraits)," ESDJF 1 (1915): 52.

The rhapsodic note sounded in this description recalls the tone of Lucie Kuss's recollections of her own lycée before the war. Almost certainly, both accounts exaggerate the degree to which girls' schools actually achieved the closeness they depict. These officials, after all, wanted to believe in the uniqueness of the institutions they had helped to pioneer. The reigning ideology of difference between the genders prompted them to look in girls' schools for qualities defined to be appropriately female. These reservations notwithstanding, a distinctive ethos did undeniably exist within these schools among the professional generation that led them through the Belle Epoque. Moreover, the commitment of directrices and teachers to their professional ideals surely touched the hearts as well as minds of some young students.

Implementing the Underside of Moralism

Lest Sévriennes' high-minded rhetoric make us forget it, though, beneath the moralizing message that their schools addressed to bourgeois families lay a deep and, on occasion, piteously severe class bias. Republicans had intended girls' secondary schools to serve a bourgeois clientele, and those in charge of carrying out their plans determined to make that vision real. The politics of this endeavor often led in devious directions. Many of the most overtly discriminatory actions had been taken by the women who preceded Sévriennes as school directrices, but wherever the presence of girls from the working classes or even petty bourgeoisie within a student body threatened to scare off more socially advantaged families, Sévriennes, too, took arbitrary steps. One favorite tactic was simply to expel girls without an acceptable social background. In 1899 the inspector at Saumur rejoiced to find that Mme Séry (Hélène Leypold, class of 1881) had "pursued the work of eliminating dubious students with great firmness and tact." "So great is her success," he marveled, "that she succeeded in getting all those who feared a forced expulsion to leave the lycée spontaneously. Thus, we find today, coming to the lycée, students belonging to a social milieu that until now refused us its confidence."[34] Other directrices, pursuing a related tactic, persuaded municipal councils to cut back on the scholarships available for their schools.[35] Marie Mangin (class of 1883) followed this strategy at Morlaix with the intended results.[36]

[34] "L'Inspecteur d'académie de Marne et Loire sur la situation du collège de jeunes filles de Saumur au 1er mai 1900," F17 6829, A.N.

[35] Mayeur, L'Enseignement secondaire, 187–90.

[36] Dossier personnel, Marie Mangin, notes, 1901, F17 23859, A.N. For a general dis-

Scholarships

Officials justified such exclusions partly on the grounds that secondary education applied to girls had little use for daughters without property. Boys' schools could comfortably adopt a policy of promoting sons with talent from the lower classes since, in theory, talent was all they needed in the public world to which the baccalauréat led. Girls' schools, by contrast, groomed their graduates for a domestic future possible only to those with dowries. The girls at Morlaix, so inhospitably treated by Marie Mangin, were in the inspector's view "incapable of profiting from the instruction and creating difficulties because of that."[37] Secondary education as conceived by its inventors had nothing to offer to the dowerless girl apart from an exceedingly narrow professional ladder, for the truly gifted student, leading to secondary teaching.

An even more pressing consideration, though, comprised the attitudes of families whom officials responsible for girls' collèges and lycées desired to attract. Bourgeois parents wanted guarantees that daughters would not encounter girls of substantially lower social origins in their schools. Apparently, some distinguished in this respect between their sons' and daughters' education. This accounted, in one inspector's view, for the difficulty that the girls' lycée at Nice experienced in recruiting from the well-to-do, while the boys' lycée drew students easily from this milieu.

> Unfortunately, the girls' lycée is not well viewed in a certain society that prefers not only convent schools . . . but even [other] lay institutions. . . . The cours secondaire that preceded it apparently had a more socially elevated clientele. The lycée attracted from the start, by contrast, the petty bourgeoisie. "Do not enroll your daughter," a nun told a woman whom I know. "She will meet there only butchers' daughters." To a good liberal, I protested his decision not to entrust his daughters to us when we had his son: "It is all right with me," he replied, "if the son of a concierge tutoie[s] my son in the lycée, but I would not want his sisters tutoyées by classmates who do not have the same upbringing."[38]

sexuality

The source of this anxiety over casual friendships with girls from lower classes centered on the issue of sexuality. The middle classes and the bourgeoisie spent enormous energy on efforts to preserve their

cussion of the policy toward girls' scholarships, see Mayeur, *L'Enseignement secondaire*, 184–87.

[37] Dossier personnel, Marie Mangin, notes, 1901, F17 23859, A.N.

[38] Académie d'Aix, inspecteur académique des Alpes Maritimes, "Rapport sur la situation de l'enseignement secondaire, 1899," F17 6892, A.N.

daughters' ignorance and innocence in sexual matters.[39] Based on the promiscuity that they believed prevailed in working-class society, they feared that girls from that stratum, once they became the confidantes of their daughters, would reveal the hidden secrets of the boudoir and the brothel. Thus, with a sigh of relief, the academy inspector at Bourg announced, after some expulsions of lower-class girls there, "It has been possible to dismiss from the lycée those whose contact might have proved dangerous."[40]

Long after the social axis of girls' schools had shifted to the solid middle class, this apprehension on the part of parents dictated vigilance on the part of school directrices. Misdemeanors would not be treated lightly, and errant girls could not get a second chance. Lucie Ravaire (class of 1884) earned the unforgiving enmity of the mayor at Nancy when she did not dismiss a student who had chalked an obscene graffito on a door inside the school.[41] Claire Poisson (class of 1884) received a censure from the ministry after an investigation at Avranches of declining school enrollments revealed that she had not expelled a girl who had pinned a sign to a schoolmate's back that read, "For hire twelve sous per night."[42] Still, for the most part, directrices were as implacable in their judgments as the ministry. Camille Porte (class of 1882) expelled a fifteen-year-old student at Montauban for telling another girl "about intercourse and the fact that one can have babies outside marriage." "Other families," her rector explained, "were threatening to take their daughters out of school."[43]

Adjusting Instruction to a Socially Mixed Clientele

Attracting even a bourgeois clientele sometimes required more than a morally and physically safe environment, however. Although this was glossed over by school prospectuses in 1900, families from the middle classes did have a keen interest in certain forms of feminine instruction—forms that did not figure in the secondary program. Failure to provide it could risk the future of a school. Alert to such a danger, directrices charged with the responsibility of making schools grow re-

[39] An important account of this effort to repress sexuality in a Victorian culture obsessed with the subject appears in Michel Foucault, *The History of Sexuality*, trans. Alan Sheridan (New York: Hurley, 1978).

[40] Conseil académique, Bourg, *Rapport sur l'enseignement secondaire des jeunes filles 1896–97*, F17 6829, A.N.

[41] Dossier personnel, Lucie Ravaire, correspondance, 1906, F17 23947, A.N.

[42] Dossier personnel, Claire Poisson, correspondance, 1911, F17 23685, A.N.

[43] Dossier personnel, Camille Porte, correspondance, 1904, F17 23792, A.N.

sponded promptly to demands for these additions. Among them figured religious education. Several heads of girls' schools arranged for local clergy to offer such instruction at their schools. Thus, as part of her campaign to attract well-to-do students to her lycée at Versailles, the Protestant directrice Léonie Allégret engaged the services of a chaplain. The results fulfilled her fondest hopes. By 1897, a jubilant inspector reported, "The lycée is up one-third in size from last year and is now recruiting from a population closed to it before, that is, among daughters of officers, formerly placed in convent schools."[44]

A second innovation, even more widespread, involved preparing students to take the brevets de capacité, degrees acquired through public examinations in each department that credentialed women as primary school teachers. By the 1880s it was fashionable in Paris and a growing practice in small towns for girls from all levels of the middle classes to get one or both of the two brevets. From a purely professional degree, the brevet supérieur had evolved in some milieus into the distinguishing possession of an educated woman.[45] Private boarding schools and normal schools alike prepared their students to pass these credentialing exams, and both parents and their daughters were enthusiastic. Far from shunning the publicity of public examinations, decried by advocates of state secondary schools as an immodest exercise for girls, increasing numbers of bourgeois parents approved such recognition for a daughter. By 1905 one Sévrienne reported, "One must have lived in a small town to grasp completely the resplendent pride of the young provincial girl whose name appears in the local paper."[46]

The brevet had other advantages over the little-known secondary diploma for girls, which the law of 1880 had created. Whereas the latter had little immediate value as a professional credential,[47] the brevets qualified the holders for a respectable feminine profession. Even girls looking for employment in the expanding service sector had better luck if their credentials included this well-known degree. Of course, the founders of girls' schools had not expected mercenary interest to affect the calculations of their students. However, as magnets for the families of the nouvelles couches, girls' secondary schools recruited from a lower social

[44] Lycée de jeunes filles de Versailles, "Rapport annuel (année scolaire 1896–7), le 18 mai 1897," F17 6828, A.N.

[45] Mayeur, *L'Enseignement secondaire*, 234–38.

[46] Anonymous Sévrienne, "Le Diplôme de fin d'études secondaires et le brevet de l'enseignement primaire supérieur," *ESDJF* 1 (1905): 152–53.

[47] The only professional position for which the diplôme qualified a woman was that of maîtresse-répétitrice at a girls' secondary school. She could not even use it to teach in a primary school.

base than Sée originally intended, including some students who came to school planning to find work after the completion of their studies. Even the moderately well-off pursued an educational strategy that was typically bourgeois, which is to say prudential. As one experienced directrice explained in 1905: "In this day and age, few fortunes are absolutely safe. People get used to thinking that fate rules their destiny and take precautions against a ruinous future."[48] To have ignored such widely based concerns when private schools met them would have risked the very survival of a collège or lycée in some places.[49] Most directrices had no choice but to accommodate their clients by asking teachers to add subjects covered on the brevets to a secondary syllabus or to teach a course geared to those exams.

When in 1902 a reform of the baccalauréat program introduced four different tracks for the first stage of this diploma, conditions changed again.[50] A few girls who had taken the feminine humanities curriculum quickly discovered that with two years or so of tutoring in Latin, they could pass the Latin–modern languages option, known as the baccalauréat "B." A new fashion threatened to catch hold among the clientele of girls' schools. Pure ambition or even sibling rivalry must have spurred some students on. In a stratum of society where knowledge of Latin and possession of the baccalauréat represented a cherished badge of masculine social status, many girls inevitably felt attracted by the challenge.[51] Yet there were also more practical considerations at work. A glut of primary school teachers in the early twentieth century encouraged girls who needed employment in respectable careers to think of the baccalauréat as an alternative.[52] For directrices a more serious problem arose when some Catholic girls' schools, recovering from the separation in 1902 of Church and state, showed signs of shifting their course of studies toward the baccalauréat.[53] Scurrying to keep up with the demand, several

[48] A. Gonnet, "Le Diplôme de fin d'études dans les lycées et collèges de jeunes filles," *RU* 2 (1905): 4.

[49] Mayeur, *L'Enseignement secondaire*, 234–38.

[50] The four alternatives in the first stage included the traditional Latin-Greek program plus a new Latin–modern languages program, a new Latin-science program, and the science–modern languages program once known as *l'enseignement spécial.* They were christened in order the "A," "B," "C," and "D" baccalauréats. The second stage of the exam limited the optional programs to philosophy and mathematics.

[51] Karen Offen, "The Second Sex," *French Historical Studies* 13, no. 2 (1983): 275–76.

[52] Mayeur, *L'Enseignement secondaire*, 234–38. The political consequences of this surfeit of primary teachers have been studied in Persis Charles Hunt, "Syndicalism and Feminism among Teachers in France, 1900–1920," (Ph.D. diss., Tufts University, 1975).

[53] Mayeur, *L'Enseignement secondaire*, 391–92.

directrices set up electives in Latin for which they charged a fee. By 1912 a few lycées received official authorization to introduce a full baccalauréat option to the diploma program.[54]

All these efforts to coax the middle levels of French society into girls' schools by accommodating their prejudices and adjusting to their needs paid off handsomely in the enrollment of new students. Their total numbers, which inched upward from 1882 to 1900, thereafter leapt every year. Between 1900 and 1907, lycées and collèges more than doubled their population, which grew from 11,994 to 27,444.[55] By 1910, girls' schools boasted nearly half as many students as boys' schools, and every year the gap between them narrowed. The greatest relative expansion came between 1902 and 1909 after a republican majority led by the Radicals closed down convent schools as part of an anticlerical backlash from the Dreyfus Affair.[56] Even after 1909 enrollments rose substantially every year until the war. By 1914, with 35,000 girls in attendance, public secondary schools for girls had turned into permanent fixtures in the educational planning of the middle classes.[57]

Opening Outward to the Community

The growing popular success of girls' secondary schools opened a new era in the relations between these institutions and the communities where they recruited students. Eager in the founding years to slip unnoticed into their locales, directrices and teachers eschewed the public sphere whenever possible. They carved a public image for their schools modeled after education in the convents. That defensive reflex gradually gave way during the Belle Epoque to more expansive views as the personnel of girls' schools reached out to link their schools to the society outside. Several catalysts worked to bring this change about. Public appreciation for the results of secondary schooling and the qualities of women professeurs made possible the movement outward. Opinion within the Université actively encouraged it. However, for directrices, whose schools began bursting at the seams, necessity acted as the moving agent.

If in the 1890s a suspicious middle class had worried school heads most, after 1900, insufficient space caused greater concern. Now that col-

---

[54] Offen, "The Second Sex," 274.

[55] Gabriel Compayré, L'Enseignement secondaire des jeunes filles; legislation et organisation, 2d ed. (Paris: P. Dupont, 1907), 120.

[56] Mayeur, L'Enseignement secondaire, 163.

[57] G. Coirault, Les Cinquante Premières Années de l'enseignement secondaire féminin, 1880–1930 (Tours: Arrault, 1940).

lèges and lycées for girls were recruiting from the middle classes, they proved more popular than even their supporters had expected. Although the state responded by founding a few schools and expanding those already in existence, local governments took the least expensive way to meet demand. Rather than creating collèges, municipalities far more often opted at far less cost to set up secondary cours. Most girls' schools, meanwhile, found lodging in abandoned and dilapidated buildings that more advantaged schools had outgrown.[58] To directrices after 1900 fell the thankless task of persuading municipal authorities to spend more money on girls' secondary education: to fund an internat more generously, to build a whole new plant, and, most important, to convert a cours into a collège or upgrade a collège to a lycée. Whatever the list of wishes she drew up, a directrice needed the goodwill of local notables to underwrite it.

These circumstances demanded new strategies and somewhat different personal reserves in a directrice from those required in earlier years. In the founding era, when directrices often had to face a hostile public, reticence in socializing could work to their advantage. Especially in the effort to establish ties with local patrons, discretion generally proved the better part of valor. Remembering those times, Louise Belugou (class of 1882) remarked, "For my part, I have always congratulated myself for refusing, on arriving at Le Havre, all invitations (which was certainly not polite), until such time as I could judge the situation for myself and get oriented to the inevitable coteries, state of mind, etc."[59] Similarly, for at least a decade after her arrival at Saint-Quentin, Marie Fourcade (class of 1887) adopted the same stance, a policy that earned her glowing accolades from the academy inspector. "On the outside," he noted with approval, "she brings great discretion to her socializing, has avoided factions, and as a result is respected and esteemed."[60] Once political passions subsided around a school, though, directrices had to change their tactics. Both to build enrollments and to attract the patrons needed to increase local funding, bridges to the outside world became essential. Parents who had put their daughters in the school anticipated consultations with the school directrice. Wives of local dignitaries expected the directrice of the girls' secondary school to court them.[61] Furthermore, attendance at large-scale official gatherings figured among a school head's

court patrons [handwritten marginal note]

[58] Mayeur, *L'Enseignement secondaire*, 163, 166–68.

[59] Letter from Belugou to Julie Lochert (class of 1882), May 8, 1892. Association des élèves de Sèvres, archives, E.N.S.

[60] Dossier personnel, Marie Fourcade, notes, 1899, F17 22869, A.N.

[61] For a lively novelist's account of these social responsibilities, see Reval, *Un Lycée de jeunes filles*.

social duties. It was not enough to live with dignity inside one's school. To be successful, a directrice had to pursue regular contacts with the surrounding social world.

Louise Belugou, whose good political sense initially restrained her social life, soon adjusted her behavior to the realities of local politicking. Eight years after her arrival, she had "acquired at Le Havre great esteem," largely because once she knew whom to cultivate, she set about the task with skill. "She knows how to attract to her establishment the patronage of leading families," applauded her academy inspector.[62] Likewise, Louise Masson (class of 1887) enjoyed success at Guéret partly because, according to her rector, "her urbanity . . . smooths the way."[63] By contrast, Marie Fourcade, whose reticence originally worked to her advantage, later became the object of complaints for "lack of amiability in her relations with families."[64] Likewise, at Epernay, Marie Gasnault (class of 1889), who "hardly ever receives parents," could not prevent a gradual desertion of her collège; while at Mâcon, "a town where public education is in great favor and the boys' school prospers," Hélène Magnus (class of 1885) watched helplessly as her lycée declined because she lived "confined in her establishment."[65]

The majority of administrators, far from losing students, faced the very different problem of finding enough room for growing numbers who enrolled. From the academic council of Poitiers came this complaint in 1900. "Recruitment is now among good families, but these establishments cannot take off as long as their physical plants remain defective."[66] At Avignon the academy inspector sounded a similar alarm. "It is sad to see the administrators of collèges so badly seconded sometimes by the municipal authorities even after they have been able to acquire and retain the confidence of families. We have not obtained either enlargements or renovations, contrary to the most elementary rules of hygiene and salubrity."[67] Even in communities where local politicians smiled on public schooling, girls' secondary schools ordinarily stood in line for handouts behind more favored institutions.[68] Elsewhere, they contended not only with the stinginess of municipal councils but also with the un-

[62] Dossier personnel, Louise Belugou, notes, 1900, F17 22602, A.N.

[63] Dossier personnel, Louise Masson, notes, 1910, F17 23861, A.N.

[64] Dossier personnel, Marie Fourcade, notes, 1900, F17 22869, A.N.

[65] Dossier personnel, Marie Gasnault, notes, 1911, F17 23995. Dossier personnel, Hélène Magnus, notes, 1911, F17 23932, A.N.

[66] Conseil académique de Poitiers. Séance 1900. F17 6829, A.N.

[67] Département Vaucluse. "Rapport sur l'enseignement secondaire en 1898. Enseignement secondaire des jeunes filles. Collège d'Avignon," F17 6829, A.N.

[68] Mayeur, L'Enseignement secondaire, 167–68.

stable political fortunes of their friends. To navigate these uncertain waters safely, girls' schools required a deft hand at the helm.

Not all schools found in Sévriennes the leaders that the task required. Some, like Hélène Magnus, lacked energy. Others, such as Marie Lépine (class of 1886), showed poor political judgment, which in her case cost both local sympathy and her job. "She made the mistake," her inspector mourned in 1901, "of joining with others from the boys' lycée who waged an unfortunate campaign against the current mayor in hopes of beating him. It was the mayor's list that triumphed."[69] Several directrices, though, managed to thread their way through the rocky shoals of local coteries with brilliance. In so doing they earned both the transformation of their schools and the respect of their immediate superiors, whose awed reports sometimes read like epic tales.

"It is known against what hostility she battled in this city where, despite all kinds of discouragements, she founded, defended, and expanded her internat, one could say, at her own risk and peril." So wrote an inspector general assessing in 1894 the success of Gabrielle Duponchel (class of 1884) in her struggle at Niort to gain the support of a hostile municipal council. Forced by the unfriendly attitudes of local bourgeois families to recruit from the surrounding region, Duponchel simply had to have an internat to fill her school, but for three years she courted local politicians to no avail. Desperation led her in her second year to take six boarders into her own home. However, once she overcame resistance to her pleas, applications to the lycée swelled. Lavish in his praise, a jubilant inspector general announced in 1896: "Internat prospers. [She] has veritably created at Niort girls' secondary education. It is to her firmness, to her devotion that we owe the results obtained." Within five years, this remarkable directrice had not only seduced the municipality into building her a whole new school; she had also lured the bourgeois daughters of Niort into its classes. An official visit in 1901 presented an inspector general with the full measure of her triumph. "Lodged in a very beautiful building, the construction of which she secured from the muncipality by her stubborn insistence after long disputes that divided the council and the town into enemy camps. . . . [She] maintains numerous relations in the city. Little by little public opinion has been brought around. The prefect has enrolled his two daughters. The clientele is recruited from the *bonne bourgeoisie*."[70] Such exceptional success had earned this directrice, he concluded, consideration for a post in Paris.

In the considerably less important town of Neufchateau, Marie Lefèvre

[69] Dossier personnel, Marie Lépine, notes, 1910, F17 23856, A.N.
[70] Dossier personnel, Gabrielle Duponchel (married name Marcourt), F17 23709, A.N.

Samuel met comparable initial opposition when she came to lead the
new cours secondaire in 1904. Recently widowed and mother of four,
this novice directrice had to contend as well with an "inexperienced and
inadequate teaching staff." Yet within a year the municipal council had
agreed to upgrade the cours into a collège. Her astonished rector presented his felicitations. "She is herself the entire collège. . . . She is everywhere and manages everything. . . . The esteem and respect for her in
town has turned opinion in favor of her school, despite shameful attacks
and anonymous calumnies. She more than justifies the confidence
placed in her by her appointment to this difficult post." Two years later,
the same rector announced, "The municipality agreed to build a new
school because it knew with her as head, the school would be successful." After the completion of the new buildings, he boasted that the collège at Neufchateau, where the directrice "cares as much for education
as instruction" and everything "is carefully maintained," had become
"the gayest" school of which he knew. Under Mme Samuel, whose "dedication knows no bounds," it had also reached its maximum enrollment
one year before the war.[71]

Almost everywhere, by 1914, Sévriennes who had become directrices
were enjoying the well-earned fruits of their exhausting labors. Public
opinion had reversed itself completely regarding girls' secondary eduction. The only exceptions to this idyllic picture were lodged in certain
small, reactionary towns where secondary schools for girls came late and
had still to pay their dues. For them, the war would bring about a change
in climate. Elsewhere, however, in the calm that settled over girls'
schools after the storm, other signs emerged that this generation of Sévriennes wanted to enlarge their schools' contacts with the outside
world. One of them involved a growing interest in turning girls' secondary schools into a launching ground for charitably active bourgeois
women.

The "Solidarist" Ideal and the Socially Active
Bourgeois Woman

By 1905, in a belated and muted fashion, some of the issues that
in the 1890s had given to republican political culture a socially activist
edge began to reach girls' secondary schools. Some members of the Université, at least, would reassess the duties of bourgeois women in society,
and among these members figured several Sévrienne directrices and
teachers. The currents from which their ideas came owed much to the

[71] Dossier personnel, Marie Lefèvre (married name Samuel), F17 24220, A.N.

social doctrine of "solidarism," enunciated by Léon Bourgeois in 1895 on the philosophical foundations laid by Auguste Comte and Alfred J. E. Fouillée.[72] This doctrine insisted on the mutuality of obligations of different social groups within society and on the responsibility of the state to use its authority, especially through the schools, to encourage moral solidarity or cohesion across the nation. For some women educators, solidarism implied the need for a more socially conscious outlook in their schools. The national debate, raging since the 1890s, over the causes of and remedies for the slow growth of the French population made the need seem all the more pressing.

The first Sévrienne to signal her enthusiasm for a solidarist cause was Marguerite Caron (class of 1887), a Protestant and agrégée who would prove remarkably attuned throughout a lustrous career to the need for innovation in girls' schools. Her initial effort to promote solidarity with workers, however, got her into trouble. "In the enthusiasm of my youth," she ruefully recalled, Caron founded at La Fère with some colleagues from the boys' lycée a program of adult education called a "workers' university," which blurred solidarist ideas of mutual social obligation with socialist goals for activating workers. "The scandal was large in the eyes of a timorous directrice, to colleagues with conservative views, even to an illiberal inspector general," she remembered. "I was the object of a thousand suspicions, a thousand vexations, a thousand pinpricks, all the ill will of a narrow-minded and petty social sphere."[73] Caron blamed the uproar on the parochialism of her milieu, but she had learned a larger lesson. Association with a masculine venture to educate male workers went beyond the parameters permitted women teachers even by the reformist republican elite. In her next ventures into social activism, Caron selected projects more closely associated with traditional female duties in the bourgeoisie: namely, charity, maternity, and child rearing.[74] In this

[72] Offen, "Depopulation," 664. The importance of this political doctrine is suggested in the title of the article by J.E.S. Hayward, "The Official Social Philosophy of the French Third Republic: Léon Bourgeois and Solidarism," *International Review of Social History* 4 (1961): 261–81. Offen has shown convincingly how French feminists at the turn of the century used this vision of national solidarity to demand more rights for women within both the family and society. "Depopulation," 648–76. For a comprehensive study of this movement, see Sanford Elwitt, *The Third Republic Defended: Bourgeois Reform in France, 1880–1914* (Baton Rouge: Louisiana State Univ. Press, 1986). See the following works by Fouillée: *Le Mouvement positiviste et la conception sociologique du monde* (Paris: F. Alcan, 1896), 326–44; *La Conception morale et civique de l'enseignement* (Paris: La Revue bleue, 1902); and *Les Elements sociologiques de la morale* (Paris: F. Alcan, 1896), 1–55, 301–78.

[73] Wurmser-Dégouy, *Trois Éducatrices modernes*, 48.

[74] Named directrice at La Fère (1895–1898), Caron negotiated with the muncipality to

form, her superiors not only approved her vision of a lycée education as "an apprenticeship in equality, in solidarity, in justice," but they even made an official effort to spread the idea through girls' secondary schools.

Several officially sponsored projects to introduce a social conscience into girls collèges and lycées developed in the years just preceding World War I. The first accompanied the introduction in 1908 of a new course on domestic science called *hygiène*. Designed to upgrade the standards of natal care and homemaking in the middle classes, the curriculum also encouraged teachers to take their students to public nurseries where they could observe directly the infant victims of deprivation and poor hygiene. Meanwhile, the rector at Lille supported public lectures on child rearing at the Faculty of Medicine to which he hoped to draw "as large a number as possible of directrices, teachers, and older students from all over the academy so that they might be . . . ready to figure in the front line of the humanitarian campaign in the department of the Nord against infant mortality." By 1909 this official encouragement in the academy of Lille had spawned "in many a lycée and collège," according to the rector, "charming organizations, either guardians for or collaborators with welfare associations or local schools for infants."[75] Elsewhere, an occasional directrice like Marie Prouhet (class of 1886) took the initiative themselves. At her lycée at Le Havre, Prouhet introduced a new course on "child rearing from birth" and made plans to found a nursery school attached to her lycée that children of working mothers would attend.[76]

Altogether these endeavors represented no more than an incipient movement in the years before the war. The actual life inside girls' secondary schools hardly changed its social thrust at all. The principal signs of a more socially responsible mood showed up not in schoolgirls' day-to-day routines but rather in the clubs organized for school alumnae. In these associations a genuinely new outlook, spawned from girls' secondary schools, had effectively emerged before the war. Borrowed from the traditions of Catholic schools, alumnae clubs first appeared in collèges

---

reserve a room where every day working-class children received a breakfast paid for by her students. The young benefactors made regular visits with a teacher to observe the good effect of their philanthropy, alerted beforehand by their teachers to the role of their contributions in the national movement to control alcoholism among the poor. Ibid., 74.

[75] Rapport lu par M. George Lyon au conseil académique de Lille dans la séance du 1 juin 1909, "Sur quelques récentes innovations dans l'enseignement secondaire féminin," RU 2 (1909): 191–92.

[76] Dossier personnel, Marie Prouhet, correspondance, 1909, F17 23870, A.N.

and lycées in the 1890s under the inspiration sometimes of a teacher, more often of a school directrice intent on making further local contacts for her school. Typically the pattern of development went as follows.

> At first members hope through meeting together regularly and conversing over tea to strengthen ties made studying together at the lycée; then from these conversations spring other ideas. . . . They think about their absent classmates . . . who perhaps need help and comforting, and they eat somewhat fewer sweets in order to build up a fund for loans to needy graduates. Then, it occurs to them that they could be working on something for the poor while chatting. . . . Eventually, they organize a sewing workroom, a course on needlework, Christmas tree parties or teas for girls whom they are trying to help. . . . that is, an entire series of philanthropic activities for the benefit of the disinherited children of the town.[77]

A considerable leap in the organizational aims of these associations occurred in 1904 when several decided to form a national federation. A Sévrienne and guiding light for the alumnae association at the lycée of Besançon, Berthe Martin (class of 1884), served on the founding committee. More important than even this new scale of operations, though, was its progressive orientation. "Women left alone," the secretary-general of the new union observed in 1904, "permit themselves too easily to withdraw into private cares and their material tasks."[78] Inspired by the example of more audacious clubs, she hoped that others would come to see their social obligations as extending far beyond the hearths and cribs of their own families. To stimulate such emulation, the union published up to the war a running chronicle of the philanthropic efforts of its members. Everywhere fund-raising events for charitable causes proliferated rapidly. Several clubs individually sponsored a society that sent children to the country or the seashore for the summer. The "workrooms" of others developed so rapidly that in 1909 the bulletin characterized those of Saumur, Besançon, and Molière in Paris "veritable workshops producing clothes of all varieties."[79] Commenting on these activities in 1910, Jeanne Crouzet-Ben-Aben (class of 1888) concluded, "Social action, properly called, the work of humanity and solidarity, is nowhere forgotten and takes its place of honor alongside artistic and intellectual pur-

[77] "Communications du comité," *BTAES* (April 1906): 2.
[78] Renée Weill, "Rapport sur l'Union française des associations des anciennes élèves des lycées et collèges de jeunes filles," *BTAES* (July 1904): 257–59.
[79] "Chronique des associations," *BTAES* (October 1909): 2–3.

suits.''[80] Her very choice of words bore witness to the links between alumnae clubs and the reigning social doctrine of the day, as well as to a more expansive mood in secondary schools for girls where those in charge had consciously set out to open windows on the world around them.

Classrooms Opened on the World and the Leçon de Chose

The new mood set up reverberations even in the classroom. Although popular approval for girls' collèges and lycées and a consequent decline in officials' timorousness paved the way for this development, the real catalyst was the new orthodoxy in republican pedagogy, summed up in the instructional concept *leçon de chose*. An approach to education first developed for primary education, the leçon de chose introduced children to abstract concepts through the medium of objects they could touch and see from the familiar world around them. At first, girls' secondary schools showed little interest in this empirical approach, largely, no doubt, because the early emphasis of girls' education had stressed its moralizing purposes so strongly. By the century's end, however, the Ministry of Education would elevate empirical demonstrations in all academic subjects to an honored place in secondary studies. Urged on by their inspectors, women teachers introduced a more vivid style of learning into girls' classrooms, making concrete objects the basis for a lesson. Science teachers put together natural collections to use as demonstrations in their classes. Geography teachers brought in maps where previously verbal descriptions had sufficed. Postcards, photographs, prints, eventually even slides brought art and history classes to life.[81] On the eve of World War I, history books in girls' schools had become "veritable art books," according to one Sévrienne who used them.[82]

Nor did these efforts end with objects brought into the classroom. After 1905, some teachers adopted excursions as a teaching aid. At La Fère, with Marguerite Caron in charge, "school walks became artistic promenades, an evocation of the past, a leçon de chose." Outings even went beyond the confines of the town: "From La Fère, they went to visit Laon,

---

[80] Jeanne P. Crouzet-Ben-Aben, "Bulletin de l'enseignement secondaire des jeunes filles," RU (1910): 151.

[81] For an early sign of this new interest, see the anonymous article: "Quelques Réflexions au sujet de l'enseignement de l'histoire de l'art dans les lycées de jeunes filles," BTAES (January 1903): 179–80.

[82] E. Flobert [married name of Emma Rémoussin, class of 1883], "Le Matériel historique et géographique: les projections," ESDJF 1 (1914): 11.

... Saint-Quentin, Latour, Amiens." When Caron was transferred to Clermont-Ferrand, she found "a group of students keenly interested in local history" and increased the number of such outings. Among them was a trip to Gergovie that became a tradition in the school. "There, high up on the plateau, teachers and students read pages from Camille Julian and understood all the movements of the Romans and the Gauls. They hoped to bring back a medal, a bit of pottery.... They visited the monuments of the town, the surrounding chateaus.... They went to Bourg, Lyon, Le Puy."[83] No doubt, the perambulations of Caron's students went beyond horizons most other Sévriennes as teachers dared to cross. Nonetheless, the idea of taking girls out of school as part of their instruction gained adherents. By 1906, Sèvres itself set the example with twenty excursions in a single year.[84] Girls' schools had come a long way from the days when, dressed in dark colors, students trouped along back streets early in the morning to avoid townspeople's notice.

A Lingering Cloistered Style

Notwithstanding these important changes, on the eve of the war, girls' secondary schools remained largely curtained off from public view. Inside their walls, little notice was taken of contemporary life. A prejudice against current events and contemporary topics of debate lingered on, even if teachers occasionally ignored it.[85] Daily papers were everywhere proscribed. "We must not let the public think," an inspector general remarked in 1911 at Versailles, "that we tolerate, and, especially, that we encourage girls to read the newspapers."[86] After 1909, a new effort by the ministry to reaffirm the modesty of girls and discourage their competitive spirit reduced the ceremonial side of graduation. Directrices now announced awards for special excellence the day before prize ceremonies and notified parents of the results by mail.[87] One disappointed directrice wrote: "Parents, especially mothers, remember with nostalgia the times gone by.... They compare the dull prize ceremonies of the girls' lycée with the dazzling celebrations of private schools ... , and in

---

[83] Wurmser-Dégouy, *Trois Éducatrices modernes*, 63.

[84] Mme Cotton-Feytis, "L'Evolution de l'enseignement scientifique à l'Ecole de Sèvres," in *Le Cinquantenaire*, 223.

[85] See the debate on this subject between H. Guénot, "L'Enseignement de l'histoire dans les lycées de jeunes filles," *RU* 1 (1909): 248–60, and the anonymous author of "Sur l'enseignement de l'histoire dans les lycées de jeunes filles," *RU* 2 (1909): 19–24.

[86] Dossier personnel, Marie Nirascou, notes, 1911, F17 23715. At the time she received this rebuke, Nirascou was a professeur at the lycée of Versailles.

[87] Crouzet-Ben-Aben, "Bulletin," *RU* 2 (1909): 438.

truth, their conclusions sadden me for public education."[88] Clearly the republic had not yet chosen definitively between two images of bourgeois women. One portrayed them modestly at home, unstinting in their familial duties, given to individual acts of charity, but shy of turning their domestic expertise to curing social ills. The other pictured them as wives and mothers first but secondarily as citizens whose tasks within the *foyer* fitted them for womanly endeavors in the forum. Sévriennes from the first generation themselves teetered between these different options. But not for long. With the advent of war and a national crisis that men could not resolve alone, this generation moved directly onto the public stage as national leaders of a new civilian female army organized from girls' secondary schools.

[88] Crouzet-Ben-Aben, "Bulletin," *RU* 2 (1910): 172.

CHAPTER

9 | Sévriennes in a Nation at War

IN THE TREMENDOUS civilian effort that the calamity of war called forth, girls' schools entered fully into the current of contemporary life. These events recast the lives of the first Sévriennes abruptly. Directrices felt the changes most profoundly, as girls' collèges and lycées became centers of organization on the civilian front. At the peak of their careers, these women found themselves transformed from leaders in their schools into local notables acting as defenders of the nation. That metamorphosis carried with it important implications for redefining accepted roles for women in society. Sévriennes from the first generation were well aware of the potential. Yet the school heads who accomplished this remarkable transformation, even as their personal influence broadened, retained the conceptual framework of society with which they had begun and with it the notion of separate social tasks for men and women. They accepted the expansion of their roles into public figures of importance to the nation. They even came to champion a larger role for women in the public sphere. However, just as their own lives represented an extension of female roles from the family to the school and later to the nation, they never lost their deep commitment to the idea that women had and should continue to have a distinctive social role.

The School in Wartime

As early as August 1914, orders from the Ministry of War to set up military hospitals throughout France swept girls' secondary schools into the mainstream of war preparations. Sometimes an entire school was requisitioned by the Office of Health Services; in other cases, only a portion of the buildings. Few, however, escaped this massive effort to prepare for the inevitable casualties of combat. Responsibility for furnishing these medical wards sometimes fell to school directrices and whomever they could enlist as their assistants: teachers, alumnae, students and their mothers, all those who made up the circle of females in and around girls' collèges and lycées. The following offers a typical account of what the task entailed.

229

> *On August first, with sad hearts and anguish in their eyes, teachers
> . . . gathered around the directrice to transform their lycée into an
> emergency hospital. With them were several alumnae, students, and
> mothers. . . . First they cleared the school of all academic materials
> and transported from dormitories . . . everything that the wounded
> could use. . . . We needed three hundred beds; we searched for them
> and found them. Some of the more ingenious spread white cloths
> over boxes, converting them into fresh dressing tables. Students
> sewed hospital shirts, pillowcases, sheets; hemmed napkins; and pre-
> pared bandages. . . . Methodically throughout August and September,
> we worked to prepare . . . whatever was necessary . . . for the regular
> operation of the hospital.*[1]

Taken from the annals of the lycée at Bordeaux, this passage depicts an
event replicated all over France.[2] These preparations anticipated the active part girls' secondary schools would take in mobilizing civilian
France throughout the war.

In October 1914, the immediate task of school officials was to reopen
their doors for classes. This presented serious problems wherever the
Ministry of War had requisitioned school buildings. Some collèges and
lycées crowded back into their former quarters alongside a military hospital; a few shared buildings with another school; several devised makeshift accommodations in rented private homes or even in the apartments
of their teachers. At Bordeaux, with 758 students, Marguerite Caron secured five separate houses in order to begin the new school year on time:

> *The arrangements were improvised and picturesque. One class of
> thirty-five students is in a hastily emptied bedroom, where a glass
> wardrobe remains, but no table, desk, or lights for the evening. An-
> other . . . is in an elegant white salon, with molding and delicate
> woodwork, its walls still hung with paintings and prints. Elsewhere,
> a long veranda with windows opening onto a shady garden is by
> turns a dining room, study hall, and classroom; it is also freezing.
> Girls keep their coats on, boarders bring throw rugs from their rooms
> to cut the cold of the flagstone, and the greatest courtesy a student
> can offer a teacher is a doormat. Classes are held right in the direc-
> trice's dining room. Meanwhile, she receives visitors in a makeshift
> office lit by one tiny window and containing huge closets from which
> appear in turn her files and her socks.*[3]

[1] "Un Lycée de jeunes filles en temps de guerre (1914)," *RU* 1 (1915): 248–49.

[2] See the reference to this article in Marguerite Caron's dossier by her academy inspector in 1915, F17 24126, A.N.

[3] "Un Lycée de jeunes filles," 249–50.

By 1917 many of the hardships of such stopgap housing disappeared. Several schools had by then reclaimed their plants from the Health Office and operated in their official buildings as before. Yet the sacrifice that those early years entailed left permanent traces on the routines inside girls' secondary schools.

The war changed many parts of school life but none more quickly than the instruction offered adolescent girls. Until then, patriotism had been a muted theme in girls' schools: implicit in a curriculum focused on French culture, a topic of discussion in la morale, but lacking the explicit celebration that training for leadership in boys' schools conspicuously inspired. Given the exigencies of war, the ministry determined to end this hesitant practice. "The role of the Université is to make the entire country understand why it is fighting, for what history and for what future, for what facts and what ideas, and in thus making clear with science the national feeling . . . to uphold it and to fortify it in an unshakable confidence and will for total victory."[4] With such statements, the director of secondary education announced a radical break with lingering efforts to distance schools for girls from modern life. Henceforth, the goal of instruction would be to keep the youth of France informed. Everywhere, it seems, teachers and directrices pursued the task with zeal. At Le Mans, where Berthe Bussard (class of 1884) directed the lycée, school opened daily with lectures on "the causes of the struggle, . . . the example of loyalty given by the Belgians, . . . or the broad outline of military operations."[5] At Avranches, weekly talks enlightened students on topics as diverse as "The Unification of Germany, the Question of Alsace-Lorraine, . . . the Balkan Wars, Serbia, the French campaign of 1914."[6] Students kept abreast of daily movements in the battlefield with the help of maps to which they pinned the flags of allied troops, while along the walls of many school halls hung regularly updated lists of dead and wounded soldiers.[7]

War gave immediacy even to traditional subjects of instruction. In physics and chemistry, for example, teachers explained "the application that these sciences received in the construction of engines of destruction . . . and in methods of combat."[8] In geography, students learned that "the

[4] "Documents officiels. Circulaire relative à la prochaine rentrée scolaire. Le 10 septembre, 1915," *ESDJF*, 2 (1915): 197.

[5] "Les Distributions des prix dans les lycées et collèges de jeunes filles. Lycée de jeunes filles du Mans. Allocution prononcée par Mlle Bussard," *ESDJF* 1 (1916): 82.

[6] "Les Distributions des prix dans les lycées et collèges de jeunes filles. Collège de jeunes filles d'Avranches. Allocution prononcée par Mlle Marie," *ESDJF* 2 (1915): 166.

[7] "Un Lycée de jeunes filles," 253.

[8] "Les Distributions des prix dans les lycées et collèges de jeunes filles. Collège Troyes. Allocution prononcée par l'inspecteur d'académie," *ESDJF* 2 (1915): 76.

life of a people is at risk . . . in the statistics of its diverse resources.''[9] In French composition classes, themes entitled "A Letter from the Front" or "The March of the Wounded" replaced such classic subjects as "A Description of a Storm.''[10] Even in the course on ethics, reports of heroic actions in the newspapers could become the basis of a moral lesson. One Sévrienne remarked, "The annals of humanity, from the most remote times up to the present era, could not offer more noble examples for our admiration.''[11]

Instruction, however, was not the only aspect of school life transformed by war. Schools also took an active part in organizing wartime charities. Earlier charitable efforts shrink by comparison with this massive effort on the part of school personnel to do their patriotic duty. Though encouraged by the ministry, the movement gained momentum through the efforts of women whose service ethos only strengthened as their field of action grew.

Everywhere the initial goal of schools was to assist as directly in the war as possible by coming to the aid of soldiers. For the wounded housed in school hospitals, staff and students displayed particular interest. Teachers and alumnae often staffed hospital services and visited bedsides; students, with the help of teachers, collected clothes and linen; and *pensionnaires* and *demi-pensionnaires* regularly skipped desserts to offer them instead to injured soldiers. At Beauvais, a visit to the hospital, where students "had the honor of joining soldiers in singing the 'Marseillaise,' " marked the high point of the school year, according to one patriotic directrice.[12] Assisting soldiers at the front brought forth still greater efforts. From Quimper came this typical description of girls' patriotic verve. "Every fifteen days, parcels leave the collège for the front . . . [filled] with caps, mittens, mufflers, and shoes; for since the reopening of school in October, sewing classes have been devoted to working for soldiers. . . . The youngest knit, the older students sew with the directrice and professeurs. After class and often on Thursday, we gather together to continue the work.''[13] Increasingly, students addressed these

[9] "Les Distributions des prix dans les lycées et collèges de jeunes filles. Lycée Toulouse. Allocution prononcée par Mme Gonnet," *ESDJF* 2 (1916): 189.

[10] "Les Distributions des prix dans les lycées et collèges de jeunes filles. Collège Digne. Allocution prononcée par Mme Brun," *ESDJF* 2 (1915): 185.

[11] "Les Distributions des prix dans les lycées et collèges de jeunes filles. Lycée Toulouse. Allocution prononcée par Mme Gonnet," *ESDJF* 2 (1916): 185. Amélie Gandon Gonnet went through Sèvres with the class of 1888.

[12] "Les Distributions des prix dans les lycées et collèges de jeunes filles. Allocution prononcée par Mlle Thomas," *ESDJF* 2 (1915): 71.

[13] "Les Lycées et collèges de jeunes filles et les victimes de la guerre," *ESDJF* 2 (1915): 9.

packages to individual soldiers. In order to personalize this effort, add to its drama, and encourage solidarity in the nation, girls' schools developed the practice of adopting "godsons" from among French soldiers. Sometimes a whole class acted as "godmother," sometimes an individual student. The choice of such quasi-familial terms to link schoolgirls to unknown soldiers constituted, in one inspector's view, "a masterpiece of feminine inspiration."[14]

Soon civilian victims of war became objects of charity in girls' schools also. Some activities aimed at immediate relief for displaced persons. Other responses to civilian dislocation shaded into welfare projects. For example, the national campaign organized under the rubric Sou des Lycées raised money to give work to women whom industrial dislocation had thrown out of work. The brainchild of an assortment of public teachers and republican reformers, including the solidarist theorist and Radical politician Léon Bourgeois, this organization set up workshops where women could earn a salary producing clothing for the front.[15] Another effort to raise money, this time for children orphaned in the war, was the Pupilles de l'Ecole. Sponsored by the Ministry of Education, this fund also expressed the solidarist message in its effort to clear the "debt" that all survivors of the war owed those who sacrificed their lives to save the country.[16] For these and other causes, schools functioned as important agents in fund-raising efforts throughout the war. Teachers gave a contribution of up to 4 percent from each month's salary; regular requests for funds went out to parents through their children; and alumnae organizations stepped up efforts to increase the profits of their charity events. Together these activities set a precedent of heightened sensitivity to social questions that, after the war, would become a permanent tradition. Girls' schools at last assumed direct responsibility for raising money on behalf of worthy causes and for training students actively for charitable activities in the service of the nation.

Sévriennes in the War

Nonetheless, merely to describe the change that occurred in girls' schools is to miss its essence as a human drama. For what the war offered older directrices and teachers was a chance to resurrect the sacrificial image that they carried of themselves as young professionals.

[14] J. Combarieu, "L'Enseignement secondaire des jeunes filles pendant la guerre: Académie de Paris. Rapport présenté au Conseil académique (Extraits)," *ESDJF* 2 (1915): 115.

[15] M. Poirier, "Le 'Sou des lycées,' " *ESDJF* 2 (1914): 193.

[16] "Pour les Pupilles de l'Ecole," *ESDJF* 2 (1915): 90.

Now, as in the founding years of girls' secondary education, Sévriennes consciously neglected personal interest for a course of action in line with higher duties, only this time they would feel the psychic strain of self-denying conduct less. Instead of silent martyrdom in isolation from society and often from their colleagues, sacrifice in war engaged these women in profoundly social acts. Inside girls' schools the sense of common purpose strengthened. Even at the largest girls' lycée in France, Fénélon in Paris, Lucie Kuss (class of 1882) reported, "We lived closer one to another."[17] More significant because unprecedented, war-related causes gave directrices and sometimes even teachers an occasion to expand their moral leadership from the confines of the school to the community and even to the nation.

Like the heroic days of their first years in teaching, war exacted a heavy toll on the health of Sèvres's oldest alumnae. Earlier, such problems affected women only in the teaching corps; now, directrices, too, fell victim at an alarming rate. At Angoulême, for instance, Cécilia Terrène Lafleur (class of 1890) "suffered distressing repercussions on her health," her inspector wrote, "as a result of the heavy increase in work and worries arising from the very important role she plays for the benefit of the wounded."[18] At Auxerre, another inspector found Anne Rollet Sausotte's (class of 1884) "health seriously undermined in recent months." "Nevertheless," he advised the ministry, "she has done her utmost to assure the opening of school . . . under particularly difficult and exhausting conditions.[19] Marie Grandjean (class of 1889) would die in 1916 at the age of forty-six, "literally a victim of the war." Her academy inspector gave this account of her unstinting labors: "The school year 1914/15 opened a period of extreme overwork: endless efforts, first to find a day school, then, later, boarding facilities; buildings separate from one another and far from the collège where she had her apartment—hence, constant comings and goings, in every kind of weather—in the long run, fatal to an already precarious health; finally, daily assistance at the hospital installed in her collège."[20] Not only directrices willingly sacrificed their health for patriotic causes. Teachers also gave up what leisure hours they had to join in relief efforts, adding thereby to the medical hazards all too present in their work already. Hélène Dubois (class of 1888) had by 1917 seriously "altered her state of health" as a result of

[17] Combarieu, "L'Enseignement secondaire des jeunes filles pendant la guerre," 107.

[18] Dossier personnel Cécilia Terrène (married name Lafleur), notes, 1917, F17 24029, A.N.

[19] Dossier personnel, Anne Rollet (married name Sausotte), notes, 1915, F17 24029, A.N.

[20] Dossier personnel, Marie Grandjean, correspondance, 1916, F17 23600, A.N.

"her generous activities";[21] while Marie Boué (class of 1889) "whose health," in her inspector's view, "justified real precautions," ignored the risks in order to "devote herself to charity for blind victims of the war."[22] Through these sacrificial gestures appeared the same commitment that had inspired ailing teachers in their youth. Only now the nation, not the school, formed the object of their altruistic actions.

Yet many of the symptoms of poor health Sévriennes experienced before the war subsided once it began. Nervous ailments, long a bane of sickly teachers, now affected almost exclusively mothers with sons away at war and wives with ailing husbands. Crushing workloads, however exhausting, did not produce much sign of psychic strain. Rather than bad nerves, the war inspired a kind of exultation that metamorphosed into firm determination as hostilities dragged on. No doubt the self-denying ethos of their training explains in part the easy adaptation by this generation to the stiff demands of war; but the deeper reason for their lack of nervous ailments must reside in the approval generated by their selfless labors. Never before nor after did the moral influence enjoyed by aging Sévriennes approach what they experienced in the war.

Teachers affirmed this influence mainly within the confines of their schools, where patriotic fervor earned them high regard from everyone. At the Lycée Racine in Paris, for instance, Angèle Coustols (class of 1887) was "greatly loved by students with whom she organized wartime charities";[23] while at the Lycée Lamartine, also in Paris, Marie Boué (class of 1889) "proved herself to be . . . a generous-hearted woman, whose patriotic ardor and devotion to our soldiers supports and fires the enthusiasm of our older students."[24] Occasionally, the influence teachers wielded over students did reach into the community. At Nice, Adèle Fourcade David (class of 1883) so thoroughly persuaded her students of the importance of the National Loan that "a certain number of families decided to participate."[25] Back in Paris, Hélène Dubois (class of 1888) achieved "unanticipated results" sending care packages to the hospital and the front because "she communicated the inspiration of her heart to all those she approached within the school and outside it."[26] Rarely, though, did teachers join in relief efforts organized outside the school.

Directrices, on the other hand, took a leading part in the increasing

[21] Dossier personnel, Hélène Dubois, notes, 1917, F17 23989, A.N.

[22] Dossier personnel, Marie Boué, notes, 1917, F17 24046, A.N.

[23] Dossier personnel, Angèle Coustols, notes, F17 24187, A.N.

[24] Dossier personnel, Marie Boué, notes, 1915, F17 24046, A.N.

[25] Dossier personnel, Adèle Fourcade (married name David), notes, 1916, F17 23985, A.N.

[26] Dossier personnel, Hélène Dubois, notes, 1915, F17 23949, A.N.

contacts between girls' schools and key figures on the civilian front. Faced with the problems of relocating schools, coping with scarcities and rising prices, sometimes even confronting invasion and enemy occupation, school heads were less than ever able to ignore the outer world. Simply operating their schools in wartime called for daily ingenuity and courage. At Lyon, the academy inspector congratulated Amélie Allégret (class of 1885) for her "commendable spirit of organization and decision" that kept her lycée going despite unorthodox locations.[27] At Nancy, where the lycée was bombarded, the rector gave Lucie Ravaire much credit for bringing her little world through. "She is an inspiration to everyone and manages to maintain the morale of teachers, students, and even families. . . . At the lycée, everyone works hard despite very frequent changes in the schedule and, especially, despite frequent alerts (descents into the cellars)."[28] Marie Rosier (class of 1884) showed the same sangfroid at Valenciennes where she continued to operate her collège under the German occupation. "By her energy and dignified demeanor," the subprefect reported, "she inspired even in the Germans sentiments of respect and acts almost of courtesy."[29] He went on to say that Rosier also conspired successfully in the escape of four French prisoners. Such heroic acts of patriotism raised the stature of directrices in their communities sharply. The more usual route to public commendation, though, led through wartime charities.

Girls' schools during the war turned into hubs of charitable activities. For the most part, this patriotic movement emerged spontaneously among the personnel of girls' schools, although the ministry immediately approved and later actively encouraged their endeavors. Even later, when national organizations like the Pupilles de l'Ecole and the Sou des Lycées had spread throughout the school system, the approach in individual schools to wartime causes remained eclectic. Almost everywhere, directrices orchestrated relief projects. "Under her stimulus, teachers and students have taken a large role in wartime charities," wrote an inspector about Henriette Maisonneuve Morin (class of 1889), directrice of the cours at Philippeville.[30] "Through her impetus," another reported of Emilie Bardenat (class of 1889), directrice at the collège in Vêndome,

[27] Dossier personnel, Amélie Allégret, notes, 1915, F17 23809, A.N. At Auch, Marie Brunaud (class of 1882) received the commendation of an inspector general for spending her own savings "so that boarders would not suffer from an increase in the cost of living."

[28] Dossier personnel, Lucie Ravaire, notes, 1917, F17 23949, A.N.

[29] Dossier personnel, Marie Rosier, correspondance, 1920, F17 23952, A.N.

[30] Dossier personnel, Henriette Maisonneuve (married name Morin), notes, 1916, F17 24016, A.N.

"students and former students participated actively in all the wartime charities."[31] Still a third remarked of Marie Gasnault (class of 1889) at Epernay, "Since the beginning of hostilities, she has multiplied the works of charity around her."[32]

This dependence on individual initiative ensured the triumph of diversity in these wartime projects. Amélie Allégret's (class of 1885) activities at Lyon provide a classic case of this eclecticism. "As soon as the lycée became a hospital," wrote her inspector, "Mlle Allégret organized a linen service in her apartment, grouping around her families and students, to make sure the hospital had everything it needed." Once the hospital was equipped, Allégret quickly turned her mind to other causes. "She displays an exemplary devotion to all efforts to help the wounded refugees and prisoners," reported her rector; "[she] applies herself actively to the young Serbs . . . ; and directs the workshop of the hospital installed in the lycée."[33] At Châlon-sur-Saône, Louise Langard Bréjoux (class of 1890) assumed the presidency of the local chapter of the Foyer du Soldat, founded under the patronage of the municipality and counting among its membership all the local public schools.[34] Marie Lépine (class of 1886) put her main efforts as directrice at Agen into the Pupilles de l'Ecole. "It is fitting," her admiring academy inspector remarked, "to be grateful for her interest in wartime charities, and I am personally obliged to her for what she has done for the Pupilles de l'Ecole. I have asked, therefore, in a meeting of both school systems, that she be named vice president of the organization for the Lot-et-Garonne."[35]

Everywhere, such undertakings improved the public image of directrices. In several towns where before the war schools had still been objects of derision, a dramatic change in attitudes occurred. As the capital of the Mayenne, Laval was one such town. On the eve of the war, the rector for the collège had written, "No doubt the Mayenne is one of the most reactionary departments in France, even more so than the department of Brittany." He blamed Marie Aulon (class of 1886), the local directrice, for doing nothing to improve the public's image of her school: "The collège at Laval is, along with that at Quimper, the establishment whose directrice leaves the most to be desired." Yet by 1915, "with no notable change . . . in the material situation of the collège," an inspector general reported, "I was happy to hear this year that Mlle Aulon has shown ini-

---

[31] Dossier personnel, Emilie Bardenat, notes, 1917, F17 23888, A.N.

[32] Dossier personnel, Marie Gasnault, notes, 1915, F17 23995, A.N.

[33] Dossier personnel, Amélie Allégret, notes, 1915, 1916, F17 23809, A.N.

[34] Dossier personnel, Louise Langard (married name Bréjoux), notes, 1915, F17 24736, A.N.

[35] Dossier personnel, Marie Lépine, notes, 1916, F17 23856, A.N.

tiative and dedication in the difficult circumstances that affect the country, and I hope that she will know how not to lose the gain in good repute which she has recently acquired among her fellow citizens." Another note from the academy inspector explained the reason for Aulon's new reputation. "At the beginning of the hostilities, Mlle Aulon founded with her personal friends and former students a workshop that has made up numerous parcels of linen and clothes for soldiers, for hospitals, and for needy children in public primary schools." Three more years of war and patriotic service turned the tide permanently in Aulon's favor. By 1918, the same inspector wrote, "Mlle Aulon has raised the prosperity of the collège at Laval to a level it has never known before."[36] The story was repeated with little significant variation in several towns in France.[37] Each time, officials attributed the improvement in a school's reputation to the charitable activities of its directrice during the war.

From one perspective, these women merely represented the last among their generation to triumph over a dying prejudice against girls' secondary schooling. As such, their victory belongs to the earlier phase of girls' schools' history when they finally won acceptance by the bourgeoisie. Yet from another angle, the war experience opened a new era, when for the first time some directrices became official members of the national elite. Before the war, this women's corps, especially its members outside Paris, lacked recognition beyond a local setting. With the war, that situation changed. Not only did women work in organizations with departmental and national affiliations; they assumed a role as leaders in a national endeavor. In so doing, they gained a qualitatively new and different public image in their own communities that placed them in the ranks of the notables. The ministry officially endorsed the metamorphosis when it decided to award to several of these women the cross of the Legion of Honor and the title *chevalier*. Eight Sévriennes of this generation, seven of them directrices, received this mark of national distinction between 1918 and 1922. If reserved for just a few, this recognition heralded, all the same, a new orientation inside this feminine profession.

Fortunately, we need not confine ourselves to inferential evidence of what changes this dramatic shift might have produced in directrices' outlook. In 1915 and again in 1916, the ministry decided to assign to heads of girls' schools the task of speaking at the graduation ceremonies for their schools in lieu of rectors, inspectors, or other dignitaries. Subsequently, Camille Sée's journal published more than forty of these

---

[36] Dossier personnel, Marie Aulon, notes, 1914, 1915, 1918, F17 22464, A.N.

[37] See for example the dossiers personnels of Emilie Bardenat at Vendôme, F17 23888; Angèle Bourgoignon at Roubaix, F17 24108; Suzanne Palaa at Lorient, F17 22559; and Alexandre Vautier at Epernal, F17 24172, A.N.

speeches delivered before an audience of students and their parents.[38] As it turned out, this proved a crucial moment to put directrices behind the lectern. For a comparison of themes informing these addresses in 1915 and in 1916 establishes the war as a crucible in which old images of women melted down and new ones took their place in girls' secondary schools.

Commencement Addresses, 1915: Women in the Family

In the commencement speeches of 1915, directrices gave several indications that they retained both for themselves and for their students a traditional notion of appropriate female conduct. In the first place, not all directrices greeted the ministry's order with enthusiasm. Several accepted the honor of speaking at commencement only under pressure, and a few prevailed on an inspector or a teacher to replace them. Marie Grandjean (class of 1889), who went ahead despite her hesitations, confessed in her address, "My first reaction, full of fear before the novelty of the task and the necessity of speaking for the first time before so imposing an audience, was to decline the honor . . . but I did not want to back away in the face of duty."[39] This remark, far from being disingenuous or falsely modest, recorded the honest alarm of someone used to exercising her authority discreetly, either behind closed doors or through intermediaries in the public sphere of men. For most directrices in 1915, the recognition that the war had turned them into public figures still lay ahead.

Discretion also made it difficult for directrices to describe the activities patriotically undertaken by the members of their staffs. Publicity offended the principle of modesty associated with a domestic sphere for women and bourgeois rules of feminine decorum. "In our lycée," Amélie Gandon Gonnet (class of 1888) insisted, "we take pride in silence." Having registered her protest, she then went on to list her school's patriotic undertakings.[40] It was the same with Madeleine Plicque (class of 1892), who began by saying, "Under some constraint, I confess, I will evoke the life of our establishment during these past ten months."[41] Obligated to describe their schools' collective actions, directrices almost never mentioned specific teachers whose contributions had been particularly note-

[handwritten margin note: Still trad. keep notion]

---

[38] These speeches appeared under the title "Distributions des prix dans les lycées et collèges de jeunes filles" in *ESDJF* 2 (1915) through 1 (1918).

[39] Directrice of the collège at Saumur. *ESDJF* 1 (1916): 6.

[40] Directrice at Toulouse. *ESDJF* 2 (1915): 255.

[41] Directrice of the lycée at Rouen. *ESDJF* 2 (1915): 261.

worthy. To have done so, several claimed, would have shocked these teachers' sensibilities. As Marie Delbosc (class of 1889) explained in recounting the patriotic deeds accomplished by her staff, "I shall not name these valiant women for fear of wounding teachers' modesty; it would require, in any case, citing all the school's personnel."[42]

The moral lesson that school heads directed at their students in these speeches was as traditional as the diffident public posture of their teachers. "Let all those who will return to us find faithfully preserved the whole tradition of the France of our old epics: heroic France and GENTLE France," Madeleine Plicque (class of 1892) urged her mostly female audience.[43] The same idea, differently expressed, reappeared in other speeches. Four of every five directrices consciously preserved the old duality that put women in the home and men outside it as protectors. The directrice at Cherbourg had this to say to girls who might have other aspirations. "The sister thinks about her brother far away at the front; what to do to resemble him; to be, like him, worthy of her country. She asks him, 'What must I become?' 'Oh, surely not an Amazon,' he replies sharply. 'Dear little sister, keep your grace, your freshness, remain the gentle image that relieves the visions of horror on the battlefield; be the good fairy who with her magic wand makes those things appear for which we have not had time to ask but that arrive just when needed most.'[44] Left behind by valorous soldiers at the front, girls and women must continue the natural feminine task of succoring men and children. As Marie Lépine (class of 1886) explained, while praising her girls' care for wounded soldiers: "To nurse, to dress wounds, to cure, to conserve, such is the role of woman in peacetime. How could she fail to do the same in the great effusion of blood that today inundates France?"[45] Viewed by these directrices, the volunteer work that girls' schools had undertaken since the war simply represented an extension of their domestic obligations, different in scale but not in kind from what women in the home had always done. None suggested in 1915 that these activities or any aspect of the war would make more than a temporary difference to the way that women lived their lives. "Your brothers," Cécilia Térrène Lafleur (class of 1890) informed her students, "will be the poets, the scholars, the artists of the new France. You will be the guardians of the foyer, you will preserve the customs: 'It is on a woman's knees that what is best in the world grows up: a man and an honorable woman.'"[46]

[42] Directrice of the collège at Carcassonne. *ESDJF* 2 (1915): 181–82.

[43] Directrice of the lycée at Rouen. *ESDJF* 2 (1915): 261.

[44] Directrice of the collège at Cherbourg. *ESDJF* 2 (1915): 270.

[45] Directrice of the lycée at Agen. *ESDJF* 2 (1915): 265.

[46] Directrice of the collège at Angoulème. She quotes Joseph de Maître. *ESDJF* 2 (1915): 79.

Nevertheless, the war did make some directrices intensely conscious of the restraints that gender placed on their activities. Anne Massen (class of 1887) could bravely reassure her students at Poitiers: "It seems to me that the abnegation of the sister is as lofty as the heroism of the brother. In any case, it is of the same nature. It is the forgetting of oneself before the Nation or before the Family."[47] But not all her colleagues judged their portion of the national endeavor in such a balanced light. To some at least, service to the family did not match service to the nation; dying for one's country moved on a diferent moral plane from raising children or tending wounded men. The contrast struck some school heads with special force in commencement gatherings with virtually all members of the school in attendance. "At this hour," the directrice of the collège at Dax pointed out, "when . . . boys' lycées and collèges piously celebrate the glory of teachers and students who are suffering and dying for the nation . . . we feel profoundly the humbleness of our contributions." This self-deprecating tone expressed an anguish also present in the speech delivered at Le Havre by Gabrielle Marcourt (class of 1884): "Our neighbors at the boys' lycée can evoke military glories. . . . We can envy the grandeur of their work; our own is different and it must be said, inferior."[48] A special note, almost of rancor, made its way into the remarks of Marie Grandjean (class of 1889) at Saumur. "How we envy them," she exclaimed, "how we would have liked, we, too, to suffer for the country, to spill our blood to the last drop for her. . . . But such is not our role, weak women that we are; we have other duties to fulfill."[49] From the daughter of an artillery commander, exposed as well to the heroic ethos taught at Sèvres, such sentiments are not particularly surprising.[50]

Nonetheless, these mournful comments do suggest a deeper crisis facing girls' secondary schools. Before the war, these schools basked serenely in the official propaganda idealizing home and family. A dual social policy based on a domestic world for women and a public sphere for men had strong attraction for women educators as long as family retained high status in the rhetoric of the state and its pivotal position in middle-class existence. However, once a world war deflated the private sphere's importance, the traditional role of women was devalued with it. Any school system as self-consciously elitist as the Third Republic's female collèges and lycées was certain to experience reverberations; but the presence of a corps of women in leadership positions, deeply committed

[47] Directrice of the lycée at Poitiers. *ESDJF* 1 (1916): 88.

[48] *ESDJF* 2 (1915): 60–61.

[49] *ESDJF* 1 (1916): 65.

[50] Dossier personnel, Marie Grandjean, F17 23600, A.N.

to the notion of female service and its social contribution, heightened the unease.

Commencement Addresses, 1916: Women in the Nation

This disorientation, sensed in certain school heads' voices in July 1915, did not last long. Twelve months later, their graduation speeches expressed a different mood. Heads of girls' schools had left behind timidity and regrets and with them many older notions of appropriate female conduct. No directrice now felt compelled to justify her presence at the lectern or to blanch on behalf of her teachers at the thought of public praise. Without exception, an air of competence and self-assurance informed these women's speeches. Experience alone cannot explain why school heads no longer felt apologetic for their presence; instead, as the realization that France might face a long and costly war swept through the country, directrices of girls' schools underwent a fundamental change of outlook.

Between 1915 and 1916, directrices as a group adopted a new perspective on the role of women in the nation. Gone, by 1916, were the domestic themes that they had presented humbly twelve months earlier. Gone also were comparisons between the social roles of men and women in which the latter figured as definitively second-rate. Instead, directrices now insisted on the importance middle-class women had as partners in the national endeavor. To the extent that they talked about domestic life at all, they linked familial and patriotic duties. "You must raise your children," Alice Bolleau (class of 1883) told students at Niort, "not for yourselves but for the country. Far from keeping them jealously near you, in conditions of every comfort, the ideal of the French bourgeoisie, you must develop in them energy, a spirit of initiative, and a love of action. These virtues must then be placed at the service of the national community."[51] Often directrices ignored familial claims on women altogether or stressed, like Louise Thuillat Manuel (class of 1891) at Limoges, the nonexclusive nature of those claims. "As good French women," Manuel warned her students, "you will not have satisfied all your obligations just because you have fulfilled your family duties. . . . You will concern yourself with all the social reforms that justice—accelerated by the miseries of war—requires."[52] Before the war and in their 1915 speeches, directrices had preached the message of volunteer work mainly to alumnae of

[51] *ESDJF* 1 (1917): 28–29.
[52] *ESDJF* 1 (1917): 35.

their collèges and lycées.[53] Now they proclaimed that this kind of service would begin in secondary schools themselves. "It is impossible to raise the generation of the war like the prewar generation," the directrice at Beauvais declared; "a new element has been introduced to lycée education: it is an apprenticeship for a worthy life within society [vie sociale]."[54] Even at a little collège like Cherbourg's, social activism within the school was a prewar ideal whose time had finally come. "Since the war," the school's directrice claimed, "school has become the place where a little girl begins her training for her social role."[55]

The newest and most striking aspect of the 1916 speeches, though, concerned the need for girls to work. The leisured lady as an ideal in girls' schools had gone distinctly out of fashion. "The type of girl, occupied by useless tasks, for whom a bit of embroidery, an hour of piano sufficed, once her studies ended, was already on the wane before the war," the directrice at Saint-Etienne commented to her listeners, "All the more reason for her disappearance today."[56] Such remarks suggest that work had become, even for women of the middle class, a national obligation. All sectors of the economy needed their assistance. At Agen, Marie Lépine (class of 1886) encouraged students "to cultivate the soil" even though, as she admitted, "it goes against your taste. This duty does not seem to befit you, but I tell you that it does because it is going to be the duty of everyone."[57] "Single women," Alice Bolleau (class of 1883) warned girls and their parents at Niort, "do not have the right to be useless and inactive. The liberal professions, the administration, commerce, even industry need their intelligence and their activity."[58] Perhaps the directrice at Moulins captured best the enthusiasm behind these admonitions in her closing remarks. "I shall end by taking the beautiful motto of our heroic defenders who cry out to one another: 'We shall go on because we must.' Let us say, instead: 'We shall work because we must.' "[59]

Such words announce a turning point in the history of girls' secondary education. Wartime conditions fossilized a school system modeled on

---

[53] See, for example, the commencement address by Henriette Vidal-Fritscher (class of 1887) at Guéret in 1915 in which she urged her students: "Apply yourself to the relief of miseries that necessarily will follow on the war. . . . Struggle energetically against all the social ills . . . for on this struggle . . . depends the future of the race. Join the leagues designed to combat alcoholism; give your help to those which attack tuberculosis or which protect children." *ESDJF* 2 (1915): 181.

[54] *ESDJF* 1 (1918): 78.

[55] Mme Martin, directrice of the collège at Cherbourg. *ESDJF* 1 (1917): 133.

[56] Mlle Thomas, directrice of the lycée at Saint-Etienne. *ESDJF* 1 (1917): 175.

[57] Directrice of the lycée at Agen. *ESDJF* 2 (1917): 233.

[58] Directrice of the lycée at Niort. *ESDJF* 1 (1917): 29.

[59] Mlle Bousquet, directrice of the lycée at Moulins. *ESDJF* 1 (1917): 71.

the exclusive and introverted bourgeois family, a system already eroded by trends in girls' schools before the war. Henceforth, girls' schools, like other public schools in the Third Republic, intended to use the classroom to shape girls into citizens first and only secondarily into dutiful members of a family. To that end, an extraparliamentary commission advised the ministry in 1917 to follow the urgings of its own inspector generals and reorder the list of subjects taught in la morale so that instruction on duties to the nation preceded classes on duties to the family.[60]

The stress on women as a national resource also placed older Sévriennes in a new position. As members of the civil service, they could themselves now claim the honor that position traditionally offered men in French society. As working women, they no longer appeared exceptions to the ideal of womanhood for which girls' secondary schools stood. Indeed, in many ways, the war prepared the way for their apotheosis as a generation. Ideally placed to make their patriotic contribution felt, teachers and directrices made manifest in girls' schools by their example what the state now called on women of the bourgeoisie to be. The self-assurance granted by official approbation came through in their activities as social leaders. It came through as well in the freedom they enjoyed from nervous ailments. But more perhaps than any other evidence, the speeches that they delivered to the community of students, parents, and alumnae gathered around their schools at graduation testify to the pride this generation took in their accomplishments and newly elevated status.

Even as their words attested to a reinvigorated sense of institutional purpose, some directrices alluded in their speeches to an altogether different need among their students. Not all of these addresses linked the themes of work and patriotism. A few speakers remarked upon the circumstances that would force growing numbers of their girls to prepare for a lifetime of work.[61] The loss of fathers and potential suitors in the war had cost an entire generation of young women the security of a male provider. Younger sisters might more easily find a husband, but once postwar inflation wiped out family savings, many would conduct the search without the benefit of dowries. For all these women, the opportunity offered by professional careers was not merely a chance to serve the country but also a way of providing for their private futures. On the whole, in 1916, directrices ignored these motivations. They chose instead to drape the modern woman in the ethical principles of another

[60] Commission extraparlementaire, "Projets de décrets et arrêtés. Exposé des motifs," *ESDJF* 1 (1917): 110.

[61] See, for example, the remarks of Alice Préjean (class of 1886), directrice of the lycée at Toulouse, *ESDJF* 1 (1918): 68.

generation. Yet this blindness to the social changes that began before the war and were sharply exacerbated by it could not persist much longer. For like the prewar leisured maiden, content with her diploma and embroidery, the ethos of duty for which these women spoke was already by 1917 out-of-date.

Unbeknownst to them and certainly without their blessing, girls' secondary schools were rushing headlong toward a radical revision of the goal for which republicans had launched this educational system, namely, to perpetuate a separate feminine culture. In less than a decade, the curricular structure designed to keep the secondary studies of girls and boys distinct received a blow from which it never would recover. The introduction of the baccalauréat program as an alternative course of study set girls' schools in this new direction. That decision, taken by the minister of education in 1924, in part responded to the rising demand for professional outlets for middle-class girls after the war. But the crisis of confidence in the notion of "different but equal" took shape in the professional world of women teachers as well. At the very moment when directrices of girls' schools presided over the most moving demonstration yet of their distinctive mission, a profound confusion over their profession's goals began to trouble teachers.

PART III
A Generation and an Institution in Crisis

Although perhaps this was not immediately clear to them, the war's end irrevocably closed the triumphal chapter in Sèvres's first generation's history. Still entrenched as teachers and directrices in the most important schools in the nation, they would soon discover that new trends within these institutions were about to pass them by. They would face, as a result, that unenviable dilemma of old leaders, protected by seniority: how to inspire confidence in youthful underlings whose outlook and values had matured in a very different age.

For a time, some of them tried to remain at the cutting edge of their profession by placing their prestige behind a movement for reform aimed at achieving equality with the men's teaching profession. In so doing, they would serve as midwives to yet one more vision of femininity, the last of three to emerge from girls' secondary schools over the course of their careers. Yet the commitment of this aging generation to the new order was ambivalent at best and actively hostile on occasion. Neither the public nor the Ministry of Education had chosen clearly among the different versions of what a girls' secondary school should be, and that vacillation would make the pressures on older teachers and directrices all the more unsettling as they slipped toward their retirement.

An account of the final years of the first Sé-

vriennes' careers unavoidably tends to poignancy, even pathos
in some cases. Nonetheless, the backdrop against which these
women's private sorrows played out is in the end the more important element of their story. What their experience reveals in
part is the important function that the meritocratic ethos of the
Université served in stimulating dissatisfaction with sex-specific
education. On the other hand, the ideology of gender difference
continued to structure public and private life so completely that
this generation never would escape it either in their professional
culture or in the world to which they would return in their retirement. Few would seriously try. For the vast majority it was
enough to have expanded the parameters of bourgeois femininity to include not just educated wives but also professional
women like themselves.

10 | A Separate and Equal Women's Profession

On March 25, 1924 Minister of Education Léon Bérard signed a decree providing for the progressive introduction of the baccalauréat program of studies into girls' secondary schools as an alternative to the regular diploma program. Within six years, that decree inadvertently produced a de facto annulment of the feminine course of studies established under the law of 1880 and with it the rationale for a feminine teaching profession trained differently from men. Reluctantly, the ministry faced up to these unintended consequences and agreed in 1930 to a gradual alignment of the two professions. Completed nine years later, this process culminated in the incorporation of the School of Sèvres into the system of higher education and its transfer in 1939 to Paris. Henceforth, women secondary teachers with the same training and credentials as men would offer the identical instruction in girls' secondary schools as boys received in their schools. The era of "égalité dans la différence" had given way to a new set of relations between the genders in secondary education based on parity within two separate institutional systems.

More startling than the replacement of this educational system was the fact that several women teachers responsible for its earlier popularity joined the charge against it. To find such women calling at the end of their careers for the abandonment of their life's work suggests at first an inexplicable rupture with the past. Many in this generation of Sèvres's alumnae, after all, had taken up the task of educating girls as a kind of sacerdotal mission. Even those less visionary in outlook had demonstrated over several decades a remarkably keen sense of professional conscience in the execution of their daily obligations. The very success that dedicated service by the entire generation had assured girls' secondary schools ought, one might have thought, to have made them fiercely loyal to the image of feminine education they had fostered.

Three separate but parallel developments explain this unexpected repudiation of their own creation by some teachers within the founding generation. One involved a growing disenchantment among the users of girls' schools with the feminine diploma. After the war, students in collèges and lycées for girls began in ever-increasing numbers to direct their

249

studies toward passing the baccalauréat instead of or in addition to the
diplôme d'enseignement secondaire des jeunes filles. This spontaneous
rejection of the degree for which their studies officially prepared girls set
the stage for a reconsideration by their teachers of the pedagogical goals
of feminine instruction.

The popularity of the *bac* does not explain, however, why women
teachers would themselves organize a campaign to align instruction in
their schools with that given to boys. This development arose less as a
result of public pressure than from considerations of professional self-
interest. Between a time early in the century when secondary teachers
first began to mobilize in defense of their material interests and 1920,
when the campaign for the baccalauréat began, women teachers proved
singularly unsuccessful in promoting their professional interests as a
group. After twenty-five years of organized pressure on the government,
they still had no official statute detailing their rights as a professional
corps nor any members seated on the Conseil supérieur or on the con-
sultative councils in the academies. As a profession, they continued to
operate under the ad hoc rulings of different ministers and their directors
of secondary education, without the benefit even of a formal avenue for
presenting their collective point of view. Gradually, the elite of the profession began to see in that lamentable condition the effect of their feminine degrees. More than any other reason, recognition on the part of
agrégées that special credentials could justify discriminatory treatment
explains why several older Sévriennes joined younger teachers in a
struggle to masculinize first the content of girls' education and then, as a
follow-up to that reform, their own profession's training and degrees.

One further new development created the intellectual preconditions
necessary to muster broad support for these demands. After 1900, a positivist obsession with objective truth invaded humanistic studies, replacing the moralizing aims of the earlier approach. This trend within the
Université undermined the pedagogical rationale for teaching the same
subject differently to boys and girls. By the time agrégées had decided to
press for the adoption of the baccalauréat, opponents could no longer
convincingly appeal to the idea, embodied in the law of 1880, of separate
intellectual spheres for men and women.

Advocates for aligning boys' and girls' instruction met serious resistance, nonetheless, even from some members of their own profession.
Heading up the opposition were those women who had long ago become
directrices of girls' schools. To most of these school leaders, especially
among Sèvres's oldest generation, the decline of feminine studies threatened to destroy the central purpose of the schools that they had crafted.
At risk from their perspective were the moralizing goals established long

ago to be the core of girls' secondary studies. As the persons most responsible for overseeing students' progress in this area, heads of girls' schools naturally opposed reforms certain to shift the focus of girls' studies away from fashioning a social personality and toward preparing for intellectually demanding national exams. In the wake of this debate, rather than united in the glorious success of their endeavors, older Sévriennes arrived on the threshold of their late careers bewildered and divided over the future of the institution they had founded.

Early Professional Associations: Separate, Different, and Unequal

The heart of the story leading up to this dispute centers on the ultimately unsuccessful efforts by women teachers to wring from the administration equality of benefits with the men's profession despite the differences in their professional credentials. This demand itself emerged late in the history of the profession and only after women teachers gained sufficient confidence in their skills to see injustice in the inferior terms of their employment. For several decades, the potential for this perception lay buried under the self-sacrificing professional ethos of the profession's most influential members, women trained at Sèvres during its founding years. Even when a more assertive outlook had developed and women teachers organized to defend their interests as a group, patriarchal values and the structure of their own profession encouraged them to see in their distinctive task and training a rationale for different conditions of employment for men and women teachers. Gradually, though, largely through association with the men's profession in a common pressure group, this readiness to accept inferior conditions eroded, and the women began to insist that difference did not justify unequal treatment.

MUTUAL AID: THE ALUMNAE ASSOCIATION OF SÈVRES

To many within the first generation of Sévriennes, it seemed as early as 1885 that school solidarity could provide the base from which to solve the problems facing isolated, inexperienced teachers trained at Sèvres. In that conviction, the first graduating class formed an alumnae association "to provide each other with mutual assistance in their careers."[1] This association with its headquarters at Sèvres had the enthusiastic support of former students from its inception. Ninety-six percent of Sèvres's alumnae belonged in 1891.[2] Eight years later, when the youngest of the

---

[1] "Statuts de l'Association des élèves de Sèvres, 1886," Association des anciennes élèves de Sèvres, archives, E.N.S.

[2] Calculated from membership lists. BMAES (November 1891): 9–13.

first ten classes had left Sèvres six years before, nine out of ten still paid ten francs a year in dues to keep their affiliation active.[3] This degree of loyalty suggests, given the financial difficulties of many fledgling teachers, that membership served some vital function. All the same, whatever the intentions of its founders, the assistance of Sèvres's alumnae organization never moved beyond an emotional to a material plane.

Mme Favre, in a speech before the inaugural assembly in 1885, announced the themes that would become the hallmark of this sororal organization. "My dear colleagues, my dear daughters," she addressed her former students,

> I am proud to call my colleagues young members of the secondary educational system who have proven themselves already as students and as teachers in the Université . . . but I am happier still to call you my daughters and to preside today over this familial reunion. . . .
> Our first reunion is quite modest; but I am sure that the few members present will make up in zeal for the absence of the others. The others, I know, share our desire to strengthen the fraternal ties between us not only for the good of our school, but especially for the success of our great work that will contribute to the progress of our beloved nation by the instruction and the education of its women. The more united we are, the stronger we will be in combating the prejudices that surround this work.[4]

Modeled after the School of Sèvres itself, this association aspired to perpetuate a sense among alumnae, long after their departure from Sèvres, of belonging to an extended family. This unity, born originally of common memories of Sèvres, would gather force through the women's collective effort to bring enlightenment to students in girls' schools while contesting the hidebound attitudes of their opponents. Meanwhile, in carrying out this historic mission, Sèvres alumnae would stand ready to support those among their ranks who found the struggle difficult and even momentarily overwhelming. Such were the assumptions that inspired the founders of this organization and its leaders for at least two decades.

The organizers envisaged two forms of mutual assistance for members of the association. One involved direct financial aid to individuals in serious pecuniary straits. This aid, financed through the dues of members and donations or legacies from friends of Sèvres, would be distributed anonymously to protect the privacy and dignity of women for

---

[3] Calculated from membership lists. *BTAES* (November 1899): 8–13.
[4] *BMAES* (May 1886): 2–3.

whom a handout even from a "fraternal" organization smacked of charity. Secondly, the association hoped to facilitate an exchange of professional advice among its members. The vehicles devised included an alumnae bulletin and an information bureau at Sèvres to which Sévriennes could send questions for referral to other members.

Nevertheless, measured against the organizers' expectations, the impact of the Alumnae Association proved exceptionally slight. Financial aid was neither large nor widely shared among the members. Most gifts did not exceed one hundred francs, hardly enough to meet the needs of Sévriennes in serious trouble.[5] In any case, the association's members demonstrated a strong reluctance to request financial help. When one alumna in the 1890s called for the creation of a *société de secours* that would pay members anonymously and automatically so as to make it more effective, the governing council rejected her proposal on two grounds. First the practical one: the association lacked the funds for such a massive undertaking. Second, the impersonality of such assistance cut against the effort to build an intimate, fraternal organization. Preserving the emotional ties among Sévriennes took precedence over all other considerations, including a more effective form of material assistance.

As for the bulletin, the major forum for professional exchange among alumnae, it nearly collapsed in the early 1890s for lack of contributions.[6] Published monthly at first, triannually from 1895 to 1914, and annually after World War I, this publication at each reduction registered its own declining usefulness to Sèvres's alumnae. The dialogue imagined by its founders never got seriously underway. Silence blanketed girls' secondary schools across the country as the reserve that was the hallmark of teachers' private lives became the emblem of their professional lives as well.[7] Faced with this neglect, the bulletin only managed to survive through the intervention of teachers based at Sèvres and Paris, whose proximity made common efforts possible and for whom the association remained an active professional center. For others, further afield, the bulletin, like the Alumnae Association itself, offered nostalgic echoes from the past but little in the way of help in coping with the present or the future of this young profession.

On the one occasion when the solidarity encouraged by this kind of

---

[5] This was the case until just before the war, when the amount of such allocations began to mount precipitously through the agency of a special fund. Minutes from the meetings of the administrative board of the association from 1887 to 1918 can be found in the association's archives under the title, "Reunion du Conseil de l'Association des anciennes élèves," E.N.S.

[6] *BMAES* (November 1891): 3.

[7] Even those who dared to send a contribution rarely signed their names.

organization might have served a useful purpose for youthful teachers in the field, an attentiveness to hierarchy interfered. In 1904, two provincial teachers proposed a solution to the problems that young graduates confronted in settling into unfamiliar towns: Sévriennes would organize reception committees composed of teachers in each school and a friendly woman patron from the town. Initially receptive, the Council of the Alumnae Association cooled its enthusiasm when a few provincial directrices complained that such a project trespassed on their prerogatives as heads of schools. The Council, whose president and four of its fourteen other members were directrices, responded sympathetically to such a caution, and the project never saw the light of day.[8] An association that tied together teachers and directrices in a common bond of solidarity was in no position to defend the interests of teachers against their school heads, however inadequately the latter executed their responsibilities.

Yet the ethos of Sèvres proved to be an even greater obstacle to mounting an effective defense of the professional interests of alumnae. Committed to the idea that a multitude of individual sacrifices were required for Sévriennes to succeed in their historic purpose, the leadership of the association lacked an outlook appropriate to aggressive self-protection. No better evidence exists of this ethical restraint than the defense of the Council's decision not to favor reception committees, given before the General Assembly by Julie Lochert (class of 1882), member of the Council, surveillante générale at Sèvres, and principal editor for the alumnae bulletin.

> The moral tie that unites former students of Sèvres is strong enough to make the organization of special committees useless. . . . Some have asked with reason to what purpose was the solid instruction and the numerous moral lessons that we received at Sèvres if not to teach us how to be alone sometimes and to view life with a certain austerity. It has been said of us that we were a kind of lay nun. Why not? For many of us the renunciation of life is the same; don't we also have our mother house represented by Sèvres and by the Alumnae Association with all that they evoke by way of memories of comradery and simple and devoted affection? The school and the association are for us at one and the same time a moral force and a material support. Unquestionably, they keep many former students

[8] The names of members of the Conseil de l'Association des anciennes élèves appear in the November issues of the bulletin from 1886 to 1901. Letters from Madeleine Sébastien Rudler (class of 1887) and Louise Belugou (class of 1882) give the background to the debate. Association des Anciennes élèves, archives, E.N.S. See also two anonymous letters to Camille Sée, the director of the journal, *ESDJF* 2 (1902): 49–53, 248–49.

*completely on their own from feeling isolated. To be alone is not to
be abandoned.*[9]

In other words, what Sèvres held out by way of aid to former students
was mainly moral solace. At the very moment Lochert spoke, however,
signs that a growing number of teachers found the sacrificial ideal insufficient had already begun to surface in their organizational lives.

SEPARATE AND UNEQUAL: THE NATIONAL FEDERATION OF AMICALES

The law of 1901 permitting civil servants to form associations opened a
period of intense organizational activity among men secondary teachers.
Rather more slowly, but with momentum nonetheless, the movement
spread to girls' secondary schools. By 1905, the staff of 40 percent of
these schools had organized amicales to enunciate and defend their professional interests.[10] Though not, like *syndicats*, charged with negotiat-
ing teachers' contracts with the administration, these organizations constituted an important vehicle for concerting professional opinion and
representing that opinion to the ministry. Their appearance in girls'
schools marked the arrival of a new outlook among women teachers. If
still committed to hard work and to the cause of feminine education,
teachers had begun to shed the heroic style of self-denial associated with
their profession in the early days.

This transformation owed much to the growing approval of secondary
studies for girls among the middle classes. As girls' lycées and collèges
won popular acceptance, assertiveness in women teachers no longer
threatened the reputation of their schools. Increasingly, the public came
to see these women as highly trained professionals with interests to protect. Once graduates of girls' schools began to pass the baccalauréat, the
difference in the public's image of men and women secondary teachers
began to blur. In this permissive atmosphere, women teachers could
more easily develop a sense of professional grievance.

This dissatisfaction grew largely out of stories of individual distress
passed along informally from school to school by mobile teachers and
directrices, alerting even unaffected teachers to injustices suffered. Actions taken by the ministry also played a part in educating teachers to
the necessity of self-protective measures. Crucial in this respect was the
law passed in 1903 changing the four-step ladder of advancement for
women teachers and directrices to a new ranking system based on six

[9] Julie Lochert, manuscript of remarks delivered to the General Assembly of the
Alumnae Association in 1904, Association des anciennes élèves, archives, E.N.S.
[10] P. Sapy, "Les Associations de professeurs de l'enseignement secondaire des jeunes
filles," *BTAES* (January 1905): 15.

classes. In the new system, each rise in rank translated into a raise in salary just as before, but the difference between the salaries paid for different ranks decreased. This meant that the ministry could give more promotions every year without incurring any more expenses. For teachers, however, the new system had one serious disadvantage. Previously, the rules regulating promotions required a minimum of four years at each rank, making it theoretically possible to reach first class in sixteen years. Under the new law, which lowered the minimum period in each class to three years while increasing the number of ranks, it would take at least eighteen years to reach the top of the salary scale. Neither figure actually represented a realistic estimate of the time teachers served before reaching the first class, since the ministry did not recognize an upper limit on the number of years a woman might be kept at any level. This had serious, long-term implications for these women's financial futures, because the ministry calculated the amount it paid in pensions on the basis of a retiring functionary's salary in the previous six years. Any woman who failed to reach first class six years before retirement would suffer the financial consequences ever after. In a profession whose leading members by now were in their forties and even early fifties, such considerations understandably caused alarm, adding impetus to the *amicalist* movement.

Nevertheless, if women secondary teachers copied men in the profession by organizing amicales, that imitation did not extend much further. A widely shared belief in the uniqueness of their professional problems and the values holding them together shaped both the way these women teachers organized themselves and the sense of grievance they expressed. In the first place, women teachers approached professional organizations in a corporate spirit. Unlike male lycée professeurs, who refused to organize amicales with *maîtres assistants*[11] in their schools or with professeurs in collèges, spokeswomen for their own movement assumed from the outset that the entire profession would organize together. "The question arises for us in the same manner it does in boys' schools," wrote Pierette Sapy (class of 1892) in Sèvres's alumnae bulletin, "but must we resolve it in the same way? Wouldn't that be a clumsy imitation of our male colleagues, one that does not at all reflect the good rapport and often even friendship which exists between teachers and répétitrices in our lycées?"[12]

Her appeal, addressed to fellow Sévriennes, reflected the professional outlook that spread from Sèvres. "Since the mission we have undertaken

[11] That is to say, academic personnel who do not teach.
[12] Sapy, "Les Associations," 16.

has above all the goal of solidarity," Sapy pointed out, "it would be il-
logical to begin it with an exclusionary measure."[13] Preached at a time
when the first graduates of Sèvres had already consolidated their position as directrices in girls' schools, the message needed no reiteration.
Indeed, some amicales went so far as to make their school directrice a
member. As for organizing the amicales of teachers from collèges and
lycées into separate federations, no one even considered such a possibility.

The only question to resolve was whether women teachers should establish their own professional group or join forces with the male profession. Hélène Dubois (class of 1889), a respected professeur in Paris, argued against affiliation on the grounds that men would inevitably
dominate a joint association and slight the demands of women teachers,[14] while Pierrette Sapy (class of 1892), a maîtresse-adjointe at Sèvres,
wrote an article for the alumnae bulletin defending the views of those
who disagreed.[15] Sapy acknowledged that women's issues might not at
first receive enough attention in a federation dominated by male teachers, but she disputed the long-term risks involved. Her main objective, to
get the women's corps a public forum, required alliance with men, who
alone possessed the right to vote in the republic. Otherwise, women
teachers would remain cut off from the arena where real political power
lay, unable even to publicize their needs. Not surprisingly, the cause of
affiliation won the day. In a profession accustomed before the war to self-
effacement in the public sphere, a strategy permitting women teachers to
depend on men to plead their interests in high places conformed to the
collective spirit. Thus, in 1905, the entire body of feminine amicales
from cours, collèges, and lycées joined the elitist masculine Federation
of Amicales of professeurs des lycées.

Nevertheless, the distinctive character of this feminine associational
movement did not reside alone in its united organization or even in the
eagerness of women teachers to rely on men to advertise their woes. In
addition, their professional complaints suggest a moral perspective on
injustice all their own. Even as women teachers emerged from the hero-
ically self-denying phase of their professional development, the code of
honor learned at Sèvres shaped the way they cast their problems. In the

---

[13] Ibid.

[14] Her views on the subject were never published because the president of the Alumnae Association, Louise Belugou (class of 1882), considered them too partisan for the
alumnae bulletin. See her manuscript article and the exchange of letters in 1905 between Louise Belugou and Julie Lochert, the editor of the bulletin. Association des anciennes élèves, archives, E.N.S.

[15] Sapy, "Les Associations," 13–19.

first place, they rejected as immoral the promotion of one group's selfish interest over any other. Even the appearance of selfish motivations concerned them. "On first glance, the list [of demands] appears to be a list of grievances," Sapy noted in her article for the bulletin on the new movement.

> Let us note, however, that the most urgent protests made by all the personnel are directed at the situation of répétitrices, the most badly treated group among them, and that often the associations of lycées, where abuses are less numerous, protest in favor of truly sacrificed establishments like cours secondaires. If at first, therefore, these demands sound a bit strong or irritated, we find on close inspection that they come out of feelings of generosity and justice as much as personal interest.[16]

In other words, women professionals organized into a single assocation would protect the needs of all their members, not just a favored elite of agrégées.

Second, to ask for parity with the male profession never occurred to women teachers in this period. Committed to a special pedagogical undertaking, they argued for reforms on the basis of their unique position within the teaching profession. Feminine amicales did not call for a dramatic reorganization of their teaching schedules to conform to those for men, who needed time to undertake research; they simply asked for a slight reduction in their teaching load from sixteen to fifteen hours per week, which would preserve their exclusive commitment to the classroom. Likewise, they pressed for representatives on the Conseil supérieur and other councils, not because male teachers sent elected delegates, but rather because the singularity of their educational enterprise required insiders, both women teachers and directrices, to speak directly for its interests. Certainly, women teachers considered their profession underpaid. They demanded both raises and salaries pegged to the actual cost of living in different places. Yet women teachers never requested their pay to be aligned with that of men or even scaled in comparable denominations from top to bottom. In this first phase of their amicalist activities, women teachers agreed that different salaries were the concomitant of their special place within the Université.

Still, women teachers had come to expect on moral grounds that the state would protect them adequately from the worst effects of their dedicated service. Time and again that expectation would be disappointed. A first promising opening occurred in 1906, when the Chamber of Dep-

[16] Ibid., 18.

uties, pressured by the rising discontent among the personnel of boys' schools, established an extra-parliamentary commission to study the complaints of all teaching personnel in public secondary schools, women as well as men.[17] In the months between the resolution and the opening of the official inquiry, a small band of women *amicalistes* polled the views of the teaching personnel and directrices of all girls' secondary schools. The results, drawn up into a single statement for each category of personnel, were presented before the Extraparliamentary Commission on January 31, 1907 by Lucie Kuss (class of 1882), representing directrices, and Camille Tollemer (class of 1884), representing teachers.[18] The demands included raises for every category of the profession except directrices of lycées, a common pay scale for teachers in collèges and cours, and an adjustment in expensive towns for a higher cost of living. In the minds of those who formulated these demands, dedicated service, wherever it occurred, ought rightly to guarantee equal material rewards.

These same witnesses raised a second and even more important issue before the commission: the treatment of aging personnel. In doing so, they signified the weight that the oldest generation carried in this first official exposition of professional griefs. The unfair consequences of the law of 1903 reclassifying the profession came in for particular attack. Teachers and directrices both demanded a system ensuring that women reached the highest class at least six years before they retired. "It is a right that we are claiming," declared one teacher, "and for the state, it is a moral obligation."[19] Witnesses before the commission attached equal importance to achieving a reform that would permit women to retire before the age of sixty, following thirty years of service, or even earlier in instances of broken health. The directrice at the lycée of Reims reported, on the subject of her teachers' health, "Too often in the eleven years that I have been in the administration, I have seen constitutions ruined even before fifty years of age, and I believe it is necessary to retire before that age."[20] Although sometimes commentators referred to the frailty of women to explain this special need, more often they attributed exhaustion to the particularly taxing nature of their work.

Despite this comprehensive hearing, women teachers had little in the end to show for the publicity they had gained. No reforms touching on the feminine profession came directly out of this inquiry. Indeed, by 1914, women professeurs still had no binding regulation governing their

[17] "Projet de Loi," *RU* 1 (1908): 229.
[18] Commission extraparlementaire, séance 31 janvier 1907, F17 12748, A.N.
[19] Ibid., 482.
[20] Ibid., 497.

sick leaves[21] or conditions of retirement, and their hours of service remained as long as ever. In addition, no teachers or directrices sat on any state academic council as representatives of the feminine profession or as spokeswomen for girls' secondary schools. All teachers had gained by this time was a series of piecemeal, minor reforms affecting specific groups within their professional corps, which the ministry had slowly handed out in previous years. These included shorter hours for répétitrices, elementary teachers, and professeurs in Paris over forty-five years of age, but not for the bulk of the profession, plus an indemnity of five hundred francs for directrices of collèges and lycées, but not of cours, for supervising boarders.[22] Meanwhile, the ministry made no provision for raising teachers' salaries, and instead of restructuring the system of advancement set up in 1903, it added another rank in 1913 called the *classe supérieure*. Once promoted to this class, women would obtain increases in their salary every year, but entry to this privileged status was reserved to older teachers of exceptional merit. With such measures the ministry eliminated a few of the most glaring injustices in girls' schools. But by avoiding all reforms that necessitated a substantial increase in the funds for operating girls' schools, it left intact most of the conditions protested by women teachers since they began to organize in amicales. Inevitably, this lack of progress raised the level of frustration within the amicalist movement.

Toward a Separate and Equal Feminine Profession

Even before the First World War, signs appeared within the Federation of Amicales of a new offensive against this discriminatory treatment. The Easter congress of 1910 marked the turning point in this development. Visibly more numerous and talkative than in previous years, women delegates at that meeting for the first time addressed the issue of their inequality with men.[23] In what proved to be the opening shot in a gathering assault on their subordinate position in the Université, women teachers asked for exactly the same treatment as the state provided men regarding sick leaves, promotions, and professional discipline.[24] No one

[21] In 1903, the minister and director agreed to apply to women personnel in practice the law of July 9, 1853 even if, legally, there were no binding guarantees. Lucie Kuss, "Rapport," *BTAES* (December 1903): 222–23.

[22] Cours secondaires continued to be at the mercy of town contracts with no ministerial guarantees.

[23] See accounts of these meetings in Crouzet-Ben Aben, "Bulletin," *RU* 2 (1910): 239 and 1 (1911): 423–24.

[24] Ibid., 1 (1910): 236–39.

for the moment mentioned salaries. Still, the longer the administration put off providing women teachers with seats on its administrative councils and a comprehensive statute regulating the terms of their employment, the greater the tendency for some among them to look to the masculine profession as a model.

This outburst of reformist sentiment in women's amicales did not bubble up from girls' schools unassisted. By 1910, the public mood in France widely favored activist collective movements. Agitational politics on the Right, strike movements on the Left, and an increasingly assertive style in the associations of civil servants all fed a growing sense in urban settings that the only way to change the status quo was through collective action.[25] Not unexpectedly, women professeurs, who throughout the Belle Epoque had sought to further contacts between girls' secondary schools and the society around them, proved open to contagion.

All the same, the sense of urgency evident in teachers' demands after 1910 had more to do with developments inside than outside girls' schools. Owing largely to the failure of lawmakers to adjust their vision of feminine secondary studies to the realities of popular demand, girls' schools had entered a period of crisis. The government had expected girls' schools to remain both small and few in number, serving the daughters of the well-to-do. Long after swelling classes proved such calculations wrong, educational budgets reflected this underestimate.[26] The results dismayed the feminine profession. Overcrowding for the first time became a serious problem; work loads for teachers steadily increased;[27] and frustration, especially inside the more disadvantaged collèges and cours, built to acrimonious levels. Even the oldest teachers, for whom stoic acceptance once had served as a professional credo, showed signs of disenchantment. "It is in this generation of teachers," claimed Jeanne Crouzet-Ben-Aben, "exhausted by several years of teaching yet

[25] For a general survey of the period, see Madeleine Rebérioux, *La République radicale? 1898–1914* (Paris: Editions de Seuil, 1975).

[26] Certainly the worst effects of this position climaxed in 1907 when the government's outlay per student fell to 68.3 francs. By 1909 the government raised to 107.8 francs per student the amount it spent on girls' schools, but this figure was far inferior to what boys' schools received. The difference translated into lower salaries, smaller staffs, fewer teaching materials, and a paucity of girls' schools. Calculations for 1907 are based on figures found in Compayré, *L'Enseignement secondaire des jeunes filles*, 136–38, and those for 1909 on figures from Maurice Faure, "Rapport fait au nom de la Commission des Finance du Sénat sur le Budget du Ministre de l'Instruction publique," *ESDJF* 2 (1919): 70, 78.

[27] No teacher-student ratios exist for 1910, but teachers in my sample had twice as many students in 1910 as in 1895. See Crouzet-Ben-Aben, "Le Surménage," 414–25.

still a long way from retirement, that discouragement and illness really rage."[28]

A few teachers, more radical in their dissatisfaction, expressed a loss of faith in the feminine professional ideal. In a society where specialists monopolized professional output and prestige, the generalist ruled an intellectual backwater, and as women teachers came in greater contact with the world, some intensely resented that position. One agrégée from Sèvres described "the cruel disappointment of a mind that understands it has been duped, that it devoted its youth to studies without depth which have not even given it the indispensable tools for further understanding." As soon as women professeurs were "no longer pitted only against each other but against the finest human minds," she claimed, they discovered that, "instead of a well-sharpened sword, all they have been given is a miserable stick. And even then, no one taught them how to use it."[29] A few agrégées in letters and history joined specialized professional societies for male professeurs to signal their objection to the generalist ideal. More commonly, women professeurs requested as a partial remedy for the dispersion of their intellectual energies that teaching assignments for agrégées reflect their field of concentration.[30]

More serious even than this dissatisfaction with their teaching obligations was a growing sense, shared by teachers and directrices alike, that feminine secondary studies as originally conceived no longer satisfied their students. Too many girls wanted more from secondary education than a diploma merely certifying their preparation for domestic life. As a result, by 1910, several large lycées were unofficially preparing some older students for the higher brevet and the baccalauréat. The pedagogical confusion thereby introduced to girls' secondary education understandably troubled the profession. An effort by the Federation of Amicales to survey members' views on a solution only pointed up the absence of agreement on the problem. Those few amicales even venturing opinions distinguished themselves above all by the diversity of their views. All agreed on the necessity of preparing some girls for the brevets; most also supported an elective course in Latin. Yet concerning the overall direction girls' studies ought to take, opinion divided sharply, with some amicales accepting the current makeshift situation, while others favored the formal introduction of three alternative educational tracks. A few proposed the far more radical solution of scrapping the girls' di-

[28] Crouzet-Ben-Aben, "Bulletin," *RU* 2 (1910): 122. See also idem, "Le Surménage," 423.

[29] F. Teutscher, "Sur quelques insuffisances de l'enseignement féminin," *RU* 1 (1911): 33–34. Félicie Teutscher, married name Stolz, was in the class of 1891.

[30] Crouzet-Ben-Aben, "Bulletin," *RU* 1 (1910): 361–62 and 1 (1912): 417.

ploma altogether for certificates offering graduates more professional outlets.[31]

Summing up the mood of women teachers in 1910, one of them concluded that a "permanent malaise" had infected the profession.[32] This
restiveness originated only partly in the uncertainties surrounding the
direction of girls' secondary studies. Official reluctance to act on demands for better benefits for the feminine teaching corps also soured feelings. Particularly galling was the decision taken in 1911 to decrease the
teaching hours required of men professeurs while women teachers'
schedules remained unchanged.[33] For the time being, though, inequities
within the women's corps proved more troubling than discrimination
against the profession as a whole. A combination of frustration over the
minimal results obtained by their collective efforts and exposure to the
elitist attitudes within the masculine teaching world undermined the
idea that moral solidarity should bind all teachers together, whatever
their professional credentials.

By 1911 the rivalries created along the natural fault lines of this bu-
reaucratically organized profession proved too much for its corporate
ethos to contain. In an atmosphere of suspicion and recrimination, the
amicales of eight collèges and cours split apart from the national federation. Shortly afterward, a few répétitrices founded a separate organization exclusively to defend the interests of assistant teachers.[34] Still committed to the collective mentality built originally at Sèvres, Jeanne
Crouzet-Ben-Aben gave the spoilers a public scolding. "It seems to me,"
she wrote in her regular bulletin on girls' secondary schools for the Revue universitaire, "that the rivalries and different viewpoints which exist between holders of the diverse feminine titles . . . have no place in
national congresses."[35] Enough women agreed with her to halt the disintegration of the federation temporarily. The coming of the war ensured
its survival even longer as professional anxieties gave way to national
concerns and a renewed sense of mission in girls' schools. But the war
could not resolve the underlying conflicts subverting the solidarity of
this profession. Quite the opposite, the impact of the war experience
merely intensified the crisis.

The central issue concerned the viability of the republican ideal of separate spheres for bourgeois men and women. If that conception of the
social order contradicted the logic of contemporary trends, the rationale

---

[31] Ibid., 2 (1910), 265–66.

[32] Teutscher, "Un Défaut de l'enseignement supérieur féminin," RU 2 (1910): 24.

[33] C. Suran-Mabire, "Le Danger des demi-services," RU 2 (1918): 105.

[34] Crouzet-Ben-Aben, "Bulletin," RU 2 (1911): 2.

[35] RU 1 (1911): 423–34.

for a uniquely feminine course of secondary studies disappeared and with it the need for a specially trained corps of women teachers. On the question of women's proper social role, the war left a dual legacy. Throughout the war official rhetoric maintained that women were serving the nation in new ways to fill in temporarily for men. Once hostilities ceased, ideally they would participate in charitable organizations as a civic duty, but their principal obligation in the nation would again become to raise a family. Most directrices, as spokeswomen for the administration, took this point of view. After 1918, motherhood as a national duty became, if anything, more important in official thinking, which pictured childbearing as a patriotic effort to rebuild the population. Still, if official rhetoric promoted the prewar view of bourgeois women in the home, the realities of postwar France pressed ever more daughters from the middle classes to accept the necessity of paid employment. An unprecedented number faced the likelihood of finding no one of their age to marry, while in many families postwar inflation wiped out savings intended to provide a daughter with a dowry.[36] Naturally, given those conditions, the prewar interest in diplomas providing access to careers quickened in girls' collèges and lycées. That in turn raised ever more insistent doubts about the professionally useless feminine diplôme and, more generally, about the purpose of secondary schools for girls.

To forestall the pending crisis, the government established in 1917 yet another Extraparliamentary Commission to investigate the problem. After months surveying professional and interested opinion, it concluded, "The war with its financial consequences, with its dreadful toll in men that makes marriage problematical, that places so many widowed women and orphaned daughters in need of earning a living, has succeeded in ruining the prestige of a disinterested education."[37] At the same time, the commission judged that sentiment within educational circles still ran heavily in favor of preserving a separate educational track for girls. Camille Sée himself appeared before the members to plead for the diplôme, as did several directrices of schools. Only two voices from the women's profession, Jeanne Crouzet-Ben-Aben and Claire Suran-Mabire (class of 1897), both teachers trained at Sèvres, spoke in favor of introducing the masculine course of studies to girls' schools, a suggestion that the commission pointedly ignored. Instead, it recommended rejuvenating the feminine track in secondary studies by making the diplôme with an emphasis on mathematics equal to the higher brevet and a diplôme with an

---

[36] For the demographic and economic impact of the war, see Philippe Bernard and Henri Dubief, *The Decline of the Third Republic, 1914–1938* (Cambridge: Cambridge Univ. Press, 1985), 78–92.

[37] "Commission extraparlementaire, projets de décrets et arrêtés," *ESDJF* 1 (1919): 98.

emphasis on Latin or science equal to the first part of the baccalauréat. Such adjustments would permit girls preparing for the diplôme to envisage secondary studies as a step toward a professional career. At the same time, the principle of difference imbedded in their distinctive educational program would survive.

In fact, this effort at adjustment to the new realities of social and economic life had virtually no chance of saving the diplôme from further challenge. Despite the ministerial reform, the baccalauréat had far too much appeal for students, especially in the large lycées where those who passed the first part of the bac rose precipitously as a proportion of the student body. Between 1919 and 1922, one out of two graduates of the girls' lycée at Nice opted for the baccalauréat over the diplôme. The ratio reached three to one in the same period at Toulouse, six to one at Jules Ferry in Paris, and nine to one at the lycée of Nancy.[38] Some impetus for this exploding interest in the baccalauréat came from the example set by Catholic secondary schools, which had resorted to preparing girls for these exams because they could not legally bestow the public school's feminine diploma. But the deeper explanation derives from the heritage of uniformity in French professional life. As long as the middle classes expected women to remain in private life, they could accept a school diploma based on separate and internally administered exams. Once graduates of girls' schools began aspiring to professional careers, the principle of merit that the Université had so successfully implanted in French professional culture took over. Against that tradition the notion of equivalent certificates had little chance of making any headway. Whatever the view within the ministry or among educators determined to defend a feminine version of secondary education, middle-class opinion recognized only one legitimate gateway into public life: the baccalauréat.[39]

Directrices of girls' schools might have managed, nonetheless, to satisfy those opting for the baccalauréat in the usual, informal way had a movement for reform not taken hold among their women teachers. This development, barely visible in 1917, when Crouzet-Ben-Aben and Suran-Mabire presented their minority position to the Extraparliamentary Commission, by 1920 had swept the cream of the profession into organized resistance to feminized preprofessional and professional exams. This remarkable reversal gave expression to a growing frustration, felt especially by the agrégées in Paris, over the ministry's discriminatory treatment of

[38] These statistics were quoted from *Les Agrégées* (March 1923), in Mayeur, *L'Enseignement secondaire*, 427n.19.

[39] Edmond Goblot, *La Barrière et le niveau, étude sociologique de la bourgeoisie française moderne* (Paris: F. Alcan, 1925).

the whole profession. If the rationale for such discrimination was that the men's degrees reflected different talents, women teachers assigned to boys' schools in the war implicitly gave the lie to that assumption. By 1916, 397 women teachers across the nation were proving daily every bit the equals in the classroom of the men whose tasks they now performed at lower salaries.[40] More and more agrégées began to see in this experience the inevitable consequence of femininized degrees. "It is a waste of time and effort to fight the indestructible association of ideas that has made the word *feminine* synonymous with the word *inferior*," Suran-Mabire would write in 1916.[41] At the time, most of her colleagues disagreed, preferring to keep their own degrees in hopes of winning better terms of work in the near future. Four years later, though, the activists among the agrégées in Paris had come to share her point of view. Tired of the title of agrégée without the privileges, the work without the pay, a group of women professeurs in Paris left the Federation of Amicales in 1920 to form the Société des agrégées, a separate, elitist organization that made the heart of its professional agenda a complete alignment with the men's profession. As a first step toward that objective, they called for the introduction of the baccalauréat course of studies to girls' schools. But their real objective was to justify the same professional training and degrees for men and women teachers, the only realistic hope, they had concluded, for equal treatment of the two professions.[42]

The response to this demand among male teachers suggested just how well these women understood their situation. Of all the amicales for agrégées, only one, the men's amicale from the lycée at Toulon, attacked the women for unseemly professional aspirations.[43] The vast majority of their male colleagues publicly supported this bid by agrégées for equal status in the Université. Such a generous attitude among the men unquestionably reflected the separate tracking of the two professions. Women with the same training and degrees as male secondary teachers did not place the latter's jobs at risk. The old imperative within the bourgeoisie that separate education for boys and girls be taught by teachers of

[40] *RU* 2 (1918): 291. The high quality of their performance in these positions finds corroboration in the reports by inspectors on the two Sévriennes in my sample who taught in boys' lycées.

[41] C. Suran-Mabire, "La Réforme de l'enseignement secondaire féminin et les associations de professeurs," *RU* 2 (1916): 208.

[42] Marthe Faure and Marguerite Schwob, "La Société des Agrégées, 1920–1948," *Bulletin officiel de la Société des Agrégées* 162 (1968): 551.

[43] Ibid., 556. The president of the amicale at Toulon sent a letter to Anna Amieux as directrice of Sèvres congratulating her on her public opposition to the introduction of the baccalauréat in girls' secondary schools and to adopting wholesale the men's professional degrees. Archives, E.N.S.

the same sex as their students, if overridden in the war, showed no signs of weakening once peace was restored. Women, therefore, would continue to teach exclusively in girls' secondary schools even with a masculine degree, unless they went on to qualify for posts in higher education. Yet this practical consideration itself might not have sufficed to win over the male profession had the idea of unique intellectual spheres for men and women still carried weight in academic circles as a rationale for two dissimilar professions. In fact, at the highest levels of the Université, that notion had already died a natural death.

The beginning of the decline of this bifurcated view of learning in the Université dated from the turn of the century, when a positivist enthusiasm for scientific methods swept through humanistic studies. Though unrecognized at first, the underlying premise of this reorientation clashed with the very idea of a separate humanities for girls. As long as educators envisioned secondary studies as an essentially moral undertaking, aimed at shaping character through inspiring examples, educating girls differently from boys possessed an intellectual rationale. Each group could, given their distinctive social tasks, prepare for adult life from a different educational perspective. Once historians, literary critics, and psychologists shifted their objectives toward a positivist search for truth, however, the justification for two distinct approaches collapsed. This happened first in literary pedagogy with the introduction of a method of critical, textual analysis called the *explication de texte*. This technique of literary criticism, which Gustave Lanson taught at Sèvres as well as the Sorbonne from 1901 to 1918, put the core of humanistic studies on a consciously scientific footing. Students were expected to approach a literary masterpiece methodically so as to understand its precise historical meaning and the techniques producing its aesthetic effect. Another teacher of literature at Sèvres, Paul Desjardins, assured his students that this critical approach need not neglect the moral uses of literature in girls' education.[44] Yet the very need to make that claim suggested how this scientific reorientation might gradually rework the goals of feminine secondary education.

Annual reports by the president of the jury for the women's agrégations in literature and history offer one easy way to trace the progress of a more scientific emphasis in girls' education. These reports summed up the strengths and weakness of contestants' performances at the agrégations each year. Through 1901, with Eugène Manuel in charge, they con-

[44] "Que doit-on se propose, au lycée, dans l'explication des auteurs? Notes prises à un entretien de pédagogie pratique—conférence de M. P. Desjardins, 1ère année," *BTAES* (April 1908): 53.

tinued to stress the importance of inspirational models in girls' education. In the examination on psychology and moral philosophy, for
example, Manuel still called in 1901 for "simple and nontechnical language,"[45] and in history, he wanted "fewer abstract analyses and more
vivid facts, more historical figures in action."[46] A year later, under a different president, Thamin, the jury turned more scientific and exacting.
Thamin filled his reports with complaints about the imprecision of contestants' answers. Regarding the exam on morals and psychology, he
complained: "Candidates know nothing about the history of moral
thought, psychology, and especially the functions of intelligence and the
laws of reasoning. . . . They imagine that a certain taste for the ideal can
take the place of all philosophy."[47] The next year he attacked contestants
for their imprecise and moralistic handling of literary texts. "Candidates
must convince themselves that the analysis of a French text, even from
the point of view of taste, is not invented and that today, when there is
no literary dogma in the name of which one distributes blame or praise,
the study of an author presupposes a rich and precise fund of knowledge. . . . Taste must be exercised on a foundation of methodical knowledge."[48] Such criticisms abated slightly between 1907 and 1911 under
yet another president, Gabriel Compayré, though even he attacked "the
tendency to look in history only for the striking examples of heroism."[49]
But with the appointment of Louis Gallouédec as president of the jury
for history and literature in 1912, the women's agrégations passed an intellectual watershed with no possibility afterward of turning back.

From 1912 through 1918, each annual report would stridently insist
on an approach to letters informed by scientific methods and the latest
learning. The days were gone when academics comfortably applauded
the idea that a field of study differed in accordance with the audience
that it addressed. "To read the exams of candidates, one would think that
child psychology has not progressed since Mme Necker de Saussure,"
Gallouédec exploded after his first exposure to the feminine agrégation
in 1912. He went on to castigate the whole approach to learning in this
area of public education. "Unfortunately, there exists in France one psychology for boys' lycées, another for elementary normal schools, and another for girls' secondary education. The last, stripped of everything that
is technical and precise . . . is, in its totality, a rather anemic psychol-

---

[45] "Rapport," *RU* 1 (1901): 112.
[46] Ibid., 122.
[47] "Rapport," *ESDJF* 1 (1904): 271.
[48] "Rapport," *ESDJF* 1 (1905): 250.
[49] "Rapport du Président du Jury," *ESDJF* 1 (1909): 121.

ogy."[50] Under Gallouédec, juries continued throughout the war to press prospective teachers of letters in girls' schools to adopt a scientific orientation in every subject. By 1919, the constant warnings and berating had borne fruit. "We are unanimous in our recognition," Gallouédec's report announced that year, "that there has been progress in grammatical analysis and great progress in the examination on morals, the analysis of texts, and geography."[51] Considerably before the Société des agrégées requested the boys' curriculum for girls' schools, the Université had renounced the idea, inspired by the social vision of political reformers, that girls should learn differently from boys.

But did the Société des agrégées speak for women teachers generally and for older colleagues in particular when it called for the baccalauréat in girls' schools? It would be hard to argue that the views of this society widely represented the teaching corps in 1920. As late as 1922, when Sèvres's alumnae bulletin asked its readers to send in their opinions on the issue of the baccalauréat, only eleven of the members replied.[52] Most teachers seem to have been indecisive rather than actively for or against the reform.[53] On the other hand, if the Société des agrégées did not reflect the unified opinion of the teaching corps, some members of every generation did share its views. At least in Paris, teachers in their fifties supported the society from the start. Three-quarters of the aging Sévriennes with teaching posts in Paris joined the founding members.[54] One of them, Elizabeth Butiaux (class of 1881), even presided over the association. Far from splitting generations, therefore, the Société des agrégées brought young and old together in an activist elite eager to convince the others that separate spheres, applied to their profession, could only undercut protection of their rights.

Watching from the sidelines, directrices for the most part disapproved of these new developments in girls' education. Even heads of schools in Paris, where the movement for reform built most momentum, objected to a drift toward masculinizing girls' education that they felt powerless to reverse. A few like Marguerite Caron, who throughout her career had

[50] "Rapport," *RU* 2 (1912): 372–73.

[51] "Rapport," *ESDJF* 2 (1919): 89.

[52] Of these eleven, seven opposed the proposition. *BAES* (June 1922): 24–27 and (January 1923): 29–33.

[53] Only two Sévrienne teachers publicly opposed the baccalauréat for girls, Louise-Amélie Gayraud (class of 1894) and H. Guénot (class of 1901), and they both taught in the lycée annexed to Sèvres. Among their articles, see Louise-Amélie Gayraud, "Pour une éducation plus intellectuelle et plus féminine," *RU* 2 (1917): 174–81; and H. Guénot, "Culture générale," *ESDJF* 2 (1921): 99–104.

[54] Together they constituted 16 percent of the membership. See the list of members published in *Les Agrégées* 1 (1920): 11–12.

shown her sensitive awareness to contemporary social trends, bowed to the inevitable with equanimity. "A directrice has no right," Caron remarked, "to follow only personal preference, even intellectual. . . . Her absolute rule must be the interest, the future of the student."[55] Far more typical, though, was the reaction of Léonie Allégret, who witnessed the collapse of a "disinterested education" and the decline of the diplôme "with anguish."[56]

Such feelings, widely shared by other school heads, might well have come from fear of losing status. The exceptional power of directrices of girls' schools derived to no small extent from the diploma program and their pedagogical role within it. Inevitably, a more specialized course of studies would limit their prerogatives, diminishing their moral influence over students and their intellectual standing with their teachers. Yet more than personal interest lay behind this opposition. The deep commitment felt by most directrices to femininized instruction sprang, above all, from their belief in uniquely feminine social roles for women.

This position did not generally proceed from rigidly unchanging views on women's place within the home. Directrices adapted their vision of the educated woman to altered conditions in the postwar years, just as they had during the war. Many stressed the need for a continued public role for women in the reconstruction of a healthy nation and sponsored projects designed to further volunteer work from their schools.[57] Nor were they blind to the obligation incumbent on their schools to guide far more of their students than before toward careers. But they continued to believe that even working women ought to preserve the cultural values handed down to them as virtuous women. Such a moral task still implied a special kind of education. "The question is very serious," intoned no less a figure than the former Sévrienne and directrice of Sèvres, Louise Belugou, in 1918. "France . . . must have women who stay women, that is, who combine the virile qualities more and more required with the virtues that properly belong to them: modesty, gentleness, charm, a quick and strong sense of family needs, a hatred for the evils that destroy it, a moral conscience in both little and important matters. It is not for women to adopt the faults of the voter but to bring to public life their womanly virtues." To preserve such female virtues within the public sphere, she argued, "We must give to our lycées a moral life that is stronger, firmer,

[55] Quoted in Wurmser-Dégouy, *Trois Éducatrices modernes*, 78.

[56] H. Guénot, "Une Educatrice: Mlle Léonie Allégret," *ESDJF* n.s., 1 (1927–1928): 27.

[57] To cite just one example, at Victor Duruy Léonie Allégret organized an infant day-care center, staffed by a doctor, nurse, and graduates of the school, for children of the working poor. Wurmser-Dégouy, *Trois Éducatrices modernes*, 41.

and more conscientious than ever."[58] This concern for moral sensitivity and its purported centrality in feminine culture was what attracted directrices like Belugou to the old diploma. The vast majority of school heads believed its fall from grace would diminish the quality of girls' education.

At one point in the campaign for the baccalauréat, even some members of the Société des agrégées became concerned that they were giving up too much by asking for the baccalauréat. Though opposed to the idea of a feminine diploma, many valued highly the girls' curriculum of modern languages and literature and fully expected that aspect of feminine studies to remain intact. Unfortunately, their campaign in favor of the baccalauréat coincided with another one by classicists within the men's profession to eliminate the modern track from the humanities. Once a proponent of that view, Léon Bérard, became minister of education in 1923, further progress toward equalizing boys' and girls' instruction hinged on introducing into girls' schools not the baccalauréat of the 1902 reforms but a new program of studies stripped of modern literature and languages.[59] When this first became apparent, consternation swept the ranks of Paris teachers.[60] Very quickly, though, the desire for professional equality overrode their hesitations. "Despite the recognized value of girls' secondary studies and regret at seeing its originality, particularly in letters, disappear, agrégées knew all too well that compromise was fatal," two apologists for their position later claimed.[61] In 1923, experience certainly gave considerable support to that contention. Despite two sympathetic directors of secondary education, Vial and Châtelet, and four years of lobbying efforts, agrégées had yet to see a single one of their key objectives met. With lower salaries and longer hours than agrégés, they still possessed no seats on academic councils, no legal recourse in disciplinary cases, and no assurance that the most prestigious teaching posts in girls' secondary schools would even be assigned to women.[62] Whatever the pedagogical costs, adopting masculine degrees continued to appear to most members of the Société des agrégées the only way to guarantee for women teachers equal treatment.

This consensus notwithstanding, victory when it came turned less on the pressure agrégées exerted as a group on state officials than on the

---

[58] "Les Carrières nouvelles ouvertes aux femmes," *BAES* (1918): 32.

[59] Offen, "The Second Sex," 280–81.

[60] Mayeur, *L'Enseignement secondaire*, 425.

[61] Faure and Schwob, "La Société," 554.

[62] Ibid., 522; Gérard Vincent, "Les Professeurs de l'enseignement secondaire dans la société de la 'Belle Epoque,'" *Revue d'histoire moderne et contemporaine* (January–March 1966): 66.

influence of well-placed individuals. The directing role in events fell to Paul Crouzet, inspector general, interim director of secondary education under Léon Bérard in 1923, and husband to one of the most vocal members of the Société, Jeanne Crouzet-Ben-Aben. In fact, both spouses were early defenders of the baccalauréat for girls, Jeanne before the Extraparliamentary Commission in 1917 and in the pages of the Revue universitaire, Paul as a minority voice on the Conseil supérieur during and after the war. Their moment of triumph finally came when Paul Crouzet joined Bérard's ministry. Bérard himself had little interest in reforming girls' secondary studies. For him, it was enough to terminate the modern alternative to Greek and Latin at the baccalauréat.[63] Yet in the view of his director, the two reforms ought rightly to occur together. Owing largely to Crouzet's persuasive powers, they ultimately did so. On March 25, 1924, by decree, Bérard ordered the progressive introduction of the baccalauréat curriculum, starting with the lowest form, as an alternative to the regular diploma program.

Just as agrégées had hoped, that decree set off a chain reaction both in girls' schools and in their own profession. As the baccalauréat curriculum gradually entered girls' schools, students began deserting the diploma option. Everywhere by 1930, the girls' degree had become a virtual dead letter.[64] With the demise of the diplôme, "equality in difference," as an official pedagogical ideal, passed into institutional oblivion. Women teachers took rather longer to excise the same principle of difference from their status in the Université. A boycott of the baccalauréat in 1927 finally forced the legislature to vote the funds for equal pay for agrégées, while the following year, they won the right to serve on baccalauréat juries. Not until 1930, however, did the ministry agree to the alignment of the men's and women's agrégations, and the process was not complete for eight more years. Meanwhile, in 1931 women teachers finally got their teaching hours reduced, twenty years after the ministry had lowered those for men. Then in December 1933, the Senate at last agreed to create five permanent seats on the Conseil supérieur for agrégées.[65] With that decision, women teachers finally reached maturity

[63] Mayeur, L'Enseignement secondaire, 424.

[64] In fact, the shift over to the baccalauréat program was only imperfectly accomplished in the interwar period due to insufficient funding for girls' secondary schools. According to Marilyn Mavrinac, many girls' schools prepared their students for the first part of the baccalauréat but not the second. As a consequence, several hundred girls got permission to attend the preparatory classes in boys' schools. M. Mavrinac, "The Anomaly of Co-education in the French Secondary System" (Paper presented at the Social Science Historical Association, Saint Louis, October 19, 1986).

[65] Mayeur, L'Enseignement secondaire, 434.

within the Université. Still separate from the men's profession, they had, by throwing off unique credentials, guaranteed their own professional corps formal equality of rights with men.

Sévriennes from the first ten classes served out their final years of service in the promise of this coming triumph. Those who had done battle for the changes could take pride in their achievement. Those opposed to the reforms would lick their wounds. Yet whichever side a woman had been on, she shared with older colleagues a common problem. Now in their fifties and sixties, one way or another the entire generation had to face the changes of the postwar era laden with values and expectations fashioned by experiences from an earlier age. That situation posed dilemmas for these women individually. But it had equally serious implications for the schools that many of them led and the classes that the others taught. As girls' secondary studies moved closer to the masculine curriculum, under the watchful eye of school inspectors, the institutional traditions of the two school systems would slowly merge as well.

11 | Aging in a Changing Professional World

BY 1920 AGING SÉVRIENNES, like the France they had defended in their schools, had passed their finest hour, and
they knew it. Now they needed to adjust to changes not usually of their making nor often to their taste. It was a shock they shared
with other members of their generation. Outwardly, little had changed in
their position. Beneficiaries of the seniority system in French schools,
they still controlled the most prestigious posts in girls' collèges and lycées.[1] Yet both their writings and their dossiers reveal a growing challenge to their professional reputations. Although for some the coming of
old age meant deteriorating skills, on the whole neither premature senil-
ity nor physical decline explained this generation's problem. Far more
serious were new expectations that emerged in girls' schools after the
war on the part of students, younger colleagues, and school inspectors.
Survivors of an earlier institutional era, the first Sévriennes had difficulty meeting or even in some cases comprehending the new demands
that others placed upon them. At the same time, their resistance to new
standards of professional conduct helped control the pace of change.
Some might describe the girls' collèges and lycées as stalemated, a term
that Stanley Hoffmann has applied to the whole of French society between the wars.[2] But this would be vastly to underestimate the transformation that the social impact of the war and the introduction of the baccalauréat precipitated in school life. What can be said is that old
traditions from prewar institutions did not altogether crumble. Neither
parents nor the administration had given up the earlier familial ideal of
feminine schooling, while the presence of older teachers and directrices
insured the persistence of values from a bygone age.

[1] One-third of girls' secondary schools had an older Sévrienne as directrice in 1920
as calculated from Ministère de l'instruction publique et des beaux arts, Direction de
l'enseignement secondaire, 5e Bureau, *Tableaux du personnel des lycées, collèges, et
cours secondaires de jeunes filles, 1920–1923* (Paris: Imprimerie Nationale, 1923). In
Paris, at some point in the twenties, Sévriennes from the first ten classes led every lycée.
[2] Stanley Hoffmann et al., *In Search of France: The Economy, Society, and Political
System of France in the Twentieth Century* (Cambridge: Harvard Univ. Press, 1963), 3–
8.

274

Directrices in Late Career: Adaptation and Resistance

Of the 147 Sévriennes in this study still professionally active in the 1920s, those in charge of schools numbered 55. Distinct in personality they surely were, but they also had in common more than age and Sèvres. All had worked as well as lived for years in school settings patterned on the family, and the experience had stamped on them a similar outlook. In their minds, girls' secondary schools were and ought properly to remain forever locked in the image of the family circle. Unfortunately for them, their late careers coincided with the disappearance of important preconditions for such an institutional goal. By 1920 perceptive directrices already understood the dangers that beset this style of schooling. Chief among them figured the explosion of the student population. "Is it truly an advantage?" Marguerite Caron (class of 1887) queried, regarding the enormous popularity of secondary schools for girls after the war. "In a lycée of 1,100, even 1,400 students, what will be the role of the directrice? Knowledge of each student, the study of their characters, of their backgrounds; the search for what will double the value to each student of her presence at the lycée: first an orientation toward her studies, later for her life; conversations with parents . . . what will become of all of that?"[3] Borrowed originally from the convent, transformed for secular objectives at the School of Sèvres, and fastened onto girls' schools everywhere by its alumnae, the maternal ideal of a directrice was clearly threatened by the coming of the vast lycée.

Size alone, however, did not exhaust the obstacles to mothering and moralizing school heads. Changes in the attitudes of students sometimes interfered as well. "Gone are the well-behaved, model young girls who imbibed everything served up to them," mourned Marguerite Caron. "We are faced with very self-confident, very deliberate young people, all the more difficult to lead because they are sometimes more pretentious than reflective. . . . Ardent at work because they know the competition and difficulties of modern life, they no longer have the suppleness of their predecessors, nor the simplicity, nor the respect, nor the courtesy. Good breeding is now rarer and so is deference. The Golden Age is past, when students were obedient and teachers were superior beings."[4]

Such dramatic changes triggered considerable public comment, for they involved boys as well as girls, dress codes as well as manners, homes as well as schools.[5] Some sought the explanation in the absence

[3] Quoted in Wurmser-Dégouy, *Trois Éducatrices modernes*, 68.

[4] Quoted in ibid., 58.

[5] See, for example, Paul Crouzet, "L'Enseignement secondaire dans l'Académie de

of the father during wartime. Others held postwar disillusionment responsible, and many put the blame on economic life. Yet whatever the source of this assertiveness, it apparently strained relations of authority in girls' schools. At Sèvres itself, where Louise Belugou (class of 1882) had passed the "holy fire" on to Anna Amieux (class of 1889), the latter instituted new and stricter rules, only to confront a real rebellion.[6] "We were," one Sévrienne from the class of 1922 informed me, "an irreverent group of students."[7]

What seemed to have invaded Sèvres and many girls' schools, too, was a pragmatic, individualistic code of conduct, in which competition played an ever greater part. Stunned professionals published frequent articles about their inattentive students, defiant toward authority or unduly reliant on their parents in their homework.[8] How was one to discipline such actions? Here again, Marguerite Caron expressed concern that other school heads shared. "What should be the attitude of the directrice toward this ultramodern child?" she inquired. "Regrets, reproaches slip right over girls to whom there is no worse a fate than to be behind the times."[9] Certainly a call to duty in the style of Mme Favre would not have worked. Yet this headmistress still maintained the answer lay in motherly persuasion. "If a little witty raillery is appropriate, how much better is indulgence, friendly reasoning. A smiling but firm discipline, an affectionate sympathy that the child senses . . . creates trust, makes her think, and . . . momentarily, at least, makes her obedient."[10] At Fénélon, her own lycée, Marguerite Caron realized this ideal in practice. "Guided as much by moral as by material interest for her children," one inspector general wrote, "she rises above the letter of the law and softens its severity."[11] That was one alternative. Unfortunately, in the large lycées and collèges of postwar France, some directrices possessed neither the talent nor the patience to adopt it. In 1928, Camille Sée's *Revue* published a clarion call to order from a teacher of a younger generation (class of 1907). "We are," she noted, "in the middle of a crisis of authority, but at

---

Paris depuis la guerre," *RU* 2 (1920): 179–98; M. Dugard, "De la jeunesse féminine d'aujourd'hui," *RU* 1 (1928): 236–43.

[6] "Cahier de traditions," archives, E.N.S. .

[7] Interview with Mme Scheid, class of 1922 (Paris, June 1976).

[8] "Réponses aux lectrices de la Revue," *ESDJF* 2 (1922): 101; A. Ecolan, "La Fraude dans les compositions," *ESDJF* 2 (1923): 145–47; A. Caring, "Correspondance," *ESDJF* 2 (1922): 245–47; M. Dionot, "Liberté et entr'aide dans les exercices scolaires," *ESDJF* 2 (1924): 206–11; H. Guénot and M. Dionot, "Lettre aux parents de nos élèves," *RESDJF* 5 (1931–1932): 33–36.

[9] Quoted in Wurmser–Dégouy, *Trois éducatrices modernes*, 58.

[10] Ibid., 58–59.

[11] Dossier personnel, notes, 1923, F17 2412, A.N.

the same time, there is a pressing need for order."[12] It was a viewpoint shared by many aging school heads. Moreover, if the conciliatory methods of the maternal figure failed to bring about obedience, directrices could always turn, true to their familial orientation, to the other domestic model of command: the dogmatic and strict paterfamilias.

Students, though, were not the only ones to threaten the authority of aging directrices. Teachers also became potentially unruly. On the one hand, there were signs in younger teachers, just as with girl students, of a disaffection with their elders' values. On the other hand, and for different reasons, aging personnel could prove obstreperous, too. Using the reports of school inspectors, we can easily establish that the conflicts noted in the early history of girls' schools had returned to trouble directrices after the war. At Lyon, a talented headmistress "had little influence on her teachers."[13] Another one at Aix had "no control over pedagogy."[14] At Cahors, the directrice had "insufficient authority over personnel and students."[15] And at Troyes, administrative authority was "completely nonexistent."[16] The directrice at Lons-le-Saunier complained that she did not find among her colleagues the help she had expected; at Amiens, the headmistress Jeanne Mehl (class of 1887) had to confront "a difficult staff stirred up against her by one or two mean-spirited teachers."[17] In all these schools, insubordination within the faculty surfaced as a problem once again.

One cause of friction was the fact that younger teachers flooded the profession in the twenties. Sèvres itself doubled its enrollment, and the decision in 1923 to admit day students increased its output further.[18] The explanation for expansion lies partly in the dramatic increase in the size and number of girls' secondary schools. Nonetheless, the hour also had arrived for the oldest generation to retire. The transfer of power took place slowly, too slowly, it appears, for some young Sévriennes, who sent an anonymous letter in 1935 to girls' lycées summoning the older women to get out. An older teacher wrote to the Alumnae Association in outrage: "Who could have written this if not some young and very mod-

[12] J. Martini, "L'Education de la femme française," *RESDJF* 1 (1927–1928): 300–303.

[13] Dossier personnel, Amélie Allégret (class of 1885), notes, 1929, F17 23809, A.N.

[14] Dossier personnel, Louise Bruneau (class of 1886), notes, 1928, F17 23979, A.N.

[15] Dossier personnel, Anne Rollet-Saussotte (class of 1884), notes, 1925, F17 24029, A.N.

[16] Dossier personnel, Gabrielle de Burrine (class of 1886), notes, 1925, F17 23744, A.N.

[17] Dossier personnel, Louise Langard (class of 1890), notes, 1926, F17 24236; dossier personnel, Jeanne Mehl, notes, 1921, F17 24013, A.N.

[18] *Le Cinquantenaire*, 205. Lists of the students in each class through 1930 can be found in the index.

ern Sévriennes whose moral and literary talents do not live up to their degrees? My first reaction was to leave a group in which I no longer recognized anything of its original spirit."[19] Her readiness to censure the younger generation outright suggests a preexisting sense of alienation. But feelings of estrangement were not the monopoly of older women. Simone de Beauvoir, in an early novel, created a young and "very modern" Sévrienne, who dismissed her colleagues in a small provincial school with the observation, "What a fine collection of fossils in this lycée."[20]

No doubt extreme, these two examples nevertheless reveal a tone in girls' schools that the remarks of school inspectors occasionally confirm. A striking case in point involved the manner adopted by Amélie Allégret (class of 1885) in dealing with her younger teachers. Noting her lack of influence on her colleagues, an inspector general wrote: "Perhaps she seems a little cold and distracted, a bit severe and partial in her judgments: she has no respect for any qualities other than seriousness of purpose and a total commitment to accomplishing professional tasks. One might almost say that certain talents—originality, brilliance—arouse in her suspicions more than fondness."[21] Something of the same incomprehension explained the problems Jeanne Mehl experienced with teachers at Amiens. "An excess of zeal," an inspector general commented, "makes her concerned with the most minute detail. This trait does not endear her to someone younger and less inclined than she to feelings of professional obligation."[22] Still, the source of trouble did not always lie in outmoded notions of professional duty. Sometimes younger teachers balked at any supervision, whatsoever. At Philippeville, for instance, the directrice Pauline Grosjean (class of 1885), whom her academy inspector considered to be "goodness incarnate," was also in his view, "unlucky in her personnel. . . . Those of her subordinates . . . who are professionally speaking the best, are the very ones over whom she has the least amount of influence and who get themselves talked about in town."[23] In this curt appraisal, something of the image of the flapper, educated and self-directed, comes to mind.

Pauline Grosjean was facing more than independent younger teachers, however. Together with other heads of girls' schools, she had suffered a real diminution in her supervisory powers. In years gone by, a teacher who aroused the local gossips might expect a dressing-down from her

---

[19] Quoted by Elizabeth Mérian (class of 1891), letter of November 15, 1936, Alumnae Association, archives, E.N.S. .

[20] *Quand prime le spirituel* (Paris: Gaillard, 1979), 73.

[21] Dossier personnel, notes, 1919, F17 23809, A.N.

[22] Dossier personnel, notes, 1926, F17 24013, A.N.

[23] Dossier personnel, notes, 1922, F17 24073, A.N.

directrice, followed, if she persisted in her conduct, by her transfer else-where. Now the worst she would encounter was a cool reception from her immediate superior. For teachers had acquired, as a by-product of the acceptance of girls' secondary schools, a truly private life. However much a reputation-conscious school head might resent it, in this matter, the precedent of boys' schools overruled her.[24] Meanwhile, the role of pedagogic counselor also slipped away from school directrices. Special-ized degrees plus the widespread practice of allowing teachers to teach a single subject removed directrices as supervisors from the classroom. With primary teachers, they might still assume a guiding role; but at the level of secondary studies, a dramatic shift in outlook gave women teach-ers, finally, the independence to which professional expertise had long entitled teachers in boys' schools.

Other factors intervened to curb the influence of headmistresses over older teachers. Of these, the high mobility of directrices compared to el-derly teachers played a crucial part, for it placed school heads at a dis-advantage vis-à-vis a much more stable teaching corps. The contrast in this regard between Sévrienne directrices and teachers is still more strik-ing at this stage than in midcareer. For if a directrice spent on average thirteen years in her final post,[25] the average teacher of the same genera-tion had been there twice as long.[26] Understandably, this longevity gave older teachers special standing in their own eyes as well as in the eyes of their directrice. For a school head not to stumble in relations with such women would take considerable tact. Amélie Gandon Gonnet (class of 1888) was one of those without it. "Extremely eager to exercise a ver-itable pedagogic influence in her lycée," a delighted inspector general reported of her in 1921, "she presides at regular faculty meetings." The following year, however, he had more mournful tidings: "She is rude to younger staff, who ought to be encouraged, and fainthearted with those who are too old."[27] Between the lines of this report of failure lurked the Scylla of the young teacher with a new professional outlook and the Cha-rybdis of the old, entrenched, and testy one.

Even if a woman managed to maneuver among competing egos in these postwar girls' schools, she still faced the ultimate threat to her authority: her own declining health. Surprisingly, that threat proved far less impor-tant than rates of illness among directrices during wartime might suggest. Assuming full recovery from that ordeal, most headmistresses had, until the very end of their careers, only minor ailments. Almost none took

[24] Wurmser-Dégouy, *Trois Éducatrices modernes*, 50.

[25] The average number of years is 12.7; the mean number of years, is twelve.

[26] The average number of years is 24.4; the mean number of years is twenty-five.

[27] Dossier personnel, notes, 1921, 1922, F17 23915, A.N.

leaves of absence after 1921. Exceptions to this rule are nonetheless instructive for the light they shed on links between a woman's health, her work performance, and symptoms of possible psychic stress.

Marie Gasnault (class of 1889), for instance, developed heart trouble as an aging directrice. Anxiety soon reduced her to a fumbling travesty of her erstwhile assertive self. Reporting on her conduct, an inspector general noted: "Age has not developed in her character the decisiveness that experience should bring. She seems more and more preoccupied by fear of accidents, a possible incident, obstacles of every sort."[28] Fortunately, her decline did not continue. Over the course of the decade, Marie Gasnault's health improved, and though she never would again become a forceful leader, enough of her old confidence returned for her to continue at her post.

Camille Porte (class of 1882) did not get off so lightly. Struck by degenerating deafness, she retired under duress four years after an inspector first made mention of her problem. In the meantime, though, she progressively lost touch with staff, her students, and the times. Recognized by her inspector as a leader "with enormous talent," she let it go to waste on the vision of a lycée every year more out-of-date. "Strong-willed and energetic, even opinionated," an inspector wrote about her, "Mlle Porte is also stubborn. Her infirmity . . . isolates her from the world and even from the surroundings where she must exercise authority. Closed in on herself and her ideas . . . she opposes any innovation and does not know how to bend with the times and changing mores. . . . She will never create of Longchamps a truly modern lycée."[29]

May we not reasonably abstract from these case histories alternative responses to the challenges facing school directrices in the twenties. For Marie Gasnault, health-related fears permitted a retreat into a faceless administration. For Camille Porte, deafness symbolized her resistance to all change. Once again, as in this generation's youth, illness thwarts facile interpretation. Is it effect or cause? Obstacle to success or a retreat from danger?

There is little doubt, in any case, that of the school heads who kept their faculties and health, many embraced one of these administrative styles. Some retreated, like Marie Gasnault, into routine administrative tasks, which permitted them a lower profile. Others adopted, like Camille Porte, an authoritarian manner designed to force the staff and students to respect their will. Among the many women to choose the former

[28] Dossier personnel, notes, 1924, F17 23995, A.N. Her heart condition was first mentioned in 1923.

[29] Dossier personnel, notes, 1921, 1922, F17 23792, A.N.

tactic figured Marie Delbosc (class of 1889). It was a strategy she had not pursued before. In 1913, her sixth year at Carcasonne, a satisfied inspector general wrote: "Nothing is neglected, not even moral guidance, which is her dominant preoccupation. Improvements jump out at you. There is not a single teacher who has not improved. Everyone works joyfully in perfect harmony. This directrice wants to lead and is capable of doing so." Yet by 1923, reports on her performance had begun to change. "She stays closed up in her office," an inspector general wrote in disapproval. "Her activity," an inspector noted six years later, "is reduced to ensuring good relations between the families of students and the lycée." Louise Graverol (class of 1882) followed a similarly descending curve of active leadership as a directrice for some thirty years. Up until the postwar era, comments by inspectors had uniformly emphasized her vigor. But by 1920, one of them complained: "She is too passive, even timid, in giving pedagogical advice and in her administration. . . . She tries not to offend anyone or to affirm anything. . . . When she talks about her faculty, she hardly distinguishes between their capabilities."[30]

Had a more impersonal style of leadership accompanied this increasing disengagement, it might have signaled far-reaching changes in girls' secondary schools. However, for most of these directrices, solicitude informed their school relations. Adrienne Prieur Bassaire (class of 1884), whose "authority" began to "lessen" by 1923 and whose "pedagogical guidance" was, in one inspector general's view, "weak more out of scruple than inability," seemed notably benevolent toward her school staff.[31] In much the same way, Jeanne Rith (class of 1881) made "a kindly disposition the principle of her authority," as she lost the "energetic" style of bygone days.[32] As for Marie Mangin (class of 1883), "whose school," in one inspector general's view, operated "largely by itself," she followed her routines with unassuming patience, "diffident and obedient toward superiors . . . friendly and gentle toward everyone else."[33] It was as if these women had consciously decided to cope with aging in a changing world by taking the path of least resistance: an affable retreat into administrative routines where they might rest on their accumulated laurels.

Not all directrices, however, proved so supine toward superiors or so timid in relations with their staffs. Some became increasingly autonomous and dictatorial as they grew older. For them, of far less moment than the chance of running into conflict was the threat of losing their

[30] Dossier personnel, notes, 1913, 1920, 1923, 1929, F17 25272, A.N.
[31] Dossier personnel, notes, F17 23738, A.N.
[32] Dossier personnel, notes, 1919, F17 23797, A.N.
[33] Dossier personnel, notes, 1922, 1924, F17 23859, A.N.

control. From the beginning, the potential for such an overbearing style existed in girls' secondary schools. But in the postwar era, a new development emerged. Now, not only staff and students might be victims, but inspectors, too, could find themselves ignored. "Jealous of her powers," an angry inspector reported of Léonie Allégret (class of 1882) in 1920, "she would like to escape controls altogether."[34] Concerning Lucie Ravaire (class of 1884), an inspector wrote this somewhat milder rebuke: "She runs her school with a jealous eye. In a less intelligent directrice, this would be more dangerous."[35] As for Angèle Bourgoignon Séverin (class of 1887), she made manifest "her scorn for paperwork and even sometimes regulations" by bothering with neither.[36] Experienced and confident of their talents, such women had the force of personality to impose proprietary claims on their own schools. Meanwhile, other women stood accused of high-handed dealings with their personnel and students. Louise Langard Bréjoux (class of 1890), a woman "utterly devoted to her school and its success," was also in an inspector general's view "harsh and authoritarian."[37] Another school head, Anne Marie Massen (class of 1887) appeared to an inspector general to be "willful, excitable, and partial."[38] As for Mathilde Dreyfus (class of 1887), one academy inspector labeled her "severe," and an inspector general thought her "insufficiently maternal."[39] Through the prism of inspectors' comments appears the image of a group of women whose rigidity, no doubt, had intensified with age, but whose authoritarian methods and occasional personal harshness may also represent one way in which aging leaders dealt with change.

Not all Sévriennes, though, fell into one or the other of these categories. Some managed to project an image of competence, vigor, and success while maintaining good relations with colleagues and superiors. Such leadership meant, above all, the adaptation of prewar institutional goals to new conditions in postwar secondary schools. Even in smaller schools, like the lycée that Hortense Daubriac (class of 1890) administered from 1914 to 1930 at Chartres, this required considerable imagination.[40] Her success earned her a special note of thanks in 1927 from the director of secondary education. "Despite the variety of her functions," which she told an inspector general in 1928 were "becoming heavier ev-

[34] Dossier personnel, notes, F17 22599, A.N.
[35] Dossier personnel, notes, 1925, F17 23949, A.N.
[36] Dossier personnel, notes, 1927, F17 24108, A.N.
[37] Dossier personnel, notes, 1926, F17 24236, A.N.
[38] Dossier personnel, notes, 1923, F17 24087, A.N.
[39] Dossier personnel, notes, 1920, 1924, F17 23834, A.N.
[40] Chartres had only a collège from 1914 to 1920.

ery year," she managed to maintain the close-knit atmosphere of prewar schools, while elsewhere curricular reform, increasing size, and the attitudes of staff and students had begun to undermine it. Many of the elements of a lost world of girls' schools appear in these descriptions.

> This excellent directrice, who is highly esteemed by local people, brings to this establishment a spirit of cooperation. She supervises classes with intelligence and provides diversions for students every Thursday, when first one group, then another organizes a little party to which professeurs are invited.

> She is delighted to show off her school, which is, from the youngest class, with its games and songs for children, to the appealing decorations of the dormitory, where light and air move freely, everywhere enlivened with some pleasing touch. . . . Mlle Daubriac loves her teachers, whose qualities she gladly boasts, she loves her students, and she loves her school.

This lycée had, according to the inspector general who suggested the congratulatory letter, "a familial atmosphere of the proper tone." At Chartres, however, with its "reactionary" municipal council and conservative bourgeoisie, the survival of a closed, familial style of school life modeled after private boarding schools of the previous century ought not to surprise us greatly. Much more striking are the cases in which directrices strove to give a major, metropolitan lycée a similar tone.[41]

Among directrices notably successful in this effort, Marguerite Caron (class of 1887) stands out in sharp relief. Not only did she head three different Paris lycées,[42] but she also managed to adapt traditional goals of prewar school directrices to postwar students' needs. "Possessed of an extraordinary memory," her biographer remembered, "she knew all the students' names by the end of the first trimester. She followed them from class to class, carefully studying their potential; then near the end of their school years, she would direct them confidently, one toward secondary teaching, another toward higher primary school teaching, still another into chemistry or electricity or pharmaceutics."[43] One can see in this procedure a lineal descent in the tradition of the mothering directrice, from director of girls' souls, to director of their conscience, to counselor for the new women's careers. Nor did Marguerite Caron restrict her interest to her current students only, anymore than had her mentor, Mme

[41] Dossier personnel, notes, 1927, 1928, F17 24131, A.N.

[42] Lycée Lamartine (1917–1919), Lycée Jules Ferry (1919–1922), Lycée Fénélon (1922–1930).

[43] Wurmser-Dégouy, Trois Éducatrices modernes, 67.

Favre. "Graduation did not divide her from her students. She kept track of them as they earned their various degrees and, later, helped them find positions. Whenever students needed reassurance and advice about the most diverse careers, always it was to her that they would come."[44] Commenting on this practice, the inspector for the academy of Paris wrote in 1928, "She exercises a morally elevated influence, even over students who have already left the lycée."[45] It was an old objective: moral influence. Whether or not the utilitarian goals of this modern directrice and her career-minded students conformed, in fact, to that ideal may be questioned. Clearly, though, Marguerite Caron did not intend to let the size of schools and the new spirit of secondary studies deflect her administration from its maternal goals.

Her success, moreover, was not confined to students. True to her ideal of a devoted staff, morally united under a directrice, Marguerite Caron took pains to win the confidence of teachers and said as much in print. "The attitude of the directrice toward her teachers determines the spirit of the school. In any lycée where a directrice treats her teachers like colleagues and not subordinates, the result will be agreement, cordiality, and a general desire within the school for each to do her part for its success." Yet within this harmonious working order, she conceived the role of the directrice as absolutely central. "Let the teacher, once out of school, take back her liberty, devote herself to personal endeavors . . . ; the directrice belongs to her lycée; she must be its soul, its conscience, its living self."[46]

In Paris, it took a particularly skillful directrice to achieve this old ambition in the twenties. Just to keep her school abreast of new ideas in this milieu required exceptional personal resources. Moreover, persuading teachers to cooperate had special problems. For in Parisian lycées, the older teachers might have been there thirty years, while the younger ones with brilliant records might easily have egos as inflated as their talent. Yet Marguerite Caron succeeded in all three schools that she directed there. At Lamartine in 1919, "she found her teachers with well-established reputations," an inspector noted. "Appreciative of their talents, she nevertheless continued to show initiative in pedagogic matters and zeal for carrying out her functions. . . . Her ideas appear to have prevailed, especially at the elementary level . . . for which she has devised a special course on early education and child psychology." In 1921, two years after she took over at Jules Ferry, the rector drew up a list of school

[44] Ibid., 68.

[45] Dossier personnel, notes, 1928, F17 24126, A.N.

[46] Quoted in Wurmser-Dégouy, *Trois Éducatrices modernes*, 56–57.

activities: "Games, gymnastics, chorus, charities, the association of students and parents, all are subject to her constant and enlightened supervision." Yet she still found time, according to her rector, "to follow elementary classes, where her suggestions led to unforeseen results, notably in teaching mathematics." To this unblemished tale of personal triumph, another inspector added, "Her staff esteems her as much as they obey her." At Fénélon, the eulogies continued. And in 1928, two years before she would retire, the academy inspector for all Paris and surrounding schools announced: "Our best directrice. Competence and rectitude explain her influence." For a Sévrienne of the class of 1887, his choice of words seemed altogether fitting.[47]

Indeed, inspectors' comments in the twenties suggest how little standards for judging a headmistress's performance had changed. Just as before the war, a lycée required more administrative talent, while a collège called for greater maternal solicitude. But in both types of schools, inspectors looked for women, above all, who could imprint their schools with their own personal style, personify it to the public, and maintain recruitment of its student body. Given these criteria, women who adopted any of the administrative styles described above might well have earned inspectors' praise. The authoritarian directrice, in particular, had little trouble. Even passive school heads could hope for acclamation as long as routine did not descend to chaos and their clientele remained content. Hence, an inspector general might write of Marie Mangin (class of 1883) on the eve of her retirement, "She lacks the qualities of a school head, having neither authority, nor industry, nor even open-mindedness." But her academy inspector, who was closer to the local situation, concluded, "She ends her career with honor, surrounded by everyone's goodwill."[48]

Of course, not all directrices had local reputations sufficient to protect them from their critics. Hélène Magnus (class of 1885) enjoyed "neither the respect of staff, of parents, nor even of her students," according to her academy inspector.[49] Likewise, Cécile Lonfier (class of 1882) was "incapable," in her inspector's view, "of the activity and constant renovation necessary to beat out the competition."[50] Naturally in such cases, superiors were anxious to see such ineffectual leaders leave the state's employ. Rarely, though, did bad reports result in the forced retirement of a school directrice. Of the twenty women whose inspectors despaired of their abilities, only four left their posts involuntarily. The general rule

[47] Dossier personnel, notes, 1919, 1921, 1923, 1928, F17 24126, A.N.
[48] Dossier personnel, notes, 1926, F17 23859, A.N.
[49] Dossier personnel, notes, 1925, F17 23932, A.N.
[50] Dossier personnel, notes, 1922, F17 22624, A.N.

was to wait for a directrice to announce her retirement or, upon her sixty-second birthday, to refuse any extension on her contract and, with great relief, to send her on her way.

However, most good-byes were occasions of honor for retiring directrices. The majority of directrices (60 percent) kept the confidence of their superiors to the end of their careers. Several even received the highest praise. Their dossiers project again the ideal that Marguerite Caron pursued.

> Extremely thoughtful of her teachers, firm and maternal with her students, she communicates to the entire school a moral inspiration completely lacking in austerity. Full of life . . . her body always in motion, Mlle Esménard does everything possible to infuse a couple of sleepy collaborators with her enthusiasm. (Julie Esménard, class of 1887, directrice until 1927)[51]

> A remarkable personality—a true directrice, with a firm and penetrating intelligence and a moral outlook as elevated as it is simple. . . . She administers her lycée with vigilance, integrity, authority, and concern for everyone's well-being. (Marie Lépine, class of 1886, directrice until 1925)[52]

> When she leaves, it is certain the school will feel the repercussions, so completely is this leader incorporated into the life of our lycée. (Camille Malou, class of 1890, directrice until 1930)[53]

The vigor in these portraits is as palpable as the commitment of the women they depict. Neither age nor time seemed to have affected their professional image.

Nonetheless, even most of those who ended their careers with honor did not get from superiors the support they had enjoyed in earlier years. Few directrices seemed indispensable. The proof lay in inspectors' parting words. Typically, instead of regretting a school head's departure, the men above them waved them off with such refrains as these.

> The lycée will no doubt gain by having at its head a younger and more energetic directrice.[54]

> The lycée must finally get a directrice reflecting its importance. And for that, we need a person as young and active as she is prudent.[55]

[51] Dossier personnel, notes, 1925, F17 23991, A.N.
[52] Dossier personnel, notes, 1924, F17 23856, A.N.
[53] Dossier personnel, notes, 1930, F17 24153, A.N.
[54] Dossier personnel, Marie Mangin (class of 1883), notes, 1926, F17 23859, A.N.
[55] Dossier personnel, Louise Masson (class of 1887), notes, 1925, F17 23861, A.N.

> *To succeed Mlle R. . . . , we need a directrice who is young, active, and full of initiative, and if I may say so, more modern.*[56]

Not just new blood but youth was what inspectors wanted. No doubt this theme expressed a valid perception that age had slowed these women down. Perhaps disparities in age between these old directrices and the younger men above them figured in. Above all, though, this viewpoint mirrored that of teachers and directrices blocked in their ambitions by a generation that had held the reins of power in girls' secondary schools for forty years. Behind closed doors and in reports that the aging directrices would never see, rectors and inspectors on the whole agreed that a changing of the guard was overdue.

Teachers in their Late Careers

Under the best of circumstances, aging complicates the task of teaching adolescents, and the 1920s offered far from optimal conditions. Just when Sévriennes from the first ten classes began to lose their strength, discipline in girls' schools became a problem. Several of the more than ninety teachers in our sample fell victim to that unfortunate circumstance. Yet this coincidence of life and institutional changes had far less consequence for aging teachers than did the introduction of the baccalauréat program. For in response to baccalauréat pressures, inspector generals began as early as 1919 to transfer wholesale to girls' classrooms teaching expectations that until then had been reserved for men in this profession. Almost to a woman, Sévriennes in their fifties showed up badly. Even teachers previously touted for their exemplary influence on their students now appeared in the reports of their inspectors only moderately competent as intellectual guides. Quite unexpectedly, this once heroic generation appeared to face an ending without glory and even, sometimes, retirement in disgrace.

Like tenured teachers elsewhere, aging Sévriennes were not without the means for their defense. Indeed, the salient feature of these women's late careers lies in the contrast between their critics' opinions and their self-evaluations. How does one make sense of this contradiction? The explanation is that teachers' sense of their success did not depend entirely on their inspectors' judgments. The members of the school community—directrices and colleagues, students and their parents—also sat in judgment on old teachers, and much more often than inspectors, they proved favorably disposed. Even if their verdict controverted a teacher's image of herself, she need not necessarily accept it. She could still appeal

---

[56] Dossier personnel, Jeanne Rith (class of 1881), notes, 1924, F17 23797, A.N.

to her professional record; in so doing, the experienced teacher invariably stood on firmer ground. On the eve of their retirement, teachers could look back on decades of correcting homework and preparing lessons, years of trekking to and from their schools, and hundreds of girls whose educations they had partly overseen. In response to critics, therefore, Sévriennes in late career had several options. They could adopt inspectors' standards; they could seek approval in the school community; or ignoring their detractors, they could retreat into a sense of their professional pride. Unable for the most part to bring off the first alternative, Sévriennes nevertheless considered they had finished their careers with honor. With or without the praise of others, the members of this first generation of women secondary teachers remained convinced of their success.

However, even a hasty survey of inspectors' standards suggests why aging Sévriennes were not actually outstanding teachers. For what inspectors wanted did not reflect the natural tendency either of experience in teaching or of advancing age. Consider the intellectual ideal for secondary teachers. Inspectors, as early as the 1880s, had made their taste for novelty in classrooms clear. Prestige depended, both for men and women, on the quality of "personal reflection." Yet creative teaching, hard enough for people starting out in their careers, is, arguably, rarer still in teachers nearing their retirement. Just as the task of teaching fundamentally depends on the repetition of the same subjects year after year, the modus operandi for veteran teachers often is routine. All the same, whenever an inspector discovered evidence of that fact, he bitterly condemned the offending party. Those who relied on their accumulated knowledge to extemporize a lecture fared no better. One peeved inspector, after watching a fifty-nine-year-old Sévrienne rely on "savoir faire" to conduct her class, announced his general rule for judging teachers: "However gifted a professeur, it is impossible to improvise good teaching."[57] Whatever a teacher's age or reputation, if she took things a little easy, it warranted the reproach of an inspector.

Perpetual renewal as a criterion of success was not, however, the only obstacle for older teachers. The pedagogy favored by inspectors suited them no better. What the ministry sought to introduce in secondary schools as early as the 1890s and insisted on by 1920, were Socratic teaching methods based on inferential reasoning. To be effective, this technique required exceptionally active teachers in the classroom. Even teachers practiced in the art found its daily use a strain when they got

[57] Dossier personnel, Léa Camourtères Bérard (class of 1884), notes, 1923, F17 23670, A.N.

older. As for Sévriennes who had not renounced a lecture style before
the 1920s, they were by now too old to change. One of them who tried
succeeded only in confusing students and in irritating an inspector general. "Used to a dogmatic style, this class has trouble following," noted
the inspector sourly, who had in previous years encouraged her to
change.[58] Thus, at sixty-one, this teacher had to show, for all her extra
work, nothing but a teaching style ill-suited to her astonished students
and exhausting to herself.

Nevertheless, the sharpness of inspectors' comments in this period had
more to do with a reorientation in their own standards of performance
than it did with the effects of teachers' aging. Neither creativity nor Socratic methods appeared in girls' schools for the first time in the 1920s.
The change that did occur was far more subtle. Rather than injecting new
criteria of success, inspector generals simply dropped a past requirement. Henceforth, the moralizing influence of a woman teacher no longer
visibly concerned them. No longer would a good rapport with students
compensate for a teacher's other faults. Now the goal preoccupying
school inspectors derived not from the notion of a separate female
sphere, with mothering as its distinctive core, but rather from the professional model of men teachers. In this transformation, the baccalauréat
acted as a Trojan horse. For inevitably, once admitted to girls' schools,
disguised or not in its "equivalent" form as a revised diploma, this rite
of passage altered standards in the classroom. Perhaps the least important of the changes it effected were those that altered the curriculum. Far
more significant was its role in spreading values from the mandarin culture of men teachers to girls' secondary schools. Once they infused girls'
education, moreover, these values changed not only the attitudes of students but also their relations with their teachers.

Given these exacting standards, it is no surprise to find few Sévriennes
in their fifties who fully satisfied inspectors in the 1920s; none succeeded in the field of letters; and when occasionally a science teacher
did excel, her success astonished even her younger colleagues. Angèle
Coustols (class of 1887) was one of these exceptions. Retired in 1931 after
forty years of teaching, seventeen of them at the Lycée Racine in Paris,
Coustols died in 1933. A memorial tribute appeared for her in Sèvres's
alumnae bulletin. "She never exhibited what is called 'professional de-
formation,'" wrote her necrologist in admiration. "She renewed her
teaching constantly. When it became necessary to organize in our lycées
a new, experimental style of teaching, those who saw her at work, like

[58] Dossier personnel, Adèle Fourcade David (class of 1887), notes, 1924, F17 23985,
A.N.

Mme Weiss, later Mlles Destrem and Châtelet, never had the feeling of collaborating with an older colleague, quite the contrary. Very often it was Mlle Coustols's enthusiasm that carried them along."[59] Far from reflecting the overindulgent memories of fond colleagues, this eulogy finds confirmation in official records. Indeed, one inspector general pronounced Angèle Coustols "among the best teachers in Paris" just before she retired.[60] Yet to judge from earlier inspectors' comments, Coustols's reputation had not always been so high.

A closer look at her career suggests an interplay of personal and institutional changes that only after considerable effort redounded to her credit. As a young professional, steeped in the ideal of dedicated service, she suffered, nonetheless, from paralyzing shyness. Eight years of teaching finally worked its cure; and from then on, inspectors every year until 1913 reported favorably on her classes. All of them did share one complaint: this teacher pushed her girls too hard and judged them much too harshly. "Her teaching is not in the spirit of the program," one inspector general grumbled; "she demands a great deal of effort, and her grades sometimes discourage students. The program is supposed to aim at general education, not at getting into Sèvres."[61]

Ahead of her time in the demands she placed on students, Coustols would shortly fall behind inspectors' expectations for herself. A move to Paris in 1913 precipitated the crisis. "Defective pedagogy," announced a prophet of the new, Socratic teaching methods after watching her in class. "She describes before doing the experiment; she draws a design, reasons, concludes, and only then goes on to test it. She never asks a question during class. It is almost a dictation." Still in her forties, Angèle Coustols responded to her critics with redoubled effort and eventually revamped her courses totally. A jubilant inspector general, returning to her class in 1918, reported the excellent results. "A few years ago her teaching was out-of-date; now it has been thoroughly modernized. She is very attentive to the experimental parts." Having once regained their confidence, Angèle Coustols never lost the capacity for renewal that inspector generals admired. In this respect, over the next thirteen years, her image as a teacher did not change. Inspector generals reported in 1922 that she was "always anxious to teach better," in 1926 that she possessed "rare dedication" and made "unceasing efforts to perfect her teaching," and in 1928 that she remained "as vigorous and effective a teacher as ever."[62]

[59] *BAES* (1933): 6.
[60] Dossier personnel, notes, 1929, F17 23187, A.N.
[61] Ibid., 1898, 1911.
[62] Ibid., 1913, 1918, 1922, 1926, 1928.

In other respects, however, the image of the model teacher projected by inspectors through this teacher's record did evolve significantly. Up to 1919, Coustols's own sense of what girls could and ought to learn inside her classroom continued to exceed inspectors' expectations. According to one of her inspectors in 1919, she still pitched "the level of instruction in her class too high." From that time forward, this criticism disappeared from her reviews. Seemingly, inspector generals had themselves accepted more exacting standards in girls' schools. Meanwhile, as approval for her demanding style increased, inspectors lost interest in Coustols's relationship with students. The last remark made on the subject appeared in the report by the inspector who discovered in 1918 her rejuvenated methods. "She is greatly loved by students," he reported, "with whom she organized several charitable activities in the war." Not until 1928 is there another hint of caring in her file, and then the object is professional. "She loves her work," an inspector general announced to sum up her remarkable career.[63] It was a fitting tribute both to this successful teacher and to the emergence of a new professional paradigm in which aggressive, intellectual ambition had pushed aside the mothering ideal.

Across this record of personal achievement, though, a shadow falls. Angèle Coustols never got the cross of the Legion of Honor that the academy inspector of Paris thought she deserved. All but eight teachers from her generation of Sévriennes who survived the war (8 percent) shared this disappointment. Yet while the dedicated services of aging women teachers went unnoticed by the nation, directrices of their vintage were every year more apt to be remembered alongside teachers from the men's profession.[64] This regard for school heads and neglect of aging women teachers suggests an issue deeper than the private rancor that it must have caused forgotten teachers. Neither category of professional had altered in any fundamental way since Sèvres their basic views on what their role as educators ought to be; significantly, their viewpoints differed very little from each other; and yet to one group came public acclamation, to the other, an undistinguished ending in the obscurity of their schools. Such glaringly unequal treatment speaks as eloquently as inspectors' reports about the changes taking place in girls' schools. With one foot in the past, the other in the future, these institutions swung uncertainly between the image of the school as a nurturing family and the reality of the classroom as a forcing ground for intellectual elites.

[63] Ibid., 1918, 1919, 1928.

[64] Thirty-six percent of the directrices in our sample had received the cross by 1935, based on lists published annually in RU.

Inspectors responsible for overseeing the consolidation of this new reality set about it with a vengeance. A strikingly harsh tone entered their reports on teachers whose competence had not been seriously in doubt before. "I've rarely heard a more insignificant textual analysis, more painfully filled with useless words," wrote an inspector general in 1920 about Céline Favre Janin (class of 1888), whom another inspector had found in 1906 "hardworking, brilliant, possessing a quick mind, with remarkable aptitudes and a firm and broad foundation of knowledge."[65] Neither Isabelle Delêtre Mallet (class of 1883) nor Amélie Bacharach Wallich (class of 1884) could boast such glowing earlier records, yet nothing in their files foretold the severity of their postwar critics either. Mme Delêtre, an inspector now announced, was "obsolete," a professor who had "not kept up with the evolution of teaching in the physical sciences over the past twenty years."[66] Mme Wallich, another inspector claimed, "has nothing that imposes or seduces, either in her person or her intellect. Nor does she possess a method or a pedagogy. She never makes a comment that either impresses by its justice or focuses the attention of the listener." He tersely concluded, "It is certain that Mme Wallich is without literary talent."[67] The denuciations went on and on, overwhelming in many women's dossiers far more flattering past evaluations that no one now recalled except the women they had praised.

Rare were the occasions when, in fairness to a teacher, an inspector general recognized her merits according to some earlier criteria. An exception appeared in a report on Léonie Bernal (class of 1889) in 1928. Rather than dismissing her abilities outright, an inspector described her as "a good teacher in the style of 1881" and then went on to note the antiquated aspects of her teaching. "By the elegance of her language, the distinction of her overstudied manners, the rather academic tone that she imparts to lessons, Mlle Bernal evokes the time when personnel had to prove to the cultivated bourgeoisie that they could send their daughters to the lycée."[68] This portrait of a rather rigid, formal, even slightly ridiculous aging teacher cannot do justice to the rich variety of Sévriennes near the end of their careers. Many teachers, certainly in their personal demeanor, did not appear so fusty. Yet the dedication caught in this description does suggest a clash of values that the criticisms of aging teachers often hid. In that respect, at least, Léonie Bernal was a model of her generation. If with her pretentious manners, she did not reflect the new

[65] Dossier personnel, notes, 1906, 1920, F17 17238, A.N.
[66] Dossier personnel, notes, 1920, F17 23830, A.N.
[67] Dossier personnel, notes, 1922, F17 24034, A.N.
[68] Dossier personnel, notes, 1928, F17 24129, A.N.

official ideal of a secondary teacher, she did manifestly personify her own image of excellence in the classroom.

Ironically, older teachers' chief defenders against the harshness of inspectors became their own directrices. Long past were the days when heads of schools had been for Sévriennes their foremost censors. Much more often now than not, directrices and older teachers shared the same perspective on a teacher's overall success, a fact that could imperil unsuspecting critics. A case in point occurred in 1920 when an inspector, outspoken in his disapproval of Jeanne Colani's technique, collided with both her amour propre and her reputation. Legendary for her success in getting students into Sèvres, Jeanne Colani relied too much, in her inspector's view, on cramming. Yet his effort to reform her produced the following effect: "When I suggested in my conversation with Mlle Colani and the directrice that she develop habits of reading and critical reflection in her history candidates, it caused considerable emotion." Backpedaling in the face of this united sense of outrage, the inspector sheepishly reported: "I pointed out that I was only offering some advice and not a criticism. In summing up, therefore, I would like to reiterate my feelings of esteem for Mlle Colani."[69]

On the surface, he had stumbled onto someone with a school reputation too solidly entrenched to admit of outside criticism. That was clearly true. But he had also, less obviously perhaps, run up against the fact that often inside schools, the criteria of success differed from the new academic standards of school inspectors. In the eyes of parents and even most directrices, if a teacher disciplined her students and ensured some basic learning, she had satisfied the essential tasks of teaching. Thus, despite what an inspector termed her "obsolescence," Isabelle Delêtre met these minimum criteria, and her directrice pronounced "the results" of her instruction "good."[70] The same applied to Amélie Bacharach Wallich, whose school directrice, in response to attacks on her by school inspectors, emphasized what Mme Wallich actually did do well. "She is the model of the honest professional. Her class is well in hand; she gets her students to work."[71] If along with such classroom fundamentals, a teacher regularly made sure her students passed some national exam as well, she might acquire in her school real prestige. Students, in such cases, would pass on from class to class stories of her triumphs and also, no doubt, jokes at her expense, until eventually she

[69] Dossier personnel, notes, 1920, F17 24437, A.N.
[70] Dossier personnel, notes, 1919, F17 24437, A.N.
[71] Dossier personnel, notes, 1922, F17 23830, A.N.

herself became an institution. It was just such a situation that tripped up Jeanne Colani's conscientious but unwitting school inspector.

Other professional accomplishments, less important and less evident to the public, also won approval from directrices, even for a mediocre teacher. What heads of schools valued most, both as administrators and professional educators, was evidence of teachers' dedication. This bias had an obvious explanation. On the one hand, dependability in teachers immensely aided a headmistress supervising school affairs. On the other hand, commitment and self-sacrifice formed the touchstone of a directrice's own professional ethos. Even inspectors were not without an occasional good word for women who possessed this quality in disproportionate measure, and the first generation of Sévriennes often did. Of the four examples cited of women in the twenties who drew inspectors' fire, three earned high marks in this regard. Jeanne Colani, of course, figured among them. But Amélie Bacharach Wallich also performed her tasks with "perfect regularity,"[72] and even Isabelle Delêtre, judged so harshly by one inspector general for the way she ran her class, received from him these grudging words of praise: "I would be unfair if I failed to mention her extreme goodwill."[73]

Unlike inspector generals, heads of girls' secondary schools also showed ongoing interest in the emotional rapport of teachers with their students, a concern frequently still expressed in terms of "moral influence." Thus, among the qualities that made Amélie Bacharach Wallich in her directrice's view "the model of the honest professional" was the fact that "her kindness" attached "her students to her."[74]

To varying degrees, all three teachers, therefore, met standards of performance valued by their colleagues and the public but lacking the intellectual rigor or pedagogical methods looked for by their school inspectors. In this regard, they did not differ from most other aging Sévriennes who taught. After years of working, usually in a single school, the vast majority of these women had complete confidence in their own professional competence as teachers. Indeed, in certain Sévriennes this feeling of mastery insulated them entirely from efforts by inspectors to reform them, even in the smallest way. Repeatedly, inspectors reported on the problem of managing these teachers' prickly egos. One wrote about an interview with Alice Préjean (class of 1890), "Doubtless the advice . . . that I offered with great politeness, knowing her susceptibilities, will not have the slightest influence."[75] Another met the same resistance from

---

[72] Dossier personnel, notes, 1919, F17 24034, A.N.
[73] Dossier personnel, notes, 1918, F17 23830, A.N.
[74] Dossier personnel, notes, 1922, F17 24034, A.N.
[75] Dossier personnel, notes, 1929, F17 24270, A.N.

Camille Tollemer (class of 1884). "Given her age," he graciously reported, "I softened my remarks as much as possible. It seemed, however, that she was thoroughly satisfied with herself, her methodology, and her experience."[76] A third inspector had no more luck with Jeanne Petit Normand (class of 1890). "Despite my extremely courteous manner," he assured the ministry, "my comments met with neither agreement nor even deference. Mme Normand stressed instead her long experience and the affection of her students."[77]

What in youth had been the style only of intrepid and foolhardy teachers became for older ones the normal pattern. Age and experience certainly help explain this transformation. Yet so radical a change in teachers' outlook also had an institutional context. Increasingly, a combination of rapid expansion and open and publicized exams for girls' schools had given women teachers an audience to balance off against inspectors. The result, much as in boys' secondary schools, brought their attitudes closer to those characteristic of the free professions than to those of functionaries in a civil service. It was the equivalent in the classroom of the change in orientation that gave birth in 1920 to the Société des agrégées.

The entrenched position of aging teachers helps explain why many remained in service long past sixty, despite the hostile judgment of inspectors. The reason was their standing in their schools. As long as neither parents nor the school directrice requested her retirement, a teacher could work until she reached the legal age limit, set at sixty-two up to 1930 and extended to sixty-five after that. Hence, of our four representative teachers whom inspectors frequently reproached, one retired early by her own choice, none retired at sixty, and two remained at work until they were brushing sixty-five.

A handful of Sévriennes did retire involuntarily, under the cloud of their inspectors' disapproval, after opinion in the school community had turned against them. Adrienne Dreuilhe (class of 1884) figured among these hapless cases. As early as 1918, an inspector general noted: "Her faults have gotten worse. She is unable to consider an idea for more than a moment or even to listen to a student's answer."[78] Nothing came of such remarks, however, until the day an irate father wrote to the directrice: "The deplorable instruction given . . . to my oldest daughter forced me to modify completely the direction of her studies. It defies good sense and is an abuse of confidence on the part of the administration to keep

---

[76] Dossier personnel, notes, 1923, F17 23730, A.N.
[77] Dossier personnel, notes, 1920, F17 24092, A.N.
[78] Dossier personnel, notes, 1918, F17 23756, A.N.

someone like this teacher, who is notoriously incapable pedagogically, in a lycée as costly as Jules Ferry."[79] Only then did her directrice decide to take some action. In a note to the rector, she explained her earlier hesitation. "Since Mlle Dreuilhe does not wish to retire until completing her fortieth year of service [still one year and five months away] and given that she is conscientious, reliable, obliging, and good-humored, one hates to draw attention to her professional inadequacy." Nevertheless, the record was well known to her directrice. "Each October," she admitted, "it is a struggle to fill her classes, and halfway through, students try to leave."[80] When at sixty, therefore, Dreuilhe at last was eligible for her pension, the directrice felt obliged to force her out.

Gabrielle Chavance (class of 1888), by contrast, had sacrificed the goodwill of her school head long before she reached retirement age. Already at fifty-six, she lacked "zeal . . . in the preparation and correction of homework," her directrice noted, and had "difficult relations" with her students. But what really irritated her directrice was this teacher's tardiness in getting to her class. "I have often hesitated," the headmistress claimed, "to point out this defect; but it is so annoying. Students profit so mischievously from the few moments they enjoy waiting for their teacher to arrive." Inspectors also noted, meanwhile, a breakdown of authority in Gabrielle Chavance's classes. "Her control is precarious," warned an academy inspector. One inspector general thought, "If she disdained appearance less and paid more attention to her clothes, it might improve her standing." Consequently, none of her superiors felt they ought to honor her request when she wanted to continue teaching after sixty.[81]

As for Marie Disdier (class of 1887), her imperfections seemed to those around her still more glaring. "She is incapable of getting anywhere on time," announced one critical inspector. "As for the negligence of her dress," he fumed, "it defies description." Students, who were of course no less observant, appeared "ironic or indifferent" in her classes. The academy inspector attributed their behavior to the fact that this teacher had "neither the necessary cleverness nor solidity of mind to redeem the ravages of age and nature." When parents, too, complained, the school directrice lost all patience. "The object of repeated censures and threats of reappointment, nothing in this teacher has improved . . . , yet she refuses to ask for her retirement, despite all efforts to persuade her." Faced

---

[79] Quoted in a letter from the rector to the director of secondary education, dossier personnel, correspondance, 1925, F17 23756, A.N.

[80] Correspondance, 1925, ibid.

[81] Dossier personnel, notes, 1924, 1927, F17 23980, A.N.

with this resistance, her directrice asked for Disdier's dismissal as soon as she turned sixty, giving her no choice but to retire.[82]

Reading these complaints, one can hardly doubt the public's loss of confidence in such teachers. Yet it is equally apparent that these Sévriennes themselves gave little credence to their critics' views. Some evidence lies in the refusal of such teachers to retire, a stubborn stand, indeed, in light of efforts by superiors to persuade them. More revealing are the accounts of their reaction to direct attacks. When Adrienne Dreuilhe was asked to resign rather than to wait until forced out, her directrice recorded her response: "Mlle Dreuilhe describes herself as 'one of the most distinguished teachers' and calls her instruction 'excellent.' "[83] Gabrielle Chavance possessed an equally flattering image of herself. "She is in everything," her directrice claimed, "sure of her perfection."[84] As for Marie Disdier, she appeared to her directrice just as shockingly immodest about what, in fact, were her disputed talents. "A difficult personality," her superior reported, "Mlle Disdier believes that she is always right."[85] Each of these three women, then, were of the opinion that professionally they performed beyond reproach. One can hardly imagine a more effective shield for teachers doubly threatened by changes in professional standards and by aging. Self-doubt, apparently, did not afflict them.

Nonetheless, their overweening confidence attests as well to the potential for self-delusion in their work. Protected by the notion of the teacher as the mistress of her class and by the rules of seniority, incompetent teachers could hide their defects over years of service, if not from others, at least, if they so wished, from themselves. As a result, stagnation might well describe the late careers of some among this old elite of teachers; but demoralization certainly did not. On the contrary, to judge from what ought to have been negative examples, the first generation of Sévriennes, far from disillusioned, survived the rapid changes of the 1920s with their professional pride intact.

Only one thing in their own opinion really jeopardized effective teaching, and that was failing health. Outstanding teachers as well as bad ones shared this basic premise and made retirement plans with reference to it. Thus, Berthes Sales (class of 1887), who throughout the twenties disappointed every one of her inspectors, still refused at sixty-one to think of quitting. "The moment for retirement has come," announced an inspector general in 1928, "but Mlle Sales, who is in excellent health and con-

---

[82] Dossier personnel, notes, 1921, 1923, 1925, F17 23832, A.N.

[83] Dossier personnel, notes, 1925, F17 23756, A.N.

[84] Dossier personnel, notes, 1919, F17 23980, A.N.

[85] Dossier personnel, notes, 1922, F17 23832, A.N.

siders herself to be as active as ever, has no desire to leave."[86] Elizabeth Butiaux (class of 1881), in contrast, chalked up in thirty-eight years of teaching an untarnished record with inspectors, yet she chose at sixty years of age to quit. "I could certainly have asked to prolong my career another two years," she wrote, explaining her decision, "but I sense a deep fatigue when I am teaching now. It would distress me to do it badly, and that is what persuades me to retire."[87] Slower to see the writing on the wall, Bertha Bastoul (class of 1886), at last gave in to mounting evidence that poor health had undermined her teaching. "Deaf, almost blind, unable to control her classes," the academy inspector reported grimly, "Mlle Bastoul is thinking seriously of retiring. She would do well to get to it as soon as possible."[88] Whereas for years this teacher had ignored complaints about her methods, she could not indefinitely do likewise with her health. Such calculations were not uncommon in late career for Sévriennes. One-third of them referred to their poor health or their fatigue when they retired. Yet the actual incidence of physical exhaustion may have run much higher, for in one respect, at least, teaching as a profession had not changed. As in the early days of girls' secondary schools, teaching went along with frequent illness.

Once again, as was the case before the war, the health of teachers compared unfavorably in the 1920s to that of directrices of a similar age, and so did the rate of their attrition. Only 5 percent of the directrices who worked after 1920 retired before the age of sixty, while one in every six teachers (16 percent) resigned during their fifties for reasons of poor health. Within this familiar pattern only the symptoms of illness changed. Neurasthenia dropped from the vocabulary of medical excuses and, more significantly, so did other names for nervous illness. Much more often now, teachers complained of ailments linked to aging—bad circulation, arthritis, poor hearing, or bad eyes—or they caught the flu. These findings signal the end of the pathology of teaching first discovered when this group of Sévriennes was young. No longer isolated from society or shaken by self-doubt, they resembled now in their afflictions any other representative group of aging women. At worst, what teaching seemed to threaten was accelerated aging brought on by physical exhaustion.

Still, if teaching aged a woman physically, reports suggest that psychologically it could have the opposite effect. Surrounded by the young, confirmed in their importance by their daily obligations, some women,

[86] Dossier personnel, notes, 1928, F17 24168, A.N.
[87] Dossier personnel, correspondance, 1921, F17 22556, A.N.
[88] Dossier personnel, notes, 1928, F17 23969, A.N.

at least, felt that teaching kept them young in spirit.[89] In a letter to the president of Sèvres's alumnae, Zénaide Génin (class of 1881) expressed the feelings of ambivalence that the prospect of retirement stirred in her. "As the hour for retirement approaches," she mused, "I sense nostalgia rising. Everything seems lighter and even easy now that I am going to leave teaching; even the ungrateful task of correcting compositions strikes me as interesting." Zénaide Génin was sixty-one when she reported these mixed feelings. Eligible for retirement the previous year, she thought at first of waiting until the summer before retiring "in order to look after" her "blind and aged mother."[90] Instead, she taught for yet another year, leaving only when, at sixty-two, she reached the legal age limit.[91] In her reluctance to quit working, Zénaide Génin resembled the majority of Sévriennes of her generation. Fifty-eight percent of the teachers and 65 percent of the directrices who worked throughout their fifties did not retire with their pensions when they had the right to do so at the age of sixty. Perhaps this simply represented a financial calculation of women on fixed incomes in a period of galloping inflation. It may also suggest their hesitation to embark on the phase of life that stretched ahead.

[89] Wurmser-Dégouy, *Trois Éducatrices modernes*, 42.
[90] Letter of June 10, 1922, Alumnae Association, archives, E.N.S.
[91] Dossier personnel, F17 22516, A.N.

12 | Retreat into the Home

*A teacher forced by age or illness to retire: how sad is a
retirement that from one day to the next thrusts you from
productive and well-loved work into idleness which you*
try vainly to escape; how sad the brutal solitude, especially, far from
the youth whose presence kept you young.

How many there are who cannot bear those long and empty hours,
the inactivity, above all, the abandonment. . . . At the same time,
with a lower income, perhaps you must curtail your modest life-style,
exchange your home, which had become over the years a part of you,
for someplace smaller, where you will be a stranger, more friendless,
more alone than ever.[1]

Such was the grim description offered by a younger teacher of the retirement facing Sévriennes in the 1920s: penury and lonely isolation. If
true, her words suggested a radical reversal of the long-term trends in
Sévriennes' experience, characterized until then by ever-widening circles of acquaintances, rising salaries, and increasing involvement in professional and charitable organizations. The effect of these developments
had been to give directrices and teachers a social status unique for
women of their generation, a social persona independent of their membership in families. Not as wives and daughters but as professional
women, they had acquired a standing in their communities. Apparently,
however, the end of their careers put that accomplishment in question.
From fixtures in their schools, it seemed retired Sévriennes might gradually deteriorate into what their detractors had predicted in the 1880s:
marginal female figures (*déclassées*) floating uncertainly in the social order.

As a realistic prediction, however, this image is considerably over-
drawn. For a teacher or directrice to move from a position of social recognition to one of poverty and neglect required more than simply taking
leave of schools and classrooms. Such a fall necessitated a full retreat
into the home, the absence of any friends or family, and the woman's
having neither the wit, the money, nor sufficient health to contrive a varied life of leisure. In fact, retired Sévriennes proved more resourceful
than this portrait would suggest, filling in the gaps left by their work with

[1] Wurmser-Dégouy, *Trois éducatrices modernes*, 42.

300

other projects, managing their finances with more success. Exceptions to this rule invariably involved a woman plagued by long and serious illness and without close family ties.

Yet one aspect of this portrait did characterize the lives of most retired Sévriennes, and that was the abrupt withdrawal into private life. Indeed, outside of Paris, directrices appeared even more prone to this development than were teachers. Sévriennes reflected in this pattern bourgeois traditions of collective life, which customarily reserved a prominent role for state officials, a lesser one for private citizens, including ex-officials, and still less for women, not even the right to vote. To leave one's post, therefore, meant for all but the exceptional woman retreat into the home, where ever fewer people remembered her professional achievements.

Sévriennes who headed schools actually hastened this loss of public recognition. Of the fifty-five directrices still in our sample at retirement, fully fifty-eight percent packed up and left the towns and cities where they had held their final posts.[2] Although their reasons for leaving often require guesswork, they are not totally obscure. To begin, at the arrival of a new directrice, retiring school heads promptly lost their homes inside their schools, which gave them a strong motive to consider other options. Some of them simply found another place in town. For others, though, accustomed to the regular rotation of directrices up the promotional ladder, other possibilities made more sense. Heads of girls' secondary schools represented that portion of the women's corps most akin to the transient professionals who constituted the men's profession. The location of their final post often represented nothing more than an accident of this process of promotion. Understandably, they sometimes had quite different aspirations when it came to settling down for good.

What then did dictate the selection of their retirement residence for former school heads? For most of them, family ties provide the answer, ties that linked them mainly to the living but sometimes just to places and to memories. A family home left them by their parents might provide the refuge. Amélie Duporge (class of 1888), dying in the lycée at Saint-Quentin, left this poignant record of the dream she never realized of going home. "I must return there," she wrote a friend about her hometown near Amiens. "My need is not just sentimental but physical, almost animal, like a wounded beast who looks for his hole to hide in. . . . I have to see my sister and her children frequently; I must go often to the cemetery to visit our graves; I need to watch the seasons pass in our garden, the

---

[2] Most of the dossiers personnels contain a retirement notice giving the pension that the retiree would receive and her place of residence in retirement. By using the address lists for alumnae that appeared periodically in *BAES* through 1949, I was able to locate places of residence as well as any change of address during a Sévrienne's retirement.

one my father cared for with such love; I want to look after the house that was my mother's kingdom; I need to live a little in the past because the present is so hard and the future will be worse."[3] Nearly one in seven directrices (15 percent) lived to make the trek back to their roots that Amélie Duporge so craved for comfort. The figure comes to one in five (21 percent) if we include those women already in their hometowns at retirement. The remaining cases of retirees who changed their residence followed the meanderings of family members or, more infrequently, of friends to new abodes. Hélène Magnus (class of 1885), raised at Besançon, directrice at Le Mans until 1927, retired at sixty "not because of illness but out of a desire to live closer to her sisters" in Mézières; Marie Bégué Laplace (class of 1885), a childless widow, brought up in the Southwest and directrice at Clermont Ferrand for fifteen years, retired to Paris to rejoin a "brother, her sister-in-law, and her nephews"; as for Louise Masson, an Alsacienne working at Rouen until 1926, she, too, retired to Paris "impatiently awaited by her sister, her brother-in-law, old friends, and former students."[4] Indeed, Paris proved a magnet for this peripatetic corps, even in the closing years of life. Only one directrice with a post in Paris left the capital to retire elsewhere, while 17 percent of the provincial directrices chose to settle in the capital. Together these statistics put more than one-quarter (28 percent) of all retired directrices in Paris, close to family often, always near some friends, and not far from an object of deep, collective loyalty: the School of Sèvres.

In striking contrast to the residential patterns of these former school heads, a majority of teachers (65 percent) settled down in towns where they last taught. For many of them, this also meant retiring in or near the places where they grew up. Unlike headmistresses, often teachers had already in the course of their careers secured appointments near the original family home. In general, the residential history of these teachers reflected a rootedness directrices never matched, and that pattern would continue into their retirement. Thus, while former school heads, in pursuit of family members, often moved to parts of France where they had never lived before, teachers retired to the part of France they knew. If originally from the North, to the North they would return; while those whose roots lay in the Midi dug in deeper. The only exception to this pattern appeared among the very ill, women often with respiratory problems. Wherever a women's place of origin or even family, she might decide for reasons of poor health to retire in the warm, dry regions of the

[3] Quoted from a personal letter in her death notice: G. Marcourt, "Amélie Duporge," *BAES* (January 1923): 4–5.

[4] P. B.-G., "Hélène Magnus," *BAES* (1931): 8; M. Audibert, "Mme Laplace-Bégué," *BAES* (1933): 5; M. D., "Louise Masson," *BAES* (1935): 13.

South. Generally, however, when teachers settled down for good, it was in homes where they had lived for years, surrounded by long-standing neighbors, and close to people, living or dead, whom they held very dear. Even when deprived of family, these were not the sort of women to drift helpless and alone into marginality or anomie.

Poverty, of course, could undermine important features of that optimistic forecast by cutting off its victims from whatever chance they had for social contact. Just how seriously it affected Sévriennes, however, is not easy to determine. One clue to follow would be a change of residence, once they had retired, for real privation might well translate into downward mobility in housing. The figures here are inconclusive, since they do not extend beyond 1949, but until that time, a mere 14 percent (21 of 143) of all retired Sévriennes changed their residences after their retirement.[5] Furthermore, a close inspection of their destinations might well suggest a reason other than financial pressure to explain their new abodes. Occasionally, a woman moved to Paris, sometimes to a town where she once had worked, more rarely to a totally new setting. Almost never, though, did Sévriennes change residences within a single town (two cases). A better explanation than poverty for such uprooting might be something like a death, an illness, or simply a change of residence for some close relative or friend.

Moreover, retired Sévriennes from this generation hardly ever made a sanatorium or an institution for retirees their "home," another indication that their personal situation was not completely desperate. The founders of Sèvres might have been surprised by that discovery. Indeed, as early as the 1890s, Mme Favre proposed a retirement home for Sévriennes and other women secondary teachers, where they could grow old together, financially secure and part of a community of old professionals. Through the efforts of a determined Sévrienne, Léonie Allégret (class of 1882), in 1923 that home finally did come into being.[6] Unlike Mme Favre's project, however, Allégret's retreat accepted women from any branch of public teaching, the postal service, and every state administration. Sèvres's alumnae Council praised its advantages for aging teachers. Yet not a single Sévrienne included in this study chose it as her home. In fact, the only Sévrienne who did retire to an institution, a decorated former school directrice, preferred the prestigious company of fellow members of the Legion of Honor in its retirement home.[7]

One further ambiguous clue to the true financial state of these retired women lies in the assistance fund that the Association des anciennes

---

[5] Based on the alumnae address lists published in *BAES* until 1949.

[6] "Oeuvres des lycées," *ESDJF* 2 (1923): 281–82.

[7] Antoinette Ecolan, class of 1883.

élèves de Sèvres developed. Swollen after the war by donations from a special fund for gifts not subject to its rules for capital investment, the alumnae gift fund grew by the 1920s to sizable proportions.[8] Instead of gifts amounting, as they had before the war, to from 100 to 300 francs per person, in the twenties, 500 francs became the average sum allotted. Given inflation, even that increase did not represent in real terms much improvement. In really dire cases, though, this amount could rise considerably higher. Indeed, in 1927/28, the association gave 5,000 francs of its total fund of 6,000 to a single person.[9] Yet despite the possibility of more substantial gifts, the number of women helped in any year as a percentage of the entire membership did not increase. Mlle Courtin, who was on the alumnae Council in this period, confided to me that the really serious cases, in any event, involved Sévriennes who had left teaching to be married and ended up in their old age widowed and impoverished.[10] Moreover, as always, even to discover hardship cases, the association relied on information passed along by the unfortunate woman's friends. At this point, someone on the Council would offer the association's help "in the most delicate possible way."[11] Sévriennes both young and old did not admit to their distress or ask for help forthrightly, which makes the task of determining their real state of affairs as difficult for us as it had always been for Sèvres's alumnae Council.

What we can with certainty establish is the inadequacy of certain women's pensions, particularly those of Sévriennes who retired before 1924. Prior to that year, the government did little to adjust the salaries and pensions of its school personnel to the rise in postwar prices.[12] Sévriennes who retired from 1918 to 1923 were granted pensions barely large enough to live on, especially by 1929, when inflation had decreased the value of the franc five times since World War I.[13] Gradually, however, the situation improved for women retiring after 1924. From a low of 4,000 francs in pension for one teacher and of 4,518 francs for a directrice prior to 1924, pensions began to rise;[14] in 1935 one of the last teach-

---

[8] Hélène Dubois, "L'Association des Elèves et Anciennes Elèves," *Le Cinquantenaire*, 309.

[9] *BAES* (1929): 35. At each meeting of the General Assembly of the Alumnae Association of Sèvres, the alumnae treasurer would give an accounting of these gifts without mentioning the names of the recipients. Her report would then appear in *BAES*.

[10] Interview with Mlle Courtin, class of 1910 (Paris, June 1976).

[11] Hélène Dubois, "Aux élèves de l'Ecole," *BAES* (January 1922): 40.

[12] *Revue des deux mondes* (1926).

[13] Philip Carr, *The French at Home in the Country and in Town* (London: Methuen and Co., 1930): 181.

[14] In 1928, the government raised salaries to compensate for inflation. "Appel," *BAES* (1928): 3.

ers from this generation retired with the astounding pension of 34,800 francs, and a directrice retired in the same year with a pension of 36,580 francs, not so much a measure for either of them of real wealth but rather of the extraordinary fall in the purchasing power of the franc over the course of the 1920s. Overall, 79 percent of the Sévriennes in our sample retired after 1923. That left only 21 percent whose pensions offered nothing as a safety net in time of crisis. Another 45 percent who retired sometime between 1924 and 1927, when both salaries and pensions were rising but not in tempo with inflation, must have had to live quite simply. Only 34 percent of the women in our group, all of whom retired after 1927, would have been reasonably well-off. Yet patchy as it is, the evidence reveals a generation determined to keep up appearances whatever the true condition of individual budgets. In their choice of homes, in their attitude toward help, Sévriennes showed themselves determined to preserve as a matter of social honor, their independence and self-reliance. However great or small their contact with the outside world, even in retirement these professional women never lost their deep concern for face.

Only a few of them, however, managed to preserve an audience for their lives larger than their intimate circle of family and close friends. Instead of seeking out some public cause or service, the vast majority slipped back for good into the private sphere whence they had emerged in young adulthood. That at any rate is the impression left by the obituaries in Sèvres's alumnae bulletin. Admittedly, the bulletin ceased to publish these memorial tributes in 1940. But it is hardly likely that this generation finally took up volunteering in their seventies. Indeed, as surprising as it seems, ex-directrices were less inclined even than were former teachers to engage in some community endeavor. Perhaps this makes more sense if we consider that many heads of schools, because they moved away, lost the contacts that might have led to volunteer work. A second explanation focuses upon the texture of local rivalries. Retired school heads, even when they did stay in the area, had a rival in the person of the new directrice. Former teachers posed much less danger for their replacements, since their role within the school had been less central and their public status depended on the students whom they had taught. Unlike the ex-headmistress, they had never served as symbols of their schools. A retired teacher, therefore, could return to serve in an alumnae club without inciting rivalries against her. In Dôle, where she had taught for thirty years, Mathilde Saugère (class of 1885) did precisely that. A friend reported: "Her industry and zeal gave new life to the organization and what a life! She transformed it into a veritable *société de bienfaisance.*"[15] Even so, Mathilde Saugère is an exception in the records we possess. Alumnae clubs were the bailiwicks of individual teachers, which limited the numbers potentially involved, and in any case, as more graduates of girls' secondary schools went on to work or study, the social life of their alumnae clubs lost vigor.

At a more general level, though, the lack of Sévrienne involvement in organized endeavors reflected less on them or even on their schools than on the organization of French provincial life. In outlying towns and cities, members of the middle class could choose among three main arenas of public service: politics, the Church, and civil or military service. Traditionally, for women in the Third Republic, these options narrowed down to two. Either they belonged to Church-related organizations, or they served the state as public teachers. Unfortunately, for women like our Sévriennes, whose professional conscience drew inspiration from the early Third Republic, only the latter route to public life lay open, at least for Catholics. Whatever their personal convictions, these women made unlikely recruits even in retirement to organizations sponsored by the Catholic church.[16] That left only their professional affiliations as a conduit to the public sphere, which, for women who retired in the provinces, was not sufficient. During the first fifty years of girls' schools' history, provincial teachers had been unable to develop professional organizations, either philanthropic or strictly professional, that were not integral to the schools where they worked.[17] To depart from that arena meant for retiring Sévriennes in the 1920s to withdraw from the pursuit of public service altogether.

Paris, on the other hand, offered retired Sévriennes many opportunities for public action. After all, in the capital the professional world of teachers extended far beyond the confines of their schools. In contrast to provincial teachers, Sévriennes in Paris had over the preceding decades developed, sometimes alone, sometimes with colleagues, organizations that bypassed the institution of the school. Sèvres itself established the precedent for extramural affiliations when it founded its Alumnae Association. Women teachers in Paris pursued a similar strategy when they organized a single amicale for all the city's lycées. But this tendency to

[15] F. P., "Mademoiselle Saugère," *BAES* (1933): 3.

[16] The only exception was Marguerite Duret Chollet (class of 1881), who joined the movement called Amis de la Bible à l'école. J. Michot-Wable, "Madame Chollet, née Lydie-Marguerite Duret," *BAES* (1936): 3.

[17] See the letter (March 30, 1921) to the Council of the Alumnae Association from two young teachers, G. Godin and G. Avare, both from the class of 1910, in which they complained because there were still no provincial chapters of the Alumnae Association. Archives, Alumnae Association, E.N.S. .

broaden affiliations came to full fruition only in the explosion of professional and quasi-professional women's organizations after the war. The
Société des agrégées was only one of these associations; yet when it made
the agrégation rather than teaching the basis of interest-group formation,
it played its part in undercutting the importance of the school. Meanwhile, at Sèvres, the Alumnae Association sought to link its members
into a larger organizational network than either school ties or professional associations offered. In 1921, it voted to affiliate with the recently
created Association des femmes diplômées des universités, together with
the International Organization of University Women.[18] Then in 1929, it
joined the feminist Conseil national des femmes françaises, ending
nearly five decades of indifference to organizations promoting women's
rights.[19] Even efforts to solve specific professional problems in this period drew Sévriennes toward a larger social world. Léonie Allégret's retirement home, which welcomed retired women office workers from all
branches of the civil service, offers one example. Another was a mutual
aid society founded by Lucie Kuss (class of 1882) in 1921 to combat the
problem of tuberculosis among the personnel of secondary schools. "In
setting up this *Mutualité* for the prevention and treatment of tuberculosis
in public secondary education," she told the General Assembly of
Sévres's association, "we did not intend to found a closed society for our
mutual assistance but rather an organization devoted, above all, to social
preservation, since we are convinced that only in this way could we attract the outside help indispensable to us. That is why our Society chose
as its objective the struggle against tuberculosis, which constitutes a peril
for the Nation."[20] This national perspective was a characteristic feature
of associational life for Sévriennes in Paris, however mixed their motives, and like the structure of their associations, it gave them both an
interest in and entrée to a public life outside the confines of their
schools.

Numerous retired Sévriennes took advantage of this rich associational
life in Paris to continue active volunteering. A favorite outlet for their
energies, of course, was the alumnae club at Sèvres. Altogether, seven
women from this generation served between the wars as members of its
elected Council, two of them as president.[21] For each of them the Council

---

[18] The Association des femmes diplômées des universités was briefly called the Fédération féminine de rapprochement universitaire. *BAES* (January 1922): 22.

[19] *BAES* (1930): 30.

[20] "Rapport de la Présidente," *BAES* (April 1922): 22.

[21] The members of the Council were Anna Amieux (class of 1889), Louise Belugou
(class of 1882), Gabrielle Duponchel-Marcourt (class of 1884), Julie Lochert (class of

seat became a sinecure to which the General Assembly voted repeatedly to return them. Other retired Sévriennes pursued equally busy lives in Paris without maintaining close ties to their alma mater. Léonie Allégret, for instance, "who never appeared more active and alive than in retirement,"[22] set up her retirement home for women teachers and civil servants with official backing but without direct collaboration from Sèvres's Council. Even less involved with Sèvres's association, Marguerite Caron (class of 1887) joined the Conseil national des femmes françaises as an individual and became within it a leading spokeswoman on the issue of women's professional training.[23] Her real passion, however, was a charity project sponsored by the Ministry of Education to teach children of the poor in private charity hospitals how to read and write.[24] Or consider the example of Jeanne François Antoine (class of 1885), "who did not abandon at retirement any of the charities that she had undertaken";[25] or Adrienne Dreuilhe (class of 1884), "whose enthusiasm for her charitable involvements never lessened after she retired."[26] Still, too much emphasis on these Sévriennes in Paris would distort our general argument. However rich their associational life, we must remember that its like was rarely accessible to those who ended their careers elsewhere, which is to say, 89 percent of the directrices and 72 percent of teachers in our group. Obituaries of women such as these reflect a life of leisure devoted less to volunteer work than to personal relations and to private interest, a life in some ways not so radically different from that of retired people everywhere but especially characteristic of the leisure of aging bourgeois women in their day.

Retirement brought the majority of these mainly single women back into a world centered to a large degree on family. Of course, by now the parents of most of them were dead, so that the composition of their family circles changed.[27] For the most part, they now depended on their siblings, their siblings' children, and even sometimes on a cousin for close familial relations. Even married Sévriennes had seen a radical transformation in their domestic lives. By the time these women retired, 38 percent of them were either widows (sixteen of forty-seven) or separated

---

1882), and Jeanne Michotte (class of 1883). Lucie Kuss (class of 1882) served as president from 1906 to 1925. Hélène Dubois (class of 1889) was president from 1926 to 1945.

[22] Wurmser-Dégouy, *Trois Éducatrices modernes*, 44.

[23] Hélène Dubois, "Rapport de la Présidente," *BAES* (1933): 22.

[24] Wurmser-Dégouy, *Trois Éducatrices modernes*, 34–35.

[25] L. Sarché, "Madame Antoine, née Jeanne François," *BAES* (1940): 6.

[26] Lucie Bérillon, "Adrienne Dreuilhe," *BAES* (1939): 22.

[27] There are many references scattered through Sévriennes' dossiers personnels referring to the death of a parent during these women's late careers. Few parents appear on personnel files as dependents in the last year during which a Sévrienne worked.

from their husbands (two of forty-seven), and their offspring had grown up and left the parental home.[28] Nonetheless, this altered family profile did not deprive these women of some regular family contact; it merely changed the nature of their duties. Rarely now did Sévriennes support one or another relative financially. Instead, their family ties involved a sentimental obligation in which they personally figured on both the giving and receiving ends of the exchange. Mathilde Saugère (class of 1885), for instance, devoted her retirement to her family. "She consecrated her entire life to others," a friend of hers reported, "to her parents, whose old age she surrounded with touching solicitude, to her brothers and to her sisters, who never lacked for her affection or assistance right up to the end."[29] Julie Esménard (class of 1887), who fell seriously ill, became, by contrast, the beneficiary of this familial charge. "She died a strangely rapid death," her obituary noted, "surrounded by her family, whose devoted care was not enough to save her."[30] Most often, though, this family obligation meant simply frequent visits, even to kin some distance away. Jeanne François Antoine (class of 1885), who lived in Paris, died while on vacation with her cousins in the Midi;[31] while Louise Belugou (class of 1882), also with a home in Paris, maintained a residence in Switzerland just so she could spend half the year near an ailing sister in the Alps.[32]

For many Sévriennes, these tangible expressions of family loyalty reflected a genuine affection. Laure Défontaine Bermyn (class of 1888), who retired with her husband "to her parents' former home," lived out her final years "simply" and "modestly," basking in her grandmotherly devotions. "She raised two children and lived to see three grandsons, the oldest of whom was the joy of her retirement."[33] In much the same way, Angèle Coustols (class of 1887), although she never married, appeared devoted to her family. "One had to see her face light up," a friend remembered, "whenever she talked about her dear parents, her brother, or later, about her long-awaited nephew."[34] Of course there were Sévriennes who harbored less than tender feelings toward their closest kin. Indeed, an enmity so open that even an inspector heard about it es-

---

[28] The conclusion is based on the fact that Sévriennes are no longer listing their children as dependents in the last year of work. Three single Sévriennes who acquired children through adoption in their midcareers or later, by taking in either a relative or an orphan of the war, also faced retirement with empty nests.

[29] F. P., "Mademoiselle Saugère," *BAES* (1933): 3.

[30] M. D., "Julie Esménard," *BAES* (1937): 5–6.

[31] L. Sarché, "Madame Antoine, née Jeanne François," *BAES* (1940): 6.

[32] H. Dubois, "Louise Belugou," *BAES* (1939): 3.

[33] M. S., "Madame Bermyn-Défontaine," *BAES* (1940): 8–9.

[34] "Angèle Coustols," *BAES* (1933): 6.

tranged one Sévrienne directrice from her eldest daughter. Yet such overt ruptures were doubtless rare. Moral pressure, on the one hand, necessity on the other, ensured that families stuck together, whatever the antipathies within them. That fact could only serve the interest of retired Sévriennes because without a family, they might well drift into painful isolation. Threatened by that fate, a Sévrienne directrice from the class of 1909 explained to me her options at retirement. "In the first place, I had to leave my home. I told myself at my age there was nothing left but an old people's home. I did not want to find an apartment by myself in a building where I knew no one and no one would know me. So I decided to retire to Grenoble near a married godchild and her children."[35] Twenty years before, Sévriennes of an earlier generation made similar calculations and ended up as she had, residing close to relatives or to someone they considered "just like family."

The need for someone to take the place of relatives was not, in fact, uncommon. One-third of Sèvres's obituaries did not refer to relatives at all among the mourners of deceased alumnae. Even those who did have family usually could not rely on such relations for a home. Unlike the parasitic Cousin Bette of Balzac's novel or the proverbial nineteenth-century maiden aunt, retired Sévriennes, unless they had a single sister, generally lived on their own.[36] Only widowed mothers possessed another option, for like their own parents before them, mothers could and often did move in with children.[37] Unfortunately, few Sévriennes could look forward to that comfort in old age, since fully 71 percent were either single or widows without offspring. Even with a relative nearby, inevitably they faced long hours on their own. Consequently, friendship sounded an important theme in Sévriennes' obituaries, but the world of friendships that these memorials reveal was as closed and rooted in the past as the universe constructed by the family.

Contrary to natural expectations, the school did not provide ex-teachers a community of friends on which to draw in their retirement. Indeed, in that respect, at least, relations inside girls' schools had hardly changed from days when young and inexperienced Sévriennes had suffered desperately from isolation. Not that the relations between teachers lacked cordiality; but they rarely led to private friendship. Interviews with Sévriennes who worked between the wars confirm a vague impression left

[35] Interview with Mlle Fontaine, class of 1909 (Paris, June 1976).

[36] For examples of women living with single or widowed sisters, see the death notices for Jeanne Michotte, *BAES* (1928): 4–6, and for H. Dubois by E. Cotton-Feytis, *BAES* (1946): 4–5.

[37] In contrast to the immobility typical of single teachers, every widowed mother who had been a teacher changed her residence at retirement.

by the obituaries. "There was not much esprit de corps within the school," one former teacher said. "In teaching and particularly among women teachers, people are, in the last analysis, highly individualistic."[38] Another one reported: "Teachers are independent people—stubbornly independent. They simply do not want to socialize together."[39] Still another, this time a former school directrice, recalled, "I have had many colleagues who were friendly and kind to me, who said nice things to me, etc." Yet she went on to note, "They did not invite me to their homes."[40]

Descriptions of friendships in obituaries suggest the truth of these assertions, for these documents detail a social world not only small in size but also mainly peopled by friends of very long duration. Sèvres itself gave birth to several of these lasting friendships. Sometimes, Sévriennes corresponded during forty or even fifty years of separation to keep these bonds intact; occasionally, a reunion during school vacation refreshed their intimacy. Overall, the accounts in these obituaries leave little doubt of the enduring strength of Sèvres's alumnae ties. In Suzanne Palaa's (class of 1883) death notice, for example, there appeared this tribute to her friendship with Jeanne Michotte, a fellow Protestant and classmate, whose career path never crossed her own: "The bond contracted at Sèvres has been one of the great joys, one of the pillars of their lives."[41] Similarly, when her fellow Sévrienne, Angèle Bourgoignon Séverin (class of 1887), died at Lille, Adelaïde Saladin (class of 1889) wrote from the Aisne, "For me it is the end of fifty years of friendship."[42] These two friends had never worked together either. The same was true for Lucie Kuss (class of 1882) and Céline Graverol (class of 1882). Yet when Lucie Kuss fell ill in 1924, she left her home in Paris to bask for the last time "in the warm sunshine and the devoted friendship" of her former classmate "Mlle Graverol," a resident of Nîmes.[43] Forged as they were in an institution modeled on the family, school friendships slipped easily into the kind of irreversible bonds that regulated Sévriennes' blood ties. At a general level, loyalty to Sèvres spawned an extraordinarily faithful membership in its alumnae club.[44] But at the level of their intimate affections, it could turn a former classmate into quasi-kin. Under certain circum-

[38] Interview with Mlle Galle, class of 1927 (Versailles, June 1976).
[39] Interview with Mme Scheid, class of 1922 (Paris, June 1976).
[40] Interview with Mlle Guiscafré, class of 1928 (Paris, June 1976).
[41] L. Belugou, "Suzanne Palaa," *BAES* (1935): 12.
[42] *BAES* (1940): 6.
[43] H. Dubois, "Rapport de la Présidente," *BAES* (January 1925): 13–14.
[44] Eighty percent still belonged to the Alumnae Association at the time of their retirement despite the fact that annual dues were raised in 1923 from ten to fifteen francs.

stances, even school life could benefit from the reverberations. A younger Sévrienne remembered a particularly "familial atmosphere" at the Lycée Molière when she was just a student, something she explained thus: "All the teachers came from Sèvres and more or less from the same classes. They were, therefore, *très amies*."[45]

For the most part, though, Sévrienne teachers had to look beyond school ties, beyond their schools, even "outside their profession" for the friendships that would sustain them in old age.[46] A Sévrienne from the class of 1900, already a directrice by 1921, described the socializing habits of her teachers: "The young ones made friends among themselves. The others were women who had been there for a long time. Often they came from the region. They had a circle of relations in the town."[47] Hastening to suggest the limits of that circle, she added, "A teacher was not a *personnage*, however."[48] Indeed, nothing in Sévriennes' obituaries would lead one to think otherwise. Typically, the main embellishments of the private lives that they described, apart from loving families, were a few enduring friendships: "[Juliette Matton] died at Pau surrounded by her faithful friends"; "[Léontine Martellière] retired . . . to Châlon [-sur-Saône] where she had a few precious friendships"; "Certain friendships had become for [Jeanne Michotte] like close relations."[49] Occasionally, a Sévrienne even moved in with another woman whose own circumstances permitted that arrangement. Angèle Coustols (class of 1887) and "her lifelong friend," Mlle Faucheux, constituted such a couple. The two companions lived together "in a little house in Vincennes [Coustols] inherited from her parents, and whenever she went out, the woman who shared her life so tenderly accompanied her."[50] Yet when I asked a Sévrienne from the class of 1922 if teachers seemed confined to the society of women, she replied, "Although the women of that period spent much of their time among themselves, the teachers whom I had myself were not the sort of women to live a cloistered life—even the unmarried ones."[51] Obituaries of retired teachers bear out the justice of her recollections. Undeniably, women dominated the circle of friends to whom these Sévriennes laid claim, particularly when they corresponded. But equally

[45] Interview with Mlle Courtin.
[46] Interview with Mlle Galle.
[47] Interview with Mlle Fontaine.
[48] Ibid.
[49] Lucie Bérillon, "Mademoiselle Matton," *BAES* (1930): 3; Lucie Bérillon, "Mademoiselle Martellière," *BAES* (January 1928): 12–13; S. C., "Jeanne Michotte," *BAES* (January 1928): 7.
[50] "Angèle Coustols," *BAES* (1933): 6.
[51] Interview with Mlle Galle.

certain is the fact that men as well as women friends were among their mourners. Indeed, news of the unexpected death of a close male friend would actually set off the illness that killed the former teacher Anne Saurou (class of 1883).[52]

Unmarried directrices, by contrast, often did not have the same close ties with men once they retired. Rather than a mix of male and female friends (amis), the intimates of former school heads appear to have been almost exclusively women (amies). In a final salute to Julie Esménard (class of 1887), for instance, her obituary read, "She will live in the hearts of her women friends and students."[53] Berthe Savery's retirement years impart the same impression, years that a close friend described as "beautiful and moving for the women friends fortunate enough to live close by."[54] Friendship appeared for Louise Graverol (class of 1882) equally specific in its gender. According to the author of her obituary, "She loved deeply both her departed women friends and those who would survive her."[55] Of course, the fact that three of every five retired headmistresses left the towns where they had worked may well have had a bearing on this finding. Perhaps directrices like Julie Esménard and Berthe Savery, who opted to migrate elsewhere, broke off their ties to local families in the process. Yet the very fact that so many school heads moved away from where they worked suggests a socially peripheral position. As one ex-directrice from the class of 1928 remarked, parents of her students, although "extremely friendly," rarely invited her to visit. She explained: "A directrice is an imposing person. I was even told sometimes that I was frightening."[56] One could imagine other reasons for this social distance. But almost certainly the experience she described differed little from that of the previous generation. Indeed, we seem to have discovered in this pattern a contradiction between the public stature of a directrice and her private isolation. However prominent her position as the principal of her school, an unmarried directrice, residing as she did inside her school, did not gain entrée to local social circles. If, therefore, we find that in retirement single ex-directrices had close relationships exclusively with women, quite likely, there was little in that conduct that was new.

Even with their friends or family close at hand, however, Sévriennes, like retirees in general, unavoidably confronted the dilemma of how to fill so many leisured hours. Perhaps the difficulties they encountered

---

[52] L. A., "Anne Saurou," BAES (January 1925): 3–4.

[53] M. D., "Julie Esménard," BAES (1937): 5–6.

[54] L. Kuss, "Berthe Savery," BAES (January 1922): 2–3.

[55] M. R., "Louise Graverol," BAES (1938): 14–15.

[56] Interview with Mlle Guiscafré.

were less trying than they often are for men; Sévriennes, in the words of one ex-school head, "at least had the upkeep of their homes."[57] Indeed, the writers of obituaries took this domesticity so much for granted that they rarely even bothered to describe it. An exception for Anna Amieux (class of 1889), the former directrice of Sèvres, allows a narrow glimpse, no doubt itself atypical, into this major aspect of Sévriennes' retirement: "In the little house on the edge of the forest [of Fontainebleau], she tended to her bees and garden . . . , looked after little children, and visited with even the humblest of her neighbors, who were always very much at ease when in her presence."[58] It is also clear, however, that Sévriennes did not reduce their lives to these domestic cares. Frequently, obituaries mention more rarefied pursuits, interests one might expect of retired intellectuals. Thus, Jeanne François Antoine (class of 1885) "gave herself over to painting," and Adrienne Dreuilhe (class of 1884), "a delicate poet in her leisure, left her women friends some charming pieces that her modesty prevented her from publishing."[59] Other, less creative women, like Angèle Bourgoignon Séverin (class of 1887), "an inveterate reader" who "kept her interest in learning right up to the end," or Louise Graverol (class of 1882), who, "despite her physical suffering and poor eyesight, forced herself until the last to read in Provost, Zweig, and other historical studies," reflected the same preoccupation with the mind.[60] Sometimes, Sévriennes' intellectual and cultural activities even struck a distinctly modern note, especially given that they were undertaken by older, single women such as Amélie Gandon Gonnet (class of 1888), who, once she became a widow, indulged "refined artistic tastes" by making trips to Italy.[61] Together with reports of other outings—to concerts, the theater, even public talks—these details of their retirement suggest that Sévriennes did not lose contact with the larger world around them. At least as interested observers, if not as public figures, retired directrices and teachers preserved their links to public life.

Nevertheless, for all their efforts to remain in contact with the world, retired Sévriennes confronted solitude in daily life. For the most part, we can only guess at how they dealt with that bleak reality. A younger friend of Anna Amieux's (class of 1889) considered that in her case, it took

[57] Interview with Mlle Fontaine.

[58] Suzanne Galle, "Mademoiselle Amieux," *Bulletin des femmes diplomées* (June 1962): 31.

[59] Ibid., 31–32; L. Sarché, "Madame Antoine, née Jeanne François," *BAES* (1940): 6; Lucie Bérillon, "Adrienne Dreuilhe," *BAES* (1939): 22–23.

[60] A. Saladin, "Madame Antoine, née Jeanne François," *BAES* (1940): 8; M. R., "Louise Graverol," *BAES* (1938): 15.

[61] E. G., "Madame Gonnet-Gandon," *BAES* (1930): 4–5.

"courage" to "stay alone in that little house on the edge of the forest . . . whose gates an elderly gardener came to lock up every night." Yet the older woman discounted, even mocked the dangers she ran. "You know, Suzanne," she said one day to my informant in regard to the old man, "he thinks he is going to find me dead in the morning. I can tell that he's afraid."[62] Perhaps her pluck derived in part from her unblemished record of good health. Illness had never been a problem for this former head of Sèvres, who retired at sixty-five and lived into her eighties. Other retirees, however, whose health gave them more trouble, left behind a rather different image of their state of mind. Anne Saurou (class of 1883), who in one year lost the two people closest to her in the world, gradually also lost her capacity to speak. According to a friend, "She stayed for months alone in her apartment, communicating only in writing with the people who looked after her." An isolation so extreme produced an equally extreme reaction in her religious life, it seems. "She bore this cruel solitude stoically, armed with an ever-stronger belief in the hereafter. This faith, which she acquired at great cost in moral suffering and which few friends of hers suspected, made her sensitive to the presence of those whom she had lost."[63] Marie-Louise Bouffaron (class of 1888), another former teacher, also developed mystic inclinations. Diagnosed before the war as a neurasthenic, she quit teaching early, only to see her health continue to decline. Her efforts to secure a pension brought her desperate straits to light after the war. "She lives alone," wrote an academy inspector to his rector, "unable to stand conversing with anyone and subject to frequent crises of tears."[64] Given a pension in 1921, she lived for six more years in "almost total isolation," her only comfort her "religious faith," which "she hoped would make her well."[65]

Suggestive as these examples are, they serve better as a litmus test of fear among such ailing, lonely women than as a proof of Sévriennes' religious faith. In the first place, not all women who were alone and sickly looked to supernatural power for relief. Some made do with science. Justine Thomas (class of 1884), who began to lose her sight while still a teacher, became in her retirement "an adept and propagator of the Coné method," a would-be cure for cataracts. As one friend later remembered, "She was convinced that by applying this technique to her condition, she would not go blind completely. Thus, on any day her eyesight seemed improved, she was lighthearted."[66] Faith in a hygienic fad met

[62] Interview with Mlle Galle.
[63] L. A., "Anne Saurou," *BAES* (January 1925): 3.
[64] Dossier personnel, correspondance 1920, F17 22554, A.N.
[65] J. Michot, "Marie-Louise Bouffaron," *BAES* (January 1927): 7.
[66] N. L., "Justine Thomas," *BAES* (1931): 7.

the same emotional needs for Justine Thomas as did prayer for Marie-Louise Bouffaron. Obituaries such as hers do not provide the only proof that in retirement Sévriennes were not religious zealots. A better indication is the absence in four of every five accounts of any reference to religious faith at all. It would be hard to see in this omission a deliberate effort to conceal a central aspect of these women's lives; for when religion did play such a part, a woman's friends alluded to that fact without apology. At the death of Jeanne Michotte, a fervent Protestant (class of 1883), her Sévrienne memorialist observed, "The idea of making herself useful to others dominated her thoughts along with the deeply spiritualist meditations she so cherished."[67] Likewise, when the pious Catholic Aline Martin (class of 1885) died, her death prompted these remarks from Marie Camus-Poirier (class of 1885): "Aline was destined to be traditional. And in point of fact, she was. Her *pays*, her family, her religious rites had hold of her in the most profound depths of her heart."[68]

On the whole, however, Sévriennes seemed to treat religion with discretion. No doubt a few rejected it completely. Marie Camus-Poirier had herself done so when still at Sèvres, though since that time her views had changed considerably. "We lived at a moment," she explained about her school days, "when faith . . . was dying in us, dying of consumption. I was in the drunken springtime of my reasoning self: since I no longer believed, I refused to worship, and I thought everyone should do the same." Much later on, she claimed to see what she believed Aline Martin "already knew" at Sèvres—"that religion was a discipline and one we needed."[69] If that discovery positioned her within a broader trend of thought inside state schools, it also placed her in her generation's mainstream. The majority of Sévriennes in retirement appeared to share respect for religion without being profoundly dependent on it.

Whatever their theological convictions, one thing is clear from Sévriennes' obituaries: the moral outlook of Christianity determined their ideal of personal conduct and the idiom in which it was expressed. Far from surprising, this observation confirms a pattern repeatedly uncovered over the course of Sévriennes' careers. Our first encounter with it was at Sèvres, where Mme Favre adapted to the secular cause of girls' education the vocabulary of a proselytizing church. The favorite borrowed terms in this initial stage included words like *mission*, *sacred fire*, and above all *duty*, a vocabulary richly resonant for students living in a Protestant-inspired milieu, embellished with the teachings of the Stoics.

[67] S. C., "Jeanne Michotte," *BAES* (January 1928): 7.
[68] "Aline Martin," *BAES* (January 1920): 12.
[69] Ibid., 12–13.

Gradually, however, as the success of girls' secondary education became less problematic and its schools sure of steady growth, the discourse surrounding Sévriennes' profession changed. *Duty* alone came to express the essence of a moral outlook whose peculiar potency for women derived from the convergence in this concept of three different and complementary discourses, one conducted by the Church, another by the family, a third by the civil service corps itself. If, in the aftermath of war, the enthusiasm that electrified this generation into using their heroic imagery again gave way to less exalted notions, it was to this old discourse on duty that these Sévriennes returned, but this time with a difference. In their late careers, confident of their experience, teachers and directrices became the arbiters of what professional duty actually required from each of them.

Following upon retirement, Sévriennes' image of a properly conducted life would shift again, albeit almost imperceptibly. Obituaries offer proof for this assertion, for in these notices, the terms of praise that eulogize retired women often refer to qualities which do not derive from obligation. All the same, this shift in moral discourse did not reflect a transformation in the generation's basic outlook any more than earlier changes had. On the contrary, aging Sévriennes relied as much as ever on Christian virtues when determining the value of a woman's life. Instead of stressing only dedication to one's duty, though, obituaries placed increasing emphasis on traits of character. "Rectitude" (*droiture*) and "kindness" (*bonté*, *générosité*), twin pillars of a Christian ethic independent of both "humility" and God, became the favorite epithets of Sévriennes who totaled up their former classmates' merits. Given what we know about Sévriennes' retirement, there is nothing unforeseen about this finding. It records in moral discourse a transformation in these women's lives that we have traced throughout the chapter. Inevitably, the idea of duty lost importance as a guiding precept for the women once they withdrew from public life and lived without dependents. At this point in their lives, moral principles applicable to individuals on their own had greater relevance.

Still more revealing of this generation's consciousness is the high moral tone of nearly every obituary. Rather than listing the deceased's accomplishments or even the posts she had held, these final tributes reported mainly on intangibles. In rambling essays, Sévrienne memorialists evoked the intellectual and altruistic interests of a former classmate or her close affective ties; above all, they described and underscored her moral qualities. Indeed, the theme of exemplary conduct ran through these eulogies like a leitmotiv. Julie Esménard's (class of 1887) "whole life was an example," wrote the Sévrienne responsible for reminding others of it. "She will live in the hearts of her women friends and students for the nobility of her soul and her perfect rectitude."[70] Another Sévrienne from the same vintage considered Amélie Gandon Gonnet (class of 1888) to be an inspiring "example," too, this time "of resignation and gentleness. . . . She provided living proof of the saying so dear to one of our professors at Sèvres: 'French gaiety gives the same beautiful results as the stoicism of the ancients.' "[71] Lucie Kuss (class of 1882), also of this generation, had this to say about Berthe Savery's (class of 1881) memorable example: "The women friends who grieve for her will, in their turn, be faithful to her memory, and in death she will remain an example for them of scrupulous conscience, dedication, courage, and kindness."[72] In other tributes, the laudable conduct of a deceased classmate served as an exemplary case by implication only, as in the case of Jeanne François Antoine, who "had not only all the highest qualities of mind but those of the heart as well; she used her ingenuity to help and comfort others."[73] One after another these obituaries read like the hagiology of women for whom ambition and success had meaning only in respect to progress toward some indeterminate state of moral self-perfection. Clearly the stamp of Sèvres was still imprinted on them. With or without the rigor of a Mme Favre, the women of this generation continued to seek purpose in their lives mainly in terms of Christian values. We have in that discovery struck the bedrock of their outlook on the world.

DEATH came to Sévriennes in different ways. For the nearly blind Justine Thomas (class of 1884), it came suddenly in the form of cardiac arrest.[74] For Amélie Duporge (class of 1888), dying undoubtedly of cancer, it moved slowly, besieging first her body, then her will. "If you only knew how tired I am of life," she wrote a friend just after an operation, "how frightened I am of what the future has in store."[75] By contrast, Marguerite Duret Chollet (class of 1881), after a long and gentle illness, simply "went to sleep" one springtime evening and sometime the following morning "ceased to breathe." And as death struck Sévriennes in diverse ways, so it also caught its victims in the full variety of social settings that this chapter has described. "Taken by surprise," Adèle

---

[70] M. D., "Julie Esménard," *BAES* (1937): 5.

[71] E. G., "Madame Gonnet-Gandon," *BAES* (1930): 4–5.

[72] "Berthe Savery," *BAES* (January 1922): 4.

[73] L. Sarché, "Madame Antoine, née Jeanne François," *BAES* (1940): 6.

[74] "Justine Thomas," *BAES* (1931): 6–7.

[75] G. Marcourt, "Amélie Duporge," *BAES* (January 1913): 3.

Tritsch (class of 1881) expired "in her residence, alone."[76] Laure Défontaine Bermyn (class of 1888), a grandmother and a widow, whose demise her relatives expected, "slipped quietly away amid her family";[77] while Berthe Savery (class of 1881), one of the few lucky enough to have a live-in friend, passed away "in the arms of the admirable *amie* who had fended off her death for seven years."[78]

Death drew another distinction, though, between its victims, a distinction that would this time produce a pattern we must make an effort to explain. Unexpectedly, directrices in retirement became by comparison with retired teachers a high-risk population. Throughout the course of their careers, with the exception of the wartime period, the opposite had always been the case: teachers had consistently exhibited higher rates of illness and mortality. Now, however, directrices would become the Sévriennes in this generation most likely to die first. By 1940 fully 38 percent of the retired directrices had died, compared to 25 percent of the retired teachers.[79] In trying to explain this turnabout, we cannot look to the effect of aging only. Retired teachers and directrices shared precisely the same average birthdate (March 1865); indeed, retired directrices who died before or during 1940 were actually younger by eight months than teachers dying during the same period. Something other than the ordinary process of deterioration must explain this rise in rate of deaths among directrices.

Perhaps, as at other critical points in Sévriennes' careers, it is again appropriate to see in a phenomenon of physical decline the effects of psychological distress. Certainly, given what we know about their retirement, directrices seem likely candidates for depression. In the first place, all without exception lost their residences, homes in which at least a few had lived as long as thirty years. Moreover, the majority added to the pain of changing domiciles an even more disruptive move out of the area. Of course, returning to the familiar haunts of childhood or the proximity of family may well have eased the strains involved in moving; that, in any case, was their transparent hope. But other emotional readjustments may have had more bearing on whether a directrice found peace of mind. Above all, we must see these women as the world perceived them and as they no doubt viewed themselves, which is to say, as leaders. Inevitably, giving up not only their authority but also their prestige caused a shock to their self-image, all the more severe for their having moved away. Re-

---

[76] L. W., "Mademoiselle Tritsch," *BAES* (1936): 4–5.

[77] M. S., "Madame Bermyn-Défontaine," *BAES* (1940): 9.

[78] L. Kuss, "Berthe Savery," *BAES* (January 1922): 4.

[79] After 1940 the difference between the mortality rates of retired directrices and retired teachers from this generation began to disappear.

tired male executives often face a similarly stressful readjustment, especially if cut off from public life. For directrices, the problems of transition threatened to be worse. For they held jobs that required their
presence twenty-four hours a day. Rarely, except for one month of vacation when schools themselves were closed, would a directrice spend a
night away from school and then only when someone else had been appointed as a sitter.[80] To break with this routine and even more with the
identification it encouraged must have caused trauma in many of them.
As administrators they suffered from the same transition pains as men
retired from authoritative posts, but as maternal figures, they experienced the reversal as would a mother whose child-rearing obligations
from one day to the next abruptly ended. Viewed from this perspective,
Marie Grun's (class of 1882) last years take on a poignant meaning. Formerly directrice at Charleville's lycée, she retired to be "near a beloved
sister and old friends" at Strasbourg. Unfortunately, a former classmate
tells us, "She proved unable to enjoy retirement. Her health declined,
and slowly her memory faded too." The friend, an erstwhile school principal herself, then goes on to add this reassurance: "In compensation, her
imaginings surrounded her with happy little girls. 'They are so nice,' she
always told us. And she passed quietly away."[81] One senses, in this
tender image, the recognition of a common bond of longing candidly expressed only in the gentle madness of her friend.

The unobtrusiveness of this Sévrienne's declining years links her obituary to others in another way. As we have seen, most of them constructed a modest image of departed comrades as women competent in
their profession and exemplary in their private moral life. The rhetoric
of heroines had disappeared. In its place, necrologists suggested a vision
of these women closer to the reality of their own profession and to the
spirit of the times. The Third Republic no longer needed martyrs to the
cause of girls' education. Its schools could even do without charismatic
leaders. Competence would suffice both in teachers and directrices to
keep the state's lycées for girls full. In addition, and equally important,
the war, in retrospect, had made heroic gestures out of fashion. Heroism
as a virtue came under withering attack from survivors of that unimagin-
able ordeal who believed their generation had been duped. But in the
humble reality of their daily lives lay the most immediate inspiration for
the style of subdued praise that Sévriennes adopted. Gone were the days

[80] Mlle Lods remarked of Anna Amieux, directrice of Sèvres from 1919 to 1935: "Feeling responsible for Sèvres, Mlle Amieux considered that she ought not to spend a night
away from the school. When something unforeseen held her up in Paris, . . . she was
extremely unhappy." Interview with Mlle Lods, class of 1927 (Paris, June 1976).
[81] L. Belugou, "Marie Grun," BAES (1936): 6.

when a directrice like Aline Martin (class of 1885)—"a victim," her memorialist claims, "certainly of the war"—went magnificently to her grave, "her casket followed by the entire town."[82] Now the funeral of the ex-directrice Louise Masson (class of 1887), to which "a few former colleagues and a handful of former students came," was more in keeping with the private setting in which this generation moved.[83] Having braved a world of hostile forces, suffered from solitude and illness, and succeeded in their task so honorably as to become within their own profession a legendary corps, these Sévriennes returned to the obscurity of their modest origins and to the anonymity of women in the Third Republic.

[82] M. Poirier-Camus, "Aline Martin," *BAES* (January 1920): 11.
[83] M. H., "Louise Masson," *BAES* (1935): 13.

Conclusion

CHRONICLING the triumphs and disappointments of a single generation of women educators throughout the course of their careers brings the ground of history vividly to life. Real people confronting the opportunities and dilemmas of their times serve as a reminder of how major historical changes translate into personal experience, recreating the human scale on which the sequence of forces and events unfurls for every generation. In the case of the first Sévriennes, however, a biographical approach yields particularly rich results because of their position in the forefront of the campaign by republican reformers after 1880 to redefine bourgeois women's place within society. That definition would continue to change over the course of this generation's working lives. Between 1880 and the 1920s, three different images of women would emanate from girls' secondary schools, each reinterpreting for successive eras how middle-class women might or should relate to the public sphere of masculine dominion. Inevitably, these shifts in orientation produced in turn new models of the ideal woman educator. In the end, this transformation would not work to the advantage of the founding generation of this feminine profession. From the cutting edge of change in feminine education, the oldest Sévriennes would slip by late career into the position in their own profession of an outmoded old guard. Far from diminishing the interest of their saga, though, this outcome enhances the usefulness of their biography as a vehicle for historical investigation. At the epicenter of the changes taking place in girls' secondary schools, this generation had a pivotal role for half a century in advancing or retarding mutations in the construction of femininity in their schools. Their personal vision of the female and the way it intersected with their own experience becomes a crucial aspect of the larger story surrounding the evolving definition of how men and women fit together into French society.

A biographical approach turns out to be exceptionally revealing since it discovers the absence of a clear demarcation between the personal and the public in the way Sévriennes conceived their obligations. For years, these women could relate to their professional environment, despite its bureaucratic organization, in terms associated with domestic life. The explanation for this continuity lies, above all, in the parallels with familial relations structured consciously into their profession. Mme Favre at Sèvres had made a crucially important contribution to that feature of

322

their professional existence. By introducing rituals and symbolic language lifted purposely from a domestic setting, she single-handedly established this profession's familial mold. Afterward, guided by her inspiration, the school's Alumnae Association kept the sororal images of Sèvres alive for former classmates in their first professional organization. More important over the longer term to the persistence of domestic values was the image that women teachers found they projected in girls' schools. In the very structure of authority inside these institutions, Sévriennes encountered a replicated vision of relations in their homes. With men in charge but only intermittently present, with a maternal figure in the person of the school's directrice implicated in every aspect of daily school life, women teachers could hardly fail to conceptualize their professional world and educative task in familial terms. This duplication of cultural forms and symbols in turn ensured an easy transfer to their outlook as professionals of attitudes embedded in home life.

Three aspects of their professional orientation showed the influence of this association most particularly. One concerned relations with their students, which teachers, just like school directrices, conceived of in maternal ways. Pressed on by school inspectors, Sévriennes would rapidly adopt a mode of discipline within the classroom modeled after techniques of control used widely in the middle classes. Typically, in that domestic setting, obedient children owed their good behavior to an internalized sense of guilt born of their affection for parental figures. The architects of republican education favored a similar style of discipline in girls' secondary schools. Women teachers were expected, therefore, to create a personal bond with students whose progress they then monitored through several years of secondary studies. Their success in that endeavor would impart to girls' collèges and lycées through World War I a distinctive character, close in spirit to Protestant and Catholic schools but fashioned consciously upon the family.

Some hope for introducing a similar tone in boys' instruction inspired critics of lycée education in the early Third Republic. There, however, elitist values, associated with the mandarin profession of secondary teaching and drummed into every schoolboy grooming for the baccalauréat, resisted a nurturing ideal. That difference between girls' and boys' secondary schools did not in fact unduly disturb reforming pedagogues since it conformed to their most cherished vision of women's contribution to the nation. Responsible as adults for moralizing family life, girls even more than boys needed a school environment focused on their personal development.

That rationale in turn helps to explain a second distinctive feature of the attitudes of the first women secondary teachers. Despite their own

(margin handwritten note: important but uniquely feminine role to play)

exceptional status in a heretofore entirely masculine profession, this generation massively supported through World War I the view that women had important but uniquely feminine roles to play within society. Nothing in that position should surprise us. Bombarded with familial imagery at work, the first Sévriennes found it easy to accept the feminist assumptions of republican progressives who championed women's education not as an expression of their individual rights but in the context of their social duties.[1] Certain aspects of Sévriennes' training, namely, the demanding series of professional competitions and exams that they endured, might have fostered a more individualistic outlook. But this potential lay buried under multiple images of themselves performing special tasks as women and meeting particularly feminine obligations. Rather than a corps of educators who aspired to professional equality with men, therefore, the School of Sèvres would spawn a generation of alumnae committed through the First World War simply to expanding the responsibilities assigned specifically to women in both familial and public life.

That preoccupation itself accounts in part for the third characteristic notable in this generation, an exceptional dedication to what Sévriennes perceived as their collective educative task. Dedicated service was not unique to women in secondary teaching. Members of both professions in the Third Republic took pride in a reputation for professional zeal, and both men and women professeurs blamed the bad health common in their ranks on selfless devotion to their tasks. Women teachers, though, had far more difficulty than male colleagues in differentiating between their needs as individuals or as a professional corps and the demands placed on them by the administration. Personally, they accepted a considerable invasion of their private lives by school officials as part of their professional obligations. Collectively, they defined themselves for years as a profession not in terms of their degrees but in relation to the public institutions they served. That orientation, in turn, would make it difficult for them to press their claims upon the state forthrightly. Implicitly, the interests of their shared endeavor on behalf of girls' education always came before their right to better treatment.

It is not sufficient to recognize in this dutiful submission to collective goals simply one more example of an attitude spread widely through the ranks of teachers in the Third Republic. Nor can the novelty of their ed-

---

[1] In a major analytical article on the history of feminism, which contrasts "relational feminism" with "individualist feminism," Karen Offen argues that the former has dominated feminist thought in Germany and France since the nineteenth century while "individualist feminism" developed its strongest cultural base in England and the United States. "Defining Feminism: A Comparative Historical Approach," 119–57.

ucational mission entirely explain this generation's high degree of self-less dedication. The deeper reason for their outlook lies in the way experiences that these women had at work reinforced perceptions of themselves developed in the home around the family. Raised to see their roles in the family in the context of familial needs, these women came to their profession predisposed to subordinate their personal aspirations to the interests of the group. This inclination only strengthened in a professional milieu where the symbolic trappings of the family draped relations with superiors, colleagues, and their students. Obligated as working wives and daughters to accommodate their families' interests in plotting their careers, Sévriennes all the more readily adopted a similarly self-denying outlook toward the duties assigned to them in their profession.

This attitude, connected as it was to a more general view of women's special social contribution, did not survive unchallenged the perturbations of the postwar years. The disillusionment with heroic gestures that war had triggered in the general population furnished the background to this shift in mood among the personnel of girls' secondary schools. Nonetheless, the more important catalysts predated 1914, reaching back to the emergence in the Belle Epoque of a fundamental contradiction between the premise on which girls' education had been founded—duality in social roles for men and women—and the principle of uniformity championed by the Université in French intellectual and public life. The ministry's decision to employ the same inspectors for boys' and girls' secondary schools inadvertently set the whole development in motion, for it insured the use of common teaching methods in boys' and girls' classrooms, which in turn permitted fluidity between the systems. This fluidity first became apparent after 1902 when the baccalauréat reform introduced a track for modern languages, and graduates of girls' schools found that with just a year or two of Latin, they could pass the baccalauréat with ease. Once offered such a prospect, ever-growing numbers refused to settle for a feminine diploma. Yet the possibility of moving between these two educational systems did not apply exclusively to students. From 1914 to 1918, more than two hundred women agrégées substituted in the boys' lycées for men professeurs away at war. Meanwhile, under the influence of positivist trends in the humanities, the jury for the women's agrégations in letters and history had gradually discarded the assumption underlying a separate educational track for girls that the content of a subject ought to vary with the gender of the student. Especially after 1912, women teachers not only were to teach like men, they had to draw in every field of secondary studies on a shared body of knowledge. Thus, through the combined effect of a centralized administration, an elitist tradition in secondary education, and a scientific slant to the humanities, girls' education moved ever closer to its counterpart in boys' schools. In the process, the structural underpinnings for a dual system slowly slipped away.

For a time, the ideological moorings for feminine secondary studies held firm, strengthened by a refurbished image of middle-class women serving both the home and nation during the war. However, in the early twenties, this rationale for educating girls differently gave way under the double onslaught of students' enthusiasm for the baccalauréat and a growing dissatisfaction among women teachers with the status of their feminine profession. Both developments originated in a recognition that broad public acceptance of the meritocratic ethos of the Université doomed holders of feminine diplomas and degrees to a permanently inferior position whenever they marketed their skills. For middle-class families that became a serious concern after the war, since so many now envisioned some professional employment for their daughters. Efforts by the ministry to shore up the feminine diploma by making it equivalent to the baccalauréat could not persuade the public to accept as a guarantor of professional advancement diplomas lacking the imprimatur deriving from a standardized exam. Many women secondary teachers came reluctantly to a similar conclusion regarding both the girls' secondary diploma and their own professional degrees.

Behind that change of heart lay a gathering frustration over the treatment of women secondary educators by the state. Once the founding years had passed, girls' schools consistently received less funding per student in annual budgets for secondary education than did their masculine counterparts. That in turn affected teachers' remunerations and the working conditions imposed upon them. Willing for years to accept the resulting hardships as part of the collective mission they had undertaken, women teachers chafed under the terms of their employment once girls' secondary studies achieved respectability and their schools began to flood with students. With growing student populations already inducing restlessness before the war, the sudden surge in students' numbers afterward, together with rampaging inflation, convinced many in the teaching corps of the necessity radically to rethink their situation. This reassessment itself took shape in contact with the men's profession. Organized since 1905 into amicales affiliated with the amicales of agrégés in boys' lycées, women teachers gradually aligned their own demands with those presented by male teachers. That strategy, once adopted, rapidly revealed the preferential treatment given to the masculine profession, which even the success of women teachers assigned to boys' lycées during the war did nothing to erase. Faced with this discrimination, agrégées within the women's corps resolved to form a separate amicale and to lobby for a full alignment of girls' secondary studies and their own profession with the masculine system. Only a decisive break with the ideal of a uniquely feminine education would, they calculated, ever guarantee equality of treatment for their schools and their profession in the Université. Moreover, given the resistance within the bourgeoisie to coeducation and male instructors for their girls, to insist on masculine degrees did not jeopardize the future place of women in girls' secondary schools. On the contrary, it promised to open new careers as school inspectors and even as professors in the universities as well.

Nonetheless, among the women who pioneered girls' secondary education, the prospect of this fusion raised ambivalent feelings. Directrices, in particular, disapproved of a reform that might refocus secondary studies away from personal development toward professional concerns. Even teachers who actively supported the idea hesitated when the ministry removed the modern language option from the baccalauréat, since this would mean relinquishing a quintessentially feminine course of study for traditionally masculine studies in Greek and Latin. For all their eagerness to claim the right of women to equality of opportunity with men in the professional world, many older teachers shared with aging school heads the conviction that the needs and interests of boys and girls differed, and that their schooling should reflect that fact. Increasingly, however, the feminine component narrowed for the prewar generation to the nurturing atmosphere properly at home in girls' schools. As one teacher expressed it, "Education is not a matter of curriculums; it depends on the school where they are interpreted, on the air one breathes there, on the spirit in which minds and hearts are won to beauty and to goodness."[2] The central task of girls' secondary schools should remain as ever, she insisted, "to give youthful hearts and minds (âmes) the chance to discover themselves and a taste for self-improvement."

In the interwar years, it would be difficult but not impossible for something of that ideal to survive the implantation of the baccalauréat in girls' collèges and lycées. Several factors favored its persistence. Approval for a nurturing style of school still ran high among the public, and that opinion influenced official thinking. School inspectors continued, therefore, to lavish praise on a directrice whose administration retained the familial tone typical of feminine institutions in the Belle Epoque. Even more important to this continuity was the fact that women whose professional training dated from the prewar years lingered on as heads of girls'

---

[2] J. Peticol, "Classes mixtes et coéducation," *RU* 34, no. 2 (December 1925): 418–29, as quoted in Mavrinac, "The Anomaly of Co-Education," 22.

schools. Seconded by older teachers who had similar values, these directrices kept the old ideal of nurturing alive in girls' schools, if sometimes only in the minds of this old guard.

Against these factors, other trends, however, worked to undermine this pedagogical tradition. The growing size of schools figured prominently among them. To keep track of several hundred students called for more than good intentions on the part of a directrice. It required vigor, an exceptional memory, and a personal style congenial with the more assertive manner of students in the postwar years. School administrators, in any case, had still more pressing new concerns after the war. The reputation of their schools to a large degree now rested on how well their graduates performed in national exams. Given that reality, directrices could hardly make promoting "a taste for self-improvement" the commanding interest of their schools. Even more pernicious were new attitudes that school inspectors brought into the classroom. While girls' studies revolved around the notion of a separate female sphere, these supervisors had considered a maternal attitude toward students a central feature of a model teacher's manner in the classroom. Yet once the baccalauréat became the standard of comparison and then the favored course of study, inspectors changed criteria for judging competence in teaching. No longer would the moralizing influence of a woman teacher visibly concern them. Their yardstick for excellence, earlier a variation on the one applied in boys' schools, now derived entirely from the masculine profession.

For a time, the presence of older teachers in the classroom helped to keep alive the nurturing values favored by the first recruits to the Ecole Normale de Sèvres. Undaunted by their inspectors and often backed by a directrice, they would execute their tasks in the same ways as before, confident in their experienced opinions. Once they retired, however, a different outlook, closer to the men's profession, was sure to enter girls' secondary schools. Younger teachers, seasoned during the interwar years, were unlikely to perceive their professional obligations in the manner of retired, former colleagues. Trained as specialists in a women's profession that soon included both inspectors and university professors, they could hardly fail to redefine ambition in more individualistic ways. When such women took over the administration of girls' schools, even the image of the school directrice would change. Girls collèges and lycées would doubtless undergo a metamorphosis with the disappearance of this founding generation. From institutions committed to adolescents' intellectual and moral maturation in an atmosphere where feelings mattered, girls' schools would become a forcing ground for intellectual elites.

Still, nurturing as a pedagogical ideal was not the only prewar tradition in eclipse in girls' secondary schools. Both staff and students were bound to lose as well habits in their discourse that limned their world out to them as feminine. With uniformity the new watchword, teachers and students alike would learn to represent themselves in language heretofore perceived as masculine. Some feminists today in France anguish over what they perceive to be their intellectual subordination to male language.[3] But for the women educators who pioneered in the creation of a distinctive feminine education, the tyranny of another gender's language posed no problems. The ethos of service, which even in retirement they continued to espouse, gave these women a vocabulary intimately connected with their conception of what it meant to be a female. However repressive from the perspective of our own, individualistic values, the idiom in which they cast their lives served many of them, furthermore, exceptionally well. Born into obscurity by their class as well as sex, they had discovered in adapting feminine domestic virtues to an expanding professional world a way to magnify their own importance. Several of them won national recognition for their pains. If after retirement these women slipped back into the publicly invisible status of their birthright, unlike most women of their generation who had modeled their lives after conventional views of femininity, they at least could reminisce on better times.

[3] See for example Hélène Cixous, "The Laugh of the Medusa," in *Critical Theory Since 1965*, ed. Hazard Adams and Leroy Searle (Tallahassee: Florida State Univ. Press, 1985), 309–31, and Julia Kristeva, "Women's Time," in the same collection, 471–85.

Glossary of Frequently Used French Terms

agrégation: A competitive, juried exam that awards the highest professional degree for secondary teachers. There were separate examinations for men and women. Only the men's agrégation permitted those who passed to teach in the university.

agrégée (agrégé):   A woman (man) who has passed the agrégation.

arrêté: Ministerial order.

amicale: Professional organization of teachers that represents teachers' interests to the Ministry of Education.

baccalauréat: Examination that terminates secondary studies and permits entry into institutions of higher learning.

bachelière: A female who has passed the baccalauréat.

brevet, brevet supérieur, brevet de capacité: Accreditation exams for primary school teachers.

certificat: A diploma that girls' collèges and lycées awarded graduates in good standing after three years of schooling.

certificat d'aptitude: A professional exam for women secondary teachers prior to the agrégation.

certifiée: A woman who has passed the certificat d'aptitude exam.

chargée de cours: A woman teacher in a girls' lycée who was not agrégée and could not hold the post of lycée professeur.

chefs: Administrators who were teachers' superiors in the public school system.

collège: Municipal secondary school under contract with the state and funded by the state and the municipality.

concours: Competitive examination.

correspondance: The correspondence file in dossiers personnels.

cours secondaires: Secondary schools for girls established and financed entirely by municipalities.

diplôme: A diploma that girls' collèges and lycées awarded graduates in good standing after five years of schooling.

dossier personnel: Personnel file kept on every teacher and directrice by the Ministry of Education.

école normale supérieure: A national school for training public teachers.

leçon de chose: A method of teaching that presents abstract concepts through experience and objects drawn from ordinary life.

licence: A professional exam for teachers in boys' secondary schools taken before the agrégation.

lycée: A state secondary school.

maitresse-adjointe: A female assistant teacher at the School of Sèvres.

normalien (normalienne): A male (female) student at a normal school.

notes: Annual reports by inspectors of teachers and directrices, which were placed in their dossiers personnels.

professeur: A teacher in a cours secondaire, collège, lycée, or university.

répétitrice, maîtresse répétitrice: A female assistant teacher in a secondary school for girls.

surveillante générale: A woman vice-principal who is responsible for general maintenance in a girls' lycée.

universitaire: Member of the Université.

Université: A professional corporation made up of all teachers in secondary schools and the university.

Sources and Bibliography

LIST OF BIBLIOGRAPHICAL SUBDIVISIONS

I. MANUSCRIPT SOURCES

A. National Archives

All the essential documentation on girls' secondary schools is located in the series F17. The following list of documents consulted is arranged according to subject matter.

DOSSIERS PERSONNELS

The staff of the National Archives provided invaluable assistance by locating for me the dossiers of 213 Sévriennes who entered Sèvres between 1881 and 1890 and afterward taught in girls' secondary schools for at least one year. In all cases the dossiers are found in cartons numbered between 22000 and 25000.

ECOLE NORMALE DE SÈVRES

8808–8811. Entrance exam for Sèvres: 1881, 1882, 1883, 1884.

8808. Minutes, subjects, evaluations, and results of entrance exam to Sèvres. Age and geographic origin of applicants.

8812–8813. Entrance exam for Sèvres. 1888–1896.

14187. Ecole Normale de Sèvres. 1882–1888.

14189. Results of entrance exam for Sèvres and geographic origin of applicants who passed the written portion.

14189–14193. Entrance exam for Sèvres, dossiers of applicants and minutes based on the oral examinations. 1882–1899.

14195. Several dossiers of applicants for Sèvres.

PROFESSIONAL EXAMS

8785–8799. Documents relating to the certificat d'aptitude and the agrégation for girls' secondary education. 1883–1896.

14195–14199. Documents relating to the certificat d'aptitude and the agrégation for girls' secondary education. Organization of exams, minutes from juries, dossiers of candidates who passed written portions. 1883–1891. Several dossiers from the entrance exam for Sèvres.

WORKING PAPERS OF THE CONSEIL SUPÉRIEUR DE L'INSTRUCTION PUBLIQUE

3211. "Rapport presenté au Conseil supérieur au nom de la commission de l'enseignement secondaire des jeunes filles par Henri Bernès." Session of July 11, 1897. Curricular revisions of girls' secondary studies.

12963–12979. Proposals for decrees relating to the entrance exam for girls' lycées and collèges, the certificat following the third year of study, and the girls' diplôme. Curricula of secondary studies in girls' lycées and collèges (July–December 1881–1904).

12964. "Rapport de M. Marion au nom de la Commission chargée d'examiner le projet d'organisation de l'enseignement secondaire des jeunes filles." December 30, 1881.

12985. The reform of the agrégation and the certificat d'aptitude, July 4, 1894.

12987. Revision of the curriculum of girls' secondary education. *Section permanente* of the Conseil supérieur. June 23, 1897.

GIRLS COLLÈGES AND LYCÉES

3372. Seniority tables for personnel of girls' secondary education.

6827–6829. Reports on the condition of secondary education by the conseils académiques, 1899/1900.

8781–8783. Salaries of personnel. 1886–1890.

12748. Extraparliamentary Commission responsible for coordinating the salaries of teachers and the regulations governing them. 1906–1907.

14185. Student population every November from 1892 to 1898. Social background of parents of students in each academy, October 15, 1899.

B. *Archives: Ecole de Sèvres*

Cahiers de traditions. 1889–1936.

Class schedules.

Minutes from faculty meetings. 1882–1885, 1906–1918, 1920.

Register of administrative correspondence. 1906–. Register of meetings of the Administrative Commission established by the decree of July 24, 1882.

Results of entrance exam.

C. Archives: Association des anciennes élèves de Sèvres

Correspondence with alumnae over *Les Sévriennes* by G. Reval. 1900.

Documents and correspondence regarding gifts to alumnae. 1892–1930.

Documents and correpondence regarding representatives of girls' secondary education on the Conseil supérieur (1900–1906, 1909) and regarding academic privileges attached to the diplôme (1906).

Dossier on the exclusion from the *Bulletin* of an article by Marguerite Dubois that was hostile to collaborating with the men's profession in an association for professeurs. 1905.

Letter from Léa Camourtères regarding the interest of Sèvres's alumnae in charitable organizations. 1907.

Letter from Marguerite Lejeune to Louise Belugou regarding attacks by the press on female professeurs in the provinces. November 12, 1890.

Letters from Madeleine Sébastien Rudler and Louise Belugou concerning the proposal to establish reception committees for teachers in the provinces.

Retirement homes for women teachers. 1902–1913.

Several letters from alumnae after Mme Favre's death. 1896.

II. PRINTED SOURCES

A. Annuaries and Dictionaries

Dictionnaire de biographie française. Paris: Letouzey, 1933–.

Ministère de l'instruction publique et des beaux arts, Direction de l'enseignement secondaire, 5e Bureau. *Tableaux du personnel des lycées, collèges, et cours secondaires de jeunes filles, 1920–1923*. Paris: Imprimerie Nationale, 1920, 1921, 1922, 1923.

B. Official Publications, Collections of Documents, Reprints of Official Documents in Journals

Bauzon, Louis, ed. *La Loi Camille Sée, documents, rapports et discours relatifs à la loi sur l'enseignement secondaire des jeunes filles*. Preface by Louis Bauzon. Paris: J. Hetzel, 1881.

Bulletin administratif du Ministère de l'instruction publique, année 1890. Enseignement secondaire: instruction et règlements. Paris: Delagrave, 1890.

Chambre des députés. Deuxième législature. Session de 1879. (Annexe du procésverbal de la séance du 27 mai 1879). *Rapport au nom de la commission nommée pour l'examen de la propositon de loi de M. Camille Sée sur l'enseignement secondaire des jeunes filles, par M. Camille Sée, député, Versailles. Paris: Cerf et fils, 1879.

"Circulaire relative à la prochaine rentrée scolaire du 10 septembre." L'Enseignement secondaire des jeunes filles 2 (1915): 197–208.

Commission extraparlementaire. "Projets de décrets et arrêtés. Exposé des motifs." L'Enseignement secondaire des jeunes filles 1 (1917): 97–123.

Compayré, Gabriel. L'Enseignement secondaire des jeunes filles; legislation et organisation. 2d ed. Paris: P. Dupont, 1907.

"Décret relatif au classement des fonctionnaires des lycées, collèges, et cours secondaires du 6 septembre, 1913." L'Enseignement secondaire des jeunes filles 2 (1913): 180–85.

"Les Droits à la retraite des élèves de l'Ecole Supérieure de Sèvres." L'Enseignement secondaire des jeunes filles 1 (1897): 181–84. Excerpt from debate in Senate in which Joseph Fabre defends rights of women secondary teachers and Sévriennes.

"L'Ecole de Sèvres depuis sa fondation." L'Enseignement secondaire des jeunes filles 2 (1900): 16–46.

"L'Enseignement secondaire des jeunes filles pendant la guerre (Académie de Paris). Rapport présenté au Conseil académique (extraits)." L'Enseignement secondaire des jeunes filles 2 (1915): 107–20.

"Instructions relatives à l'enseignement de l'histoire et de la géographie dans les lycées et collèges de garçons et de jeunes filles." Revue universitaire 1 (1908): 314–17.

Ministère de l'instruction publique et des beaux arts. Direction de l'enseignement secondaire. Instructions concernant les programmes de l'enseignement secondaire (garçons et jeunes filles). Paris: Delagrave, [1910].

————. Enseignement secondaire, instructions et règlements, année 1890. Bulletin administratif du Ministère de l'instruction publique. Supplement to no. 922. Paris: Delagrave, 1890.

————. Instructions concernant les programmes de l'enseignement secondaire (garçons et jeunes filles). Paris: Delagrave, 1909.

"Projet de loi relatif à l'avancement des fonctionnaires de l'enseignement secondaire." Revue universitaire 1 (1908): 228–31.

Proposition de loi de M. Camille Sée sur l'enseignement secondaire des jeunes filles. Discours prononcé par M. Camille Sée, rapporteur de la commission. Séance du 19 janvier 1880. Paris: Delagrave, 1880.

Sée, Camille, ed. Lycées et collèges de jeunes filles. Documents, rapports et discours à la Chambre des députés et au Sénat. Décrets, arrêtés, circulaires, etc. Tableau du personnel des lycées et collèges par ordre d'ancienneté. . . . Préface par M. Camille Sée. Paris: Cerf, 1884. The seventh edition for the International Exhibition of 1900 includes prospectuses from several girls' lycées and collèges.

"Tableau des traitements du personnel enseignant, du personnel administratif, du personnel du service économique et du personnel de la surveillance des lycées et collèges de jeunes filles, 1904." Revue de l'enseignement secondaire des jeunes filles 1 (1904): 43.

Villemot, Antoine. "Etude sur l'organisation, le fonctionnement et les progrès de l'enseignement secondaire des jeunes filles en France de 1879 à 1887 (extrait)." Reprinted in *L'Enseignement secondaire des jeunes filles* 1 (1905): 57–83, 114–34, 164–84, 209–16, 258–63.

————. *Exposition universelle de 1889. Enseignement secondaire. Documents, publications et ouvrages récents relatifs à l'éducation des femmes et à l'enseignement secondaire des jeunes filles.* Paris: P. Dupont, 1889.

C. Journals

Bulletin de l'Union française des associations d'anciennes élèves des lycées et collèges de jeunes filles. 1900–1910.

Bulletin mensuel de l'Association des élèves de Sèvres, 1887–1894, became *Bulletin trimestriel de l'Association des élèves de Sèvres,* 1895–1917, and then *Bulletin de l'Association des élèves de Sèvres,* 1917–1939.

L'Enseignement secondaire des jeunes filles. Published monthly from July 1881 to January 1919 with Camille Sée as editor. After his death, his son Pierre Sée edited the journal until 1927. In that year the name was changed to *Revue de l'enseignement secondaire des jeunes filles* and published by the Delalain press through 1939.

Famille et lycée. Publication of the Fédération des associations de parents d'élèves des lycées et collèges, founded in 1906. Issues consulted: 1914–1920.

Revue universitaire, founded January 15, 1892. Issues consulted: 1892–1939.

D. Selected Publications by First-Generation Sévriennes

I will not include in this list the death notices written by Sévriennes for their deceased friends that appeared in the Alumnae Association bulletin or the speeches given by Sévrienne directrices at the prize ceremonies in 1915–1917. Those cited in the study appear in the footnotes.

Allégret, L[éonie]. "L'Internat des lycées des jeunes filles et l'Université." *Revue universitaire* 2 (1912): 19–26.

Amieux, Anna. "Chez les Sévriennes." *Revue des deux mondes* 3 (1928): 87–105.

————. "Enquête sur les tendances actuelles de la jeunesse en France." *Bulletin de l'Association des élèves de Sèvres* (1929): 62–69.

————. "L'Enseignement des sciences dans les lycées de jeunes filles et la réforme des classes préparatoires." *Revue universitaire* 1 (1910): 311–20, 437–47.

————. "Le Problème de la natalité et l'éducation secondaire des jeunes filles françaises." *L'Enseignement secondaire des jeunes filles* 2 (1921): 193–201.

Anonymous. "A propos des Associations de bienfaisance des lycées et des collèges de jeunes filles." *Bulletin trimestriel de l'Association des élèves de Sèvres* (April 1899): 6–8.

Anonymous. "Bureaux de bienfaisance des lycées et cours d'adultes." *Bulletin trimestriel de l'Association des élèves de Sèvres* (January 1899): 10–13.

Anonymous. "En attendant . . . restons secondaires." *Revue universitaire* 2 (1912): 200–211.

Anonymous. "Notes de lecture. Le jeune professeur en province (J. J. Weiss)." *Bulletin mensuel de l'Association des élèves de Sèvres* 29 (1890): 7–10.

Anonymous. "Note sur un article de Mlle Dugard. La question des parents." Bulletin trimestriel de l'Association des élèves de Sèvres (March 1900): 3–8.

Anonymous. "L'Oeuvre de Madame Jules Favre à l'Ecole." *Bulletin trimestriel de l'Association des élèves de Sèvres* (May 1986): 1–5.

Anonymous. "Quelques Réflexions sur le professeur." *Bulletin mensuel de l'Association des élèves de Sèvres* 38 (April–May 1890): 1–3.

Aron, Marguerite. "Le Journal d'une Sévrienne." *L'Enseignement secondaire des jeunes filles.* 1 (1901): 5–; 2 (1902): 5–.

———. *Le Journal d'une Sévrienne.* Paris: Alcan, 1912.

———. "La Mode et les examens dans l'éducation féminine." *L'Enseignement secondaire des jeunes filles* 2 (1912): 248–53.

———. "Pour l'amélioration de l'enseignement féminin." *L'Enseignement secondaire des jeunes filles* 1 (1912): 200–203.

Bastoul, B[erthe]. "Devoirs-confidences." *Revue universitaire* 1 (1913): 29–40.

———. "Lycées mondains." *Revue universitaire* 1 (1912): 29–41.

———. "Les Sanctions des études secondaires féminine: baccalauréat ou diplôme." *Revue universitaire* 2 (1910): 386–97.

Belugou, L[ouise]. "A propos du diplôme de fin d'études." *Bulletin trimestriel de l'Association des élèves de Sèvres* (April 1905): 68–71.

———. "Les Carrières nouvelles ouvertes aux femmes." *Bulletin annuel des élèves et anciennes élèves de Sèvres* (1918): 30–45.

———. "Madame Jules Favres." Preface to Mme Jules Favre, *La Morale de Plutarque.* Paris: Henry Paulin, 1909.

———. "Pour l'après-guerre: carrières qui s'ouvrent aux élèves de lycées et collèges de jeunes filles." *Bulletin de l'Association des anciennes élèves de Sèvres* (January 1917): 47–52.

Belugou, L., J. Michotte, and J. Lochert. "Compte rendu de l'inauguration du buste de Madame Jules Favres le 31 Mai 1898." *Bulletin trimestriel de l'Association des élèves de Sèvres* (1898): 1–15.

Ben-Aben, Jeanne. "Souvenirs de Sèvres." *La Grande Revue* 42 (May 24, 1907).

Bérard, Léa [Camourtères], *Ce qu'il faut savoir du féminisme en 1924.* Agen: Revue féministe du Sud-ouest, 1924.

———. *Héroisme au service de la France. Les décorées de la Grande Guerre, 1914–1919.* Paris, S.A.D.A.G., n.d.

———. "L'Université et le féminisme: le rôle des éducatrices dans le féminisme." *La Française* (March 15, 1908): 1.

Bérard, L[éa Camourtères], and Eugène Blun. *Cours de morale théorique et notions historiques pour l'enseignement secondaire des jeunes filles.* Paris: Alcan, 1903.

Bérillon, Lucie. *La Préparation au bonheur (essai de psychologie appliquée).* Paris: Jouve, 1933.

Caron, M[arguerite]. "Cinquante Ans de vie de l'enseignement secondaire féminin 1881–1931." *L'Enseignement secondaire des jeunes filles* 1 (1931): 398–409.

————. "Les Demi-services dans l'enseignement féminin." *Revue universitaire* 1 (1918): 352–55.

————. [published anonymously]. "Un Lycée de jeunes filles en temps de guerre 1914." *Revue universitaire* 1 (1915): 247–60.

————. "Quelques Remarques à propos de la réforme de l'enseignement secondaire des jeunes filles." *L'Enseignement secondaire des jeunes filles* 1 (1924): 322–26.

Colani, Jeanne, and M. E. Driault. *Histoire nationale et notions sommaires d'histoire. Troisième année.* Paris: Alcan, 1908.

Crouzet-Ben-Aben, Jeanne P. "Bulletin de l'enseignement secondaire des jeunes filles." *Revue universitaire.* This was a regular publication that appeared in every issue beginning in 1909.

————. "Monographie d'une éducation masculine de femmes." *Revue universitaire* 1 (1917): 331–40.

————. *Souvenirs d'une jeune fille bête. Souvenirs autobiographiques d'une des premières agrégées de France.* Paris: Debresse, 1971.

————. "Le Surménage du personnel féminin." *Revue universitaire* 1 (1910): 414–25.

Dreyfus, Mathilde. *Leçons d'hygiène et d'économie domestique.* Paris: Alcan, 1903.

Dubois, H[élène]. "Sèvres et Fontenay." *L'Enseignement secondaire des jeunes filles* 1 (1896): 145–47.

Ecolan, A[ntoinette]. "Du régime de l'internat pour les jeunes filles." *L'Enseignement secondaire des jeunes filles* 1 (1897): 193–98.

————. "L'Education de la femme française: la discipline par l'affection." *L'Enseignement secondaire des jeunes filles* 2 (1928–1929): 40–42.

————. "L'Enseignement de la morale dans les lycées et collèges de jeunes filles." *L'Enseignement secondaire des jeunes filles* 2 (1897): 5–10.

————. "La Fraude dans les compositions." *L'Enseignement secondaire des jeunes filles* 2 (1923): 145–47.

————. "Nos Maîtresses d'internat." *Revue universitaire* 2 (1911): 209–14.

Ecole Normale Supérieure de l'enseignement secondaire de jeunes filles. *Le Cinquantenaire de l'Ecole de Sèvres 1881–1931.* Paris: Printory, 1932.

Flobert, E[mma Rémoussin]. "L'Inauguration du buste de Monsieur Camille Sée à l'Ecole Normale Supérieure de Sèvres," *L'Enseignement secondaire des jeunes filles* 1 (1919): 181–203.

Israël-Wahl, Berthe. "La Fête du Trocadéro." *Bulletin trimestriel de l'Association des élèves de Sèvres* (December 1908): 139–43.

Kuss, L[ucie]. "Le 25e anniversaire du Lycée Victor-Hugo." *L'Enseignement secondaire des jeunes filles* 2 (1921): 29–39.

Lacharrière, M[arie]. "Les Récréations dans les lycées de jeunes filles." *Bulletin mensuel de l'Association des élèves de Sèvres* (November 1888): 1–5.

Lejeune, M[arguerite]. "L'Enseignement moral: lettre de Mlle Lejeune." *L'Enseignement secondaire des jeunes filles* 2 (1897): 49–52.

Lhullier, M[arie-Louise]. *Leçons de chimie.* Paris: Mony, 1898.

Masson, L[ouise]. "De l'education du goût dans les classes de lettres." *L'Enseignement secondaire des jeunes filles* 1 (1896): 241–56.

———. "De l'education du raisonnement dans les classes de lettres." *L'Enseignement secondaire des jeunes filles* 1 (1896): 61–77.

Michotte, J[eanne], and J[ulie] Lochert. "Compte rendu de l'inauguration du buste de Madame Jules Favre le 31 mai 1898." *Bulletin trimestriel de l'Association des élèves de Sèvres* (October 1898): 1–15.

Réval, G. [Gabrielle Logerot.] *La Grande Parade des Sévriennes*. Paris: Fayard, 1933.

———. *Un Lycée de jeunes filles*. Paris: Ollendorf, 1902.

———. *Les Sévriennes*. Paris: Ollendorf, 1900.

Rudler, Madeleine Sébastien. *Enseignement ménager*. Paris: Félix Juven, 1911.

Salomon, A[lice Caen]. *Leçons d'arithmétique*. Paris, 1900.

Sapy, P[ierette]. "Les Associations de professeurs de l'enseignement secondaire des jeunes filles." *Bulletin trimestriel de l'Association des élèves de Sèvres* (January 1905): 13–19.

Teutscher, F. "Sur quelques insuffisances de l'enseignement féminin." *Revue universitaire* 1 (1911): 33–37.

———. "Un Défaut de l'enseignement supérieur féminin," *Revue universitaire* 2 (1910): 24–27.

Vigié, Madeleine. *Pour servir à l'histoire des lycées de jeunes filles*. Etampes: La Semeuse, 1913.

Vigié-Lecocq, E. *La Poésie contemporaine*. Paris: Société du Mercure, 1896.

E. Articles and Books by Contemporaries or Earlier Commentators

Anonymous. "De Mme Clément–Baumann à Mme X . . . Shanghai." *L'Enseignement secondaire des jeunes filles* 2 (1904): 196–200.

Anonymous. "L'Ecole de Sèvres." *L'Enseignement secondaire des jeunes filles* 1 (1896): 193–208.

Anonymous. "L'Egalité des traitements masculins et féminins dans l'enseignement secondaire." *L'Enseignement secondaire des jeunes filles* 1 (1907): 193–97.

Anonymous. "Les Lycées et collèges de jeunes filles et les victimes de la guerre." *L'Enseignement secondaire des jeunes filles* 1 (1915): 97–113.

Anonymous. "Oeuvres des lycées." *L'Enseignement secondaire des jeunes filles* 2 (1923): 281–82.

Anonymous. "Pour nos professeurs-femmes (isolement, solitude et solidarité)." *L'Enseignement secondaire des jeunes filles* 2 (1902): 49–53, 198–202.

Anonymous. "La Question du relèvement des traitements du personnel secondaire féminin." *L'Enseignement secondaire des jeunes filles* 2 (1906): 254–55.

Anonymous. "Réponses au questionnaire relatif à la réforme de l'enseignement secondaire féminin." *Bulletin de l'Association des Élèves de Sèvres* (January 1923): 29–33.

Anonymous. "La Spécialisation des professeurs d'histoire et des professeurs de lettres dans l'enseignement secondaire des jeunes filles." *Revue universitaire* 2 (1909): 299–304.

Beard, George M. *A Practical Treatise on Nervous Exhaustion (Neurasthenia)*. New York: W. Wood, 1905.

Beauvoir, Simone de. *Quand prime le spirituel*. Paris: Gaillard, 1979. She wrote this novel in the 1920s, but it was not published until 1979.

Bouveret, Dr. L. *La Neurasthénie: épuisement nerveux*. Paris: Baillière, 1891.

Bréal, M. *Quelques Mots sur l'instruction publique en France*. Paris: Hachette, 1872.

Brisson, Adolphe. "Jules Ferry et l'enseignement secondaire des jeunes filles." *L'Enseignement secondaire des jeunes filles* 1 (1893): 164–70.

———. "La Question du pot-au-feu et l'éducation de la future maîtresse de maison dans les lycées et collèges de jeunes filles." *L'Enseignement secondaire des jeunes filles* 1 (1885): 132–35.

———. "Soixante ans de souvenirs (Monsieur Legouvé)." *L'Enseignement secondaire des jeunes filles* 1 (1887): 252–81.

Combarieu, J. "L'Enseignement secondaire des jeunes filles pendant la guerre: Académie de Paris. Rapport présenté au Conseil académique (Extraits)." *L'Enseignement secondaire des jeunes filles* 1 (1915): 49–53, 2 (1915): 107–20.

Crouzet, Paul. "L'Enseignement secondaire dans l'Académie de Paris depuis la guerre." *Revue universitaire* 2 (1920): 179–98.

Daubié, J.-V. *Des Progrès de l'instruction primaire*. Paris: Imprimerie de Mme Claye, ca. 1862.

———. *La Femme pauvre au XIXe siècle*. Paris: Guillaumin, 1866.

Delluc, Elodie. "Le Cours de morale de 3e année dans l'enseignement secondaire des jeunes filles." *L'Enseignement secondaire des jeunes filles* 2 (1897): 11–17.

Deprez, Mlle. "Contribution pour l'enseignement secondaire féminin français." *L'Enseignement secondaire féminin français* 2 (1913): 150–59.

Desparmet-Ruello, J. *Les Programmes de sciences dans les lycées des jeunes filles: réponse à M. Camille Sée*. Paris: Guillaumin, 1884.

Dionot, M. "Liberté et entr'aide dans les exercises scolaires." *L'Enseignement secondaire des jeunes filles* 2 (1924): 206–11.

Dugard, M. "De la jeunesse féminine d'aujourd'hui." *Revue universitaire* 1 (1928): 236–43.

———. "Du surmenage des femmes professeurs dans l'enseignement secondaire des jeunes filles." *Revue universitaire* 1 (1895): 107–38.

Dupuy, Paul. "L'Ecole Normale de Sèvres." *L'Enseignement secondaire des jeunes filles* 2 (1882): 32–33, 151–57.

———. "L'Etat actuel de l'enseignement secondaire des jeunes filles d'après une publication récente." *L'Enseignement secondaire des jeunes filles* 1 (1887): 241–58, 1 (1888): 5–18, 121–34, 2 (1888): 193–202.

Ecole Normale Supérieure. *Le Centenaire de l'Ecole Normale 1795–1895*. Paris: Hachette, 1895.

Ecole Normale Supérieure d'enseignement primaire de Saint-Cloud. *Livre-Souvenir (1881–1906)*. Paris: Alcide Picard et Kaan, 1906.

Fabre, Joseph. "Discours prononcé aux obsèques de Mme Jules Favre, Directrice de l'Ecole de Sèvres." *L'Enseignement secondaire des jeunes filles* 1 (1896): 84–87.

Favre, Mme Jules. Preface to Jean Paul Richter, *Sur l'Education*, 1–35. Paris, 1886.

Fénélon, François de Salignac de la Mothe, Abp. *Fénélon on Education: A Translation of the "Traité de l'éducation des filles" and Other Documents Illustrating Fénélon's Educational Theories and Practice.* Edited by H. C. Barnard. Cambridge: Cambridge Univ. Press, 1960.

Fouillée, Alfred J. E. *La Conception morale et civique de l'enseignement.* Paris: La Revue bleue, 1902.

———. *Les Elements sociologiques de la morale.* Paris: F. Alcan, 1896.

———. *Le Mouvement positiviste et la conception sociologique du monde.* Paris: F. Alcan, 1896.

Gaultier, Paul. "La Crise de la charité." *La Revue bleue* 4 (1905): 187–91.

Gayraud, Amélie. *Les Jeunes Filles d'aujourd'hui. Enquête de "L'Opinion."* Paris: Oudin, 1914.

Gayraud, Louise-Amélie. "Pour une éducation plus intellectuelle et plus féminine." *Revue universitaire* 2 (1917): 174–81.

Ghinijonet, L. *Précis de l'éducation des jeunes personnes dans les pensionnats et autres établissements d'instruction.* Paris: H. Casterman, 1860.

Godlewski, Dr. A. *Les Neurasthénies.* Paris: A. Maloine, 1904.

Gonnet, A. "Le Diplôme de fin d'études dans les lycées et collèges de jeunes filles." *Revue universitaire* 2 (1905): 1–18.

Gréard, Octave. *L'Enseignement secondaire des filles: mémoire présenté au Conseil académique de Paris dans la séance du 27 juin 1882.* Paris: Delagrave, 1882.

Guénot, H. "Contre l'identification des programmes masculins et des programmes féminins." *Revue universitaire* 2 (1916): 118–26.

———. "Culture générale." *L'Enseignement secondaire des jeunes filles* 2 (1921): 99–104.

———. "L'Enseignement secondaire des filles et l'avenir de la race française." *Revue universitaire* 1 (1918): 1–11.

Guénot, H., and M. Dionot. "Lettre aux parents de nos élèves." *L'Enseignement secondaire des jeunes filles* 2 (1923): 145–47.

Laurent, Dr. Emile. *La Neurasthénie et son traitement vade-mecum du médecin praticien.* Paris: A. Maloine, 1895.

Lavisse, Ernest. "Discours: les fêtes des lycées et collèges de jeunes filles." *Revue universitaire* 2 (1907): 58–63.

Legouvé, Ernest. *Dernier travail, derniers souvenirs. Ecole Normale de Sèvres.* Paris: Hetzel, 1898.

———. *La Femme en France au XIXe siècle.* Paris: Hetzel, 1873.

———. *Histoire morale des femmes.* Paris: Sandré, 1848.

———. *Nos Filles et nos fils. Scènes et études de famille.* 9th ed. Paris: Hetzel, 1881.

———. *La Question des femmes.* Paris: Hetzel, 1881.

Lemonnier, H[enry]. "L'Ecole de Sèvres depuis sa fondation (1881–1900)." *L'Enseignement secondaire des jeunes filles* 2 (1900): 5–12.

———. "L'Inauguration du buste de Mme Jules Favre, Discours de M. Henry Lemonnier." *L'Enseignement secondaire des jeunes filles* 2 (1898): 30–32.

Levillain, Dr. F[erdinand]. *La Neurasthénie: épuisement nerveux*. Paris: A. Maloine, 1891.

———. *La Neurasthénie: maladie de Beard*. Paris: A. Maloine, 1891.

Marion, Henri. *La Pyschologie des femmes, cours professé pendant plusieurs années à la Sorbonne* Paris: A. Colin, 1900.

Martini, J. "L'Education de la femme française." *Revue de l'enseignement secondaire des jeunes filles* 1 (1927–1928): 300–303.

Mathieu, Dr. A. *Neurasthénie (épuisement nerveux)*. Paris: J. Rueff, 1892.

Michelet, Jules. *Du prêtre, de la femme et de la famille*. Paris: M. Lévy, 1845.

Misme, Jane. "L'Université et le féminisme." *La Française* (March 1908): 1–2.

Parmentier, Mathilde. "Les Retraits des fonctionnaires de l'enseignement secondaire des jeunes filles." *Revue universitaire* 2 (1907): 26–30.

Petit, Edouard. "Situation et role des associations d'anciens élèves et d'anciennes élèves." *Revue universitaire* 2 (1900): 344–59.

Poirier, M. "Le 'Sou des Lycées.'" *L'Enseignement secondaire des jeunes filles* 2 (1914): 193–99.

Proust, A., and B. Ballet. *L'Hygiène du neurasthénique*. Paris: Masson, 1897.

Renal, E. *La Réforme intellectuelle et morale*. Paris: Calmann-Lévy, 1871.

Rousselot, Paul, ed. *La Pédagogie féminine*. Paris: Delagrave, 1881.

Roy, E. "La Spécialisation des enseignements." *La Française* (November 1906): 3.

Sée, Camille. "Une Lacune à combler." *Revue de l'enseignement secondaire des jeunes filles* 2 (1908): 118–19.

Sonday, Paul. "Henri Marion." *L'Enseignement secondaire des jeunes filles* 1 (1896): 177–79.

———. "Mme Jules Favre." *L'Enseignement secondaire des jeunes filles* 1 (1896): 78–83.

Strepeno, E. "L'Education pratique dans l'enseignement secondaire des jeunes filles." *L'Enseignement secondaire des jeunes filles* 1 (1892): 193–200.

Suran-Mabire, C. "La Réforme de l'enseignement secondaire féminin et les associations de professeurs." *Revue universitaire* 2 (1916): 203–17.

Szejko, Dr. Jadwiga. *L'Influence de l'éducation sur le développement de la neurasthénie*. Lyon: A. Rey, 1902.

Vigouroux, Dr. R. *Neurasthénie et arthritisme*. Paris: A. Maloine, 1893.

Weill, Renée. "Rapport sur l'Union française des associations des anciennes élèves des lycées et collèges de jeunes filles." *Bulletin trimestriel de l'Association des élèves de Sèvres* (July 1904): 257–61.

———. "L'Union française des associations d'anciennes élèves des lycées et collèges de jeunes filles." *Revue universitaire* 1 (1905): 114–18.

Wurmser-Dégouy, Henriette. *Trois Éducatrices modernes*. Paris: Presses universitaires de France, 1930.

Wychgram, Dr. Jacob *L'Instruction publique des filles en France*. Translated by E. Esparcel. Paris: Delagrave, 1885.

Zola, Emile. *Au bonheur des dames*. Préface d'Armand Lanoux. Paris: Fasquelle, n.d.

III. SELECTED SECONDARY WORKS

Abbot, Andrew. *The System of Professions: An Essay on the Division of Expert Labor*. Chicago: Univ. of Chicago Press, 1988.

Acomb, Evelyn. *The French Laic Laws, 1879–1889: The First Anti-Clerical Campaign of the Third French Republic*. New York: Columbia Univ. Press, 1941.

Adams, Hazard, and Leroy Searle, eds. *Critical Theory Since 1965*. Tallahassee: Florida State Univ. Press, 1985.

Agulhon, Maurice. *Le Cercle dans la France bourgeoise: 1810–1848*. Paris: A. Colin, 1977.

Anderson, Robert. *Education in France, 1848–1870*. Oxford: Oxford Univ. Press, 1975.

Auspitz, Katherine. *The Radical Bourgeoisie: The Ligue de l'Enseignement and the Origins of the Third Republic, 1866–1885*. Cambridge: Cambridge Univ. Press, 1982.

Baker, Donald N., and Patrick J. Harrigan, eds. *The Making of Frenchmen: Current Directions in the History of Education in France, 1679–1979*. Waterloo: Historical Reflections Press, 1980.

Beauvoir, Simone de. *The Second Sex*. Translated and edited by H. M. Parshley. New York: Bantam, 1961.

Bell, Susan Groag, and Karen M. Offen. *Women, the Family, and Freedom: The Debate in Documents*. 2 vols. Stanford: Stanford Univ. Press, 1983.

Bledstein, Burton. *The Culture of Professionalism: The Middle Class and the Development of Higher Education in America*. New York: W. W. Norton, 1976.

Bourdieu, P., and J.-C. Passeron. *Reproduction in Education, Society and Culture*. Translated by Richard Nice. London: Sage Publications, 1977.

Brumberg, Joan Jacobs, and Nancy Tomes. "Women in the Professions: A Research Agenda for American Historians." *Reviews in American History* 10, no. 2 (1982): 275–06.

Canovan, Margaret. "Rousseau's Two Concepts of Citizenship." In *Women in Western Political Philosophy*, edited by Ellen Kennedy and Susan Mendus, 78–105. New York: St. Martin's Press, 1987.

Carr, Philip. *The French at Home in the Country and in Town*. London: Methuen and Co., 1930.

Charle, Christophe. *Les Elites de la République 1880–1900*. Paris: Fayard, 1987.

Charrier, Edmée. *L'Evolution intellectuelle féminine*. Paris: Editions Albert Mechelinck, 1931.

Clark, Linda L. "A Battle of the Sexes in a Professional Setting: The Introduction of *Inspectrices Primaires, 1889–1914.*" *French Historical Studies* 16, no. 1 (1989): 96–125.

―――. *Schooling the Daughters of Marianne: Textbooks and the Socialization of Girls in Modern French Primary Schools.* Albany: State Univ. of New York Press, 1984.

Coirault, G. *Les Cinquante Premières Années de l'enseignement secondaire féminin, 1880–1930.* Tours: Arrault, 1940.

Cott, Nancy F. *The Grounding of Modern Feminism.* New Haven: Yale Univ. Press, 1987.

Darrow, Margaret. "French Noblewomen and the New Domesticity, 1750–1850." *Feminist Studies* 5, no. 1 (1979): 41–64.

Daumard, Adeline. *La Bourgeoisie parisienne de 1815 à 1848.* Paris: S.E.V.P.E.N., 1963.

Davidoff, Leonore, and Catherine Hall. *Family Fortunes: Men and Women of the English Middle Class, 1780–1850.* Chicago: Univ. of Chicago Press, 1987.

Elshtain, Jean Bethke. *Public Man, Private Woman.* Princeton: Princeton Univ. Press, 1981.

Elwitt, Sanford. *The Making of the Third Republic: Class and Politics in France 1868–1884.* Baton Rouge: Louisiana State Univ. Press, 1975.

―――. *The Third Republic Defended: Bourgeois Reform in France, 1880–1914.* Baton Rouge, Louisiana State Univ. Press, 1986.

Eros, John. "The Positivist Generation of French Republicanism." *Sociological Review* 3 (1955): 255–73.

Farge, Arlette, and Christiane Klapisch-Zuber, eds. *Madame ou Mademoiselle? itinéraires de la solitude féminine 18e–20e siècle.* Paris: Editions Montalba, 1984.

Faure, Marthe, and Marguerite Schwob. "La Société des Agrégées 1920–1948," *Bulletin officiel de la Société des Agrégées* 162 (1968): 551–60.

Foucault, Michel. *The History of Sexuality.* Vol. 1, *An Introduction.* Translated by Alan Sheridan. New York: Hurley, 1978.

Furet, François, ed. *Jules Ferry, fondateur de la République: actes du colloque.* Paris: Editions de l'Ecole des hautes études en sciences sociales, 1985.

Geison, Gerald L. *Professions and the French State, 1700–1900.* Philadelphia: Univ. of Pennsylvania Press, 1983.

Gerbod, Paul. *La Condition universitaire en France au XIXe siècle.* Paris: Presses universitaires de France, 1965.

―――. *La Vie quotidienne dans les lycées et collèges au XIXe siècle.* Paris: Presses universitaires de France, 1968.

Glazer, Penina Migdal, and Miriam Slater. *Unequal Colleagues: The Entrance of Women into the Professions, 1890–1940.* New Brunswick, N.J.: Rutgers Univ. Press, 1987.

Goblot, Edmond. *La Barrière et le niveau, étude sociologique de la bourgeoisie française moderne.* Paris: F. Alcan, 1925.

Goldstein, Jan. "The Hysteria Diagnosis and the Politics of Anticlericalism in Late

Nineteenth-Century France," *The Journal of Modern History* 54, no. 2 (1982): 209–39.

Gontard, Maurice. *L'Enseignement secondaire en France de la fin de l'Ancien Régime à la loi Falloux, 1750–1850.* Aix-en-provence: Edisud, 1984.

Hacquard, Georges. *Histoire d'une institution française: l'Ecole alsacienne.* Vol. 1, *Naissance d'une école libre, 1871–1891.* Paris: Editions Garnier Frères, 1982.

Harris, Barbara J. *Beyond Her Sphere: Women and the Professions in American History.* Westport, Conn.: Greenwood Press, 1978.

Haskell, Thomas L. *The Authority of Experts: Studies in History and Theory.* Bloomington: Indiana Univ. Press, 1984.

Hause, Steven C. "Anti-Protestant Rhetoric in the Early Third Republic." *French Historical Studies* 16, no. 1 (1989): 183–201.

Hause, Steven C., with Anne R. Kenney. *Women's Suffrage and Social Politics in the French Third Republic.* Princeton: Princeton Univ. Press, 1984.

Hayward, J.E.S. "The Official Social Philosophy of the French Third Republic: Léon Bourgeois and Solidarism." *International Review of Social History* 4 (1961): 261–81.

Higonnet, Margaret, et al., eds. *Behind the Lines: Gender and the Two World Wars.* New Haven: Yale Univ. Press, 1987.

Hoffmann, Stanley, et al. *In Search of France: The Economy, Society, and Political System of France in the Twentieth Century.* Cambridge: Harvard Univ. Press, 1963.

Horvath-Peterson, Sandra. *Victor Duruy and French Education: Liberal Reform in the Second Empire.* Baton Rouge: Louisiana State Univ. Press, 1984.

Hufton, Olwen. *The Poor of Eighteenth Century France, 1750–1789.* Oxford: Clarendon, 1974.

———. "Women and the Family Economy in Eighteenth Century France." *French Historical Studies* 9, no. 3 (1975): 1–22.

Hunt, Persis Charles. "Syndicalism and Feminism among Teachers in France, 1900–1920." Ph.D. diss. Tufts Univ., 1975.

John, Angela V., ed. *Unequal Opportunities: Women's Employment in England, 1800–1918.* Oxford: Basil Blackwell, 1986.

Karady, Victor. "Normaliens et autres enseignants à la Belle Epoque. Note sur l'origine sociale et la réussite dans une profession intellectuelle." *Revue française de sociologie* 12 (1972): 35–58.

Knibiehler, Yvonne. *Nous les assistantes sociales.* Paris: Aubier-Montaigne, 1980.

Kunzel, Regina G. "The Professionalization of Benevolence: Evangelicals and Social Workers in the Florence Crittenton Homes, 1915 to 1945." *Journal of Social History* 22, no. 1 (1988): 21–43.

Landes, Joan. *Women and the Public Sphere in the Age of the French Revolution.* Ithaca: Cornell Univ. Press, 1988.

Langlois, Claude. *Le Catholicisme au féminin.* Paris: Cerf, 1984.

Legrand, Louis. *L'Influence du positivism dans l'oeuvre scolaire de Jules Ferry: les origines de la laïcité.* Paris: M. Rivière, 1961.

Lévy, Marie-Françoise. *De mères en filles: l'éducation des françaises 1850–1880*. Paris: Calmann-Lévy, 1984.

Lewis, Jane, ed. *Women's Experience of Home and Family, 1840–1914*. Oxford: Basil Blackwell, 1986.

Lougee, Carolyn. "Noblesse, Domesticity, and Agrarian Reform: The Education of Girls by Fenelon and Saint Cyr." *History of Education Quarterly* 14, no. 1 (Spring 1974): 87–114.

McBride, Theresa. "A Woman's World: Department Stores and the Evolution of Women's Employment, 1870–1920." *French Historical Studies* 10, no. 4 (1978): 664–83.

Margadant, Jo Burr. "Aging in a Changing Profession: Girls' Secondary Schools in the 1920s and 1930s in France." Paper presented at the Social Science Historical Association Conference, Saint Louis, October 19, 1986.

————. "Ambition in a Women's Profession: The First Generation of Sévriennes, 1881–1930." Paper presented at the American Historical Association, San Francisco, December 29, 1983.

————. "Are Women Different? The Medical History of Women Educators in the Third Republic." Paper presented at the French Historical Studies Association, Los Angeles, March, 1985.

Martin-Fugier, A. *La Bourgeoise. La Femme au temps de Paul Bourget*. Paris: Grasset, 1983.

Mavrinac, Marilyn. "The Anomaly of Co-education in the French Secondary System." Paper presented at the Social Science Historical Association Conference, Saint Louis, October 19, 1986.

Mayeur, Françoise. *L'Education des jeunes filles en France au XIXe siècle*. Paris: Hachette, 1979.

————. *L'Enseignement secondaire des jeunes filles sous la Troisième République*. Paris: Presses de la fondation nationale des sciences politiques, 1977.

Moch, Leslie Page. "Government Policy and Women's Experience: The Case of Teachers in France." *Feminist Studies* 14, no. 2 (Summer 1988): 301–24.

Moody, John. *French Education since Napoleon*. Syracuse: Syracuse Univ. Press, 1978.

Nye, Robert A. *Crime, Madness, and Politics in Modern France: The Medical Concept of National Decline*. Princeton: Princeton Univ. Press, 1984.

Offen, Karen. "Defining Feminism: A Comparative Historical Approach." *Signs: Journal of Women in Culture and Society* 14, no. 1 (1988): 119–57.

————. "Depopulation, Nationalism, and Feminism in Fin-de-siècle France." *American Historical Review* 89, no. 3 (1984): 648–76.

————. "Ernest Legouvé and the Doctrine of 'Equality in Difference' for Women: A Case Study of Male Feminism in Nineteenth-Century French Thought." *The Journal of Modern History* 58, no. 2 (June 1986): 452–84.

————. " 'First Wave' Feminism in France: New Work and Resources." *Women's Studies International Forum* 5 (1982): 685–98.

————. "The Second Sex and the Baccalauréat in Republican France, 1880–1924." *French Historical Studies* 13, no. 2 (1983): 252–86.

Okin, Susan Moller. *Women in Western Political Thought.* Princeton: Princeton Univ. Press, 1979.

Outram, Dorinda. *The Body and the French Revolution: Sex, Class and Political Culture.* New Haven: Yale Univ. Press, 1989.

———. "Le Langage Mâle de la Vertu: Women and the Discourse of the French Revolution." In *The Social History of Language,* edited by Peter Burke, 120–35. Cambridge: Cambridge Univ. Press, 1987.

Padberg, John W. *Colleges in Controversy; The Jesuit Schools in France from Revival to Suppression, 1815–1880.* Cambridge: Harvard Univ. Press, 1969.

Pedersen, Joyce Senders. *The Reform of Girls' Secondary and Higher Education in Victorian England: A Study of Elites and Educational Change.* New York: Garland, 1987.

Perrot, Marguerite. *Le Mode de vie des familles bourgeoises 1873–1953.* Paris: A. Colin, 1961.

Perrot, Michelle, ed. *Histoire de la vie privée; de la Revolution à la Grande Guerre.* Vol. 4. Paris: Editions de Seuil, 1987.

Pitts, Jesse R. "Continuity and Change in Bourgeois France." In *In Search of France,* edited by Stanley Hoffman, 235–305. Cambridge: Harvard Univ. Press, 1963.

Pope, Barbara Corrado. "Angels in the Devil's Workshop: Leisured and Charitable Women in Nineteenth-Century England and France." In *Becoming Visible: Women in European History,* edited by Renate Bridenthal and Claudia Koonz, 296–324. Boston: Houghton Mifflin, 1977.

Prost, Antoine. *L'Histoire de l'enseignement en France, 1800–1967.* Paris: A. Colin, 1968.

Quartararo, Anne Therese. "The *Ecoles Normales Primaires d'Institutrices*: A Social History of Women Primary School Teachers in France, 1879–1905." Ph.D. diss., Univ. of California, Los Angeles, 1982.

Rebérioux, Madeleine. *La République radicale? 1898–1914.* Paris: Editions de Seuil, 1975.

Roche, Daniel. "L'Intellectuel au travail." *Annales (économies, sociétés, civilisations)* 37, no. 3 (1982): 465–80.

Rossiter, Margaret W. *Women Scientists in America: Struggles and Strategies to 1940.* Baltimore: Johns Hopkins Univ. Press, 1982.

Rowbotham, Sheila. *Women, Resistance and Revolution.* New York: Vintage, 1972.

Scott, Joan Wallich. *Gender and the Politics of History.* New York: Columbia Univ. Press, 1988.

———. "Gender: A Useful Category of Historical Analysis." *American Historical Review* 91, no. 5 (December 1986): 1053–75.

———. "Women in History: The Modern Period." *Past and Present* 101 (November 1983): 141–57.

Sewell, William H., Jr. *Structure and Mobility: The Men and Women of Marseille, 1820–1870.* New York: Cambridge Univ. Press, 1985.

Shafer, John. "Family, Class and Young Women: Occupational Expectations in

Nineteenth-Century Paris." In *Family and Sexuality in French History*, edited by R. Wheaton and T. K. Hareven, 180–96. Philadelphia: Univ. of Pennsylvania Press, 1980.

Singer, Barnett. *Village Notables in Nineteenth-Century France: Priests, Mayors, Schoolmasters.* Albany: State Univ. of New York Press, 1983.

Smith, Bonnie G. *Ladies of the Leisure Class: The Bourgeoises of Northern France in the Nineteenth Century.* Princeton: Princeton Univ. Press, 1981.

Smith, Robert J. *The Ecole Normale Supérieure and the Third Republic.* Albany: State Univ. of New York Press, 1982.

———. "Normaliens of the Rue d'Ulm: An Elite of the Third Republic." Unpublished manuscript, 1976.

Stock-Morton, Phyliss. *Moral Education for a Secular Society: The Development of Morale Laïque in Nineteenth-Century France.* New York: State Univ. of New York Press, 1988.

Struminger, Laura S. "L'Ange de la Maison: Mothers and Daughters in Nineteenth-Century France." *International Journal of Women's Studies* 2, no. 1 (1979): 51–71.

Sussman, George. *Selling Mothers' Milk: The Wet-Nursing Business in France, 1715–1914.* Urbana: Univ. of Illinois Press, 1982.

Talbott, John E. *The Politics of Educational Reform in France, 1918–1940.* Princeton: Princeton Univ. Press, 1969.

Thibaudet, Alfred. *La République des professeurs.* Paris: B. Grasset, 1927.

Tilly, Louise A. "Three Faces of Capitalism: Women and Work in French Cities." In *French Cities in the Nineteenth Century*, edited by John M. Merriman, 165–92. New York: Holmes and Meier, 1981.

Tilly, Louise A., and Joan W. Scott. *Women, Work and Family.* New York: Holt, Rinehart, 1978.

Vicinus, Martha. *Independent Women: Work and Community for Single Women 1850–1920.* Chicago: Univ. of Chicago Press, 1985.

Vincent, Gérard. "Les Professeurs de l'enseignement secondaire dans la société de la Belle Epoque." *Revue d'histoire moderne et contemporaine* 13 (January–March 1966): 49–86.

———. "Les Professeurs du second degré au début du XXe siècle, essai sur la mobilité sociale et la mobilité géographique." *Mouvement social* 69 (1969): 124–27.

Walsh, Mary Roth. *"Doctors Wanted: No Women Need Apply": Sexual Barriers in the Medical Profession, 1835–1975.* New Haven: Yale Univ. Press, 1977.

Weisz, George. *The Emergence of Modern Universities in France, 1893–1914.* Princeton: Princeton Univ. Press, 1983.

Wright, Gordon. *France in Modern Times.* 3d ed. New York: W. W. Norton, 1981.

Zeldin, Theodore. *France 1848–1945.* 2 vols. Oxford: Clarendon, 1973, 1977.

Index